About Pearson

Pearson is the world's learning company, with presence across 70 countries worldwide. Our unique insights and world-class expertise comes from a long history of working closely with renowned teachers, authors and thought leaders, as a result of which, we have emerged as the preferred choice for millions of teachers and learners across the world.

We believe learning opens up opportunities, creates fulfilling careers and hence better lives. We hence collaborate with the best of minds to deliver you class-leading products, spread across the Higher Education and Test Preparation spectrum.

Superior learning experience and improved outcomes are at the heart of everything we do. This product is the result of one such effort.

Your feedback plays a critical role in the evolution of our products and you can contact us - reachus@pearson.com. *We look forward to it.*

Political Theory

Political Theory

An Introduction

Updated First Edition

Edited by

Rajeev Bhargava
Ashok Acharya

Senior Editor—Product: Anindita Malhotra
Senior Editor—Production: C. Purushothaman

ISBN 978-93-615-9850-0

First Impression, 2024
Second Impression, 2025

Published by Pearson India Education Services Pvt. Ltd, CIN: U72200TN2005PTC057128.

Head Office: 1st Floor, Berger Tower, Plot No. C-001A/2, Sector 16B, Noida - 201 301, Uttar Pradesh, India.
Registered Office: Featherlite, 'The Address' 5th Floor, Survey No 203/10B, 200 Ft MMRD Road, Zamin Pallavaram, Chennai – 600 044.
Website: in.pearson.com, Email: companysecretary.india@pearson.com

Compositor: DigiWorld Creative, Pune, Maharashtra
Printer: Rajkamal Electric Press, Kundli, Haryana-131 028.

Contents

PART IV POLITICAL ARGUMENTS

Preface to the Updated First Edition

It is extremely satisfying to know that a set of introductory essays conceived as a textbook of political theory has been received enthusiastically not only by postgraduate and undergraduate students for whom it was originally written in the early 2000s but also by succeeding generations. It is reassuring that this book has done consistently well all over the country and has been translated into other languages. There can be nothing more gratifying than to learn that our youth are keen to learn about key normative concepts, multiple ideologies, and modes of public reasoning and argumentation, for all these are indispensable not only for scholars but also for strengthening the foundations of a robust and engaged citizenry.

When the idea of an updated edition was first mooted, it was taken to all the contributors who instantly agreed to swiftly make the most unavoidable, minor revisions to their papers. A big thanks to all of them. Since the book was first conceived plenty of work on Indian political theory has that deserves several chapters. We have not been able to do so but have incorporated significant parts of an article published by Rajeev Bhargava in 2010 that covers some important questions neglected in the previous edition. We hope to bring forth more such important theme-based topics in subsequent editions.

We trust that this revised, updated edition will continue to make a difference to the teaching and learning of political theory.

Rajeev Bhargava
Ashok Acharya
June 10th, 2024

Preface to the Updated First Edition

Preface to the First Edition

This introductory book is meant primarily to help Indian students learn to do and evolve an Indian political theory. This is a bold and somewhat controversial objective and requires elaboration.

Indian universities tend generally to be lukewarm to social and political philosophy, partly because of a lack of interest in normative issues but also because of certain features of mainstream, academic political philosophy. Notwithstanding the occasional universal content, the form of mainstream political philosophy (MPP) is largely parochial. MPP takes little inspiration from non-Western societies, makes hardly any references to their problems and takes scant notice of how cross-cultural issues acquire a distinct inflection in different cultures. Most of the examples discussed in MPP have no immediate relation to these societies. Besides, there are few non-Western philosophers who could be role models for an Indian student. These difficulties are compounded by the unavailability of good political theory journals. No wonder that Indian academics evince disinterest in political philosophy and Indian students, though enthused by political philosophy, do not display self-confidence or competence at it.

How do we transform this condition? Do we need and can we evolve an Indian political theory? Allow me to clarify straightaway that by Indian political theory I do not mean a theory born out of and reflecting the 'genius' of Indians, or something uniquely Indian. Neither the editors nor any of the contributors to this volume believe in this kind of political theory. We do believe, however, that if we are engaged in our social and political practices and are properly concerned about issues that grow out of them, if we reflect on them and if creatively use the multiple traditions of theorizing regardless of where they are born, then something like an Indian political theory, a political theory with a distinctive contextual flavour, is bound to emerge. The difference between this political theory and political theory in other parts of the world, particularly in Europe and in the United States, may be tiny. But since the devil is in the small detail, these little differences are bound to make a big difference to how our own political theory is shaped.

A bit of personal history might help illustrate and extend my point further. I have taught political theory for 25 years. If I draw from this experience, I may divide this period into two phases. In the first phase, say between 1979 and 1989, political theorists were generally obsessed with reading and thinking about Western texts. We were commentators, at best, analysts of texts that make up the canon of Western political philosophy or that emerge out of the context of Western societies. In this period, I frequently heard a complaint from some of my own students and several colleagues: what is the applicability or relevance of political theory? I used to find this refrain odd, tiresome and, frankly, very irritating. It was particularly frustrating to find a change in the attitude of good students. Several of them who glowed with enthusiasm in their class and took optional courses in political theory in their MA began to show indifference or impatience when they moved up to do their M.Phil. Never failing to mention how much they enjoyed our classes, they shied away from *doing* political theory. An unbridgeable gap opened up between us as two camps were forged, one *for* political theory and the other *against* it.

But with hindsight, I feel that this division grew from a collective inability to understand the complex nature and function of political theory. Neither camp really properly distinguished two different questions: (*a*) What is the relevance of political theory? (*b*) what is the relevance of the kind of political theory that then occupies many of us? The fact is that a general scepticism about political theory must be kept entirely separate from the more specific scepticism directed against particular kinds of political theorizing. The pro-political theory camp should have realized that they ended up defending not only the more worthwhile and relevant forms of political theory but also its considerably less-significant variants. The anti-political theory camp made the same mistake and quite sweepingly attacked not merely the largely indefensible versions but even their indispensable cousins. What was the point of endlessly explicating what this or that Western thinker said or meant? No doubt, this is a small component of studying and teaching political theory, but is this all there is to this important human practice? Even if we were interested only in normative issues, why could we have not turned to a sustained defence of democracy, of the autonomy of institutions, of what it means to have a committed judiciary or bureaucracy? Why were we not able to properly distinguish an honourable religious sensibility from an ignoble communal assertion? Why were we unable to distinguish different forms of equality or justifiable inequalities from those which were morally illegitimate? Why had we not constructed a proper moral argument in favour of affirmative action or minority rights? Why were only platitudes on secularism available to us? Why had we forgotten the moral worth of many of our constitutional provisions?

By the end of the1980s, the climate, I am pleased to report, began to change and by the early 1990s, in what from a purely personal point of view is the second phase, several of us were beginning to get an idea of what kind of political theory is necessary and relevant to our context. In short, a new kind of political theory was taking birth. This textbook is written in this period of transition, in a phase when the world of a purely Western-oriented political theory is dying and a new political theory rooted in our own world is emerging.

This textbook would never have seen the light of day had I not moved to the University of Delhi (DU). In Jawaharlal Nehru University (JNU), somehow its need was never felt as acutely. In DU, it was experienced instantly and with lightning urgency. So, when Kamini Mahadevan, the ever patient commissioning editor of Pearson Education approached me with a proposal to write a textbook, I jumped at what I thought was a terrific idea. Alas, I also knew that I did not have the time to do so. I first proposed that we should get someone to tape classroom lectures. This did not happen. Instead, we agreed to give a small remuneration to a group of students who were to take down notes with the unambiguous objective of seeing their handiwork transformed into a textbook. The result, I must confess, was pretty disastrous, though I would never know whether it was due to the poor quality of my teaching or the even poorer note-taking ability of students. It took just three classes for me to realize that my original proposal was unworkable. I then suggested that we have other editors—Ashok Acharya, who agreed, and Nivedita Menon, who tried hard to find time for the work it entailed but could not—and put together a team of contributors. The two criteria of inclusion were (*a*) they should have fresh experience of teaching particularly in an undergraduate college, which effectively meant that they should be from the University of Delhi; and (*b*) that they should work in a democratic spirit as a team loosely knit together by the unity of the purpose outlined above.

No specific guidelines were given by the editors to the contributors. The only relevant instruction was that all must adopt the point of view of a good teacher. Good teachers enable students to enter the conceptual world of the text, to see the point of view of its author, and provide the broader context within which it is written. They are able to draw students into the loop of the argument, where there is one, and to help understand an issue from the inside of both its defenders as well as its opponents. Good teachers must connect well with students, something assisted by a conversational style, though one that is not entirely informal. They do so by a rich use of examples from their own context. Given this simple but clear understanding of good teaching and despite the knowledge of an unbridgeable gap that stretches between the written and oral text, our attempt was to try and replicate face-to-face teaching in the textbook.

Other qualities of good teachers were also kept in mind. For instance, though they never cease to be political, they are always careful not to be over-ideological. This is particularly important in the case of political theory. Indeed, it is important that teachers not wear their politics on the sleeve, if only on grounds of prudence. No one in the class must feel that the teacher has erected such an ideological wall in the course of teaching that it cannot be breached. But what if students themselves create such a wall? To my mind, the tone, demeanour and stance of the teacher, indeed his entire manner of teaching should be such that it enables students to themselves break it. Teachers must create an open space not only between themselves and the students but also amongst students so that every viewpoint can be articulated, discussed, debated, and collectively deliberated. An over-ideologically charged teacher may temporarily carry some students along, may even convert a few, but would eventually fail because of an unwillingness to create an open space for conversation. This textbook marks an attempt to re-create this flavour of the classroom—an open space for conversation and argument—inside its covers.

In the last instance, though, this book is driven by one unflappable motivation: to make available to good students the textbook they deserve. These books must not only be accessible but also be something to which a student can easily relate. We realize that we may not succeed in stopping every single student from relying on *kunjis* but we hope that a majority of them would not lean only on them. We are guided by the belief that the eventual purpose of the text is to contribute in a small way to help each student to do a bit of political theorizing on her/his own.

Political theory is increasingly becoming inter-disciplinary. It is, therefore, our hope that this book will be read not only by students and, I dare say, teachers of political science, but also historians, sociologists, anthropologists, economists, even natural scientists—anyone interested in socio-political concepts, arguments and perspectives.

This book is dedicated to all the students from whom the editors and contributors have learnt during the course of their teaching.

Rajeev Bhargava

PART I

What Is Political Theory and Why Do We Need It?

CHAPTER 1

What Is Political Theory?

Rajeev Bhargava

Chapter Outlines

Introduction

A cursory glance at the newspaper brings us face-to-face with dozens of political issues. The Supreme Court pronounces that there should be no reservations in private colleges, university students demonstrate against the government to demand the proper implementation of the Rural Employment Guarantee Act (REGA), women's organizations complain bitterly about the unequal treatment of women and girls in our society, trade-union leaders condemn police brutality against workers, animal-right activists demand better protection for endangered species of tigers, the prime minister apologizes to the Sikh community for moral indifference and neglect by the Congress Government at the time of the 1984 massacre of Sikhs, the government gives up the sale of public sector units (PSUs), the Rajya Sabha passes a bill to grant Hindu women an equal right in ancestral property, the chief minister of Gujarat insists that Gujarati identity and pride is wounded by opponents of the Sardar Sarovar project.

What in your opinion makes all these issues political? Do all these issues have some one thing in common which defines them as political? Consider the examples that refer to reservations, REGA, the massacre of Sikhs, equal rights to women in ancestral property and the sale of PSUs. All these refer to some institution of the state: the judiciary, the government, the legislature, the office of the prime minister. They also refer to the decision-making power of these institutions. Does it follow that the term 'political' refers to any public agency with the power or authority to take decisions? Notice, too, that all these decisions possess the potential to have an impact on almost every member of the society in question. Even when a particular decision appears to target a specific group, it relates to and has an impact on other groups. Does the term 'political' then refer to the common power to take decisions about the common life of a society?

It would be a mistake to confine this term only to this common power of state institutions. Consider once again the example of women's organizations protesting against the exclusion or unequal treatment of women. On the understanding of 'political' arrived thus far, this action of a group of women is not political. Why so? Because women's organizations are clearly not part of the state. But, surely, on any intuitive understanding of a political act, such a protest by a women's group is political. If so, this must compel us to change or broaden our understanding of the term 'political'. This protest is political not merely because it is a collective act by a group against some continuing social practice or an earlier decision of the government but also because the very object of this protest, namely the unequal treatment of women, is part of what we understand by the term 'political'. And why is this so? Because to treat women unequally is to exercise power over them—men make women do things which, left to themselves, they may not do. This exercise of power is also part of what we mean by 'political'.

A closer look at most of the examples points to another feature of the political. The political is that domain or dimension of our collective life where we fight for our interests, make claims (including moral claims) on each other, where important and urgent issues are contested. But demands, claims, protests and complaints cannot but generate conflict. The political, it appears, is inherently conflictual. Finally, we might look at the political in a still different sense. Implicit in almost every example is a vision of a future world, one where all are equal, or where even animals are treated with some respect, or where force is replaced by deliberation and so on. The political, then, is also where new worlds are imagined. Clearly, the term 'political' has no fixed or unique meaning. It has multiple, though related meanings. One objective of these introductory chapters is to enhance our understanding of the political and to draw the attention of the reader to its multiple meanings.

Our second task is to understand what we mean by the term 'theory'. Though not easy, it is important that this be done so that eventually we can put the terms 'political' and 'theory' together and have a better grasp over what is meant by political theory. Consider once again the examples in the first paragraph. Many of us have an opinion on most of these issues. Some of us are interested in seeking an explanation of the actions of the police, the Supreme Court and the government. Are there any motives behind the actions of these agencies? Do their actions serve the interest of the entire community or the narrow interests of a class or perhaps a tiny political elite? For instance, some might argue that the issue of a 'Gujarati' identity is used to further the interests of rich peasants. Others may claim that identity is a non-issue, that the real motive underlying every public action is class interest. The academically minded amongst us may claim that there exist structural reasons underlying these actions. For example, the slow implementation of REGA might be due to systemic institutional biases hidden from the consciousness of power wielders.

Is doing political theory the same, then, as explaining an act, practice, event or process? This does not appear to be so. Although explaining is part of political theory, surely, it is not the whole of it. And this, for two different reasons. First, because an explanatory statement does not on its own constitute a theory. If I say that I fell down because I stumbled unknowingly upon a stone, I have offered an explanation of why I fell down, but have I offered a theory of what has happened? Or, if I said that the United States has invaded Iraq in order to have easy access to oil, I would have offered some explanation of why the United States government acted the way it did. But is this the same as articulating a theory of it? No. Why so? Second, although explaining may be part of theorizing, it is not the whole of it. There are other functions of theory. For example, theories offer justifications of actions. Take the examples of the first paragraph again. Some of us might silently condemn equal rights to women in ancestral property or justify police brutality. Others may disagree. They might denounce police action as violative of the most basic human rights or rejoice that equality now covers an important gender issue that had hitherto been neglected. These justificatory statements do not constitute theory but they may be its crucial components. Moreover, in denouncing police action, we are necessarily evaluating it negatively. All justifications presuppose evaluation. Behind these evaluative judgments are deeper issues. Why should women and men be treated as equals? What is the appropriate response of the government to mass-killings? What is the connection between ensuring employment to everyone and social justice? What is the proper function of the police in a modern democratic state? Workers are beaten up, apparently for disobeying the state? But why should we obey the state at all? Why should we be law-abiding citizens? Similarly, we might ask; why should tigers who sometimes turn man-eaters still be protected? Such questions have to do with right and wrong, good and bad, in short, with ethics and morality, with the normative. Admittedly, answers to these questions may not on their own constitute theory, but what additional features are necessary for them to be deemed theoretical?

As *theory*, political theory must share features with theories of other phenomenon. It may even have some features in common with theories of the physical or the biological world. However, by virtue of being *political* theory, it must possess characteristics that are distinctive. Some of these distinctive features separate it from theories of nature but not from theories pertaining to human affairs more generally. But its truly distinctive features must flow from its focus on the political. In what follows, therefore, we outline the more general features of any theory and in particular elucidate features of a theory of human condition and action. In order to do so, we relate theory to and differentiate it from other forms of systematic reflections such as art, literature and religious worldviews. Finally, we ask the question what is political and outline the specific features of political theory.

What is Theory?

Humans as Concept-bearing Animals

Let us begin with some truisms. No one denies that we are physical creatures, part of the physical universe and subject to the same laws as any physical object. Nor will anyone deny that unlike purely physical objects, but like other biological creatures, we are sentient creatures: we breathe, we eat, we grow and have sensory experiences. However, what distinguishes us from most, though not all, biological creatures, is that we are concept-bearing animals. As conceptual creatures, we are born in a world that is already arranged thoughtfully in particular ways. Consider the following. A child is told to sit on a chair. From a purely physical point of view, chairs are just wood, nothing else. But it would be odd to tell the child to sit on a piece of wood. What we wish to convey to the child is that a particular piece of wood when crafted in a particular manner serves a particular purpose, that it is something on which we sit or with which we can do certain things such as eating, reading, writing, talking and so on. It is these purposes that we wish to convey to the child, purposes which would not exist unless conceptually formulated. This is true not only of objects—such as chairs, tables, blackboards, chalk, the classroom in the school building—but also of human beings themselves. A student interacts with the person standing in front of the blackboard and talks to her not as if she is any odd person but as one who is there to perform a certain role, that of a teacher. Once again, no teaching is possible unless all of us already have a rough idea of the social role of students and teachers. The same is true of bus conductors, drivers, ticket inspectors, shopkeepers, government officials and so on. A society cannot function without these elementary understandings and so every child is initiated into the social world by an informal instruction in these concepts. Unlike the purely physical, chemical or the biological world, the human world is conceptual through and through. Plants and most lower order animals live in this world and sense it, but by virtue of living the world through concepts, humans do not merely have sensory experience. Because their experience is mediated by images, concepts and representations, we might say that human experience is always thoughtful. Humans do not merely live but have a thoughtful experience of living—what we might call *lived experience*.

Concepts Embedded in Practices

As hinted above, most concepts that we use in everyday living are not formally learnt in the classroom but are acquired by participating in various practices. Since we use concepts, we may liken them to tools but this should not lead us to think that we have mental boxes in our head from which we pick them out as and when we need them. Much of our conceptual understanding is available to us as a practical skill or is directly embedded in practices. We are not even aware most of the time that we possess this skill or understanding. This may appear implausible to you at first. But really, the matter is quite simple. Several activities you do routinely are not thoughtless but are mostly absent in the stream of your consciousness. (How many times do you really interrupt the flow of your activity and think?) You just do them without explicitly thinking about them, just as the bus driver changes gears without first asking himself whether or not he should. You see the object in front of you as a table or a book and you understand that what you are doing is sitting at the table and reading. When we see a person entering the poll booth and approaching the ballot box, we understand that he is voting. This understanding is direct and practical, not inferred from something that first takes place in your consciousness. It is usually the same with people and social relationships. We might call this an embedded understanding of things, practices, people and relationships.

Human Expressions

All humans have the ability not only to have thoughtful experiences but to express these thoughts in different media. A child experiences a piece of wood as a chair or a table but she may express this experience in a drawing, by representing these objects on paper. An actor, a mime artist or a dancer may use her body to say the same thing. A photographer may use the camera for the same purpose. There are multiple ways of expressing an experience, some word dependent and others not. Besides, we may express this experience in words to other people: 'Hey! I see a table there.' Or I may express it to myself, privately, 'That's a table, isn't it?'. So, some of these expressions are in the outer world, in public spaces and some may occur inside, privately as ideas in our heads. These private expressions may be called subjective reflections, a kind of mirroring of the world in our own heads.

Ad hoc and Systematic Reflections

All expressions, including subjective reflections, may occur randomly, on the spur of the moment or be arranged systematically. All of us, from time-to-time have spontaneous and random reflections. The chalk with which I unthinkingly and effortlessly write on the blackboard keeps crumbling one day. When that happens, I may interrupt the flow of my action, examine the chalk and ask if I could not have a chalk of better quality. I have an embedded understanding of what a chalk is and practical knowledge of what is to be done with it; but confronted with a piece of chalk literally melting in my fingers into dust, I may think to myself, just what it is made of, whether it really is what it is meant to be. 'Is this really a piece of chalk?' Such, random thoughts may occur and then disappear for no ostensible reason, but they arise invariably when there is an unexpected interruption of my activities, when I am faced, for example, with a problem.

Word-dependent and Word-independent Reflections

Suppose then, that I don't let this thought disappear: I engage with it, indeed pursue it obsessively. Suppose that I now examine not merely the chalk in hand but the entire box, indeed not just one but all the boxes bought by the department of my college, and arrive at the conclusion that the entire lot is defective. I identify the manufacturer and begin to look at the quality of other lots used elsewhere. Quite obviously, I have begun a kind of sustained and systematic empirical enquiry. When I write a report on chalk produced by the manufacturer, it becomes an expression of systematic reflection on an issue selected for sharper focus. A report is systematic and word-dependent. But humans have the ability to systematically reflect and express themselves in a variety of non-linguistic media. Systematic expressions and reflections on the world and on ourselves are also found in music, sculpture, painting, dance, pottery, architecture and so on. A filmmaker or a painter may reflect on the human condition, on a social environment, on the problems of a society in transition, on the predicaments of modernity or on the futility of war but without deploying words to convey their meaning. Have you seen the paintings in Ajanta caves? Or Madhubani and Worli paintings? Or a replica of the Spanish painter Pablo Picasso's *Guernica*? Many of you may have heard Amir Khan's rendering of *Bhairavi* or Kumar Gandharva's rendering of *Bhim Palasi*. These, too, are systematic reflections. Other forms of systematic reflections use language but in interestingly different ways.

Varieties of Word-dependent Reflections

Word or language-dependent systematic expressions or reflections can also be accomplished in multiple modes, in interestingly different ways. The essay is one form; a written dialogue is another, poetry is yet another. Newspaper articles, a mixture of short description and analysis, provide another form. A record of one's experience in a village, the ethnography of a good anthropologist is a systematic expression of collective lived experiences. Folk tales, moral fables, myths and legends, epic poetry, short stories and novels are all systematic reflections.

What has all this got to do with theory? I propose that theory, too, be seen as a particular form of language-dependent systematic expression different from, but related to, other forms of systematic reflections on the world. Like other expressions, a theory articulates in a particular medium a conceptual world lived practically by a specific set of human agents. Moreover, it does so in its own distinctive way. What marks a theory out from other language-dependent systematic expressions? I propose that there are six such features, four of which it necessarily shares with philosophy and two that are specific to it.

The Distinctiveness of Theory

The *first* feature is an almost obsessive and self-conscious concern with the internal structure of concepts, with how concepts relate to one another and come in clusters, and how in turn, they mark their own boundaries. A philosopher or a theorist—for my purpose I will often use these terms interchangeably—focuses on the meaning of words, on the different ways in which the words are used so that she can eventually answer questions, such as 'what is justice?' What is the meaning of the phrase 'social revolution' and how is it different from 'social reform' or 'social engineering?' What is the core idea of freedom, if there is one? What are the different interpretations of this core idea? What is the relationship between freedom and equality? And, between freedom, equality, and justice? What distinguishes power from influence, force, violence or persuasion? In ordinary life we use words more or less unself-consciously and we are not normally compelled to ask such questions. But philosophers must raise these questions and understand them in a particular way. When asked what 'Time' is, we don't expect philosophers to look at their watches and tell us the precise time of the day. Philosophers are expected to convey to us what the meaning of time is and what it is for us to live in time. Likewise, if a philosopher is asked a question about basic needs, he is not expected to supply us with a list of our most urgent desires but rather to make us understand how needs are different from ordinary desires and what the distinction is between our most inescapable and significant needs and others that at least temporarily we may live without.

As long as our purpose is served, we don't ordinarily care whether a word is used literally or metaphorically, or both. Poets, novelists, essayists use words self-consciously and with extreme care, but it is not their business to elucidate why they have chosen to use this rather than some other word or to make explicit connections between different concepts. The job of a philosopher and insofar as philosophy is part of theory, the job of a theorist is to accomplish precisely this. A full-blooded sensitivity to the entire web of concepts and a commitment to its articulation is the first feature of theory.

Let me illustrate this further with an example. Suppose that someone gives a call for freedom: 'We should all be free'. What are people to make of this call? For a start they must understand what it means to be free. Once they have understood the meaning, or rather, the different meanings of freedom, they may ask why they should be free or at least why they should be free in this rather than in some other sense. To be free of, or from, something is to get rid of it. What you wish to get rid of must be something that you evaluate negatively. In the literature on freedom such things that you wish to get rid of are usually called constraints. So, to be free is to be free from constraints. But what is the nature of these constraints? Surely, our ideas of freedom will depend upon our understanding of what these constraints are. Are these constraints purely physical? Take the paradigmatic example of freedom: a man is in chains. Get rid of the chains and he is free. The same is true of birds in a cage. The cage imprisons, restricting the flight of the bird, that which it is most prone to doing and is its nature. To set the bird free is to get rid of the cage. In the same way prisoners are set free when they are released. Have you noticed that our notion of constraint may already have changed with this last example? For at issue here is not merely the idea of physical but of legal constraints. A person may have been put behind bars because he has been caught stealing. He stole because he was physically free to steal and yet he was imprisoned because it is illegal to do so. Appropriating a thing that by law belongs to another is illegal and it is because of the presence of this legal constraint that the man was put in jail. To be free then is to be free not just from physical but from legal constraints.

Is this all there is to freedom? Notice that both physical and legal constraints are external to the agent. Can a person be unfree not because of the presence of physical and legal constraints—there may be none—but by virtue of psychological barriers, obstructions that are present within his mental make-up. So, consider a slave who is set free and who is now pronounced as formally equal to his former master. Suppose that they both compete in an open exam, and while the former master always does well, the former slave simply cannot perform. Centuries of slavery have taken away from him the basic self-confidence required for a good performance. He is unable to achieve his objectives not because of physical or legal constraints but due to internal psychological ones. A conception of freedom in purely physical or legal terms is unable to capture the mechanism of unfreedom which is at work here. We can similarly talk about constraints which are neither purely external nor purely internal but a bit of both—I mean social constraints. A person is physically and legally free to enter the higher education system. He has done well in his school examinations, well enough to get a place in a decent college. But higher education is costly. There are no subsidies or scholarships. The person is confident that he would do well and he has every reason to feel so. And yet, he cannot get higher education. He is severely handicapped by his relative poverty which is a major socio-economic constraint on what he wishes to do. Implicit in this is a still different conception of freedom: freedom from not merely physical, legal and psychological but also socio-economic constraints.

Hitherto we have focused on constraints. However, our conception of freedom changes with our ideas about what we should do once freed from constraints. Some argue that it is enough that we are able to fulfil whatever we happen to currently desire. So, if I desire to smoke and no constraints exist to prevent me from doing so, then I am free. Others argue that by a focus on current unevaluated desires we misunderstand what is really at issue in discussions of freedom. Such people work with a less instrumentalist, more robust conception of reason and argue that one is free only when there is absence of constraints and a real opportunity to do what we evaluate to be good for us. On this view, if information that cigarettes are gravely injurious to health is available to us but we continue to both desire smoking and fulfil this desire, then we are not really being free. We are not free because we succumb to a habit or addiction, completely bypassing, ignoring or evading what our reason says is good for us. To fall prey to one's current unevaluated desires, in this view, is to be in a state of unfreedom. Freedom is a condition of leading a life and of doing things that are evaluated to be good for us, to fulfil desires that are judged to be worth having in the first place. This view slowly leads to the idea that freedom is identical with self-realisation. The detailed elaboration of different conceptions of freedom is one task of political theory. The other one is to reason why we should choose one rather than the other conception; why, if at all, one conception is better than others.

This brings me to the *second* distinctive feature of theory or philosophy, i.e. that it is a rational enterprise, where the term rational is understood very broadly to mean that the conclusion arrived or hinted at has some discernable structure of reasons behind it. To say this is not to imply that philosophers or theorists do not rely on instincts, emotions, or flashes of insight. Nor does it mean that a philosophical or theoretical enquiry must possess a definite argumentative structure of the kind made familiar by logicians, although some philosophies and theories may have some such pattern. However, it does mean that philosophers and theorists are not satisfied with bland assertions, the flat announcement of a claim or the presentation of a readymade proposal. When they make an assertion or proposal, they must state why they do so. In other words, they must give a reason. Indeed, they cannot be satisfied with providing one reason and stopping the process of questioning at this point. There can be a reason for a reason already supplied and a reason for the reason for the initial reason. In other words, whether stated explicitly or not there is a chain of reasons that is discernable in a theoretical or philosophical work. Does this mean that we can reach the final reason, a reason beyond which there is no reason—the foundation of all reasons? Some philosophers appear to be obsessed with this idea of ultimate cause or justification of an event or act. But I doubt if we humans can ever get to the bottom of all things.

Take the example of scientific theories. Suppose that it is claimed that water is a compound. This must be backed by some evidence demonstrating that it is composed of two elements: hydrogen and oxygen, and that this composition is not a mere mixture of features of both but rather a new substance with features of its own. Furthermore, this evidence must itself be supported by more general claims about the mechanism by which such a process takes place. Similarly, suppose that it is proposed that all children must be provided elementary education, and suppose in answer to the question 'Why?' it is asserted that education is a fundamental right, then it must also be argued that at least in modern times there is a connection between education, employment, and a life of dignity and, further, that a dignified life is a crucial component of human well-being and so on. This rational structure of theories, their internal requirement that they persistently ask for reasons makes them, albeit with some qualifications, subversive—with the potential to transform societies.

The rational component of theory also illuminates another of its important features, namely, its aspiration to truth and objectivity. This claim must be made very cautiously but clearly. The truths that theories, particularly social and political theories, aspire to are not valid for all times and all places. The truth of most theories is context-dependent and therefore limited to specific times and places. Only the very exceptional theories have a reach that cuts across time and space. Nor is this very achievable but limited truth in any way final. We must rid ourselves of the illusion that like God, we humans can stand outside all perspectives and attain God-like objectivity or an eternal truth of the matter. The truth that we achieve is dependent on the collective reasoning of human beings and even if all rational persons can agree at any given point of time that they have arrived at the truth of a certain matter, new information or a flaw in an argument detected much later by other reasonable beings can force us to revise our earlier truth-claims. Human knowledge can neither altogether escape subjective viewpoints nor be imprisoned within the subjective biases of wealthy classes, powerful political blocs or even intellectuals. Such views may pass off as knowledge for some time but sooner or later their limitations are bound to come to light. We might, then, arrive at some acceptable version that can be rightfully claimed as the truth of the matter, an achievement not possible without the use of reason, although reason alone cannot help us attain it.

A *fourth* feature of philosophy/theory is that it is committed to unearthing the background assumptions and presuppositions of our statements, beliefs, actions and practices. For example, the force of gravity is presupposed by all our situated action. We don't always articulate this nor are many of us aware that this is so. Yet, without the force of gravity, embodied persons cannot exist on this earth. Similarly, when we set out to attend a class we make many assumptions which remain in the background, as part of our pre-reflective understanding. For example, the classroom is exactly where we left it on the previous day, that the teacher would arrive to take the class, that at least some other students would be present, that the teacher will give the lecture in a language that we speak or understand and so on. All of us exist, think and act with these assumptions and presuppositions but do not always articulate them. To take another example, in 17th century England, politicians had begun to think and speak of politics without appeal to religious principles. But frequently, they did not acknowledge this. It was left to Hobbes to articulate these new background assumptions and to show that it was possible to conduct politics in a purely secular manner. Thus, within reasonable limits, philosophers and theorists are committed to articulating these background assumptions and presuppositions.

The *fifth* feature of theory—and here philosophy and theory may begin to diverge—is this. A theory aspires to some degree of generality and abstraction. It does so because it aims to cover a wide variety of related but disparate phenomena. This does not mean that all theories must be universal in scope. But it does mean that a theory cannot deal only with a concrete particular, something in the singular. Thus, we have a theory of motion that applies equally to planets as it does to rolling stones. Such a theory has a very high degree of generality appropriate to the object of its study. There cannot be a theory exclusively for rolling stones. Likewise, we could have a descriptive study of Indian nationalism or an empirical study of the causes of Indian nationalism. But, it is unlikely that we will have a theory of nationalism that applies to India and to India alone.

Finally, a *sixth* feature of theories, one that is a product of modern conditions and has emerged more particularly with the birth of modern science, has to be mentioned. Modern theories cannot be purely speculative and must pass through and then transcend the empirical world. They cannot bypass the empirical world altogether. This feature is related to the point mentioned above. The data collected by the sciences, the collective lived experiences of a people captured in the work of insightful observers, socially engaged thinkers or consummate social scientists cannot be ignored by theorists. These general and inter-connected reflections must take into account all of these. For this very reason a theory must be simultaneously rooted in and transcend the lived experience of a people, the collective practices of a society, and the embedded understandings and common sense of a community. There is no theory if there is mere description of lived experience and common sense, but we have theory only in name if theoretical propositions are altogether disconnected from experience, practices and the data collected by sound empirical enquiries.

Let me sum up. A theory is a form of systematic reflection with six features. (*a*) Conceptual sensitivity, (*b*) rational structure, (*c*) aspiration for a humanly achievable truth and objectivity, (*d*) generality, (*e*) an explicit mandate to unearth assumptions and presuppositions, and (*f*) strong non-speculative intent—the need not to bypass results of micro-enquiries into the particular. It is not identical to any one feature but must possess all six. Thus, a theory must be distinct from ad hoc reflections, speculation, empirical enquiry into the particular, rich insights, imaginative but fictive prose and other related narratives. It must also be distinguished from ideology, worldview and cosmology—a point that will emerge more clearly below. A rare specimen of theory may be universalist or reach the foundation, but on the whole, the constitutive features of a theory do not include a commitment to foundationalism or universalism.

Cosmologies and Common Sense

I have used the terms 'embedded understandings' and 'common sense' above. Let me remind the reader what I mean by them. I made a distinction between conceptually organized lived experience and reflection on that experience. This distinction presupposes that though conceptual, lived experience may not be present in our consciousness. We may use our concepts in practice but be unable to speak about them, quite like a skilful cook who can make delectable dishes without quite being able to tell us how. (Conversely, the possession of a good recipe book is not sufficient to make a good cook.) By embedded understanding, I mean, this practical knowledge that remains pre-reflective and inarticulate. It is an understanding we acquire by being initiated into the practices of a society. The term 'commonsense' is broader and covers embedded understanding but also, at the very least, our spontaneous and ad hoc reflections, including reflections that are closely aligned to our practices, which might be called practical reflections. It usually also includes stories, epics, folk tales, legends, myths that have been passed on from one generation to another and with the help of which we make sense of and evaluate the entire universe. Such nearly systematic but non-theoretical reflections which knit together in a seamless web the physical, biological, social, mental and spiritual worlds may be called cosmologies. Cosmologies frequently in-form and become part of a society's common sense.

If this is true of the relationship between cosmologies and common sense, can it also be true of the relationship between theories and commonsense? Can theories shape and inform our common sense? Though they can do so (indeed, good theories must aspire to do so), the two remain and perhaps must remain distinct entities. The common sense of a society is the collective possession of an entire people. A theory is a specialized activity or product dependent on and generated by specific skills. Does this mean that theorizing is an elite activity from which the common man will remain forever estranged? I don't think so. First, distance does not mean estrangement. Many cricket lovers in India have never played cricket. Some do play it but quite badly. Still others play well but are not exceptional. But all of them can love or admire the skills of a Sachin Tendulkar or Azharuddin. In some ways they are distant from them but surely no one can claim that distance here necessarily means estrangement. Second, and more importantly, though the practice of theory involves skills, these can be acquired, in principle, by anyone who has some talent and a lot of opportunity and commitment. Just as cricket is not the preserve of a special class or caste of people, so also theory is not the monopoly of a particular kind of people. To think so is to be committed to a deplorable and outdated form of casteist Brahminism. We must avoid both the view that theory is the monopoly of the special, naturally talented or genetically endowed group and the claim that it is available effortlessly to the masses. To the objection that there is a sense in which everyone is a philosopher or a theorist, an appropriate response is to draw the distinction between having a philosophy/theory and doing it. Though all of us have a philosophy, we do not all *do* philosophy. Everyone may have a systematic world-view, a theory of the world, a philosophy, but it does not follow that all these are the result of his or her own theorizing philosophizing.

The emphasis on the distance between theory/philosophy and common sense as also between theory and practice should not be misunderstood or exaggerated. As I pointed out earlier, there is also a close relationship between theory and common sense and between theory and practice. As we will see in Chapter 2, the most fundamental questions asked by philosophers are the same to which answers are implicit in our practice and in common sense. A philosophy of the human world articulates what is already implicit in human practice. In this sense and unlike what many believe, philosophy is down-to-earth. Yet, it is also up there. It takes flight and is up there because like other systematic reflections—and this close relationship between theory and the arts is equally worth emphasizing—it frequently tries to do more than merely describe human practice. *It also attempts to explain and justify it in general terms and less directly to endorse, modify or change it.*

What is Political?

The term 'political' has multiple meanings. The first goes back to classical Greece and is derived from the word 'polis' which literally means the city, but is better, more properly understood as a place with a common world or even more simply, a community. 'Political', then, pertains to whatever is done within or by the community. More specifically, it refers to *decision making* within and about the community. Decision making itself has a specific connotation. To be political, to live in the polis, as Hannah Arendt tells us, means that everything is to be decided through words and persuasion and not through force and violence. The term 'political' then points to a specific mode of decision making—by words, not force. However, the term 'political' also refers simultaneously to what decisions are about. When we use the term 'political' in this first sense, we speak not merely about life but necessarily about the *good* life of a community. Thus, we may ask, given that we live by a certain conception of the good life, who is to be a member of the community and why, who is to rule, i.e. take fundamental decisions about the community and for what reasons, how resources are to be distributed, to whom and why. In this conception, as we can see, the empirical and the normative are completely intermeshed. Nor has the distinction emerged in this context between political and social spheres. Nothing that we now consider to be merely social, i.e. falling between the public-political and the private-household is outside the political. On this classical view then, there is no distinction between social and political theory. Political theory is about how and with what justification decisions are made concerning the good life in a community.

Over a period of time and particularly with the advent of modernity, the meaning of the term 'political' appears to have changed. To understand this change let us go back to what I said above. In classical Greece, the term 'political' had to do with fundamental decision making about the affairs of the community. To make decisions, however, one must first have the power to do so. If the entire community is involved in decision making, then decision making presupposes the collective power of the entire community. The term 'political' then may also refer to this collective power, to the use of this power to make decisions, and political science or philosophy may be viewed as the study of this collective power. However, as is well known, even in Greek societies, decisions were not made by everybody. Power was not exercised by everyone. Slaves, women and aliens were excluded from the decision-making process. One might then say that decisions about the entire community were taken by some, only by excluding others from the processes within which they were made. Some people had the power to make decisions about everyone only on condition that they also exercised power over some others. Of course, this can be said only with hind-sight. People living at that time did not see their own condition as we now describe it.

With the advent of modernity, this meaning of the term 'power' became far more explicit. Indeed, the classical meaning of power as the collective capacity to decide about the community was almost completely obscured and replaced by the second meaning of power as the capacity of some people to act in a manner that thwarts the significant interest of others, that marginalizes and excludes them, so that they are left with no ability or capacity to take decisions about themselves or about the whole community. Power came simply to mean power over others. Correspondingly, the term 'political' refers to this power *over* others. Political science, then, came to mean an empirical enquiry into the exercise of this power. And political theory, the most general reflection on the processes, mechanisms, institutions, and practices by which some people are excluded by others from significant decision making.

Yet another related meaning emerged under conditions of modernity when major sites of decision making were relatively separated from the rest of society and were concentrated in a specific set of institutions designated by the term 'state' (this is related to the point that a new concept of the social emerged which was distinguished from the political). If politics, considered as a comprehensive enquiry, is the study of decision-making power, then the birth of the modern state naturally implied that the major object of study of political science and political theory is the state. Indeed, the term political was itself identified with anything pertaining to the state rather than to the entire society. Political science and political theory studied the institutions of the state—the government, the judiciary, the bureaucracy, the military, the police and so on. Sociology and social theory, on the other hand, studied all those structures, processes and institutions that fell outside the state. Some people continued to believe that a study of the state was the study of how power was exercised on behalf of and in the interest of all the individuals who make up a particular society. Others, cynical of this view, saw political science and political theory as the study of how these institutions take major decisions on behalf of a small elite or the dominant class to the exclusion of the interests of the subordinate classes or subaltern people.

To summarize, the term 'political' has multiple meanings: (*a*) The collective power to take decisions about every aspect of the good life in the community. Notice that 'political' here refers both to power and to ethical values. (*b*) The power of some groups to control or subordinate others in order to realize not the good of the entire community but their own narrow interests. In short, to get others to do things that might go against their own interest. Here, the term 'political' is used to relate power and self-interest. It also refers to power embodied in a separate institutional apparatus, i.e. the state and, therefore, (*c*) to state power used to realize the common good/values, or (*d*) state power used to exercise domination by one group over others.

But how can (*a*) or (*c*) coexist with (*b*) or (*d*)? How can the entire community take decisions when a group excludes others from collective decision making? Well, in this case we might say that a split has occurred between the empirical and the normative. The subordinate group may be excluded from decision making but may have the desire to forge a new world where everybody is involved in taking decisions about shared interests and values. Then (*a*) and (*c*) become normative/ethical notions capturing something which is hitherto unrealized or realized very marginally while (*b*) and (*d*) capture what really exists on the ground. A final meaning is related to but still different from how we have hitherto conceived (*a*). The reader may have noticed that so far (*a*) refers to the good life of the community, to values of specific communities. But what if we begin to use the term 'political' for values common to the entire humanity in abstraction from both power and specific communities? What if it refers to values common to all living species? Here, polis coincides with cosmopolis.

So (*a*) splits into two and gives us a fifth meaning of the political. This meaning, (*e*), refers to values common to the entire humanity, even all living species. Recall that the political sphere may also include the art of imagining new values and devising new worlds. Therefore, (*e*) is maximally abstracted from really existing lives. Thus, today, we use the term 'political' in each of the five senses and as both an empirical and a normative concept.

Political theory then is a particular form of word-dependent systematic reflection on any or all of the following: (*a*) the collective power to take decisions about the good life of a community, (*b*) the mechanisms by which power is exercised by one group over another, (*c*) the use of state power to achieve the good of the community, (*d*) the use of the state by one group to exercise power over another, and (*e*) on the values by which a particular community governs its life. Finally, (*f*) there can be a grand political theory that reflects on the general condition of the entire humankind or the values by which the entire humanity may govern its life.

Points for Discussion

1. A child complains to his father that he has got fewer chocolates than his brother. Women's organizations complain to the state that women are often given unequal pay for the same job. Are both these acts political?
2. Can you think of things in the world which are not 'concept-bearing'? Is concept-bearing a unique feature of human beings? Can you think of worldviews which reject this idea?
3. Do you think that even in our ordinary life we are frequently engaged in explaining or justifying our acts? Can you think of examples?
4. The term 'political' refers both to power and to values, sometimes together and at other times separately. Do you find this puzzling? Can you explain why?

Reading List

Ball, Terence, James Farr and Russell L. Hanson (eds), *Political Innovation and Conceptual Change* (Cambridge: Cambridge University Press, 1989).

Barry, Brian, *Political Argument* (Hemel Hempstead: Harvester Wheatsheaf, 1990).

Dryzek, John, B. Honnig and Anne Philips (eds), *A Handbook of Political Theory* (Oxford: Oxford University Press, 2006).

Goodin, Robert E. and Philip Pettit, *A Companion to Contemporary Political Philosophy* (Oxford: Blackwell, 1995).

Kleinberg, Stanley S., *Politics and Philosophy* (Oxford: Blackwell, 1991).

Lukes, Steven, 'Power and Authority', in Tom Bottomore and Robert Nisbet (eds), *A History of Sociological Analysis* (London: Heinemann, 1979).

Nagel, Thomas, *What Does it All Mean? A Very Short Introduction to Philosophy* (Oxford: Oxford University Press, 1987).

Wolff, Jonathan, *An Introduction to Political Philosophy* (Oxford: Oxford University Press, 1996).

CHAPTER 2

Why Do We Need Political Theory?

Rajeev Bhargava

Chapter Outlines

Introduction

What in general are theories meant to do? What are the functions of theory? In the first chapter, some of these functions have already been listed. However, here we ask a different, deeper question. Do we really need political theory? One may ask how this question is different from the one mentioned in the previous line? Consider then the following: doctors of modern, Western, allopathic medicine undeniably perform a function in our society. However, we might ask, in the critical spirit of Gandhi's *Hind Swaraj*, if we really need doctors who practise modern Western medicine? Can the function of healing and restoration of health not be performed by other practices and their practitioners? Analogously, we might ask: can the function of political theory be better performed by something else, say ideologies or cosmologies? Why do we need political theory?

I propose that this question cannot be answered unless we ask the big questions of human existence and collective life. I suggest that many of these answers are now provided, though not exhaustively, by natural-scientific theories and the social sciences. However, this was not always the case. Most of these answers were once provided only by religions, cosmologies and philosophy. Moreover, political philosophy simultaneously performed both explanatory and normative functions. In what follows, I suggest that political theory now performs three key separate functions. It explains at the most general level possible, it evaluates and tells us what we should do and it speculates about our current and future condition. It also tells us who we are. In some sense, these functions are no different from the tasks performed by cosmologies and ideologies. Yet, I argue that political theory is distinct from both. I also try to claim that political theory has a special function under modern conditions. Far from being dead, it not only lives but needs to flourish.

The Big Questions of Human Life

Consider the following abstract but significant questions:

- What is there/going on in the world? (Understanding)
- Why are things there/going on in the world? (Explanation)
- Will something that is currently going on continue to go on in the future? (Prediction)
- Is that which is there/going on good or bad, right or wrong? (Ethics)
- What am I to do? What is to be done? (Normative)
- Who am I? Who are we? (Metaphysical self-knowledge)

Human life is virtually impossible without the availability of answers to each of these questions. One might say that one becomes a human being, or at least a certain kind of human being, as answers to these questions are learnt. Humans can live in a society only if they have some understanding of what the nature of the society is. For example, it is crucial that in a hierarchical society a person has an understanding of his own rank as well as the social standing of others. A person who is part of the 'lower' order has a practical understanding of this status and knows that he must be deferential to someone superior to him. A member of this society understands what is going on when a person stands bowing his head and lowering his eyes before another man. He also understands why this is going on; he knows that a person must bow before another person *because* he is inferior. Such understandings and explanations are part of common sense and crucial to the functioning of the society. Similarly, members of such a society have some idea of what is in store for them in the future, indeed what they can hope for. For the lower castes, practically nothing. For the upper castes, the permanence of privilege. And all this is linked further to a fairly common understanding of what is right and wrong, good and bad in that society and to a certain self-understanding. Given that I am a member of the lowest caste and therefore inferior, I must perform this action. In a properly functioning hierarchical society, the person deemed inferior believes that bowing before his superiors is the right thing to do, that it would be wrong to violate this norm. Thus, the possession of answers to all these questions is vital to the working of a hierarchical society. The availability of different answers to roughly the same questions makes possible a functioning egalitarian society.

Of course, to possess a fairly comprehensive understanding of one's society does not mean that this knowledge is available *as answers* to questions. As a matter of fact, we do not first have questions for which we seek answers. We begin to have an understanding of our world that is reformulated as answers to these big questions when, as reflective creatures, we learn to raise these questions. But what are the circumstances in which we learn to raise these questions? There are many reasons why this might happen. I mention three. It might happen first if, for whatever reason, an individual or a group is alienated from the rest of the community. It might then be asked by alienated persons: do I really belong here? Who really am I? This estrangement leads to a crisis of mutual understanding. Second, this could occur with the entry of the stranger whose opaque actions provoke curiosity and internal dissonance. Why is that man doing whatever it is that he is doing? How should we relate to him and others like him? Third, it may be caused by unpredictable changes in the natural world: disease, flood, earthquake, any natural disaster. Why do such dramatic changes occur in nature? Why do they cause suffering in this world? Why is there suffering in the world? Why are we born at all if we *must* suffer?

Now, I want to suggest that small communities develop their own local cosmologies in the face of any of the three changes mentioned above. Unpredictable changes in nature, the coming of the stranger, the possibility of the break-up of the community—all of these lead human beings to seek re-familiarization with what has become unfamiliar. In order to make a fresh sense of the world and their own place within it or to lend larger, deeper significance to our somewhat shaken existence, revisions in common sense become necessary.

Cosmologies perform this function and help us tell a story about ourselves and our relations to others and to nature and make sense of the existing chaos. By making sense of something that is going out of control, becoming meaningless or discordant, they help in endowing it with meaning, make it harmonious with other things and bring it under some semblance of control. Cosmologies inform and re-fashion common sense. They frequently extend and even challenge the common sense of the day by raising some of these questions afresh. Is the world that is apprehended by our senses real? (A question remarkably similar in form to: is the chalk that is crumbling and falling through my fingers really a piece of chalk?) Does life end with the physical destruction of the body? Am I to be identified exclusively with the physical body? Several cosmologies provide negative answers to these questions and thereby oppose our common sense. The world of senses is illusory or there is a life of the soul after death, they say. Whatever the case, cosmologies are never identical with common sense.

The Emergence of Western Modernity

Several ancient cosmologies tied to relatively small communities tended to see these questions as pertaining to one unified universe. A distinction between the human and the natural world was neither drawn sharply nor seemed significant. Metaphysical self-knowledge was believed to be related to an understanding of the whole universe including nature. As Charles Taylor points out, identities in these worlds were not self-defining but defined in relation to the rest of the universe. Moreover, ethics frequently pertained not merely to human action but also to natural events. There was no distinction between science and philosophy and certainly no clear lines were drawn between a philosophy of the natural and the human world.

This judgement might seem over-simplistic about all cosmologies. But it is certainly true of several European cosmologies and Aristotelian sciences and it is not too off-the-mark to claim that elements of such cosmologies are present in virtually every 'pre-modern' cosmology, including in several world religions. Let me stick, however, to 'pre-modern' European cosmologies. For example, before the rise of modern science, much of what we call the Western world believed that the universe is a meaningful whole signifying something higher than humans or embodying some important purpose, goal or final cause and that everything which exists was moving towards the fulfilment of that cause. This was the great design or pattern in the world. Moreover, some cosmologies believed that this design was part of the intention of a transcendent God. To find fulfilment, human beings simply had to relate to this pattern, one that existed in society, nature and the whole of the universe. This pattern could be known either by revelation, by the grace of God, or by pure reason.

Explaining Human and Non-human Nature

Around the 15th century, a change began to occur in the intellectual climate of several Western societies. For many of its members, nature no longer appeared to be meaningful. It expressed neither an idea nor perhaps the intention of some transhuman subject.

Aristotelian physics was challenged by a new perspective. The elements of nature were no longer believed to be purposeful. Fire does not move upwards because this is its purpose; likewise water does not flow downwards to serve this purpose. It is mistaken to understand nature in terms of final causes, as if its design was pre-ordained. Rather, for the moderns, nature was composed of discrete things, in themselves meaningless and independent of one another. They were not related to one another by virtue of some overall design. If related, this relation was more accidental. A ball moves because one hits it with one's foot, not because it is destined to fit into some larger cosmic pattern. Its movement in a particular direction is not pre-ordained. It is due to a variety of contingent reasons, i.e. that a person happened to hit it with his foot and the ball remains hit, keeps moving till some other force stops it. How does one find this out? Not, by relying on cosmologies that talk of deeper significance. This interpretative move, the 'moderns' felt, must first be jettisoned. Instead, one discovers this by 'seeing' the world unmediated by these meanings. One observes what an entity is like, how it happens to relate to other entities. If they happen to relate regularly, then this observed, *de-facto* regularity is what constitutes causation. There are no final causes at work here. Explanation is nothing but recording this pattern of regularity. By recording regularities one can explain not only why something occurred in the past but also why it is likely to occur in the future. If you go near the fire and feel warm and this happens each time you have been there, then this is also likely to happen at a future time. This fact can be predicted. Thus, these new sciences are not just telling stories about nature but, so it appeared to modern thinkers, also explaining and predicting it.

Before the birth of modern empirical sciences, the only form of rational enquiry abroad was philosophy, which used the *a priori* method of reasoning to arrive at answers to each of the six important questions concerning both the worlds taken together. In other words, a speculative, largely non-empirical mode of enquiry was expected to answer all the questions. With the birth of modern natural science, the traditional role of philosophy was transformed. For it now transpired that reason by itself cannot arrive at knowledge of the natural world. It could not by itself answer questions concerning the nature and activity of the physical world, nor to explain or predict what goes on within it. This could be done only with some partnership with the human senses. Some considered this a partnership between unequals, with reason playing a subsidiary role. Others thought that reason and the senses were joint authors of our cognitive world. What the precise nature of this partnership is remained contested but the sole authority of reason had been permanently de-bunked. This meant that philosophy became, in the now famous words of John Locke, 'a hand maiden of science'.

Several thinkers—Hobbes, for example—tried to apply to human behaviour what was earlier applied to natural phenomena. Hobbes tried to replicate the idea of a unified universe, by talking of an all-embracing materialism. To him, it appeared that what held true for the physical world was also true of the socio-historical world. Later, some philosophers drew the conclusion from this Hobbesian standpoint that a rational enquiry of the moral world or the self was impossible. As in the natural world, the task of the rational enquirer was to seek the guidance of the senses, to gather data about the social world and to try and understand its structure, and to explain and predict all the manifold events that take place within it. Theory was a more generalized form of explanation, rooted in and dependent upon data-based enquiry into the particular. Direct observation yielded a knowledge of particular things. Reason saw connections between all these different things and offered generalized explanations and predictions. These generalized explanations were theories of both the natural and the social world.

Understanding Humans

However, soon a second perspective emerged in which the universe began to be segmented into at least two worlds. Though some questions were relevant to each, their form became different. Other questions could be raised only in relation to one of these worlds and not to the other. Modern understanding allows for a much sharper distinction between at least two worlds: the non-human natural world—the world of physical and chemical objects, and the world of plants and animals—and the world of humans that is already constituted by pre-reflective and reflective understanding. To admit the existence of two worlds does not imply that they are completely disconnected from one another. But no matter how deep the relationship between the two, there also exist some fundamental differences.

The Difference between the Human and Non-human Worlds

One such difference is this; while the natural world in principle exists independently of human beings, the human world is largely constituted by and is therefore dependent on human action. The force of gravity is not contingent on whether or not we exist. Neither is the movement of planets. Even if the entire human species were to perish tomorrow, rainfall, thunder, a flash of lightening will still occur. Not only are these independent of our actions, they are also independent of our thoughts. There is rainfall whether or not it is apprehended by us, whether or not we have a concept of it. This is not the case with the human world, which is both action-dependent and concept-dependent. Let me explain.

Consider the act of raising one's arm. This is already different from the expression, 'the upward movement of the limb'. The latter is a purely physical description, while the former is an intentional *act*, a movement guided by or possessing an intention. To raise my arm, I must already be in possession of the concept of an arm and I must know what it means to raises something. The concept of raising something is constitutive of the physical movement of the hand going upwards. Now focus on the phrase 'raising my arm'. This, in turn, may mean different things in different settings, i.e. in different conceptual worlds. In the classroom it means that the student wishes to raise a question or offer a comment on what she has heard. In the board meeting it may signal the act of voting on an issue. On the cricket field it signals a bye and so on. Outside these settings it is simply the raising of the arm. In other settings, it signifies questioning, voting or signalling a bye. In each of these settings, therefore, the relevant concept of questioning or voting or signalling a bye is constitutive of the purely physical upward movement of the arm and involves an enrichment of the simple idea of raising one's arm.

All human actions, practices and situations are *constituted* by concepts. To understand them is to understand these concepts. This is why an *interpretative* component is crucial to what we mean by the empirical in the human sciences. Understanding the human world is to grasp the complicated structure of concepts that partly constitute it. This is not true of the understanding of the natural world. So, this is the first qualitative difference between empirical social sciences and natural sciences; indeed, the word 'empirical' itself has an entirely different connotation in the human sciences. The term 'empirical' is related to experience but the nature of our experience of the natural world is different from experience in the human world. The natural world cannot be apprehended without concepts but it is not constituted by them. In this sense, the natural world exists independently of the concepts we have of them. As I said, it existed even before we had any concepts of them, before we even existed on this earth. This is not true of human or social phenomena.

What is true of human sciences in general is also true of social and political studies. The state is not just an ensemble of material things and movements. To describe it materially is absurd. Besides, such a purely physical understanding fails to distinguish the state from other social and political institutions. The modern state is a form of public power, relatively independent of the ruler and the ruled, embodied in an apparatus that has virtual monopoly of violence in a particular community or territory and that functions to reproduce the conditions of existence and perpetuation of that community. This is just one way of understanding of the state but notice how many different types of concepts we must have already learnt in order to grasp the concept of the state: power, ruling, the distinction between ruler and ruled, monopoly, violence, community, conditions of existence and so on. Take a relatively simple example: A man called John F. Kennedy has just died. Physically speaking, a living body has turned into non-living matter. But we humans describe this event as death. The person in question was no ordinary man, however. He was the President of the United States. To understand this fact about Kennedy is to already grasp a complex institutional setting. Moreover, we must ask: is it true that President John F. Kennedy simply died? Yes, and No. To say that he has died does not convey that he has been killed. Indeed, to say that he was killed still does not capture what has happened. For one can be killed in an accident. Would it then be right to say that he was murdered? This, too, is true but only up to a point. For Kennedy was a President of the United States of America and his murder had a political motive. He was murdered probably by a network of rival political groups, state agencies and the mafia. His was a political assassination. When a person says that Kennedy was assassinated, we assume that he understands the distinction between dying, being killed, murdered or assassinated. Each of these concepts and the distinctions among them are part of, and implicit in the event of Kennedy losing his life.

Thus, we arrive at the following conclusions:

- The question of understanding, explanation and prediction about the non-human natural world is answered by the natural sciences.
- Given the difference between human and non-human nature, the question pertaining to the understanding, explanation and prediction about the human world is answered by the human sciences (by political science, sociology, anthropology, economics, etc.), though always aided by humanities and the arts.

What then is the proper role of social and political theory? Why do we need it? Let me straightaway elucidate two functions of political theory which it shares with social theory. Indeed, the *first* is not a separate function but an integral feature of all social sciences, including political science. If all human phenomena are constituted by pre-reflective or conceptual understanding and if philosophy/theory helps us understand this and make it explicit, then given the first feature mentioned above of political philosophy or political theory, the latter is an integral part of empirical social science. You can neither identify what you wish to explain nor what you are to explain it by unless you have a conceptual grasp of what these are. Philosophy is not merely a handmaiden of the human sciences but its integral feature. This is the interpretative and explanatory role of political theory.

The second function of political theory is this. Some social and political phenomenon have such a large scale that no specific empirical enquiry can do justice to it. Nor can it result from a collection of all the empirical detail. Data gathering and controlled enquiry can never suffice for the understanding of large social formations and for the explanation of changes within them or changes from one type to another. So, the explanation of the rise of capitalism or the transition from feudalism to capitalism can never be understood or explained without some degree of speculation which is independent of empirical enquiry. Nor can we fully understand the nature of modernity or the variety of human predicaments in the modern world or the general attributes of subordination in a society that is colonized by another society merely by controlled empirical enquiry. This job is best done by social and political theory. The object of this enquiry itself is identified at a very general level and its fuller understanding or explanation cannot be properly controlled by empirical data but requires a speculative jump. Political theories must perform this second function of providing insight and understanding into the most general pattern of human practices and social change. Bhikhu Parekh calls this the contemplative role of political theory.

To grasp the *third* function of political theory, it is important to register the second qualitative difference between the natural and the social world and therefore between the natural and the human sciences. It makes no sense to ask moral and self-related questions about the physical world. It is no longer sensible to ask: how do we morally evaluate the force of gravity? Is there anything good or right about the laws of motion? Do chemical compounds have self-knowledge? However, such ethical and normative questions are at the heart of the human world.

Why is this so? Consider once again our claim concerning the action-dependence of the human world. Also, consider any human action. It is true that human action can be explained and to explain it is to provide the reason for why it was done. In this respect, explaining an action is no different than explaining any natural event. But in the case of human action we could ask another question. Is the reason for action a *good* one? Now, to say that it is a good reason is to endorse the action, to justify it. An action is not merely explained, it is also justified and as I said this justification is always accomplished in the light of some idea of good and bad, right and wrong.

This idea of justification can be explained in another way. Take the example from cricket again. When a batsman faces a ball bowled outside his off stump, he also faces a number of distinct possibilities. He can leave the ball alone or flash at it. If he decides to hit the ball, he must make a quick decision whether to drive, slice or cut it, to hit the ball towards long off, to cover drive or square cut. If he is audacious, he can even pull it towards midwicket. This judgement must be made on the spot, within a split second. Now suppose, the ball is a perfect out swinger, the batsman flashes at it, gets an edge and is caught behind. He must ask himself if he had good reason to go after the ball, whether or not he made a correct judgement. Could he justify what he did to himself, to his captain, his team, the team's coach? Indeed, he is answerable to a much wider public. He is answerable because he could have acted otherwise. There is a reason why he got out. But it is not a *good* reason. His rash act can be explained but it cannot be justified.

Now, I want to draw a general conclusion from this example. To say that the human world is action-dependent is to say that it is grounded in one set of reasons from among several available and that the choice to act on one rather than another is made in the light of the person's own understanding and judgement of what is good or right for the agent in the context. This understanding can be evaluated by others. We can ask if the person's judgement of what is good is really so. Moreover, what is true of human action is also true of the state of affairs it brings about. Anything which is a result of human action is out there from among many possibilities and part of the reason why it is there is because the agent or agents in question undertook it in the light of their own understanding of what is good or right. Human action and the world it creates must be necessarily evaluated because a normative component is an integral part of it.

The example I took involves an evaluative but not an ethical dimension. But cricket does possess an ethical aspect, too. Consider once again a bowler who has been hit for three consecutive fours. This assault is not merely on his bowling but on his own reckoning also on his sense of self-esteem and dignity. As he goes towards his bowling mark, he is angry and resentful. Indeed, he is so angry that he cannot contain himself. It occurs to him that to avenge the treatment meted out to him, he should bowl a beamer. Should he, really? He has a second to decide whether to do so or not. Should he use unfair means to remove the batsman from the crease? This is not all. A bookie has offered that if he is hit for four consecutive fours, he would earn twice the match fee paid to him by the Board. Should he succumb to this temptation? He must assess these reasons in the light of some conception of the good life, some idea of right or wrong. A cricketer has this choice. So do all other human beings in their respective contexts. In short, a human being has some degree of ethical or moral autonomy.

Similar ethical considerations also arise in politics. Consider that the state is withdrawing from the public sector, say public educational institutions. The policy of reservations is predicated upon the availability of seats or jobs in the public sector. If admission or employment opportunities get limited in this way, the policy of reservations becomes practically toothless. What must now be done for those who have been historically disadvantaged? At least two options are available. One is to pretend helplessness and to become indifferent to the plight of the 'Scheduled Castes'. The other is to compel the private sector to have, for example, a proportion of seats or jobs reserved for them. Whatever policy the state adopts will be guided by some reason. The question is whether the reason guiding the policy is a good one. And whether it is really good or not must take into account the policy makers' understanding of what is good or bad, right or wrong and the assessment of this understanding by others. It will depend upon whether these considerations are given any weight at all, which itself is a matter of ethics. To fail to assess one's reason in the light of any ethics is itself unethical, if ethics has a bearing on these issues.

Decline of Political Theory?

This view that all human actions including public policy can be evaluated in the light of ethical considerations was not accepted by scientific-minded early modernists and resistance to it has somehow persisted to this day. A number of persons believe that a rational evaluation or enquiry of the moral world is impossible. The moral and political philosophy of yesteryears expressed merely the opinions, tastes and preferences of the individual enquirer and did not deserve the status of knowledge. Our experience yielded a wide variety of forms of self-understandings and moral opinions which cannot be rationally evaluated. If they come into conflict, reason cannot arbitrate between them.

Perhaps for this reason, several philosophers in the Anglo-Saxon world began to claim that political theory was in an irretrievable decline. If political theory is a rational and normative enterprise, as indeed classical political philosophy from Plato to Hegel had sought to be, then after the 'new discovery' about the impossibility of such an enterprise and the rise of the empirical sciences, political theory was believed to have no future. Indeed, as someone put it, it was already 'dead'.

This view, associated with Positivism, is now widely believed to be deeply mistaken. Everything seen, heard or touched by human beings is already constituted by concepts and therefore everything in the human world has to be properly understood even as it is observed. Moreover, most of these concepts carry a normative import. The human world has to be, to some degree and extent, good or bad and human action, right or wrong. There is no feature of the human world entirely free from evaluative significance.

Of course, from this we could draw two different conclusions. If values are impervious to reason but constitute the human world, then all we can have is subjective opinion of this world. This means the impossibility of social sciences. This is a radical conclusion that the positivists did not reach because they rejected the first premise, namely, that facts and values are intertwined. Alternatively, we must abandon the assumption that values are beyond reason, and that therefore, it is possible to have objective knowledge of the human world. If values can be known and rationally assessed, then their permeation in the human world is no barrier to its understanding or rational assessment. This not only brings out the difference between the character and method of the natural and social sciences but also paves the way for a kind of systematic reflection that is exclusive to the human world, namely normative, moral or ethical theorizing.

So, in addition to two functions of political theory mentioned above, we have a third function, one that is special because exclusive to human phenomena: to bring out the normative import of concepts embedded in social practices and used in social sciences and to subject them to detailed critical reasoning. Indeed, for some people this has become the defining, perhaps even the sole function of political theory. Much of Anglo-Saxon political theory focuses only on the normative at a sufficient level of generality. In contrast, political theory on the Continent refuses to separate the normative from the explanatory/interpretative and the contemplative.

Continental political theory has a broader scope for another reason which needs explication and brings into relief the *fourth* function of political theory; to tell us who we are. Recall the point made earlier that in a hierarchical society, people perform actions in accordance with their social role, what in contemporary parlance we might call their identity. A person stands bowed with folded hands or walks at a safe distance from others, given that he is from a lower caste and the other has a much higher rank in the caste hierarchy. What he does now depends on what goes on in society and who he is. More generally, almost everywhere what one should do and who one is are related issues. When we ask the question, what are we to do? There is another question that we do not always ask. The implicit form of the question is: given that this is what we are, what are we to do? Classical political philosophers almost always asked these questions together: given the essence or purpose of human beings, what should they do? In contemporary theory, these questions are separated. Thus, political philosophy remains both a practical philosophy, i.e. one that has an action-guiding character and a systematic enquiry into the self, a kind of metaphysical self-knowledge.

At the cost of repetition, let me once again answer the question: What is the function of political theory? Given that empirical political science is meant primarily to understand, describe and explain how decisions are taken in a society and how some individuals, groups or classes are excluded from such decision making, one task of political theory is to help empirical political science to perform this role. However, it performs three roles not undertaken by the social sciences. First, to offer a general reflection on 'the human condition', on the predicament of modern societies, on who we are and so on (in Chapter 1, see point [e]). Second, a general reflection on a relatively narrow topic: the exercise of power in societies and the mechanisms by which power, i.e. domination is exercised by some over others. This includes the most general reflection on state power but if power resides in the capillaries of a society, then political theory is a reflection not only on the state but on the myriad capillaries in society (in Chapter 1, points [b], [c] and [d]). Third, it is the study of how this power should be wielded, by whom and why, and in the light of which values and ideas of the good life. This is a prescriptive, normative and broadly ethical enterprise. (In Chapter 1, point [f] and partly [a]). These three constitute the distinctive functions of political theory.

We can put the point differently by once again examining the six big questions. If the first three are answered primarily by the natural and the human sciences, the next three questions, of ethics and normativity and of metaphysical self-knowledge are answered by normative political theory along with philosophy, humanities and the arts.

Types of Political Theories

Allow me to elaborate in somewhat greater detail these three different types of political theory.

Explanatory

Suppose that we wish to understand the birth of capitalist socio-economic formations. In the social sciences we have several different explanations. For example, Marx offered a general theory of fundamental social change. In one version of this theory humans have a fundamental interest in improving their material well-being and, therefore, in raising their level of productivity. Thus, Marx believed that this interest explains why there is a constant improvement in the level of productive forces. However, he also believed that a thing became a productive force only in use, and the use of productive forces presupposes that human beings relate to each other in particular ways. Marx called these relations social relations of production. Marx proposed the thesis that a certain type of social relations of production is appropriate, roughly speaking, to a particular level of development of productive forces. For Marx, a particular type of social relations of production facilitates the development of productive forces. However, beyond a point these very relations begin to hinder the further development of these forces. The level of productivity fails to rise, productive forces get into crises and yet the human urge for better material well-being does not cease. In short, a contradiction develops between the ever-developing productive forces and the existing but outdated relations of production. This contradiction, according to Marx, is resolved not by preserving the level of the development of productive forces but rather by changing the social relations of production. The new set of social relations of production comes into existence in order to facilitate the further development of productive forces. Marx developed this general theory to explain the rise of capitalism, which he defined largely in terms of the relation between capital and labour mediated by a free market. Such relations had to come into existence in order to increase human productivity at the time of the emergence of capitalism. Other thinkers offered different explanations. For example, Weber argued that capitalism could not have come into existence without a change in the cultural climate, in the attitudes of a specific set of people. This change of attitude was a component of and was brought about by a transformation in the dominant religion of particular societies. For Weber, the Protestant ethic that emphasized a certain degree of this-worldly asceticism and disciplined work was crucial both for the accumulation of capital and an efficient labour force, both of which were crucial for the emergence of capitalism.

Normative

Suppose that in a poverty-stricken country such as India, there is a demand that the right to work and therefore, that the right to an adequate minimum income be entrenched not just as a desirable goal but as a legal guarantee. Suppose also that there is a great deal of resistance to this idea. For example, it might be argued that while social justice is important, it should not take precedence over the decisions of elected representatives and that therefore the government of the day, backed by the parliament may, from time to time, decide to have welfare schemes for the poor, and no welfare measure should be guaranteed by law. Thus, we have two broad positions on this issue, one for the right to work and the other against it. How do we break the deadlock? How do we advance further to resolve this dispute? We can settle the dispute in a number of ways. One, by a simple recourse to power. A position that is backed by greater power may override the other, irrespective of its moral strength. A pro-poor government may enact a law that entrenches the right to work as a judiciable right. Alternatively, a coalition of wealthy classes may buy off the fence sitters and block the constitutional entrenchment of this right. Both sides may arouse passion and let the matter be decided in the heat of the moment. In all such cases, a decision is made in favour of one or the other position without examining the merits of the case, without a detailed review of possible justifications in favour of either of the two positions. Normative political theory does not accept this way of proceeding on this issue. While it does not disregard the importance of emotion, rhetoric, negotiation and even power, it begins with the assumption that rational argument, in whatever form, must play a pivotal role in decisions on such matters.

So how would a normative political theorist proceed? A brief account may be as follows. The normative political theorist must begin with assumptions that most people can endorse. For example, few would deny that all citizens have a basic interest in living a minimally decent life. Nor would anyone deny that absence of physical suffering is part of a minimally decent existence. Thus, a modicum of material well-being is important for everyone, regardless of caste, religion, gender, inherited wealth and so on. We all have an equal moral right to a minimally decent existence. Once these assumptions are accepted, we are left with the more contentious issues. Does minimal well-being include simply the absence of physical suffering that can be remedied by welfare schemes or does it include the guarantee of work? Here we have to bring in two further issues. First, whether or not the democratically elected government of the day can be relied upon for initiating these schemes? Second, whether apart from the avoidance of physical sufferance, dignity is also an important component of well-being? What psychological impact does merely receiving benefits have on the poor? Is it not important that even the poor feel not that they are living on charity but that they have earned what they receive? Once dignity is included in the concept of well-being, which, if we think of humans not just as biological organisms but as persons, we must, we are committed to the view that, at least in modern societies, work is crucial for well-being. Therefore, a right to well-being, a right to be free from suffering must include the right to work.

To go to the second issue now: can we rely on democratically elected governments of the day to guarantee well-being? This is to be decided partly by the political history of societies and our understanding of the behaviour of people with wealth and power. My own answer is that the government of the day cannot be relied upon for such guarantees. This may be true even for governments with the best of intentions. Indeed, this assurance is even less likely in democratic societies where governments may change every four to five years, and people have to live with a government that might initiate policies that go against their interests. Democratic governments cannot be trusted with the promises they keep, no matter how sincere they are. If so, such guarantees must be made an integral part of the constitution so that every democratically elected government is constrained to ensure the fulfilment of the right to work. An argument such as this neither undervalues democracy nor presents itself as the final word on the matter. It shows that this is one way in which we might proceed in democratic societies. In the last instance, it is meant to take a brief glance at and to illustrate how normative political theory may be done.

Contemplative

In her famous book, *The Human Condition*, Hannah Arendt begins by drawing our attention towards how in 1957, a satellite, an earth-born, man-made object stayed in skies, circled the earth and 'dwelt and moved in the proximity of the heavenly bodies as though it had been admitted tentatively to their sublime company'. She spoke of how for many this was the first 'step toward escape from men's imprisonment to the earth'. She also spoke of other new developments: the splitting of the atom as well as of the birth of a new language of mathematical symbols that contains statements which cannot be translated back into speech. With these introductory remarks, she proposed that in her new book she would offer a 'reconsideration of the human condition from the vantage point of our newest experiences and our most recent fears'. For Arendt, political theory was not reducible to its explanatory or normative functions, although clearly these functions are part of its defining features. Political theory for her, as indeed for many others, continues to be what it was for classical thinkers: a deeply contemplative enquiry into the general condition of humankind either over a very long period or at a certain stage of their changing existence.

Little Theories, Grand Theories

I have claimed that there are three types of political theories, explanatory/interpretative, normative and contemplative. All theories contain each of these dimensions. However, most of them implicitly emphasize either the explanatory (e.g., Weber's theory on the rise of capitalism or Marx's historical materialism) or the normative dimension (e.g., liberalism). These might be called little theories. On the other hand, some explicitly possess both. Let these as well as deeply contemplative theories be called grand theories (e.g., there are traditions of Marxism that claim to have each of the three features). Grand theories need to be distinguished from ideologies, worldviews and cosmologies that possess *one* of the six features mentioned above, namely, generality. In addition, they may possess one or two other features, but rarely all. For example, they may attempt conceptual clarity or possess a rational structure but simply ignore the requirement to unearth hidden presuppositions. Besides, unlike theory, their commitment even to these is half-hearted. They may start off with conceptual elaboration or the construction of an argument but stop mid-way—arbitrarily and abruptly. Almost always, they bypass controlled enquiry into the particular and are, therefore, largely speculative.

Theory and Ideology

The relationship of normative political theory and by implication of grand theories to modern ideology is particularly complex. Both try to persuade—in a crude sense, if we believe that we are roughly equal, we all try to convert one another to our own viewpoint. But there are important differences. While political theory tries to give the fullest possible reason for why a certain stand-point must be adopted, or why an act must be performed on the basis of one set of principles rather than another, ideology lacks a commitment to spell out all reasons. Reason is short-circuited and principles reduced to formulae. This is true of nationalism and fascism but also of liberalism and Marxism when they function as ideologies.

The case of liberal and Marxist ideologies shows that an ideology need not be entirely disconnected from reason. It may have a strategic connection. But it is in the nature of strategic connection that it is snapped if it no longer serves a specified end. As explained above, theory has an intrinsic commitment to reason that an ideology does not have. When liberalism and Marxism function as ideologies, they have merely a strategic connection with reason. This is not so when they function as political theories. It is possible then for Marxist or liberal political theory to come into conflict with Marxist or liberal ideology.

If all that I have said above is true, then political philosophy is even more different from another mode of persuasion and conversion, i.e. propaganda. For in propaganda, conversion is sought by opaque, manipulative methods. Advertising is a good example because here anything goes. Not only is transparency abandoned and reason short-circuited but everything hinges on pure rhetoric. Lies are permitted, so are half-truths. The bad points of a product are never mentioned and the good ones are exaggerated.

Before I end this section, one misunderstanding must be dispelled. Grand theories do share with ideologies and cosmologies another feature; they all perform one function—all of them attempt to formulate a common understanding of the world as well as provide a common normative orientation. When they do both, they provide a common self-definition, an identity. In the performance of this function, grand theories, ideologies and cosmologies may on the one hand compete with, rival, and substitute one another and on the other hand be mutually complementary. Thus, I am not suggesting that ideologies should be replaced by political theory. This can never happen. Ideologies have a function in society. Nor am I saying that we must always be rational and that there should be no place in the public sphere for emotion, rhetoric, or even condensed statements or formulae. But none of these should have such an overwhelming place in society that political theory is seen or made to be entirely redundant.

Cosmologies and Political Theory

I have proposed that there is something distinctive about political theory and implied that something socially valuable is lost without it. In other words, I have suggested that we all need political theory. This might seem an odd claim. After all, many societies have lived without political philosophy or theory. At least, political philosophy has not existed as a separate entity in most societies. At best, we might say with hindsight that it lies hidden within cosmologies. My claim would be more defensible if it was made in favour of cosmologies for it is hard to imagine any society that is not accompanied by a cosmology.

One might then ask why cosmologies alone cannot suffice for the functions I have claimed for social and political theory? This brings us to the question of the difference between cosmologies and theories. And to why in modern societies, cosmologies probably do not suffice. I have three reasons to offer in support of theories. First, cosmologies are local and too tightly tied to contexts. Under modern conditions, however, we live in several contexts at once. Moreover, these contexts are not insulated from one another. They interact, intersect, inter-communicate. In these circumstances, anything with a purely local significance will not do. We need inter-contextual thinking. We need something which does not merely pretend to be general but is really so. Since theories possess this inter-contextual generality, they are better likely to serve us in these conditions. Furthermore, we live in times and in places where people with remarkably different cultural backgrounds and cosmologies have been thrown together. This has happened not merely with globalization but much earlier with the formation of nation-states. Despite their claims of cultural homogeneity, nation-states have had to deal with diverse local traditions and deep cultural heterogeneity. Nation-states bring together strangers. Recall my point that cosmologies are required to re-familiarize what was once familiar and is currently not. Now, this condition of almost permanent unfamiliarity with everything around us, including other human beings with whom we interact, is pervasive in modern societies where, frequently, the very distinction between insiders and outsiders collapses.

Second, the situation in our times is one of a near-permanent crisis of mutual understanding and common agreement. Nation-states are built around a rough consensus on some issues, a mixture of indifference and forgetting on the part of its members, a fair amount of illegitimate force and huge areas of difference and disagreement. Such large societies can hardly be stable. But they are unlikely to survive without a good deal of open communication among its diverse people. Conceptual clarity enables better communication. Through argument, differences which are the norm in our societies can be managed if not resolved. We need to give reasons to one another for and against why some policy is to be initiated. We need to be more critically self-aware of why we are doing what we do. The rational structure embedded in theories appears to offer some hope towards a possible resolution of some of the most significant differences that remain between us. Third, modern societies no longer have one locus of authority. In the past, community-based cosmologies frequently gave answers in a manner that gave the impression that they were emanating a single authoritative source. Some theories which imitate these cosmologies give the same impression. But the truth is that such a source does not exist anymore. We have multiple sources of authority and to communicate amongst them, we need a space where reasons are offered, examined, questioned, challenged, endorsed, rebutted or mediated. A theory provides such a space which local cosmologies may be unable to provide. Apart from these, there is a wholly separate reason: Questions answered by normative political theory need to be even more urgently addressed. There are no easy answers to the questions: 'how are we to live?' 'What am I?' 'What are we to do?' These questions have acquired urgency because old certainties are gone, everything is up for grabs and therefore, everything needs to be justified. Nothing today can be taken for granted. Secularism, democracy and equality cannot simply be assumed. Their ethical importance will always be questioned. Their value has to be justified not only to those who oppose but also to those who defend them. Besides, these concepts do not come in one unique form. Therefore, we have to justify which conception of secularism or democracy or equality is worth having in our context. Normative political theory is meant to do just that.

To sum up, both the task of general understanding and prescribing are crucial in modern societies. A theory of both how power is really exercised and how it should be used is crucial for two reasons. First, because modernity disperses communities and yet connects societies in such an intensified manner that understanding and explanations of specific groups and societies will never yield a relevant, comprehensive understanding of any issue. Disparate but related phenomena must be brought together under a general rubric to give us a satisfactory knowledge of them. Second, traditional knowledge systems and older cosmologies are unable to tell us what we need to do and in the light of which values. Modern political theory appears to have the potential to do so, as long as it performs this task with modesty and with the help of social science, humanities and the arts.

History of Political Thought and Political Theory

I need to address one final issue before bringing this discussion to a close. I have written of political theory as if its history is irrelevant. If I have given that impression, it is because of paucity of time and space. Let me address it very briefly. Consider a social practice. Suppose that it is being challenged by a group but you are not among those who oppose it. You wish to defend the practice and therefore ask the legitimate question: what is the good embedded in the practice. In fact, you may be more neutral and may wish to examine and evaluate the practice so that it may be critiqued or endorsed. But before you begin to do so you must identify it. You need to articulate both what it is and the underlying point behind it. This, however, is not as easy as it seems. Sometimes that with which you are excessively familiar, that which appears to you to be obviously valuable is among the least understood. It is not properly understood because it has receded into the background, almost merged with it. It is so much taken for granted that one does not even notice that it exists. After all, this is precisely what is meant by taking something for granted. This excessive familiarity has then become an obstruction to its proper understanding and to an understanding of its underlying values. If we are to better understand it, a change of stance towards it becomes mandatory. To begin to notice it, we need to make it unfamiliar, to defamiliarize it. Some strategy of radical estrangement is required to counter an already existing familiarity. We need to introduce a part-existential and part-reflective disquiet about the practice. Only then will we begin to better recognize it. Among the strategies of estrangement and re-familiarization is to place the practice along with other similar yet related practices. Locating a practice among others may be accomplished either by the use of one's imagination or by cross-cultural comparison. When this is done one gains the awareness that it is one among several practices, one of the several ways in which the objective or value underlying the practice is accomplished. One realizes that what had appeared natural, what one had taken for granted is one of the many possible ways of doing roughly the same thing and that it is not a natural, permanent phenomenon but a social construction carved out of one set of choices.

Now, this defamiliarization can be accomplished not just by travelling in space, that is, by moving from one cultural location to another existing at the same time but also by moving back in time. In short, by asking the question: what were the analogues of this practice in the past that achieved if not the same, other similar values, values that belong roughly to the same family? Or else, we can go back not to the very distant past where we would find entirely different practices for comparison but to that moment of transition when this very practice began to first take shape? Indeed, to go back to its moment of origin is useful for another reason. It is useful because when the practice was born, there may have been something startlingly new about it. Therefore, it must have been noticed by everyone. This is precisely the time when it was least taken for granted, when those in favour of it were keen to offer a fully explicit defence on its behalf and those opposed to it were equally keen to rebut it. At that period and in that context it is likely that a very rich set of arguments surrounded the practice, one that by now is forgotten. By going back in time, we retrieve those arguments, that one must remember, are once again desperately needed, now that it has become contentious. Rather than put all our labour into a *de novo* articulation of the conceptual and normative structure of the practice, understanding the history of the practice is a more economical way of achieving the same result. We re-articulate what is currently in a hopeless condition of inarticulacy. This remembering is also a process of recovery of the richness of that practice. This is why a proper political argument about rights must take us back to the writings of John Locke, a proper understanding of nationalism must compel us to return to Herder, and in order to properly debate about Western modernity and colonialism, we cannot set aside Gandhi's *Hind Swaraj*. For a full disclosure of all the complex reasons for and against a practice, for the values that inspired it and the murk in which it was entangled we need to uncover the origins of that practice and to fully grasp these origins we need to do the history of political philosophy.

In this chapter, I tried to answer the question what theories in general are meant to do. I suggested that, in their own distinctive way, theories also answer the big questions of human existence. I then suggested that some of these answers are now best provided by systematic empirical enquiry and natural-scientific theories. The natural sciences understand, explain and predict events and processes in the non-human natural world. Scientific theories do the same at the most general level. The social sciences—including political science—understand, explain and seek to predict events and processes in the human world. Political theory is then left to perform three important functions: the explanatory function at the most general level, but more distinctively the contemplative and the normative. In this chapter, I also (*a*) distinguished between political theory on the one hand, and ideologies and propaganda on the other; (*b*) claimed that political theory may be able to respond to our needs under conditions of modernity somewhat better than cosmologies do; (*c*) briefly explained why in the 1950s, there was widespread belief that political theory was either dead or in decline, and; (*d*) explained the relationship between contemporary political theory and the history of political thought.

Points for Discussion

1. Charles Taylor has called humans 'self-interpretating animals'. Gadamer says that interpretation is the distinctively human mode of being. What sense can you make of these statements in the light of what you have read in this chapter?
2. There is a widespread belief that all evaluations are subjective. Good and bad, right and wrong are relative to each individual, at least to every society. This makes normative political theory impossible. Discuss.
3. If cosmologies can explain, understand, evaluate and give effective answers to questions about who we are, then modern political theory is redundant. Discuss.
4. Deep down, political theories are ideologies. Therefore, political theory is an intellectual passion of the elite. Discuss.

Reading List

Arendt, Hannah, *The Human Condition* (Chicago: University of Chicago Press, 1958).

Cohen, G. A., *Karl Marx's Theory of History* (Oxford: Clarendon Press, 1978).

MacIntyre, Alisdair, 'The Indispensability of Political Theory', in David Miller and Larry Siedentop (eds), *The Nature of Political Theory* (Oxford: Clarendon Press, 1983).

Parekh, Bhikhu, 'Political Theory: Traditions in Political Philosophy', in Robert Goodin and Hans-Dieter Klingemann (eds), *A New Handbook of Political Science* (Oxford: Oxford University Press, 1966).

Plamenatz, John, 'The Use of Political Theory', in A. Quinton (ed.), *Political Philosophy* (London: Oxford University Press, 1967).

Taylor, Charles, 'Philosophy and its History', in Richard Rorty, J. B. Schneewind and Quentin Skinner (eds), *Philosophy in History* (Cambridge: Cambridge University Press, 1984).

———, *Philosophical Papers I* (Cambridge: Cambridge University Press, 1985a).

———, *Philosophical Papers II* (Cambridge: Cambridge University Press, 1985b).

Weber, Max, *The Protestant Ethic and the Spirit of Capitalism* (London: George Allen and Unwin, 1930).

CHAPTER 3

Indian Political Theory

Rajeev Bhargava

Chapter Outlines

Introduction

When contemplating whether political theory still holds relevance in the Anglo-Saxon world, one might ponder if it ever truly emerged in India. This inquiry stems from the culturally and historically constructed identity of political theory, which differs significantly from Western constructs. While, recognizing that political discourse in the subcontinent diverges from Western paradigms, it is equally plausible to argue for the absence or underdevelopment of a critical tradition of political theory in India. While India boasts a rich heritage of political and moral treatises spanning centuries, it is arguable that it fails to align with contemporary understandings of political theory.

Absence of Political Theory

To elaborate on this point, let's consider the example of the Indian constitution. Arguably, at last until very recently, a political theory perspective is notably absent in any examination of the constitution. What does this entail? Firstly, existing analyses lack sufficient depth in elucidating the conceptual framework, showing minimal interest in exploring the constitutional implications of or analysing terms such as 'rights', 'citizenship', 'minority', or 'democracy'. Additionally, there's a failure to construct a societal and political vision based on an interpretation of key concepts within the Indian constitution. Secondly, there's a deficiency in grasping the underlying ideals structured within the constitution. While some works acknowledge the values upheld by the constitution, they often lack thorough articulation or critical interpretation. For instance, Gavin Austin discusses Isaiah Berlin's distinction between negative and positive liberty and their influence on the Indian constitution yet stops short of deeper analysis of normative values. Delving deeper into this aspect is a must. Thirdly, in order to refine, elevate to a higher theoretical level, and justify these underlying values, it is essential to examine the Constituent Assembly debates alongside the constitution. A philosophical examination of values remains incomplete without a detailed justification. When the framers of the constitution chose to guide Indian society and polity by particular values, they presumably did so with reasons, many of which remain implicit. Despite the sketchiness and incompleteness of the argument, it's improbable that such considerations were absent. It is therefore imperative that these reasons be made explicit by a thorough examination of the CA debates.

Need for Indian Political Theory

Political theorists need to articulate and refine these arguments to facilitate an informed and meaningful debate on the essence and significance of the Indian constitution. Furthermore, they should identify the broader contextual conditions that enabled the emergence of a constitution-bound society, first among the elites and later among the wider populace.

This absence of rigorous analysis extends beyond the study of the Indian constitution. Numerous concepts in Indian social and political discourse remain under-examined, with only a handful of arguments systematically thought through. Once again, until recently, there had been a notable lack of effort to reimagine the intellectual landscape shaped by major thinker-activists in India. Those who label themselves as political theorists seldom engage in conceptual history, history of ideas, or analysis of social and political thought. Similarly, historians often fall short in providing a non-reductive history of concepts. The impact of colonial modernity sparked diverse streams of thought among various thinkers, yet our understanding of the world shaped by their ideas remains inadequate. While some figures like Gandhi and Bankim Chatterjee receive attention, others, including Nehru, remain largely unexplored. [1]Moreover, the works of social reformers and anti-colonialists remain largely untranslated, further hindering the development of Indian political thought as a discipline within social sciences, humanities, and philosophy.

The absence of political theory not only hinders efforts to foster dialogue between contemporary Western and Indian political theory but also undermines the development of politically theoretical frameworks with transnational potential. This deficiency is evident in contemporary political theory, where while some of its content may have universal applicability, its form remains largely shaped by Western paradigms. Current political philosophy largely overlooks inspiration from non-Western societies, rarely addressing their unique challenges or considering how cross-cultural issues manifest differently in various contexts.

Despite discussions of pluralism and multiculturalism within Western political theory, there is minimal engagement with how these concepts are understood and addressed in places like India. Furthermore, political philosophers display limited curiosity about the experiences of non-Western societies. For instance, in the philosophical discourse on Affirmative Action, the Indian experience, which predates that of many countries by several decades, is often neglected in favor of a focus on the American context. This trend extends to other significant issues as well.

One might argue that Western political theory remains Eurocentric or even Anglo-Saxon-centric. To counteract this bias and to better understand the profound diversity inherent in Indian daily life, political theorists worldwide should consider immersing themselves in intensive courses on Indian society and politics. Debates concerning group rights, self-determination, differentiated citizenship, gender equality, secularism, and constitutionalism would undoubtedly benefit from incorporating insights gleaned from the Indian experience. Without such cross-references, the search for transcultural ideals remains incomplete.

However, the responsibility for this state of affairs cannot be solely attributed to Western political theorists. Indian thinkers have also played a significant role in perpetuating this situation.

---

[1] In the past few years some rectification has happened with the publication of books on Mohammad Iqbal, Savarkar, Maulana Azad and Lala Lajpat Rai.

The prevailing focus on Western political theory has led to a disregard for the diverse experiences and perspectives of countries outside this sphere, such as Indonesia, Senegal, India, Belgium, and Switzerland. This narrow lens limits our understanding of global political dynamics and perpetuates a form of ethnocentrism that overlooks alternative viewpoints.

For instance, while Western countries like Britain, the USA, France, and Germany receive exclusive attention, the experiences of other European nations like Belgium are often ignored. Similarly, the interface of religion and language in Switzerland and its impact on politics is seldom recognized.

This issue extends beyond mere oversight. It results in the adoption of derivative political theories that may not accurately reflect the unique cultural and political contexts of non-Western regions. These borrowed theories often fail to address the complexities of local dynamics and can distort or obscure the interests of their new users.

To rectify this, efforts should be made to promote inclusivity and diversity in political theory and comparative studies. This could involve encouraging scholars to explore non-Western contexts, fostering collaboration between researchers from different regions, and amplifying marginalized voices in academic discourse. Such initiatives can contribute to a more comprehensive understanding of global political phenomena.

Influence of Culture

How many of us care to comparatively explore conceptions of religion——state relationships in, say, Indonesia and Senegal? We have unthinkingly pursued an agenda shaped entirely by the concerns of a few western countries—mainly Britain, the USA, France, and Germany. Exclusive attention bestowed on a small number of western countries is a matter of concern and self-reflection. Indeed, blindness to other European countries is shocking. Consider the Belgium experience on the issue of language. India and Belgium can certainly learn a thing or two from one another about deep cultural differences that emanate from linguistic diversity. But can we think of a single book that discusses the comparative experience of linguistic diversity in India and Belgium? Has political theory been even faintly affected by the mutual experience of these two countries? Or take Switzerland. How many of us are aware of the interface and overlap of religion and language in Switzerland and their impact on Swiss politics. Quite clearly, the West towards which we remain almost permanently oriented comprises a handful of hegemonic countries.

So, we here have a conundrum. Existing, mainly western political theory is excessively ethnocentric but there appears to be nothing at hand to replace it. Whatever political theory exists in the rest of the world, including India, is largely derivative. Now to say of something that it is derivative means that its real source lies somewhere other than where it is currently located, made, or used. To be sure, derivative entities need not always be imports; in a sense, they could even be made by recipients who are among its current users. Yet, these users do not make them under background conditions that facilitate their generation. The conceptual structure of these entities is usually out of sync with the new contexts in which they are made. This dislocation may be minor or major, be easily corrected or align with new background conditions with great difficulty or indeed not at all. The original producers and users of entities have a shrewd idea of what purpose they serve. The borrowers and imitators may use it in ways and for purposes for which they were not designed. Many derivative entities not only thwart the autonomy but also distort or obscure the real interests of their new users.

It sounds like one is highlighting a significant issue in the field of political theory and comparative studies. The dominance of Western perspectives, particularly those from countries like Britain, the USA, France, and Germany, often leads to an oversight of other regions and their unique experiences. This lack of inclusivity not only limits our understanding of global political dynamics but also perpetuates a form of ethnocentrism that disregards alternative viewpoints.

Examples of Indonesia, Senegal, India, Belgium, and Switzerland illustrate how diverse cultural, linguistic, and religious contexts shape political landscapes differently across the world. Yet, existing political theory often fails to adequately address these nuances, resulting in derivative theories that may not fully capture the complexities of non-Western contexts.

The notion of derivative entities, in this case, political theories, suggests that they are borrowed or imitated from Western models and may not fully align with the cultural and political realities of their new contexts. This misalignment can lead to distortions or misunderstandings of local interests and dynamics, ultimately hindering the autonomy and development of political thought in these regions.

Is Indian Political Theory Derivative of Western Models?

Let's tentatively put forward a set of reasons that might explain why social and political theory in India has frequently been derivative of western models. First, as already mentioned, a well-developed tradition of social and political theorizing has never been available to us as a steady cultural resource. We have often been tempted to classify modes of expression and cognition in India as falling within four broad categories. First, those for which one can legitimately claim a long, well-developed, and, more or less, continuing tradition, real or invented. Surely, classical and folk music, epic poetry, theories of grammar, logic, and metaphysics belong to this category. Second, those that belong to a tradition that once existed but has now broken so that their practices are invented either in ferocious opposition to older, fossilized forms or appear to many to be radically deracinated. Here, some forms of poetry, painting, architecture, and theatre come to mind. Third, those for which a tradition could not have existed in the past but does now and is thriving, that is, for example, cinema, film music, and novels. Fourth, practices where a tradition neither existed in the past nor has been invented; probably, autobiographical writing.

Second, unlike cinema, why have we not built a new tradition of social and political theorizing? Here several reasons can be cited. The site where traditions of social and political theorizing develop are almost wholly occupied by vibrant, deeply entrenched cosmologies that continue to orient people to define their world and to normatively view it in ways that inhibit critical theorizing (cosmologies are speculative, non-rational, thrive on ambiguity and polysemy, and are disinclined to examine their own presuppositions or assumptions). In their identity-constituting function, existing cosmologies and Grand theories compete for the same space. Extant cosmologies restrict the development of Grand social and political theories. This in turn impacts the growth even of little theories.

A third possible reason why theorizing in India cannot but help being derivative is the lack of self-confidence and self-esteem, crucial to the development of a new tradition of social theory built on equal terms with the West and appropriate to our conditions. Ashis Nandy has argued that colonialism should not only be viewed in economic and that colonialism should not be solely viewed through an economic lens but also as a factor influencing the psyche, contributing to this lack of confidence.

The impact of colonialism extends beyond political and economic realms to encompass socio-psychological dimensions as well. Even after the end of political and economic colonialism, socio-psychological colonialism may persist. In fact, it can be argued that a new phase of colonialism commenced in India upon the departure of colonial rulers. With newfound liberation, the educated class shed self-imposed inhibitions and uncritically adopted Western cognitive categories. Ashis Nandy suggests that colonialism relies on a shared cultural code that facilitates cultural co-option, akin to what psychoanalysts term "identification with the aggressor." The wholesale embrace of Western conceptual systems exemplifies this psychological phenomenon.

However, this process is not purely psychological; it is also institutional. Specifically, it begins with the academization of Indian intellectual life. Modern Indian universities have adopted Western practices and discourses, perpetuating a form of colonial power. Within the academic sphere, traditional cosmologies coexist with Western political theories disseminated through academic institutions, books, and journals. Accessing the world depicted in Western political theory becomes straightforward for English-speaking individuals, yet discerning this textual world from lived reality proves challenging. The fallacy of misplaced concreteness leads to the misconception that the ideal world of Western political theory mirrors reality in the West and, consequently, becomes the imagined reality for Indians. As a result, one can become a "non-resident Indian" without leaving the country.

Furthermore, the groundwork for social and political theory in pre-independent India surpasses that of post-independent India due to the lack of academization and professionalization in intellectual life during that era. It is often argued that as intellectual life becomes professionalized, it becomes self-referential, severing ties with the external world. Intellectual debates predominantly occur within academia, isolating them from broader societal contexts.

Role of Academia

In academia, peer recognition and career advancement are paramount concerns. While this perspective holds weight, it falls short in the Indian context. Professionalization in academia offers focus, rigor, and depth within specific fields of inquiry, albeit at the cost of disconnecting academics from the broader societal landscape. While Western academia may sometimes take professionalization to extremes, a moderate degree of it is beneficial, particularly in fields previously dominated by amateurs. However, in India, the process of academization has not been accompanied by a commensurate level of professionalization.

This under-professionalization, especially in the social sciences, presents a significant challenge. It leads to an over-ideologization of academia and the public sphere. Ideology, as Clifford Geertz points out, serves as a structured system of cultural symbols that organize social and psychological processes, facilitating purposeful action. Ideologies blend facts and values, rationality and ambiguity, connecting them to the wider world. However, over-ideologization impedes rational critical thinking and controlled inquiry. It manifests as opposition to critical engagement with one's preferred ideology, dogmatic attitudes, manipulation of language to bolster one's viewpoint, and reluctance to consider counter-evidence. Emotion and rhetoric dominate discourse, rendering every statement rhetorically charged.

The under-professionalization of academia hinders direct engagement with the political realm, leading to an overly ideological approach among academics. This impedes nuanced understanding and complicates efforts to navigate complex political realities.

Additionally, over-ideologization within academia can incite extreme responses from some scholars, ranging from detached macro-speculation to a zealous quest to dismantle perceived certainties. This represents a form of negative dialectic at its most extreme.

Moreover, the pursuit of calculated tactical thinking for immediate gains inhibits the impartial reflection necessary for theoretical development. Paradoxically, the democratic process itself, which has fostered a commendable wave of social equality, encourages calculated thinking for short-term advantages. The influx of newly empowered individuals into local and national public spheres, each bringing their own cultural norms and perspectives, has multiplied the diversity of opinions and norms. Consequently, contemporary India grapples with profound uncertainty regarding the very principles it proudly upholds. The confidence with which these principles are defended coexists with underlying anxiety and doubt.

Human psychology reveals that in the face of numerous uncertain principles, individuals often cling to material interests and prejudices for stability. Amidst the transience of ideologies, material interests and prejudices endure, providing a semblance of stability. However, discussions of principles persist, albeit often disguised as interests or prejudices. This tendency leads individuals to believe that their opinions, tastes, values, and lifestyles are superior, serving as the universal standard. Consequently, skepticism regarding general standards of excellence and the absence of commonly agreed-upon criteria for judgment ensue. In such a milieu, rational inquiry suffers, and fragmentation becomes inevitable, with isolated groups lacking cohesive networks for connection.

This network is crucial because new and original traditions of thought emerge not as gifts from historic individuals, but through sustained public discourse and debate. This process relies on interconnected and intercommunicating public spaces, which foster the exchange of ideas and perspectives. However, in India, older public spaces are often dominated by ideologies, while new public arenas are primarily driven by market values.

The principles governing the public sphere differ markedly from those governing the market. In the market, individuals choose between options based on how they affect themselves, whereas in the public sphere, individuals must consider how their choices impact others. The intrusion of market values into the public sphere privatizes it, hindering its function as a space for liberal discourse. This phenomenon has been evident in the distortion of intellectual life by electronic and print media over the past two decades. The expansion of liberal public spaces is essential for the development of social and political theory.

In summary:

Due to the absence of a tradition of social and political theorizing as a cultural resource and the influence of colonialism's second phase, there is a tendency to rely solely on Western theory. Many people fail to recognize the culturally specific aspects of Western theory, as its universalistic language often obscures its cultural origins.

Academic institutions are heavily influenced by Western categories, potentially perpetuating systems of domination.

For most people, identity is better served by older cosmologies than by grand theories. The marginalization or indifference toward grand theories contributes to the stagnation of smaller-scale theories.

Over-ideologization undermines critical and rational inquiry, leading to a distrust of theory.

The development of theories relies on a commitment to broadly defined standards of impartiality, facilitating consensus across diverse interests.

Indeed, pervasive individual or communal egoism can hinder impartiality and impede the development of theories, as personal biases may distort perspectives and undermine objective analysis.

Moreover, there has been an inundation of ad hoc reflections and solution-centered approaches, often driven by ego-focused motivations, which dominate public discourse and academia. This flood of immediate problem-solving responses leaves little room for sustained and systematic reflection.

In the absence of sustained micro-inquiries crucial for theory-building, the existing systematic thinking tends to be highly speculative and aligned with prevailing cosmologies.

How then can we overcome this condition? Can political theorizing in India break free from being derivative? Fortunately, there are signs of change already underway.

Reflecting on the observations from the late 70s to end of 80s, political theorists were predominantly focused on studying and analyzing Western texts. During this time, there were frequent questions regarding the applicability or relevance of political theory. Many political observers showed signs of indifference or impatience as they progressed to advanced studies. This division led to two camps—one in favor of political theory and the other against it. This division stemmed from a collective failure to understand the multifaceted nature and function of political theory. Neither camp properly distinguished between the questions of relevance of political theory in general and the relevance of specific types of political theorizing. The pro-political theory camp inadvertently defended less significant variants along with more worthwhile forms, while the anti-political theory camp indiscriminately attacked both defensible and indefensible versions.

The endless explication of Western thinkers' ideas and meanings has been a significant component of studying and teaching political theory, but it does not encompass the entirety of this vital human practice. Even within the realm of normative issues, our focus did not consistently center on sustained defenses of democracy or institutional autonomy. We often failed to discern and properly distinguish between honorable religious sensibilities and ignoble communal assertions, or to differentiate between various forms of equality and reflect on which inequalities might be justifiable.

However, the climate began to shift in the early 1990s. Several political theorists began to explore the kind of political theory that was necessary and relevant to our context, opening up a new world of political thought. The mid-1980s witnessed context-sensitive empirical theory emerge with Partha Chatterjee, Sudipta Kaviraj, Ashis Nandy, D.L. Sheth, Upendra Baxi, Suhas Palshikar, and Yogendra Yadav. This continued with Javeed Alam and Pratap Bhanu Mehta, alongside Nivedita Menon and Aditya Nigam, bridging empirical and normative approaches. Simultaneously, normative theory arose with Achin Vanaik, Gurpreet Mahajan, Valerian Rodrigues, and Gopal Guru addressing India-specific issues. Scholars like Pratap Bhanu Mehta, Javeed Alam, Neerja Gopal, and Neera Chandoke traversed both domains. Normative theory solidified further with Neera Chandoke, Gurpreet Mahajan, Valerian Rodrigues, Thomas Pantham, Sarah Joseph, Gopal Guru, and Peter de Souza linking societal issues to rights and democracy.

How do we assess political theory in this phase? How original or derivative was it? This we need see in perspective. When multicultural discourse was first examined in India, several scholars argued that it would not align with the crisscross, amorphous pluralism characteristic of traditional India.

The diffusion of ideas to Australia, America, and Britain was evident. However, this perspective diverged slightly. Primarily, because we may not align with the rigid tenets of the sociology of knowledge, which tether concepts and theories steadfastly to specific interests. Instead, one may perceive many concepts and theories as possessing a degree of adaptability and versatility, allowing for diverse applications beyond their original contexts. Critics of multiculturalism often over-contextualized it, viewing it as an alien framework.

Contrary to this critique, our argument is basis certain facets of multiculturalism that find their roots in the practices of modern India more profoundly than anywhere else. Multiculturalism, as practiced, is inherently Indian. Internationally, where multiculturalism conveys a quest for authenticity, India boasts a longstanding tradition of a shared yet distinctive civilization, distinct from cultural nationalism. Additionally, there exists a multicultural nationalism that vehemently opposes narrowly conceived Hindu and Muslim nationalism. Furthermore, within the nation state, practices stemming from constitutionally recognized, group-specific cultural and religious rights prevail.

Despite the formulation and discussion of multiculturalist practices in India, their theorization remained elusive. Why did we turn to the Canadian experience for theories? While theories often emerge from practice, the mere presence of certain practices or casual reflections on them doesn't suffice for theory generation. We must draw upon traditions of theorization and foster a culture of learning from them. While such traditions and institutional frameworks exist in the West, they are lacking or fragmented in India. Without their revival or creation in India, original theories cannot emerge.

This leads to a challenging, somewhat pessimistic conclusion. What should be done in the interim? Most theories originating in the West inherently bear the stamp of their origins initially.

However, by rejecting the stringent framework of the sociology of knowledge, we recognize that concepts and theories can be disentangled from their original contexts, relocated, and endowed with new meanings and nuances. This intricate process of disentanglement and recontextualization must be actively pursued. Understanding how to disentangle requires drawing upon available theoretical traditions, while a firm grasp of our own social practices guides us in determining what precisely needs recontextualization.

This elucidates why multicultural practices don't always necessitate accompanying multicultural theories. It also explains why our multicultural theories, such as Indian political theories, for now, are likely to be co-produced by Indians in collaboration with thinkers like Taylor or Kymlicka. Thus, we may have Indian political theory in a somewhat diluted form, mainly Western theories infused with a distinctively Indian essence. Through engaging in political practices, reflecting on arising issues, and creatively employing traditions of theorizing regardless of their origin, something akin to an Indian political theory is likely to emerge. While the disparities between this and political theories elsewhere, particularly in Europe and the USA, may seem minor, these nuances significantly shape the character of our Indian political theory.

Though a step in the right direction, this may not go far enough. It is not here proposed that we strive for theories born solely from and reflecting the 'genius' of Indians, something uniquely Indian. However, current circumstances imbue me with the confidence to suggest that we can have Indian political theory in a more robust sense. This confidence stems from certain global historical developments, indicating that the era of second colonization may be nearing its end. Gandhi's Hind Swaraj remarkably foreshadowed many aspects of the current juncture, marked by the dramatic, nearly irreversible erosion of the hegemony of modern Western civilization.

The ideas and practices associated with the modern West have long been subject to critique, viewed with suspicion, and sometimes rejected in the past. However, never before has this critique wielded such profound impact, ushering in a transformation in the social and political imagination of a large portion of the global populace. Recent times have set in motion a new historical dynamic that fundamentally alters the relationship between former centers and their peripheries. In essence, the decentralization of power has commenced. The persistent challenges posed by alternative viewpoints and the consequences of its own actions have nearly brought about the demise of Western hegemony.

We find ourselves in a world where hegemonies are in constant flux. The modern West is now just one among many cultures, with its own strengths and weaknesses, in need of improvement like any other. It has been dethroned from its pedestal. While the West still possesses wealth and the capability for coercion, it can no longer assert its superiority over other civilizations. This shift has created an opportunity for genuine cultural and civilizational equality between a significantly weakened hegemon and a previously dominated world.

The emergence of modern Indian political theory

For political theorists, this moment presents a unique opportunity to rethink their approach. Previously, much attention was paid to how concepts originating in the West were adapted and utilized in India, examining the meanings and nuances they acquired. However, the more pressing question now revolves around the internal dynamics of concepts developed in India and how they were impacted by colonial modernity. This necessitates closer collaboration between political theorists and Indian social anthropologists, sociologists, historians, as well as scholars of Sanskrit, Persian, and regional languages, including Hindi.

In the following sections of this chapter, we shall outline what such an endeavour might entail. Let's begin with an example from early Indian history. There is often discussion about tolerance or toleration in Indian civilization. What did this concept truly entail at its best? Tolerance implies refraining from interfering in the morally objectionable beliefs and practices of those being tolerated, even when one has the power to do so. Was this the practice during Ashoka's reign, for instance? Evidence from Ashokan edicts paints a different picture. Many of these edicts recognize the presence of diverse religions as natural occurrences. All religions are deemed deserving of respect and support. Non-Buddhist faiths are not viewed as errors but rather as integral components of a morally productive society. The subjects are advised to avoid excessively praising their own faith while disparaging others', except in appropriate circumstances. Consequently, a moderate critique of other faiths is deemed acceptable, with the assumption that such criticism is made from the perspective of one's own faith, thereby implying its marginal superiority. According to Ashokan edicts, all religions are expected to coexist within a space where they can mutually respect and engage in dialogue with one another. However, acknowledging and respecting other religions does not necessarily imply according to them equal respect. Respect can still be compatible with hierarchy, which is why the term 'toleration' in the context of Ashokan edicts is partly fitting. Ashoka's edicts seem to articulate something beyond mere toleration but fall somewhat short of advocating for equal respect for all religions. This concept transcends neat categorizations of Western political theory.

More can be said on Ashoka's ideas on free speech. Should members of one religious community have a right to freely criticise other religious communities? Why not? Indeed, they must. Should this right be absolute? No right is absolute, but if our speech never upsets other groups, then why have it as a right? So, does discussion on the subject end here? No, because having a right is different from exercising it. So, we need to ask if there are circumstances when it is wise not to exercise but waive it instead? And if we feel compelled to criticise others, in what form must we do so? Should there not be some informal social norms or an ethos that helps us judge when and how to exercise the right to criticise other groups?

Ashoka addressed these issues 2300 years ago. For a start, as already mentioned above, there was great religio-philosophical diversity in his time (Vedic Brahmanism, Upanishadic philosophers, Jains, Ajivikas, Buddhists, to name just a few groups). These included those who made ritual sacrifice central to their ethic and those who didn't, those who believed in gods and goddesses and those who did not, those who thought ritual sacrifice was sufficient for a good life and those who differed, those who believed in the theory of karma and others who didn't, those who evaluated karma negatively (to act is to acquire demerit) and those who did not, those who affirmed and those who denied radical asceticism and those who linked self-fulfilment to compassion towards others and those who did not. This deep diversity must have generated conflict, particularly because Ashoka tried to ensure that all these groups lived together, sharing the same public domain, rather than live separately in ghettoes.

What form did conflicts take? In Ashoka's time, writing was virtually non-existent. Everyone lived in a vibrant oral culture. The entire complex of art, philosophy and religion- poetry, our deepest metaphysical thoughts, acts honouring gods and goddesses.- were spoken, composed, recited, sung, chanted and heard. Words were believed to have magical potency. They could beckon gods to help us tide over problems, create something out of nothing, empower or disempower others, turn them into stone or even kill them. They could be a weapon or an elixir, soothe or cause grievous hurt, bring us together or pull us apart.

In such a strong oral culture, social conflict frequently took the form of verbal duels between adversaries in intellectual combats. Moreover, vitriolic reciprocal name-calling existed alongside fulsome expression of self-praise and excessive bragging about one's own prowess. If words fall off the tongue effortlessly and tumble out inadvertently—worse, carelessly—it is imperative that unguarded speech be checked, that words be enunciated with great care and thought in public. And that is exactly what Ashoka advised—free speech must be regulated by *vācāguti* (the artful management of the tongue), a social norm of a specific kind of *samyama* (self-restraint). While coexisting religious communities might invariably find each other irksome, this negative response, Ashoka argued, must not be privatised or repressed. It should be expressed in the public domain but only upon meeting certain conditions.

To begin with, speech critical of others may be freely expressed only if there are good reasons to do so. Second, even when good reasons exist for criticism, one may criticise only on appropriate occasions. And finally, even on an appropriate occasion, one must never be immoderate. Critique must never belittle or humiliate others. Only moderate criticism on appropriate public occasions is justified. Thus, there is a multi-layered, ever-deepening restraint on negative speech against others—self-restraint for the sake of others.

With this, Ashoka had evolved an original norm of civility, but he did not stop here. He further asserted that one must not extol one's religion/philosophy without good reason. Undue praise of one's community is as morally objectionable as unmerited criticism of the other. Moreover, even when there is good reason to praise one's own perspective, it too should be done only on appropriate occasions, and even then, never immoderately. Excessive self-glorification is a way to make others feel small.

Indeed, blaming other groups out of devotion to one's own world view and unreflective, uncritical self-praise, argued Ashoka, damages one's own community. By offending and thereby estranging others, such speech undermines the capacity for mutual interaction and possible influence. Thus, there must equally be a multi-textured, ever-deepening restraint on oneself—self-restraint for the sake of one's own self. For Ashoka, our duties towards others cannot be neatly separated from the virtues we cultivate in ourselves. Our moral concern for others can't be hived off from our ethical regard for ourselves. So, if Ashoka were alive today, he would argue that a crucial precondition for exercising one's right to free criticism of other groups is a robust ethos of self-restraint and self-criticism. A social norm of self-reflective civility in public speech is a perfect antidote to the mutual estrangement between communities now creeping into our society.

Since Dumont introduced the essentialist notion that Indian society should be perceived as an organic whole characterized by a hierarchical caste system, and partly because this mirrored the nineteenth-century social reality in India, it has been challenging for scholars to conceive that a form of equality existed as a conceptual foundation in our traditions. However, it did. Despite the Mahabharata being commonly associated with endorsing the caste system, it contains verses urging the Brahmin Kaushika to learn about dharma from a lower-caste person engaged in trade. Implicit in this is the notion of some form of dharmic equality. Moreover, Buddhism's challenge to Vedic Brahminism arguably positioned it as one of the earliest proponents of the idea of social equality, thereby creating a conceptual space that would be later embraced by low-caste Shudras and outcastes.

Between the seventh and thirteenth centuries, various movements, collectively known as 'bhakti', embodied egalitarian principles. One such movement, the Virasaivite movement led by the Karnataka saint Basavanna and popularized by vachana writers in the twelfth century, was particularly radical. Despite being a Brahmin, Basavanna rebelled against Brahmanical orthodoxy, ritualism, and caste- and creed-based discrimination. His movement accorded special status to women and played a significant role in challenging Brahmanical supremacy and, to some extent, patriarchal values.

In the context of the Virasaivite movement, women gained prominence for their roles in creation and nurturing, surpassing the importance traditionally accorded to men. Additionally, individuals from lower castes, lacking the trappings of wealth and power, were considered closer to the divine than Brahmins. Worshiping Shiva, the movement rejected Vedic authority regarding cremation rites, advocating burial instead. It advocated for widow remarriage, condemned child and arranged marriages, and did not consider women polluted during menstruation.

Women saints, often dedicated to God from a young age, challenged many male-centric norms. They resisted parental pressure and avoided marriage through various means, including steadfast devotion, adopting the life of a courtesan, transforming into an unmarriageable elderly woman, or even assuming a male identity. Similar to Buddhist and Jain women of the past, they had the liberty to explicitly renounce marriage. While the initial radicalism and anti-Sanskritization of the Virasaivite movement waned after the twelfth century, and socio-economic disparities persisted, reinforcing caste hierarchies, patriarchy, and gender inequality, several aspects stood out in its early phases.

Firstly, it defended social equality and rejected caste and gender hierarchies. Secondly, it emphasized individual choice and responsibility in religious matters, advocating for liberation unmediated by social authority or institutions, thereby laying the groundwork for socio-religious freedom for individuals. Lastly, this freedom not only challenged established authority but also provided a platform for radical dissent.

We have highlighted the emergence of conceptual frameworks where ideas of religious tolerance, social equality, and individual freedom flourished in early Indian history. Moving into the Sultanate and Mughal periods, my focus shifts towards notions of Sharia, state authority, and justice.

Scholars argue that political exigencies prevented Afghan and Turk rulers from imposing Sharia law on their entire kingdom populations. Instead, they followed Quranic injunctions advocating for peaceful coexistence between Muslims and non-Muslims, recognizing religious diversity. However, this policy of political expediency wasn't universally accepted among the ruling elite and religious clergy. Rulers often yielded to pressure from religious orthodoxy. For instance, Ziauddin Barani emphasized the duty of rulers to protect Islam and Muslims, considering any action taken in the interest of Islam as praiseworthy, even if detrimental to others. According to Barani, a decision that disregards Sunni Islam is deemed tyrannical, while royal actions in support of Islam cannot be despotic.

Similarly, Ali Hamdani argued for the differential treatment of Muslims and non-Muslims by Muslim rulers. Non-Muslims were to be protected by the state only if they refrained from constructing public places of worship, and even their private religious structures were to be accessible to Muslim travelers. Public displays of non-Muslim rituals were not tolerated, and the jizya tax imposed on non-Muslims served as both a financial burden and a symbol of inferiority, often incentivizing conversions to Islam. Hindus, in particular, were reminded of their subordinate status within an Islamic state.

However, this perspective doesn't capture the full picture. It overlooks how Sharia law was reinterpreted and how justice, rather than religious law, became a fundamental value underlying the state. In contexts where rulers' religious beliefs diverged from those of their subjects, dissenters within Sunni Islam reshaped the interpretation of Sharia to legitimize a diverse and inclusive city, where various religious and social practices coexist harmoniously. An ideal ruler, in this view, prioritized the well-being of all people, irrespective of their religious affiliations.

For these dissenters, Sharia was not to be narrowly interpreted solely within the realm of jurisprudence but rather through a broader philosophical lens. It evolved into a more adaptable concept of practical political philosophy rather than a rigid legal doctrine. In the narrow juridical interpretation, exemplified by the works of Barani and Sirhindi in the sixteenth century, the rule of Sharia implied not only the dominance of Muslims but, if not the eradication of infidelity, at least the subjugation of non-Muslims. However, for those who adopted a more philosophical interpretation of Sharia, such as Abul Fazl, Sharia became synonymous with Namus, or divine law. Its primary objective was to maintain a balance of conflicting interests, foster harmony among different groups and communities, and ensure non-interference in personal beliefs.

Furthermore, dissenters within Sunni Islam developed a concept of a state founded on justice, which, while not entirely divorced from Sharia, was nonetheless compatible with it. This perspective is evident in the Nasirian tradition, particularly in texts like Akhlaq-i-Nasiri. Akhlaq texts focus on human beings, their livelihoods, and the temporal world. While human perfection requires devotion to divinity, it also necessitates a well-organized and cooperative society. Social cooperation relies heavily on justice. In the absence of justice, individuals pursue their own self-centered desires, undermining social cohesion. To foster cooperation, a balancing mechanism is essential. Sharia serves this purpose, but it requires the administration of a just ruler whose primary duty is to govern with affection and fairness.

In the Akhlaq literature, justice in an ideal state equates to social harmony and the equitable resolution of conflicting claims among diverse interest and religious groups. This concept of justice entails not only the fair distribution of resources but also the nurturing of mutual love and cooperation among individuals and communities. In essence, social harmony is achieved through the equitable sharing facilitated by justice administered in accordance with the law, upheld and promoted by a ruler who governs with compassion, favors, and justice rather than authoritarian decree.

Since humans adhere to diverse religions, conflicts may arise. The role of the perfect divinely appointed figure, known as Namus or Sharia, is to prevent such conflicts. Justice further dictates that no individual should receive either less or more than they deserve based on their class. Both excess and deficiency disrupt the natural order of societal relationships and companionship. This emphasis on the importance of justice is argued from a secular ethical standpoint, advocating for fairness for all and opposing discrimination based on faith. Kings are advised to regard their subjects as "sons and friends" regardless of their religious affiliation, demonstrating that justice serves the genuine public interest. A non-Muslim but just ruler is deemed more beneficial to society than an unjust Muslim sultan. The ancient Sassanid kings, despite being fire worshippers and non-Muslims, maintained power for 5,000 years. The concepts of justice in Akhlaq and Mutazilite theories shared similarities, although the former was rooted in divine will while the latter relied on human reason. While the Sunni tradition predominantly favored the former, elements of the latter, whose ethics closely resembled the former, also influenced the tradition.

Akbar took progressive steps in this regard. As the de facto caliph in India, every Muslim ruler relied on the religious guidance of ulema. In 1579, Akbar reduced the authority of the Sadar-us-Sadur, the chief theologian responsible for interpreting and applying Sharia. Akbar asserted that as a just ruler, he was not bound by any particular interpretation of Sharia and had the authority to issue legally binding interpretations in cases of disagreement. This stance exhibited clear secular overtones. Additionally, Akbar abolished the tax on Hindu pilgrimage centers and the jizya tax on Hindus. While some argue that these actions were primarily motivated by state exigencies rather than religious tolerance, this assertion is more applicable to the early part of his rule.

Over time, Akbar unfolded his philosophy of Sulh-I-Kul, meaning 'absolute/universal peace,' through a composite approach of socio-religious tolerance. He introduced Din-i-Ilahi, an independent belief system, separate from orthodox Islam or Hinduism, which questioned both religions using neutral terminology to address intra and inter-religious controversies. This philosophy was heavily influenced by pantheism, asserting that while God creates visible differences, the ultimate Reality remains the same. Akbar implemented policies prohibiting forced conversions to Islam, relaxed restrictions on temple construction, and appointed Hindus to prominent positions in his administration. He organized religious dialogues open to Muslims, Hindus, Jains, Parsis, and Christians alike. Translations of Hindu scriptures like the Mahabharata and the Upanishads into Persian were commissioned, and various Hindu festivals were celebrated in Akbar's court.

In personal matters, Akbar followed Hindu yogic practices such as abstaining from meat and shaving the center of his head. He adopted the term 'chelas' for his household servants, reminiscent of the disciples of yogis, and appointed a Brahmin to translate Khirad Afza. He demonstrated interest in the worship of fire and the sun, permitted his Hindu wives to worship their idols within the palace, and showed curiosity about the concept of reincarnation. Additionally, he revered the Virgin Mary and allowed the construction of churches.

These actions stood in stark contrast to the prevailing religious bigotry and intolerance elsewhere in the world. The 'Age of Akbar' coincided with a period of bloody religious wars in France and other parts of Europe, including the St. Bartholomew's massacre in 1572.

Conversely, the Ottoman emperor emphasized the enforcement of Sharia as a crucial aspect of state policy. Akbar's tradition of equal or near-equal respect and impartiality towards all religions was continued by the British. It's plausible to conclude that while Europeans learned the idea of tolerating other sects from their own experiences, the conceptual foundation for impartiality towards all faiths was established in the Indian subcontinent and possibly transmitted to Europe through colonial encounters and the legacy inherited from colonial subjects' polities.

The ongoing discussion not only elucidates concepts within different periods of Indian history but also contributes to an anti-anachronistic, non-teleological understanding of the evolution of modern secularism in India. This perspective offers a preliminary framework outlining how various traditions, including popular Hinduism, Buddhism, Jainism, Sufism, and court Islam, created conceptual spaces that paved the way for later generations to develop a distinct conception of India's secular ideals. Buddhism, for instance, fostered ideas of minimal material well-being and equitable social relations, while the history of India showcases a persistent narrative of religious toleration and freedom alongside accounts of religious oppression. Similarly, principles of human equality can be discerned in Buddhism, bhakti and Sufi movements, popular Islam, and intermittently in Akbar's eclectic religious practices. Additionally, elements supporting a principled separation between state and religion can be traced back to India's deep religious diversity dating back to at least the fifth century BCE, further reinforced during the Sultanate and Mughal periods.

Conclusion

Preliminary accounts are not without their internal challenges. Firstly, there is a risk of adopting an overly triumphalist stance, wherein the emphasis is placed more on the conditions conducive to the development of secular ideals rather than on those that undermine them. Secondly, chronological narratives carry the potential for teleological bias and an unwarranted belief in progressivism. Thirdly, such accounts may inadvertently mirror the modernist vocabulary inherent in the social reform movements of the nineteenth and twentieth centuries, thus falling prey to anachronism. For instance, the claims made regarding the Virasaivite movement's advocacy for widow remarriage and rejection of arranged marriage, as well as their belief in the purity of women during menstruation, prompt questions about the distinctions between life in the eleventh and twelfth centuries and contemporary society. Without addressing these questions, it's difficult to fully comprehend the differences between historical and modern contexts.

Even if we entertain the notion that there were intriguing developments occurring in certain regions of southern India during the twelfth century—long before the onset of Western modernity—we still lack a comprehensive understanding of the historical context, social dynamics, and cultural and political mindset of that era. Our grasp of how historical actors perceived and articulated their actions and intentions is inadequate, leading to anachronistic interpretations and a failure to appreciate the profound disparities between their world and ours.

Another challenge arises from the interpretation and translation of critical terms. When terms like "equality" are translated, what precise meanings are implied? How do we interpret claims that religious reformers like Kabir aimed to eradicate the caste system? How do we conceptualize notions of individual agency and accountability? In essence, we are confronted with the need to reject absurd notions that ideas of individualism, freedom, and equality originated solely in the modern West and were absent elsewhere. However, we must also avoid falling into the traps of ethnocentrism and anachronism. It's imperative not to project modern Western conceptions of freedom, equality, or individualism onto India's historical narrative. Instead, we must unearth a new language and vocabulary, excavating buried treasures to reassess not only non-Western history but also to reframe the narrative of Western history.

The primary challenge lies in the fact that the conceptual framework within which we operate—terms like "secular," "state," and the notion of church-state separation, implicit in "political secularism"—has largely evolved within the context of Western Christendom and modernity. A deeper, conceptually nuanced examination of historical sources might reveal entirely different concepts and categorical frameworks, fundamentally challenging the terms we currently utilize. This underscores the formidable task of evolving a form of political theory that resonates with our own context while also engaging with and reshaping Western political theory. However, the underdevelopment of political theory in India could be advantageous because, unlike the heavily professionalized discipline of Western political theory, Indian political theory can draw inspiration from real political struggles and conflicts. Indeed, the ongoing debate on secularism in India has been fueled less by academic disputes within the discipline and more by the looming spectre of religious majoritarianism in the late twentieth century.

Indeed, without promptly cultivating a scepticism towards prevailing dominant theories, embarking on more detailed micro-inquiries that are highly targeted, and, crucially, delving into the traditions of reflection accessible to us from pre-independent India and earlier periods, the development of a political theory capable of addressing our pressing and enduring challenges is unlikely to materialize.

Points for Discussion

1. What are the main challenges and pitfalls associated with interpreting historical narratives through a modern lens?
2. In what ways might the underdevelopment of political theory in India offer unique opportunities for the development of new perspectives on political thought?

3. How do you interpret the author's call for a deeper engagement with traditions of reflection from pre-independent India? What specific traditions or thinkers might be relevant in this context?
4. How might a more nuanced understanding of historical contexts and terminology contribute to the development of a political theory that speaks to contemporary challenges?
5. What implications might the author's critique of anachronism and ethnocentrism have for how we teach and study political theory?
6. What steps can individuals and institutions take to promote the cultivation of alternative perspectives on political theory within academic and intellectual communities?

References

A version of this paper entitled 'Notes on Derivative Theorizing in India' was presented at a workshop organized by the Architectural Forum at Mohile Parekh Centre, Mumbai in early 2002.

Bhikhu Parekh in 'The Poverty of Indian Political Theory', unpublished paper that is part of the Hull papers in Indian Politics (edited by Noel O'Sullivan), undated, p. 1.

Gavin Austin, The Indian Constitution: Cornerstone of a Nation, New Delhi: Oxford University Press, 1999, p. 51.

Alfred Stepan, 'The Multiple Secularisms of Modern Democracies', in Craig Calhoun and Mark Juergensmeyer (eds), Rethinking Secularism.

Ashis Nandy, The Intimate Enemy, 1989, Oxford: Oxford University Press.

C. Geertz, The Interpretation of Cultures, New York: Basic Books, 1973, pp. 216–18.

Jon Elster, 'The Market and the Forum: Three Varieties of Political Theory', in Robert Goodin and Phillip Pettit (eds), Contemporary Political Philosophy, Oxford: Blackwell, 1997, pp. 128–42.

Shail Mayaram, 'Recognizing Whom? Multiculturalism, Muslim Minority Identity and the Mers', in Rajeev Bhargava, Amiya Kumar Bagchi and R. Sudarshan (eds), Multiculturalism, Liberalism and Democracy, New Delhi: Oxford University Press, 1999, pp. 380–99.

K. Scheible, 'Towards a Buddhist Policy of Tolerance: The Case of King Ashoka', in J. Neusner and B. Chilton (eds), Religious Tolerance in World Religions, Pennsylvania: Templeton Foundation Press, 2008, p. 321. Also, see Romila Thapar, 'Asoka and Buddhism as Reflected in the Asokan edicts', in Romila Thapar (ed.), Cultural Pasts, New Delhi: Oxford University Press, 2000, p. 432.

V. Ramaswamy, Divinity and Deviance: Women in Virasaivism, New Delhi: Oxford University Press, 1996, pp. 147, 192.

K. Jones, Socio-religious Reform Movements in British India, Cambridge: Cambridge University Press, 1994, p. 11.

Vinay Dharwadker, The Collected Essays of A.K. Ramanujan, New Delhi: Oxford University Press, 1999, pp. 271–8.

P. Mukta, Upholding a Common Life: The Community of Mirabai, New Delhi: Oxford University Press, 1994.

K. Sangari, 'Mirabai and the Spiritual Economy of Bhakti', Economic and Political Weekly, 7 and 14 July 1990, pp. 1464–75, 1537–52.

M. Alam. 2004. The Languages of Political Islam in India c. 1200-1800, Delhi: Permanent Black. p. 59.

R. Aquil, Sufism, Culture, and Politics, New Delhi: Oxford University Press, 2007, p. 232.

I. A. Khan, 'The Nobility under Akbar and the Development of His Religious Policy, 1560-80', in Richard M. Eaton (ed.), India's Islamic Traditions, 711-1750, New Delhi: Oxford University Press, 2005 (reprint), Ch. 5.

S. A. A. Rizvi, 'Dimensions of Sulh-I Kul (Universal Peace) in Akbar's Reign and the Sufi theory of Perfect Man', in I. A. Khan (ed.), Akbar and His Age, New Delhi: ICHR, 1999, pp. 3–21; I. Habib, 'The Mughal Empire', in J. S. Grewal (ed.), State and Society in Medieval India, New Delhi: Oxford University Press, 2005, p. 79.

M. Athar Ali, Mughal India, New Delhi: Oxford University Press, 1996.

E. Vanina, 'Meeting of the Oceans', in her own book, Ideas and Society in India 16th–18th Centuries, New Delhi: Oxford University Press, 2004 (second reprint; first published 1996), p. 82.

S. Chandra, 'Historical Background to the Rise of the Bhakti Movement in Northern India', in his own, Historiography, Religion and State in Medieval India, New Delhi: Har-Anand Publications Pvt. Ltd., 2004 (third reprint; first published in 1996), pp. 110–31.

Rajeev Bhargava, Beyond Toelration: Civility and principled coexistence in Asokan Edicts, in Alfred Stepan and Charles Taylor (eds) The Boundaries of Toleration, Columbia University Press, New York, 2014

PART II

Concepts

CHAPTER 4

Liberty

V. Sriranjani

Chapter Outlines

Introduction

Consider the following sentences—

The BA class wants to have a free period (state of affairs).
I feel free to talk to my teacher (perception).
I am totally free to choose my career (choice).
Even in the 21st century, a substantial part of South Asia's population is not free from the clutches of poverty (denial of material needs).
No country should be denied its freedom (denial of a sense of dignity).

Now, let us substitute the term liberty wherever 'freedom' has been used in the above instances. Each of these sentences brings to the fore a different dimension of the concept, defying a single definition of liberty. They also highlight concepts other than liberty—equality, right, justice, etc. How does one then delineate and distinguish the concept of liberty?

Meaning

Let us take the following sentence as an example—'I am at liberty to learn how to drive a car.' To begin with, it means there are no hindrances to your decision. Nobody physically stops you from learning how to drive a car. Second, the existence conditions for learning how to drive a car are available and accessible. So, you would have to have access to a car, a person who is willing to teach you how to drive, streets where it is safe for you to practise driving, etc. Third, and in a certain sense this precedes the first two, you have a choice to learn how to drive a car. So, the concept of liberty carries three connotations—the notion of *choice*, the *absence of constraints* to make and exercise such a choice, and the *existence conditions* that enable you to actuate the choice.

Evolution of the Concept

Liberty as a concept has been viewed variously by thinkers in various stages of the history of political thought. Each of these views expresses the thinker's understanding of the historical phase in which the concept evolved and is in sync with the larger philosophical outlook of the thinker. Let us understand the views of the various thinkers and see to what extent each of them mirrors the three connotations of liberty—choice, absence of constraints, and existence conditions.

Read the following sentence and observe the meanings that it gives rise to—'I am free to take my political theory exam.' Invariably, the first thing that comes to one's mind is that one is not restrained from taking the exam. Now, let us look at the reasons for which one wants to take the exam. Broadly, one wants to take the exam to clear it and secure career prospects. Two immediate reasons can be stated—first, it is necessary to take the exam if one has to be promoted to the next level; second, if one does not take the exam, one is declared to have failed the paper. So, the fear of failure impels one to take the exam. Let us take the example further. My future security depends on clearing the exam. But I am not prepared for the exam. In this context, if I am at liberty to take my exam and do whatever I can to secure my future, does it include the liberty to cheat in the exam?

It is this understanding of liberty that is put forward by **Thomas Hobbes** in his fictional state of nature. According to Hobbes, liberty or freedom signifies the absence of all impediments to action that are not contained in the nature and intrinsic quality of the agent. As Hobbes would explain, it is proper to state that the person who is tied with chains wants the liberty to leave, as the impediment is not in the person but in his chains, whereas that cannot be said of one who is sick or lame, because the impediment is in oneself. Fear and necessity, for Hobbes, are the motivating factors in human nature that impel them towards liberty. As he explains, a man sometimes pays his debts only for fear of imprisonment, which because nobody hindered him from detaining, was the action of a man at liberty.

Two issues emerge. One, can the act of one to preserve oneself be justified as an act of liberty even if it violates the safety of another human being(s)? Two, do you think the action of a person based only on fear or necessity is an act of liberty? Would you say that the act of begging due to the fear of starvation or the necessity to eat one square meal a day is an act based on liberty? After all, the beggar is not physically restrained by anybody in the act of begging.

While such an understanding of liberty does take into account the 'absence of constraints' aspect, it totally undermines the notion of choice and does not recognize any kind of moral framework. Going back to our example of wanting to learn how to drive a car, one may want to learn to drive a car as there is no other mode of transport available or because one is coerced into it. However, for it to be a decision based on liberty, the decision has to be based on the fact that one wants to learn or does not want to learn driving. It is this notion of choice that is conspicuously absent in the examples by which we understand Hobbes's view of liberty. The beggar does not have a choice on whether s/he wants to beg or not. Similarly, a dacoit cannot rob or kill anyone and explain it as an act of liberty to preserve herself/himself.

Hobbes' understanding of liberty, based on considerations of fear and necessity rather than choice, does not make a clear distinction between acts of liberty and acts under the threat of coercion. For choice to be exercised in the exercise of liberty, existence conditions have to exist. Such conditions can include material resources as well as a moral framework. The scope to exercise choice in a moral framework finds place in Locke's understanding of the concept.

Let us reconsider the example of choice cited at the beginning of the chapter—'I am totally free to choose my career.' This basically throws up two points—'no one should dictate to me what my career should be. So, if I want to be a VJ (video jockey) or a writer,

I should not be forced to become an IAS (Indian Administrative Services) officer or do an MBA course. However, my choice of career should not harm anybody. So, I should not choose a career as a thief or murderer.'

It is this view of liberty as choice exercised in a moral framework that comes across in **Locke's** understanding of the concept. This moral framework is based on the Laws of Nature of which equality is a central tenet. The Law of Nature, according to Locke, is that no one ought to harm another in his life, health, liberty, or possessions. Liberty as a natural right, for Locke, is no more than the liberty to do what the Law of Nature allows—in other words, what is morally permitted. For Locke, each individual is free to the extent the exercise of freedom does not violate the tenet of equality. The exercise of liberty should not be at the cost of equality.

Now, what does liberty as a natural right imply for Locke? As a natural right, liberty is a universal right. It is a right held equally by all in the state of nature. It is also a right that is bestowed by nature along with the right to life and property. As a natural right, liberty is innate in human nature, is universal and can be apprehended by reason. As a right bestowed by nature, Locke views it as inalienable. In other words, one cannot waive from one's person the right to liberty. As Locke states, 'Every One … *is bound to preserve himself,* and not to quit his station wilfully; so by the like reason when his own Preservation comes not in competition, ought he, as much as he can, *to preserve the rest of Mankind*' (Locke 1988: p. 271, emphasis added).

As a natural right, liberty precedes civil and political society in Locke's thought. The contract of civil society is drawn to preserve natural rights, including liberty. While the political society regulates liberty, it has no power to constrain it. The Lockean individual is guided by the faculty of reason in the exercise of freedom in conditions that are alterable. So, the Lockean individual will not seek the freedom to want to fly like a bird but will seek the freedom to be heard even if in a minority.

While the moral framework of Locke ensures existence conditions that qualify the 'absence of restraint' and the element of choice, it does not specify ways to bring about existence of conditions to facilitate choice. Let us understand this through the earlier example—I am free to choose my career. In the Lockean scheme, this will amount to the following—Nobody has a right to dictate to me my choice of career. I have as much right to choose my career as any other person. My choice should not harm anybody.

These implications, however, do not take into account restraints on choices that are not natural. Again, going back to the example of a beggar who begs for a living—nobody need have dictated the beggar to choose begging for a living and neither does it harm anyone. Does it mean that the beggar chose to beg as a natural right?

Till now, the concept of liberty or freedom has been discussed basically at the level of the individual. Also, the exercise of liberty is either preserving oneself (Hobbes) or operating within a moral framework (Locke). But neither of these conceptions addresses the hindrances of hierarchy and inequality in the exercise of liberty. While Locke does consider natural equality as a prerequisite, social inequalities are not addressed at all. It is this hindrance to liberty that is addressed in Rousseau's thought.

Consider the instance that some of us own a vehicle and travel by it in the city. This can have two possible effects. One, it introduces a hierarchy between those who own a vehicle and those who do not. Two, it increases pollution levels that is harmful to all. So, liberty here can be understood as liberating the people of the city from the hierarchy and inequality between a few people owning vehicles and those who do not. Liberty is also choosing the right option, in this case, a pollution-free option.

Rousseau considered freedom as a collective venture, and as freeing oneself from selfish motives towards a larger good for the entire group. His conception of liberty liberates human beings from the hierarchical and unjust inequality of society. Rousseau views this inequality as the constraint in the realization of liberty. Unlike Hobbes and Locke, liberty is not a natural right for Rousseau. Liberty for him is liberation from a state of unfreedom which comes into being with the emergence of civil and political society. Constraints on liberty refer to the constraints of one's baser nature that does not facilitate human nature to think of the good of all. Constraints also refer to the inequality in society that does not allow for the exercise of liberty.

A people is liberated only through obedience to law. Law is equated with the expression of the general will of the whole community. The individual in obeying the laws obeys one's own self as the author of those laws, authored by virtue of the capacity of uniting with others in the community. An individual can be free only by being a part of a free people who obey laws.

For Rousseau, one is liberated when one is free of personal servitude. His way out is to make individuals dependent not on other individuals or institutions, but upon the whole community, which protects the goods and persons of every citizen with the united force of all. The individual is liberated from subjection to one's lower nature in uniting with the whole community. As Rousseau states, 'a free people obeys, but it does not serve, it has leaders but no masters; it obeys the laws, but it obeys only the laws, and it is due to the strength of laws that it is not forced to obey man'. It is the understanding of freedom through obedience to law that is captured in the famous phrase of Rousseau in *The Social Contract*—'Man is born free, but everywhere he is in chains.'

The element of choice in Rousseau's thought is quite interesting. It appears that he seems to equate choice with the right to choose the right option, where the *right option* is pre-decided. For example, driving a car can be seen as something that contributes to pollution. Pollution is harmful to all. It can then be decided that the right option is to ride a bicycle rather than drive a car. So, the existence conditions would be tailored not towards conditions that enable them to drive a car but conditions that are friendly to cyclists and pedestrians as also conditions that would check pollution levels and be in the interest of the larger good.

The word freedom may also have a parallel, though simplistic, reference to the idea of pleasure. Utilitarians see a positive correlation between freedom and pleasure. Freedom is about seeking pleasure and avoiding pain. This is best captured in Bentham's works. Liberty for **Bentham** is viewed through the utilitarian maxim of 'Greatest Happiness of the

Greatest Number'. In this view, the liberty of the rapist or the murderer comes into practical competition with that of the victim.

Let us look at two examples of pleasure giving activities—

(*a*) Watching sunset is an activity that gives me pleasure. I should be free to watch the sunset.

(*b*) Taking drugs gives me pleasure. I should be free to take drugs.

Since the utilitarian understanding of freedom does not make any distinction between different kinds of pleasures, there is no difference between the kind of pleasure felt under (*a*) and (*b*).

There can be four possible reasons because of which one can't endorse such a view of freedom in an unqualified manner. One, such an understanding of freedom is not accompanied by a sense of moral responsibility. The drug addict may indulge in anti-social activities that may cause pain to a large number of people. Two, it violates the harm principle—that one's exercise of liberty should not harm the life, liberty and possessions of others—that Locke qualifies his understanding of liberty with. Three, because the pleasure of one person (the drug addict) can cause pain to several people, the utilitarian maxim of the 'Greatest Happiness of the Greatest Number' is violated. Four, this understanding though very similar to the Hobbesian understanding of liberty, does not have the sole qualification that Hobbes sets for the exercise of freedom, namely, self-preservation. So, the drug addict's freedom to take drugs as it gives him/her pleasure may even be a self-destructive move.

This simplistic understanding of liberty within the utilitarian framework has been fine-tuned to a great extent in the work of Bentham's disciple—J. S. Mill's *On Liberty*. This view will be discussed in detail in the next section.

J. S. Mill on Liberty

Look at yet another example cited in the beginning of the chapter—The BA class wants to have a free period. On the face of it, it appears as a collective decision of the class. Now, there might be a few students (as few as even one student) who may want the lecture to take place. What do you think should be the decision of the teacher? An almost immediate response may be that since a majority of the students do not want the class to take place, the opinion of a few students (or one student) who want to attend the lecture should not be considered. This can generally be justified as a democratic decision. Such a 'democratic decision', however, is at the cost of suppressing the individual decisions of the students who want to attend the lecture.

The liberty not to have one's individual opinion suppressed by collective decisions of society and state is at the core of J. S. Mill's understanding of liberty.

Mill's views on liberty are based on his understanding of utility 'in the largest sense grounded on the permanent interests of man as a progressive being'. His essay *On Liberty* seeks to protect individual liberty from the interference of state and society. He takes the concept of liberty beyond the utilitarian doctrine of Bentham by holding the view that a proper conception of happiness includes freedom as individuality. For Mill, individuality was a prerequisite for the cultivation of the self. This would enable society to progress as each individual is useful in proportion to the extent they differ from the rest.

J. S. Mill qualified utilitarianism with two considerations—(*a*) in applying the principle of utility, consideration has to be given both to the quality and quantity of pleasure, and (*b*) utilitarianism need not involve a radical break with traditional morality. Instead, everyday rules of morality can be seen as the utilitarian thumb rule.

It is almost inevitable for conflicts to emerge from these qualifications. After all, it is very difficult to prove that watching a classical dance recital is more pleasurable than eating *bhelpuri* on the streets (or vice versa). Conflicts can emerge even for Mill's second qualification. Take the statement 'Honesty is the best policy.' One can find arguments as to how this will result in greater pleasure as well as greater pain. Liberty for Mill can be regarded as a principle that mediates such conflicts. Freedom or liberty, for Mill, is also valuable as an end in itself. This is not to say that even a 'wrong' act is to be valued if it is freely chosen. What it indicates is freedom as an essential component of the ideal of individuality. It is by virtue of the freely chosen actions that an individual is regarded as a worthy person.

Mill discusses liberty under three aspects—liberty of thought and discussion, principle of individuality, and limits of authority over an individual's action.

Liberty of thought and discussion is often understood as freedom of expression. It is not just the right of an individual to express an opinion but also includes the right of individuals to hear opinions expressed. So, while freedom of expression is sought to be exercised minimally at the level of an individual, the good derived from the freedom is for humankind at large.

Mill enumerates four reasons in favour of the freedom of expression. They are—

(*a*) If an opinion is suppressed as against the prevailing notion and the suppressed opinion is right, then humankind stands deprived of its benefit. And, even if it is the prevailing notion that is right, suppression of the 'wrong' deprives humankind of the opportunity to reinforce what is right. So, to facilitate the expression of opinions, true or false, that are against the prevailing notions in society, freedom of expression is needed.

(*b*) In the field of social and political belief, truth rather than being of one view or the other, emerges from the conflict of two or more opposing views. It is only freedom of expression that facilitates the airing out of several views.

(*c*) Freedom of expression can throw up right views as well as wrong. But even views that are wrong or false should not be suppressed as they may contain elements of truth. Such elements of truth may be lost to humankind if freedom of expression is not exercised.

(*d*) Even prevailing views that are true and right need opposition to reinforce their truth and to prevent themselves from being frozen into inert clichés. Indeed, it is only by being exposed to contradictions that views become reliable guides for action.

According to Mill, it is the clash of views facilitated by the freedom of expression that provides the intellectual impetus for thought, discussion, and progress. Mill is convinced that without such freedom society finds itself enfeebled by dogma. Beliefs held by such a society degenerate into prejudices and opinions lack a rational foundation.

Individuality enables a human being to choose rather than blindly follow accepted modes of behaviour, customs, and practices. There is no pre-decided concept of the 'right' or 'wrong' way of life. The content of 'right' choices depends on the kind of person one is.

Mill defends the principle of individuality against governmental interference and social tyranny. The sphere of non-intervention in an individual's life is demarcated by drawing a distinction between self-regarding and other-regarding activities. Self-regarding actions are actions over which the individual is sovereign. Whether an action is other-regarding or is of concern to others depends on whether such action is harmful to others. Now, there can be several instances where the boundaries between self-regarding and other-regarding actions are quite blurred. For example, addiction of an individual to drugs is as much a self-regarding as an other-regarding issue. To counter this, some readings on Mill state that a self-regarding action cannot be viewed as other-regarding if it causes offence, it can be viewed so only if it causes injury. This exempts intervention in self-regarding action on grounds of moral beliefs as to the appropriate form of social behaviour.

Liberty: A Liberal Good?

It is often felt that liberty is a concomitant value of liberalism. As a multifaceted concept, the value of liberty or freedom is present in the writings of even those who are not considered liberals. Of the thinkers we have discussed so far, Rousseau is one such example. Yet another thinker is Karl Marx. Marx's understanding of liberty is through instances of what is not liberty.

Let us go back to our example—'I am free to choose my career'—to understand the way in which Marx perceives the absence of liberty. Let us be more specific—'I view myself as a writer and want to choose writing as my career.' Now, let us assume that due to lack of the right material existence conditions, in order to survive I have to work as a factory worker. To have a career as a writer would be to realize the writer in myself. My job as a factory worker disables me from relating to myself. In that sense, my own labour confronts my sense of self and alienates me.

According to Marx, what defines human nature is the ability to express creativity. The circumstances that create situations of inability of expression of self are those that deny liberty. Marx explains the denial of liberty, what he terms alienation, as a four-stage process. The agent is alienated from the product, from productive activity, one's own human nature and from other human beings. Marx explains this by saying, 'As a result, therefore, man (the worker) no longer feels himself to be freely active in any but his animal functions—eating, drinking, procreating or at most in his dwelling; and in his human functions he no longer feels himself to be anything but an animal.'

Marx's understanding of the term 'liberation' is leading a life of self-realization. Self-realization can be defined as the full and free actualization and externalization of the powers and abilities of the individual. Marx held capitalism responsible for the lack of opportunities for self-realization. He also emphasized, however, that capitalism creates the material bases for another society in which the full and free self-realization of each and every individual becomes possible.

Capitalism hinders self-realization in two ways. One, the formation of desires occurs through a process the individual does not understand and with which one does not identify. Often, one's own desires appear as alien powers, not as freely chosen. Two, the realization of desires is often frustrated by lack of coordination and common planning. The aggregate outcome of individual actions appears as an independent and even hostile power, not as freely and jointly willed. The non-identification with one's desires and confrontation of one's self by those desires is what he termed alienation.

Classification: Negative and Positive Liberty

Let us have another look at the example—The BA class wants to have a free period. Now, the students of the class do know that this may mean that they may not cover their course before the exam. This will cost them their marks and affect their future career prospects. Nobody is forcing the class to miss the lecture. Yet, the temptation to have some free time stops the class from doing what it ought to do—attend the class. In this example, no one is stopping the students from bunking the class and in this sense the students in the class are free. On the other hand, if being free is being self-determined and entails control over temptations to take care of real interests, then the students of the class are not free.

It is to explain this distinction that the concept of liberty was classified in 1969 as negative liberty and positive liberty by Isaiah Berlin in his celebrated work—*Two Concepts of Liberty*.

Negative Liberty

The term 'negative' in negative liberty indicates injunctions that prohibit acts that restrict freedom. Popularly understood as freedom from interference, the scope of negative liberty is the answer to the question 'Over what area am I master?' (Berlin 1969: 121–22). Berlin further states, 'If I am prevented by others from doing what I could otherwise do, I am to that degree unfree: and if this area is contracted by other men beyond a certain minimum, I can be described as being coerced, or, it may be, enslaved' (Berlin 1969: 121–22). For example, if an individual who is otherwise qualified to contest elections is prevented by others from doing so by the use of coercion, the liberty of the potential candidate is being infringed. Berlin, however, makes it clear that incapacity to attain a goal is not unfreedom. As he states, 'only restrictions imposed by other people affect my freedom'.

Negative liberty rests on two main axioms—

(*a*) Each one knows one's own interest best. This is based on the assumption of the individual as a rational agent with a capacity to deliberate and make an informed choice.

(*b*) The state has a limited role to play. This follows from the earlier axiom: with the individual agency foregrounded, the state cannot decide ends and purposes for the individual.

For Berlin (1969), negative liberty as freedom is the opportunity to act, not action itself. As 'opportunity concept of freedom' it focuses on the availability rather than exercise of opportunity. The central problem with the negative concept of liberty is its indifference to the quality of action. For example, it makes no distinction between being liberated to pursue the occupation of one's choice and the liberty to starve. Indeed, poverty is not always seen as an infringement of freedom in negative liberty.

Two thinkers who illustrate negative liberty in their writings are Frederick Hayek and Robert Nozick. Hayek views liberty as a negative concept, because 'it describes the absence of a particular obstacle—coercion by other men', and it becomes positive only through what we make of it. This is complimented by Hayek's definition of individual freedom as 'the state in which a man is not subject to coercion by the arbitrary will of another'. Hayek does not view negative liberty as exhaustive of the concept of freedom as he postulates a necessary connection between liberty, justice and welfare. He explains this by stating that 'the conception of freedom under the law rests on the contention that when we obey laws, in the sense of general abstract rules irrespective of their application to us, we are not subject to another man's will and are therefore free'.

In Nozick's conception, the primary threat to liberty is the imposition of obligations to which one has not consented. Liberty is to be safeguarded by keeping such obligations to a minimum, leaving the greatest possible scope for voluntary agreements and exchange. The idea that respect for individual liberty requires consent is a necessary condition for all obligations beyond the requirements of a minimal framework of rights.

Positive Liberty

The concept of positive liberty proceeds with the idea that each self has a higher self and a lower self. The higher self, the rational self, should attain mastery over the lower self for an individual or a people to be liberated in the understanding of positive liberty. As Berlin (1969) states, 'The positive sense of the word 'liberty' derives from the wish on the part of the individual to be his own master.... I wish to be the instrument of my own, not of other men's acts of will.... I wish, above all, to be conscious of myself as a thinking, willing, active being, bearing responsibility for his choices and able to explain them by reference to his own ideas and purposes'. It does not just refer to non-interference, but includes the idea of self-mastery where the higher self is in command of the lower self.

Positive liberty is the *freedom to* do. It is what can be called the 'exercise concept of freedom'. It is exercising and availing of the opportunities while negative freedom is just having opportunities. Unlike negative liberty, positive liberty is open to the idea of directing the individual either by law or an elite. As long as the law directs the individual towards rational ends, it liberates rather than oppresses the individual's personality. Rousseau is a votary of positive liberty when he states that true liberty is in obedience to moral law. He also refers to it as the function of the will of the enlightened people. From a neo-Marxist perspective, Herbert Marcuse also favours a positive conception of liberty. The reason given is that the working class is incapable of seeing its true end and needs to be directed towards liberation by the revolutionary elite.

Positive liberty also includes the idea of collective control over common life. Maintaining a pollution-free environment is a collective effort for the common benefit. While this may allow a certain degree of coercion, it is usually justified by the larger good involved.

Many liberals, including Berlin, have suggested that the positive concept of liberty carries with it a danger of authoritarianism. Consider the fate of a permanent and oppressed minority. Because the members of this minority participate in a democratic process characterized by majority rule, they might be said to be free on the grounds that they are members of a society exercising self-control over its own affairs. But they are oppressed, and so are surely unfree.

J. S. Mill and Negative and Positive Liberty

Mill, often viewed as a defender of the negative concept of freedom, compared the development of an individual to that of a plant: individuals, like plants, must be allowed to grow, in the sense of developing their own faculties to the full and according to their own inner logic. Personal growth is something that cannot be imposed from without, but must come from within the individual.

Critics, however, have objected that the ideal described by Mill looks much more like a positive concept of liberty than a negative one. Positive liberty consists, they say, in exactly this growth of the individual: the free individual is one that develops, determines and changes her own desires and interests autonomously, and from within. This is not liberty as the mere absence of obstacles, but liberty as self-realization.

While the emphasis on non-intervention in the life of the individual tends to classify Mill as a theorist of negative liberty, the defence of individuality to facilitate deliberate cultivation of certain desirable attitudes, does not preclude the possibility of understanding Mill as a theorist of positive liberty.

Insufficiency of Negative Liberty: Charles Taylor

While Mill does not limit himself to the negative concept of liberty and Berlin discusses the role of positive liberty as self-mastery that complements the view of negative liberty as non-interference, Charles Taylor points out why negative liberty may be a necessary pre-requisite but not a sufficient condition for freedom. Taylor discusses the two types of liberty as the opportunity concept of freedom (negative liberty) and as the exercise concept of freedom (positive liberty). For Taylor, the concept of freedom is inclusive of the concept of self-realization. This notion of self-realization is unique to each individual and can only be worked out independently. Taylor feels that a pure opportunity concept of freedom is inadequate to attain freedom inclusive of self-realization. As Taylor states, 'We can't say that someone is free, on a self-realization view, if he is totally unrealized.' For example, if you have the potential to sing well, to the extent that nobody goes out of the way to deny you opportunities, your sphere of negative liberty has not been violated. However, you are not liberated till you don't exercise the freedom to realize your potential as a singer.

This exercise of freedom is further qualified. Merely exercising freedom does not lead to the attainment of self-realization. There are certain conditions put on one's motivation to qualify the exercise concept of freedom as a quest for the attainment of self-realization. One is not free if one is motivated 'through fear, inauthentically internalized standards, or false consciousness'. So, if you exercise your potential to be a good singer because somebody coerces you, or you think it will elevate your social standing or you think of it as a way to be popular among friends, then the quest for self-realization is a motivated one. Taylor also states that the subject cannot be the final authority on whether one's desires are authentic. This is because others may know us better than we know ourselves.

On the one hand, one has to be cautious that the quest for self-realization, even if decided by the subject, is not motivated by fear or false consciousness. On the other hand, since the subject is vulnerable to having her/his quest for self-realization motivated, the question arises as to who decides the authenticity of the quest for self-realization. One way out is the Rousseauan way, where the 'right' path helps in the realization of one's higher self. This, however, can have authoritarian, totalitarian implications. For, if the subject is to realize a good that is pre-decided by someone other than her/him as consonant with one's higher nature, it is an anachronic situation in which the subject needs to relinquish the freedom to make an independent judgement of the 'right' path to attain freedom.

Taylor acknowledges that the concept of positive liberty, understood in the Rousseauan framework is prone to totalitarian manipulation. However, according to him, the quest for self-realization need not be subject to totalitarian manipulation. The reason given by him is that since each person has his/her original form of realization, nobody can possess a doctrine or a technique to manipulate with a totalitarian intention as such a doctrine or a technique cannot in principle exist if human beings really differ in their self-realization.

Liberty: Freedom as a Triadic Relation

As Gerald MacCallum (1967) pointed out, there is no simple dichotomy between positive and negative liberty; rather, we should recognize that there is a whole range of possible interpretations or 'conceptions' of the single concept of liberty. He explains liberty as a triadic relationship in the following manner—X is free from Y to do or become (or not to do or become) Z. According to MacCallum—a subject, or agent, is free from certain constraints, or preventing conditions, to do or become certain things. Freedom is, therefore, a triadic relation—that is, a relation between *three things*: an agent, certain preventing conditions, and certain doings or becomings of the agent. Any statement about freedom or unfreedom can be translated into a statement of the above form by specifying *what* is free or unfree, *from what it* is free or unfree, and what it is free or unfree *to do or become*. Any claim about the presence or absence of freedom in a given situation will, therefore, make certain assumptions about what counts as an agent, what counts as a constraint or limitation on freedom, and what counts as a purpose that the agent can be described as either free or unfree to carry out.

Indeed, as MacCallum says, a number of classic authors cannot be placed unequivocally in one or the other of the two camps. Locke, for example, is normally thought of as the father of classical liberalism and, therefore, a staunch defender of the negative concept of freedom. He, indeed, states explicitly that '[to be at] liberty is to be free from restraint and violence from others'. But he also says that liberty is not to be confused with 'licence' and can be exercised only within a moral framework (Locke 1988: paras 6, 57). Locke also seems to endorse an account of MacCallum's third freedom-variable (Z) that Berlin would call positive, restricting this to actions that are not immoral (liberty is not licence) and to those that are in the agent's own interests (I am not unfree if prevented from falling into a bog).

Liberty and Other Concepts

Liberty and Equality

The concepts of liberty and equality conflict or complement each other depending on how they are defined. The most common reason for the conflict is scarcity of resources and the nature of its distribution. To understand the nature of conflicts between equality and liberty, let us start with an example. Let us take the example of a family with meagre resources to be divided between the education of two siblings, one of whom wants to become a doctor and another an engineer—arguably both incur fairly high expenses. Either the family can divide the resources in an equal way between the two siblings or allow one of them to pursue her/his vocation of choice. However, the resources are divided, the values of equality and liberty end up in a relation of conflict.

Liberty and equality conflict with each other when equality is understood as equality of outcome, and liberty is understood as freedom to choose. Equality as equality of outcome tends to work as a levelling mechanism. This consequently reduces the freedom of choice by restricting the availability of outcome. In the above example, if the resources are divided into two equal halves, what is achieved is an equal outcome with both siblings having the same amount of resources. This equality is, however, accompanied by the fact that neither can pursue the vocation of their choice. The stress on equality of outcome, thus, is at the cost of the liberty to choose.

Liberty and equality also tend to conflict with each other when either concept is equated with fairness. A fair state of affairs is, however, very subjective. Any state of affairs can be fair if some arbitrarily believe it to be fair and vice versa. In the example discussed above, giving all the resources to one of the siblings can be seen as fair to the extent that at least one of them can exercise the freedom of choice. The same situation can also be seen as unfair as the other sibling is totally deprived of any share of resources. An equal division between both the siblings, too, can be arbitrarily described as fair (as neither is totally deprived of her/his share) as well as unfair (neither is now capable of pursuing the vocation of their choice).

Equality and liberty can also conflict with each other when the practice of one is at the cost of the other. The extent to which liberty is attained can be gauged by the extent to which a trade-off has taken place with the concept of equality and vice versa. Again, going back to the example above, the liberty of any one sibling to pursue the vocation of her/his choice is in proportion to the extent of equality that is violated by the other sibling's equal share of resources. The liberty of each sibling is violated to the extent that the equal division of resources has limited their choice.

John Rawls, a social contract theorist of the 20th century, attempted to reconcile the values of liberty and equality through his 'veil of ignorance' argument. The motive behind this was as much to secure the inviolability of liberty as welfarist and redistributivist ideals of equality.

Rawls developed a scheme of basic liberties in his work, *A Theory of Justice*. The basic liberties are those that free and equal persons with the relevant moral capacities would choose in what he calls the 'original position'. This original position is a position where individuals divide liberties and resources in society without knowing their placement in society (see the chapter on Justice). According to Rawls, these basic liberties consist in freedom of thought and liberty of conscience; the political liberties and freedom of association, as well as the freedoms specified by the liberty and integrity of the person; and finally, the rights and liberties covered by the rule of law. To resolve conflict between various liberties, Rawls suggests that the institutional rules that define these liberties must be adjusted so that they fit into a coherent scheme of liberties. This scheme is secured equally for all citizens. In the Rawlsian scheme, redistribution of resources to bring about equality is qualified by two conditions—that the basic liberties will not be infringed upon and that increase of resources at any level should not be at the cost of the worst-off person.

Equality and Liberty: A Complementary Relation? A complementary relation between equality and liberty also depends on the way they are defined. To examine the possibility of a complementary relation liberty can be understood as being in control of one's life. This implies three things—

(*a*) Leading one's life according to one's beliefs, desires and purposes
(*b*) Being able to examine and revise them
(*c*) Being able to pursue alternative paths

Equality can be understood as non-discrimination. As non-discrimination, it entails elimination of disadvantages of those who suffer from them, yet are not responsible for them. It entails protection of essential interests that are harmed by such disadvantages. Without an equal opportunity to be liberated, neither equality nor liberty can attain its purpose in totality.

Equality accompanies the concept of liberty in the view of most thinkers. For Locke, natural rights (inclusive of liberty) are regulated by natural law characterized by equality. For Rawls, any method of distribution of liberties or social resources has to conform to the norm of equality.

Liberty and Rights

While there is a strand in Western political thought that equates the concept of right with the concept of liberty (Hobbes, Locke, Nozick), contemporary theory is of the opinion that they are two distinct concepts. The traditional view understood the equation between the two concepts as the idea of having a right to do or be something is the same as the freedom to do or be something. Later, it was felt that while liberty cannot be equated with the concept of right, a right is a liberty in a restricted sense—a liberty that is protected, recognized or allowed by the law (Holmes 1881; Lamont 1946).

The concept of liberty differs with the concept of right in at least three ways.

(*a*) There can only be a right to something, whereas freedom can be freedom to, as well as, freedom from. One does not have a right from something (this is distinct from a right not to do or be something).

(*b*) There are degrees of freedom, but not of rights. One can be more or less free, but one cannot have more or less of a right.

(*c*) Liberty cannot be delegated, transferred or waived unlike a right.

In contemporary theory, Dworkin admits that the concept of liberty can be related to a concept of right in a weak sense. As he explains, someone has a right to liberty if s/he either wants it or if it is good for her/him to have it. But a right to liberty cannot be always sustained in a stronger sense of right. As in, if someone has a right to something, then it is wrong for the government to deny it to her/him even though it would be in the general interest to do so.

The Concept of Liberty in India

The term closest to liberty in the Indian tradition is *mukti*; its connotations, however, are entirely other-worldly. Understood either as renunciation or as deliverance from the chain of rebirths, the initial understanding of *mukti* did not refer to freedom from social restrictions.

Ideas of modern liberty entered colonial India through three different routes—colonial legal arrangements accompanied by tacit understandings of rights and freedoms of individuals, institutional spread of Western-style education, and intellectual influence of Western social thinking. With the rise of the middle class and spread of non-ancestral salaried jobs, freedom began to be expressed in an individualistic manner. Women were elevated from their hierarchically subordinate position in the joint family to that of a companion. Freedom was also expressed in the religious sphere through the formation of associations. Voluntary associations were also formed for the establishment of educational projects, advancement of women, sports clubs, etc. However, opportunities to form and enter these associations were limited to the upper-caste elites. Two pioneers of freedom from social restrictions in India—Rabindranath Tagore and Raja Rammohun Roy—were a part of this elite.

In western India, unlike Bengal, thinkers from lower-caste groups began to use ideas of social freedom to attack caste hierarchy, notably Jyotiba Phule and later, B. R. Ambedkar. The meaning of freedom came to be located in the everyday life of caste indignities. Freedom had two aspects to it—liberation of lower castes from upper-caste domination, and affirmative action with regard to jobs in the colonial administration. This strand remained in a state of potential conflict with the nationalist strand—freedom from colonial rule. By the first decade of the 20th century, the meaning of freedom came to be dominated by the idea of freedom from colonial rule.

Both the strands of freedom found a place in the views of Gandhi. Gandhi adopted the term '*swaraj*' as an analogue to the concept of freedom. The very term *swaraj* carries with it the two main components that it embodies—*swa* as in 'self' and *raj* as in 'rule' and can be understood as 'self-rule' in two senses—'rule of self' and 'rule over self'. Gandhi understood and sought to apply freedom as *swaraj* in both senses of the term. *Swaraj*, in the context of the freedom struggle in India, referred to freedom as a constitutional and political demand, and as a value at the social-collective level. It meant not just freedom from British rule, but also freedom from the cultural authority of the West.

It is the understanding of *swaraj* as 'rule over self' that was highlighted by Gandhi in his work *Hind Swaraj*, where he states, 'It is *swaraj* when we learn to rule ourselves'. *Swaraj*, in this understanding, is about redeeming one's self-respect, self-responsibility, and capacities for self-realization from institutions of dehumanization. Understanding the real 'self', and its relation to communities and society, is critical to the project of attaining *swaraj*. Such an understanding of *swaraj* advocated that people must continuously strive to create a different set of institutions, structures and processes consistent with diverse cultures, traditions as well as principles of the natural world. Gandhi believed that the development that follows would liberate both individual and collective potentialities guided by the principle of justice.

Liberty and the Indian Constitution

The Indian Constitution discusses liberty in Part III of the document under Fundamental Rights. These rights are primarily in the form of negative injunctions rather than positive directions to the state. While the rights are fundamental, they are not absolute. Liberty as a principle, is protected not just by the right to freedom and the right to personal liberty, but also by the Directive Principles of State Policy.

While Article 19 of Part III of the Constitution—Right to Freedom—enumerates the various freedoms, Article 21 defines the scope of the liberty principle.

Article 21—worded in the following manner: *No person shall be deprived of his life or personal liberty except according to procedure established by law*—is the only article in the entire gamut of Fundamental Rights that does not have exceptions or qualifications to its application. In fact, one need not even be a citizen of India to invoke Article 21. In not demanding the criterion of citizenship, the Indian Constitution has elevated the right to life and personal liberty to the status of a human right.

Judiciary in India and Article 21 Statutes do not cover every conceivable case, and even when a statute does control a case, the courts may need to interpret it. Judicial decisions are known collectively as case law. A judicial decision legally binds the parties in the case, and may also serve as a law in the same prospective sense as does a statute. In other words, a judicial decision determines the outcome of the particular case, and also may regulate the future conduct of all persons within the jurisdiction of the court.

It is instructive to note the way courts in India have understood and applied the concept of liberty. Its multifaceted aspects as mirrored in the application of law facilitate the structure of reality and prevent liberty from being restricted to the abstract realm. The Indian judiciary is replete with instances of case law on the concept of liberty. Through its judgements and observations it has substantially contributed to the expansion of the right to life and personal liberty. The four instances cited below indicate the role of judicial decisions in the expansion of the scope of liberty.

The judiciary initially restricted itself to limiting the concept of liberty to tangible constraints. The Supreme Court in 1963 in the Kharak Singh case pointed out, that 'in dealing with a fundamental right such as the right to free movement and personal liberty, that only can constitute an infringement which is both direct as well as tangible and it could not be that the constitution makers intended to protect or protected mere personal sensitiveness'.

A far more expansive understanding of liberty was visible in 1981 when a Supreme Court judge observed (Francis Coralie Mullin *v.* Administrator, Union Territory of Delhi) that

> the right to life includes the right to live with human dignity and all that goes along with it, namely, the bare necessities of life such as adequate nutrition, clothing and shelter and facilities for reading, writing and expressing oneself in diverse forms, freely moving about and mixing and commingling (*sic*) with fellow human beings. Of course, the magnitude and content of the components of this right would depend upon the extent of the economic development of the country, but it must, in any view of the matter, include the right to the basic necessities of life and also the right to carry on such functions and activities as constitute the bare minimum expression of the human self.

The expansive understanding was further reiterated in 1984 in the Bandhua Mukti Morcha case—the scope of Article 21 was broadened by drawing on the Directive Principles of State Policy. The judgement noted—

> This right to live with human dignity (as) enshrined in Article 21 ... must include protection of the health and strength of workers ... of tender age of children against abuse, opportunities and facilities ... to develop in a healthy manner ... in conditions of freedom and dignity, educational facilities, just and humane conditions of work and maternity relief.

A holistic interpretation of Article 21 was put forward in 1989 (Ramsharan *v.* Union of India) where it was held that 'all that gives meaning to a man's life including his tradition, culture and heritage, and protection of that heritage in its full measure would certainly come within the encompass of an expanded concept of Article 21 of the Constitution'. In a 1991 judgement, the Supreme Court went on to include 'the right of enjoyment of pollution-free water and air for full enjoyment of life' under Article 21.

Points for Discussion

1. Peer pressure often colours our preferences on many issues ranging from consumer brands to career choices. To what extent do we exercise our liberty as freedom in making choices?
2. Liberty loses its meaning as well as legitimacy when viewed outside the civil and political system. Do you think unquestioned obedience to law will ensure the right to enjoy liberty?
3. According to Marx, capitalism hinders self-realization. Which ideology do you think best ensures the right to liberty as self-realization?
4. In 1996, the renowned painter M. F. Husain portrayed goddess Saraswati in the nude. Again, in 2000, the film director Deepa Mehta tried to shoot *Water*, a film on the plight of widows, in Kashi. In both cases, conservative elements went on a rampage, and declared these efforts as obscene, as against Indian culture and ethos. How would you discuss these incidents against the reasons enumerated by Mill under the freedom of expression?
5. It is necessary to speak against and resist the practice of dowry. Can you apply Mill's views on the freedom of expression, individuality, and limits on social coercion to this instance? Would Mill be regarded as a theorist of positive or negative liberty?
6. Can you see a correlation between the judgement of the judiciary in India and the manner in which the concept of liberty evolved in political theory?

Reading List

Berlin, Isaiah, *Four Essays on Liberty* (Oxford: Oxford University Press, 1969).

Chappell, Vere (ed.), *Hobbes and Brahmall on Liberty and Necessity*, *Cambridge Texts in History of Philosophy* (Cambridge: Cambridge University Press, 1999).

Dworkin, Ronald, *Taking Rights Seriously* (London: Duckworth, 1977).
Elster, John, *An Introduction to Karl Marx* (Cambridge: Cambridge University Press, 1986).
Gray, John, *Liberalism: Essays in Political Philosophy* (London and New York: Routledge, 1989).
Hayek, F. A., *The Constitution of Liberty* (Chicago: University of Chicago Press, 1960).
Kaviraj, Sudipta, 'Ideas of Freedom in Modern India', in Robert H. Taylor (ed.), *The Idea of Freedom in Asia and Africa* (Stanford, CA: Stanford University Press, 2002).
Locke, John, *Two Treatises of Government* (Cambridge: Cambridge University Press, 1988).
Lukes, Steven. 'Equality and Liberty: Must they Conflict?' in David Held (ed.), *Political Theory Today* (Cambridge, UK: Polity Press, 1991).
Rousseau, Jean Jacques, *The Social Contract*, ebook available at http://ebooks.adelaide.edu.au/r/rousseau/jean_jacques/r864s/
Scanlon, Thomas, 'Nozick on Rights, Liberty, and Property', in Jeffery Paul (ed.), *Reading Nozick: Essays on Anarchy, State and Utopia* (Oxford: Basil Blackwell, 1981).
Taylor, Charles, 'What's Wrong with Negative Liberty', Nigel Warburton (ed.), *Freedom: An Introduction with Readings* (London and New York: Routledge, 2001).
Ten, C. L. (ed.), *Mill's Moral, Political and Legal Philosophy* (England: Dartmouth Publishing Company Limited, 1999).
White, Alan R., *Rights* (Oxford: Clarendon Press, 1984).

CHAPTER 5

Equality

Ashok Acharya

Chapter Outlines

Introduction

Among the billions of human beings in this world, innumerable inequalities abound. People are different and unequal in many respects. They belong to different races, religions, sexes, and so on. Their physical, genetic and mental endowments are also dissimilar. People differ with regard to their dispositions and abilities and the ways in which they lead, and are taught to lead, their lives. The range of inequalities and disparities that humanity displays is indeed very wide and this *is* an empirical fact.

Yet, as humans, we believe, and rightly so, that we are essentially equal and possess equal worth especially when it comes to realizing this ideal in social, economic and political structures of our society. We invoke the concept of equality when we want to be counted as an equal, to be treated—and aspiring or claiming to be treated—as an equal, to be equally entitled to social goods. But what does it mean to be treated as an equal? What sense do we make when we say that irrespective of our differences and certain inequalities—whether as Brahmins or Dalits, black or white, men or women—we, as humans, possess *equal* worth? We are clearly here not referring to anatomical similarities, save the difference between men and women, and the common facts of our social existence that we, as *humans*, possess: to wit, the use of language, ability to reproduce, living in societies, and so on. But we are alike in more fundamental respects. Our capacity to feel pain or to suffer, capacity to experience affection for others and to be able to bear relevant consequences of the same are capacities that have a moral resonance. As Bernard Williams (1962) highlights, these are *moral* capacities that are universal to humanity. However, there are other characteristics as well that we possess and these connect us to other humans in important ways. One of these would be a 'desire for self-respect', which helps us unravel our own goals without being instruments of others' will. In short, there is something common in our collective experience that forms the core of our egalitarian beliefs. This makes certain causes worthy of pursuit and helps realize the significance of some of our struggles against unequal relationships and social order. Along with other political values such as justice or liberty, equality offers us a moral framework that we draw upon to make political judgements, and explain, prescribe or criticize certain political views and forms of political action.

The concept of equality lies at the heart of normative political theory. In a very general sense, equality is a relationship between two or more persons or groups regarding some aspect of their lives. The idea of equality is not, however, a simple one and hence it is not always easy to speak with accuracy what that relationship ought to be and in respect of what. There is no one way in which we may define a relationship between two or more persons (or groups), determine the goals of the relationship, and give primacy to one aspect of it over another by attaching pre-eminent value to the same. There are multiple ways of doing so. In other words, the suggestion here is that the concept of equality can yield various *conceptions* depending on how we unpack the building-blocks—relationships, persons, relevant attributes—and propose an appropriate relationship between them.

Evolution of the Concept

The history of political philosophy is replete with many references to the ideal of equality. Starting from the ancient Greek civilization till the 20th century, notable for its many egalitarian experiments, the idea of equality has evoked some of the strongest human passions. The content of the concept has undergone momentous transformations across centuries shaping, and being shaped by, the millions of people that have been inspired to fight various political battles sometimes against an autocrat, at other times against unjust social conditions, and on other occasions against undemocratic regimes or policies.

Tracing the history of an idea is fraught with difficulties, one of which is the problem of recovery of an interpretive exercise. Quite a lot has already been said on how we should go about interpreting texts and events, the focus of disagreement being on whether or not we can successfully employ contemporary lenses to judge contributions of past authors. Some say we can, and others claim this is impossible. Those who deny the possibility suggest that in order for interpretation to be authentic, it needs to be contextual, not textual. There are merits on both sides and many scholars are persuaded to adopt a pluralist approach, or at least concur to the validity of the same. The one further issue that remains, however, is that either the recovery of an idea can promise progressive revelation culminating in some contemporary set of ideals or it may very well be an account of degeneration concluding in a set of dangerous trends visible in contemporary times. The project of recovery, in other words, is laden with either hope or despair.

Most exercises of recovering the history of normative concepts in political theory aim at a progressive revival, noting in the process how ideas widen and deepen in scope. This is usually helped by drawing on the role that other ideas or values have also played in enriching the one under study. Thus, an account of the idea of equality cannot be separated from parallel accounts of liberty, justice, rights, popular sovereignty or democracy from which it feeds and is inspired by.

In what follows, we will selectively use some thinkers (Aristotle, Hobbes, Rousseau, Marx, and Tocqueville) who had decisive roles in giving shape to the idea of equality. If we consider the fact that the idea of equality also derives its strengths from similar normative concepts, we may well find other chapters in this book complementing the present exercise.

Alexis de Tocqueville, the author of the classic *Democracy in America,* writes that there is something irresistible and inevitable about the spread and progress of equality in the history of humankind. 'The gradual progress of equality is something fated', he declares. The main features of this progress, he claims, are its universality and permanence and the fact that the ideal 'is daily passing beyond human control, and every human and every man helps it along' (Tocqueville 1969: 12). How did something that is now 'universal' and 'permanent' 'begin its journey?

Aristotle

In what by now are well-known facts of the Greek experiments in popular rule, we are well aware of how citizens exercised an equal voice in the governance of their city-states.

Aristotle's *Athenian Constitution* contains many references of egalitarian reforms initiated in Athens that prepared the passage for testing the democratic ideal. At the heart of the reforms were attempts that sought to reduce inequalities in many spheres of social life including, most importantly, the ending of aristocratic stranglehold over land, power and honour. Practices of equality established by law were a *sine qua non* of democratic rule. A word that competed in common usage with *demokratia* in ancient Athens was *isonomia*, meaning equality before and within the law, a form of political equality that secured the equal participation of 'the many' who were poor in the regime.

Yet, ancient Athens also had other classes of people who were excluded from the domain of citizenship: *metics* (foreigners), slaves and women. Aristotle's *Politics*, both documents and justifies this exclusion. Aristotle's conception of equality, it is evident, was limited to the class of citizens only. The political equality of citizens lay in acknowledging the virtue of 'ruling and being ruled in turn.' In Book III, Chapter 9 of *Politics*, Aristotle draws a straightforward correlation between justice and equality when he says that 'justice is held to be equality, and it is, but for equals and not for all; and inequality is held to be just and is indeed, but for unequals and not for all'. This is the first classic statement of *formal equality*, reiterating the dominant conception of legal equality of treating like cases alike, and unlike cases unlike. However, unlike other conceptions of formal equality which are generally shorn of substance, this conception captures Aristotle's defence of natural inequality among men to rule. Note that in Aristotle's view, nature, which does nothing in vain, divides people into the ruling and the ruled, where, to belong to the ruling category one must have rational, deliberative and authoritative capacities (true for some men, but not all). This inequality between the ruling and the ruled—the unequals—is just.

Hobbes

If Aristotle defends natural inequality and then proposes a corresponding political equality between some humans (usually male citizens), Hobbes, who quarrels with Aristotle the most, defends a view of the natural equality between all humans in the state of nature. In *Leviathan*, his most famous work, Hobbes claims that

> (n)ature hath made men so equal, in the faculties of body, and mind; so that though there be found one man sometimes manifestly stronger in body, or of quicker mind than another; yet when all is reckoned together, the difference between man, and man, is not so considerable, as that one man can thereupon claim to himself any benefit, to which another may not pretend, as well as he. (Hobbes 1968: 183)

As to the strength of the body, Hobbes proclaims that even the weakest has enough strength to kill the strongest either by secret plot or by conspiring with others. In addition, as to the faculties of the mind, Hobbes argues that prudence, borne out of experience, is equally bestowed upon men. What Hobbes proposes is the equal ability of individuals in the state of nature which gives rise to an equality of hope to achieve our ends. What drives individuals is an equal ability to work as well as an equal and irresistible passion for power. From this condition of equality, beset, however, by the passions of self-glorification and competition for more power, emerges the first threat to equality when men try to dominate and subjugate others. In this quest for more power, men forgo the need for security and live in a state of depravity. Unless men agree to cede a part of their power to the political authority and accept to lead a civilized but equal existence under the domination of authority, they can never be fully secure. In the Hobbesian vocation, it is important to acknowledge the achievement of natural equality among men freed from all non-political sources of authority, including the religious.

Rousseau on Inequality

In his *Discourse on the Origin and Foundations of Inequality* (also called the *Second Discourse*), Rousseau speculates on human psychology and the history of social institutions. This is where he delves deep into the issue of human inequality, describing its various types that exist among human beings and determining which kind of inequality are 'natural' and which ones are 'unnatural'. Rousseau presents his analysis of society and the origins of inequality as a historical narrative. The narrative is relatively simple but bears a powerful message. For Rousseau, man in his state of nature is essentially an animal like any other, driven by two key motivating principles: pity and self-preservation. In the state of nature, which is more a hypothetical idea man neither is a rational creature nor possesses the concept of good and evil, has few needs, and is essentially happy. The only thing that separates him from the beasts is some sense of unrealized perfectibility. This notion of perfectibility is what allows human beings to change with time, and according to Rousseau, it becomes important the moment an isolated human being is forced to adapt to his environment and allows himself to be shaped by it. When natural disasters force people to move from one place to another, make contact with other people, and form small groups or elementary societies, new needs are created, and men begin to move out of the state of nature towards something very different. Rousseau writes that as individuals have more contact with one another and small groups begin to form, the human mind develops language, which, in turn, contributes to the development of reason. Life in the collective state also precipitates the development of a new, negative motivating principle for human actions. Rousseau calls this principle *amour propre*, and it drives men to compare themselves to others. This drive towards comparison with others is not only rooted in the desire to preserve the self and pity others, but it also drives men to seek domination over their fellow human beings as a way of augmenting their own happiness.

Rousseau states that with the development of *amour propre* and more complex human societies, private property is invented, and the labour necessary for human survival is divided among different individuals to provide for the whole. This division of labour and the beginning of private property allow the property owners and all those who live off the labour of others to dominate and exploit the poor. Rousseau observes that the poor resent this state of affairs and will naturally seek war against the rich to end their unfair domination. In Rousseau's history, when the rich recognize this, they deceive the poor into joining a political society that claims to grant them the equality they seek. The universal consent of humanity is needed to justify the institution of private property. The rich suggest that everyone associate together to use their common force to 'secure the weak from oppression, restrain the ambitious, and secure for everyone the possession of what belongs to him'. The naïve and unsuspecting poor 'ran to meet their chains thinking they secured their freedom, for although they had enough reason to feel the advantages of a political establishment, they did not have enough experience to foresee its dangers' (Rousseau 1964: 159–60). Instead of granting equality, however, the rich sanctify their oppression and make an unnatural moral inequality a permanent feature of civil society.

In the progress of inequality through the different epochs of civilization, Rousseau notes how the changing nature of institutionalized inequality transforms the dynamic of social relations. If the right to property and the establishment of law was the first stage, it authorized the status of rich and poor. The institution of magistracy was the second stage and it established the relations between the powerful and the weak. The last stage effected the transformation of legitimate power into arbitrary power (which we just discussed above) that authorized the existence of masters and slaves. In Rousseau's inequality-continuum, the property owners or the rich amass power and become masters. For the poor the metamorphosis would follow: poor→weak→slaves. That is a powerful statement but is soon followed up by Rousseau's claims that when no more inequality is possible and things have been stretched to their limits, 'new revolutions dissolve the government altogether or bring it closer to its legitimate institution' (Rousseau 1964: 172).

Rousseau's argument in the *Second Discourse* is that the only natural inequality among men is that which results from differences in physical strength, for this is the only sort of inequality that exists in the state of nature. As he explains, however, in modern societies the creation of laws and property has corrupted natural men and created new forms of inequality that are not in accordance with natural law. Rousseau calls these unjustifiable, unacceptable forms of inequality. It is, in other words, moral inequality, and he concludes by making clear that this sort of inequality must be contested. From this analysis and the prescribed prognosis of 'new revolutions', a straight road leads to the work of Karl Marx.

Marx

At one level, Marx's views on equality can best be described as a critique of liberal equality. In his polemic against the prevalent socialist conception of equality, Marx derided his contemporaries for their inability to account for the materialistic conception of history. It was necessary for Marx to correct popular misconceptions surrounding the ideal whose uses were more in the interest of the bourgeois. In *The German Ideology*, Marx seeks to unravel the ideological bind that certain concepts have in a historical period. A ruling class has its own ideology to which society subscribes. The parallel between Rousseau and Marx here is pretty evident. As Rousseau laments how the poor get duped by the promises made by the rich to secure the consent of the former to institute 'legitimate' power, Marx also shows how the ruling class produces a legitimating ideology to perpetuate the system of economic exploitation. Towards that end, the division of labour in the ruling class of a capitalist society will ensure a division between mental and material labour, and correspondingly the division between the 'the thinkers of the class' and the capital owners will emerge. The former are 'the active, conceptive ideologists, who make the perfecting of the illusion of the class about itself their chief source of livelihood'. All historical epochs provide their own ruling ideas: 'during the time the aristocracy was dominant, the concepts honour, loyalty, etc., were dominant, during the dominance of the bourgeoisie, the concepts freedom, equality, etc.' (Marx 1978: 173). These concepts are abstract and hold sway by taking on the form of universality to which even some socialists sometimes fall prey. But they are hollow and bereft of substance unless accompanied by a communist vision.

What Marx envisions for the final stage of history—the communist, classless society—becomes clear only when we understand the impossibility of human emancipation under conditions of exploitative social relations. The question of human emancipation is linked to freedom from economic inequalities. The capitalist system intensifies and heightens economic inequality. In the transitional socialist stage, emancipation is not complete but equal access to the means of production is ensured. In this transitional stage many capitalist practices, including the necessity of labour and material incentives, do not vanish. The distributive principle in operation during the stage is guided by the principle of 'to each according to his work'. Socialism, in the transitional phase, realizes the ethical principle of liberalism. Here, man is seen only as a worker. In his *Critique of the Gotha Programme*, however, Marx declares that in the final phase of communism, society would be able to inscribe on its banner: 'From each according to his ability, to each according to his needs!' (Marx 1978: 521). Under communism, man will no longer be regarded simply as a producer but as a person with needs and desires, which, rather than his contribution of labour, will be the basis for the distribution of goods. The distribution of goods, properly understood, is the consequence of the distribution of the conditions of production. Scarcity and conflict of economic interests are contingent aspects of class societies. These will disappear with the inauguration of communist society.

Tocqueville

The central thrust of Tocqueville's work was to study equality as a tendency of modern history. His study of the American democratic revolution was designed to understand the historical transition from feudalism to democracy in the Western society as a whole. His study was not meant to just identify the transition, but to account for it as well. Why was the triumph of equality inevitable? The project involved explaining the gradual and progressive development of social equality. Equality as an ideal appeals to people who wish to escape conditions of servitude and dependence. It makes democratic life possible. In comparing aristocracy with democracy, Tocqueville notes: 'Aristocracy links everybody, from peasant to king, in one long chain. Democracy breaks the chain and frees each link' (Tocqueville 1969: 508). In democracies, men prefer equality to liberty, and hold on to it tenaciously. 'The charms of equality are felt the whole time and are within the reach of all; the noblest spirits appreciate them, and the commonest minds exult in them. The passion generated by equality is therefore both strong and general' (Tocqueville 1969: 505). However, Tocqueville warns us of the dangers of excessive equality. There are times when the passions for equality may turn into a delirium. Tocqueville is equivocal about the consequences of social equality on political life. Although passions for equality may be found to exist very strongly in democracies, it is vital, in his view that a single-minded pursuit of equality at the expense of liberty may prove detrimental to the political health of democracies.

Why Equalize?

Reduction of inequalities may be considered as the primary objective of equality. But, why reduce inequalities? The objective of inequality-reduction can be inspired, for example, by a commitment to the ideal of uniformity. One way to bring about uniformity in an unequal world is to fix for everyone equal income irrespective of the individuals' abilities, or to design and distribute identical houses irrespective of the size of the family. This we know raises more problems than helps resolve. For instance, the idea of an equal income militates against what we deserve by way of differential talents, skills, occupations and efforts. No one can make a plausible argument that irrespective of our social positions we all deserve equal income. No one as well can make a convincing case that every family, whatever the size, gets to have a two- or three-room house. Or, for that matter, no one would ever argue that irrespective of performance in the examinations, every student should get the same grades.

Uniformity, in spite of some of its attractions, cannot be the end of equality, at least the way we understand and extend the latter in distributional terms. Equality must appeal to some other and better standards. However, a caveat is in order. Uniformity is a valuable standard when we speak of fair procedures. The idea here is that, rich or poor, high or low-ranking, each one of us is entitled to the uniformity of equal treatment, say, in the court of law, where our wealth or social rank should not affect the dispensation of justice. The usefulness of the yardstick of uniformity, however, ceases to have a moral significance in the distributional sphere.

Equality achieves certain ends and, by doing so, augments its moral appeal and its separate standing as an autonomous value. Equality is valuable for fulfilling four different ends to which it has an intrinsic connection. First, *equality is sometimes required in order to be fair*. If there are benefits or burdens to distribute, then, other things being equal, it is unfair to distribute them unequally. It is unfair, say, to award unequal marks or grades to two equally talented students who have performed identically in their examinations. In the absence of good moral reasons for an unequal distribution, fairness requires equality.

Second, equality is desirable because *some measure of equality is necessary for self-respect*. People may belong to different positions in society but that should not reflect on how they perceive each other. When a person feels that in spite of the status differences that she shares with others she is as good as none, her self-respect is in danger. A fundamental way of understanding the need for self-respect is to acknowledge that the gap between a person's self-image and how others who are better off perceive that person is not too huge. Often, this calls for correcting unjust external conditions—by way of, for example, ensuring a minimally just material condition—that have a bearing on a person's self-image.

Third, equality enjoins *a duty to show respect to others*. The ability to possess self-respect is not the only thing that matters, but how one treats others. Showing equal respect implies recognizing that all people have capacities to deliberate for themselves and to engage in activities and relationships that are considered intrinsically valuable.

Finally, equality is necessary *to foster fraternity*. Conditions of equality induce some measure of solidarity among the inhabitants of a society by way of removing systematic barriers to social intercourse. Most commuters in buses and on trains do not worry about the caste or religious affiliation of their fellow passenger. Across caste and communal divide, people join hands to fight various forms of injustice. This is possible because we believe in the ideal of equality. Inequalities are objectionable in part because they place barriers to friendship, community and love.

All the above four justifications for equality are complementary to each other. Together, they capture different reasons for a general defence of equality and each separately highlights a special aspect as significant. The argument to be fair on grounds of distributive justice focuses on the *equal satisfaction of basic needs*. The argument from the perspective of self-respect makes a case for *equality of status* by requiring that material inequalities should not be glaring. The case for equal respect demands prerequisites of *equal opportunities for self-development*. Finally, the argument from the perspective of fraternity makes a case for *social equality* (Miller 1996).

Equality of What?

In contemporary political philosophy, a lot of discussion surrounds the 'equality of what?' debate. Any attempt to apply the principle of equality between individuals must first come to terms with what exactly we must be concerned to equalize. In addition, the 'what' of equality has a distributional aspect to it; we are chiefly talking here about *distributional* equality. Although the final word on the debate on 'equality of what?' is yet to be said, scholars generally identify three metrics of equality: welfare, resources and capabilities.

Besides the above, there is an alternative conception of equality that is less a competitor to distributional equality and more of a complement. This is the idea of complex equality. We shall examine each one of them below.

Equality of Welfare

Utilitarians generally argue that the project of distributional equality amounts to the distribution of welfare. 'Welfare' here is primarily understood in two ways. According to the classical utilitarian thinking, as espoused by Jeremy Bentham (also see Chapter 3), welfare refers to the happiness which is understood as the net balance of pleasure over pain that the individual experiences. According to this view, in assessing how well-off someone is in life, we should look at how happy he or she is, that is, at the net balance of pleasure over pain in his/her life. In more recent writings, however, welfare is identified with desire or preference-satisfaction; people have more or less welfare, and so have better or worse lives in a fundamental sense, depending on how far they satisfy their desires or their preferences. In deciding which preferences matter most to a person, the person must be able to form his/her own judgements independently and with full information without any scope for errors of reasoning.

A society that believes in distributing welfare equally will not worry much about how much resources individuals get, but whether or not these resources are instrumental in securing for each individual a level of satisfaction or happiness (whether in terms of pleasure or preference-fulfilment) equal to everyone else. Under such a scheme, it is imperative that we fulfil everyone's welfare equally irrespective of the inequality entailed in the distribution of resources. Someone who has a taste for an expensive car or jewellery is to be treated at par with someone who is happy riding a bicycle or owning a lantern. There is a moral issue here, however, that is bound to engage our intuitive notions of fairness. Should our society subsidize people's expensive tastes? Why should those who are unhappy without expensive cars have more of a claim on social resources than those who are content with bicycles? Or, for that matter, why should a society underwrite a gambler's professional risks and treat it at par with someone who needs much fewer resources to be trained as a car mechanic? Demands to treat preferences equally can at times be morally worrisome and unsustainable. The ideal of equality of welfare, let us be clear, certainly does not promote the cause of fairness, self-respect, or fraternity. In many ways, the ideal is considered morally objectionable by most liberals and is held to be unattractive as a yardstick for social policy.

Equality of Resources

The resourcist view of equality or 'resource egalitarianism' is most expressly identified with the views of John Rawls, Ronald Dworkin and Eric Rakowski. Equality of resources, Dworkin maintains, holds that a distributional scheme treats people as equals 'when it distributes or transfers so that no further transfer would leave their shares of the total resources more equal' (Dworkin 1981: 186). But one needs to know when precisely equality of resources is likely to be achieved. Dworkin suggests a two-stage process: (i) the ambition-sensitive auction, and (ii) the insurance scheme. But let us start with a simpler story, a story—much like a philosopher's fiction—that Dworkin himself uses.

Imagine we are shipwrecked immigrants washed ashore on a deserted island. Let us further assume for the moment (though we will qualify this later) that everyone has the same natural talents. Huddled together in an island with abundant resources and no native population, we set upon the task of equally dividing the available resources. We elect one amongst us to affect an equal division of resources. The division will follow the auction procedure. In view of the fact that our goals in life may differ, we need to exercise our choices on which resources we need and hence bid for. To that extent, we are each given 100 clamshells to bid for all the available resources in the island that are up for sale in a perfectly competitive market. Each one of us is likely to have different preferences and our preferences will determine on what we wish to spend our clamshells. Someone who wishes to engage in farming will spend a major part of the clamshells on agricultural land, and those others who wish to spend time near the sea will bid for the beaches. And a person who wishes to set up a dairy farm will bid for cattle and some grazing land. In this manner, each one will bid for different resources in accordance with one's ambitions and each will end up with a bundle of resources that he or she would not wish to trade away with someone else's. The division, so effected by the purchase of a different but equal bundle of resources in the auction, meets the *envy test*, which implies that 'no division of resources is an equal division if, once the division is complete, any immigrant would prefer someone else's bundle of resources to his own bundle' (Dworkin 1981: 285). We could say that if the envy test is met, then people have been treated with equal consideration, and differences between them owing to different bundles of resources are a reflection of their different ambitions.

We have just met the requirement of choice in the resource egalitarian conception. However, in the real world it is difficult to imagine that everyone would be similarly endowed in natural assets. We are re-opening an issue that we had assumed to be non-existent earlier. Will the envy test succeed if we assumed that people were differently endowed? Suppose some of us are physically challenged and are born with natural handicaps, say, without eyesight. Now, in the auction scheme where all of us enjoy equal ability to bid for equal bundles of resources, no two persons with different natural endowments will find themselves under conditions of equal circumstances. A person who is physically challenged, for instance, will have special needs and the resources that she purchases with her 100 clamshells will leave her less well-off than others. She shares the burden of unequal circumstances. Where the more fortunate than her make more meaningful choices with their resources, a disproportionate amount of her resources will be spent in meeting her special needs. This is not fair considering that her handicap was involuntarily acquired. How do we then meet the envy test?

One way out would be to compensate for her natural disadvantage from the common pool of resources before we start the auction process. In order to be fair to her we may be required to design a distributional plan that offsets her brute luck before giving her a fair go at the auction. The plan is simple: we need to be *both* endowment-insensitive and ambition-sensitive. This is another way of acknowledging, as Dworkin suggests, that people's fates in any distributional scheme is as much determined by their choices as by their circumstances. Hence, although the auction takes care of people's choices, compensating people—or, better still, securing insurance for them against brute luck—is morally required. However, the matter is not as simple as it may first seem. One cannot simply concede that we compensate all natural disadvantages of the unlucky. Some disadvantages cannot just be compensated, and some need not be a cause of great concern. And in cases where compensation is due we can only partially equalize unequal circumstances—not wholly—no matter how much we compensate. We need to strike a balance somewhere between being fair to people's choices and taking moral responsibility for their disadvantages. An ambition-sensitive auction needs to be balanced by an *insurance* scheme that takes care of natural, undeserved inequalities. Before the auction can take place, all of us may be required to put aside, say, 25 or 30 clamshells to meet the obligations towards the disadvantaged and then bid for the available resources. A central objective of Dworkin's proposal is to invite us to see the parallels between what we commit ourselves to in an ideal setting, and what the transposed implications are to the non-ideal, real world. A rough parallel of the insurance scheme in the real world is the practice of progressive taxation. Taxing the rich proportionately more than the poor enables the state to secure welfare for the disadvantaged. A resourcist conception of equality lays emphasis on the centrality of state responsibility towards remedying unequal circumstances among people.

Equality of Capabilities

The economist Amartya Sen pioneers the idea that distributional equality should concern itself with equalizing people's capabilities, instead of emphasizing on resources or incomes. We should be able to, Sen argues, focus on the real freedoms that people enjoy such as being able to read, being healthy, having self-respect, being politically active, being able to take part in the life of the community, and so on. The proper focus should be on what people are able to be and do, that is on their functions, and not on how much resource is allocated to them. Resources only secure for us what makes us happy, lead valuable lives, and are therefore, to be considered as means of well-being.

In contrast to the resource approach, Sen proposes the notion of well-being understood in terms of *function*. Reading is a function vital to leading a valuable life. However, Sen does not argue that social policy should be concerned with function. Social policy, according to Sen, should instead focus on *capabilities*. A capability is the ability to achieve a certain sort of function. For example, literacy is a capability, while reading is a function. In a society where people are illiterate, a state should actively promote people's ability to read, i.e. literacy. Whereas a resource egalitarian may insist that resources such as books and educational services may be provided for in regions that are deficient in literacy, the capability advocate would argue that more than a provision of external means what matters is the capability—

an internal ability—of the target population to read and write. This way of addressing the problem of inequality is indeed a novel one.

The novelty of the capability approach is further brought home by Sen's observation that a proper analysis of inequality needs to go hand-in-hand with facts of human diversity. We are, Sen argues, 'deeply diverse in our internal characteristics (such as age, gender, general abilities, particular talents, proneness to illnesses and so on) as well as in external circumstances (such as ownership of assets, social backgrounds, environmental predicaments, and so on).' (Sen 1993: xi) To take one example of an internal characteristic (gender) made worse in the presence of some adverse external factors (discrimination and patriarchal institutions), Sen points to the mortality differential between males and females (that also accounts for the phenomenon of 'missing women' in countries such as China and India), especially among rural families in Asia and Africa (Sen 1993: 122–25). If other social characteristics such as identity and social disadvantage are factored in, our understanding of inequality deepens. Hence, it will be plausible to maintain, for instance, that beyond the simplistic account of gender inequality, most Dalit women are worse off than other women in terms of high mortality. However, the buck may not stop here. It will be a real test to determine further whether Dalit women of Delhi, for example, fare as badly as, say, widows from upper-caste rural Rajasthan. Some would argue, and with good reasons, that the latter—due to rigid external constraints—are probably worse off than the former. We need to be sensitive to such differences and not be misled by appearances. Since many characteristics can impinge on people's functioning, it is essential that policy makers amass as much information as possible before they design suitable policies to equalize people's capabilities. Social policy must be attuned to facts of human diversity. A simple-minded approach (for example, of equalizing incomes) towards correcting complex modes of inequality will simply not do.

Complex Equality

Michael Walzer gives currency to the idea of complex equality. Walzer is an egalitarian but finds himself ill at ease with the intellectual enterprise involved in identifying the single most important metric of equality—welfare, resources or capability. This enterprise, to him, is somewhat misplaced. It is misplaced due to the egalitarians' unrelenting insistence on a single point of access to the *plurality* of distributive arrangements. This needs unpacking. Often, in our quest to distribute goods, we harp more on the principles of distribution and less on what meaning we attribute to goods. Walzer argues that people conceive of and create goods, which they then distribute among themselves. It is important that we shift our attention from distribution to the conception and creation of goods. We give meanings to goods, which determines their social value. The same goods have different meanings in different societies. There is no single set of basic goods which could be universally conceived of and given the same value. Rawls, Walzer would argue, was off the mark when he suggested that what mattered was how a set of primary goods needed to be fairly distributed across societies. If one knew how goods were socially created, one would have difficulty agreeing with Rawls in giving a universalist account of justice that would apply across time and space. 'All distributions are just and unjust relative to the social meanings of goods at stake' (Walzer 1983: 9). These meanings change across time and space. For instance, the idea that childcare is solely a family responsibility no longer holds true in some societies unlike in others. Every society will give value to goods in a particular way, and will be sustained by a shared understanding among members.

What, however, is typical to the understanding of how goods ought to be distributed is that when meanings given to goods are distinct, distributions must be autonomous. Every set of goods constitutes a distinct distributive sphere within which only certain criteria of distribution are appropriate (Walzer 1983: 10). Economists may be right to impute a certain measure of rationality and acquisitiveness to the behaviour of people in the markets. However, the same does not hold true in all social domains. Fathers and mothers are supposed to be loving, trusting, caring and altruistic. Citizens are supposed to be equal, impartial, and motivated by views of the collective good. Resources within families are not distributed as wages; political offices in a democracy ought not to be distributed among relatives. Walzer maintains that there is no reason to expect that the same distributive standards must prevail in different 'spheres' of social life. Thus, the spheres of the market and political power, to take two examples, are distinct and separate. The norms for distributing goods within each are internal to each and ideally should not spill over. Critics, however, may reason that this is easier said than done. Of course, inequalities from economic life do spill over into political life and vice versa. Wealth can buy votes, and elected representatives can misuse their offices to further the interests of business. This, Walzer would be quick to point out, is highly undesirable. Nations do indeed erect barriers, with limited success, to restrict the extent to which wealth leads to political power.

Within each sphere, there might well be inequalities and there is nothing wrong with that. If the distributional norm in the economic domain lays emphasis on effort and because of which inequalities emerge between those who work hard and those who do not, the indolent or the lazy cannot expect to be similarly rewarded as the diligent. This inequality is acceptable with the caveat that hard work at times goes unrewarded in some societies. What is not acceptable, however, is when people who enjoy a certain pre-eminence in other spheres are disproportionately rewarded in the economic sphere. A case in point could well be to ask whether reward for work should be related to religious affiliation. In Walzer's scheme, it is clear it cannot be. But, what if it does? That would lead to *tyranny*. Tyranny is the disregard for the distinctness of spheres and the principles internal to them and in ways in which it multiplies inequalities. Some groups can monopolize a particular category of goods and then use their monopoly to achieve unequal distribution of other goods. That would lead to *dominance*. Our effort should be on the reduction of dominance. Equality requires a diversity of distributive criteria that mirrors the diversity of social goods.

Complex equality is the opposite of tyranny. 'It establishes a set of relationships such that domination is impossible. In formal terms, complex equality means that no citizen's standing in one sphere or with regard to one social good can be undercut by his standing in some other sphere, with regard to some other good' (Walzer 1983: 19). The idea of complex equality is a refreshingly different perspective than those struggling over the metrics of equality. In contrast to the abstractions of individual responsibility and person hood that characterizes the three conceptions we discussed above, Walzer's approach focuses attention on the social meanings of goods and the plurality of the spheres of justice.

In Conclusion: The Politics of Equality

The politics of egalitarianism in the 20th century was instrumental in justifying the idea of a welfare state, among other things. That idea, successful in its heyday, has declined over the past two decades. What went wrong? We cannot detail all the causes, but a short checklist may help. Many democratic societies today are witnessing the rise of right-wing politics. This trend started in the 1980s when governments headed by Ronald Reagan and Margaret Thatcher unleashed a backlash against the welfare state. The legitimacy of the welfare state was called into question and it was largely discredited for having given short shrift to individual responsibility, creativity and economic efficiency. Right-wing politics in recent times is sustained by citizens who wish to pay less tax and consequently vote to power parties (usually right-wing) who promise less tax. In the global political landscape, moreover, one notices a decisive ideological shift toward the right. The politics of globalization has further caused a setback to the practice of redistribution and the idea of welfare-state policies.

Yet another distinct political phenomenon is also visible: the political struggles of identity groups. This parallels new concerns in normative political theory, too. The 'equality of what?' debate is being replaced by 'equality of whom?'. Egalitarians are increasingly shedding their individualist bias and are keener to engage in concerns surrounding inequality between groups that owe more to non-material factors. The struggles for greater equality by women, minorities, Dalits, linguistic groups and others are a pointer to the continuing relevance of the bases of social equality and a corresponding search for new paradigms of group-sensitive equality.

Points for Discussion

1. In drawing up a will between five children with different tastes and ambitions, how would a parent divide the inheritance among them? The following information is provided about the children:

    One is blind.

    One does not wish to work and has expensive tastes.

    One is a prospective politician with expensive ambitions.

One is a teacher with humble needs.
One is a fashion designer who works with expensive material.

2. As a representative of your class, you have been invited by the college Governing Council to discuss policy issues related to
   (a) The translation of the most popular English textbooks to your native language
   (b) The expansion of Braille resources in the college library for visually challenged students
   (c) The provision of wheelchair access to the entire college premises

   Would you justify any of these policies? Why and how?

Reading List

Aristotle, *Politics*, trans. Carnes Lord (Chicago: The University of Chicago Press, 1984), an ebook version from MIT available at http://classics.mit.edu/Aristotle/politics.html

Cohen, G. A., 'On the Currency of Egalitarian Justice', *Ethics*, 99(4), 1989: 906–44.

Dworkin, Ronald, 'What is Equality? Part 1: Equality of Welfare', *Philosophy and Public Affairs*, 10(3), 1981: 185–246.

———, 'What is Equality? Part 2: Equality of Resources', *Philosophy and Public Affairs*, 10(4), 1981: 283–345.

Hobbes, Thomas, Leviathan (London: Penguin Books, 1968), complete text available at http://ebooks.adelaide.edu.au/h/hobbes/thomas/h68l/

Kymlicka, Will, *Contemporary Political Philosophy: An Introduction*, Indian Edition (New Delhi: Oxford University Press, 2005).

Lakoff, Sanford A., *Equality in Political Philosophy* (Boston: Beacon Press, 1964).

Marx, Karl, The Marx-Engels Reader, ed. Robert C. Tucker (New York: W. W. Norton and Co, 1978).

Miller, David, 'Arguments for Equality', *Midwest Studies in Philosophy*, 7, 1996: 73–88.

Pojman, Louis P. and Robert Westmoreland (eds), *Equality: Selected Readings* (New York: Oxford University Press, 1997).

Rousseau, Jean Jacques, *The First and Second Discourses* (New York: St Martin's Press, 1964).

Sen, Amartya, *Inequality Re-examined* (Oxford: Oxford University Press, 1993).

Tocqueville, Alexis de, *Democracy in America* (New York: Harper and Row, 1969), entire text and background available at http://xroads.virginia.edu/~HYPER/DETOC/home.html

Walzer, Michael, *Spheres of Justice: A Defense of Pluralism and Equality* (New York: Basic Books, 1983).

Williams, Bernard A. O., 'The Idea of Equality', in Peter Laslett and W. G. Runciman (eds), *Philosophy, Politics and Society*, Series II (Oxford: Basil Blackwell, 1997).

CHAPTER 6

Justice

Krishna Menon

Chapter Outlines

Introduction

Procedural theories of justice do not make a distinction between production and distribution. Such theories contend that there can be no abstract principle of distribution that takes the whole society into account. Such theories work with the idea of individual entitlements. In this context, the chapter deals with the principles of justice formulated by Robert Nozick and John Rawls, as well as with a critique of Rawls' work. The last part of the chapter discusses feminist accounts of justice that have opened up a completely new way of arguing about issues such as justice.

The concept of justice that we will discuss in this chapter is closely related to the concepts of liberty and equality discussed in the preceding chapters. In everyday life, justice is seen as an attribute of law. But if we think closely, we shall realize that all laws are not always just. In fact, many great political and social movements the world over have focused upon opposition to unjust laws, e.g. the movement against the apartheid laws in South Africa.

The other commonly held belief about justice is that it is always impartial—we only need to think of courtroom scenes in popular Hindi films where the camera inevitably focuses upon the statue of the goddess of justice, who is blindfolded and holds the scales of justice in her hands. Thus, impartiality and fairness are understood to be aspects of justice.

One of the earliest accounts of justice is found in Plato's *Republic*. In this book, Plato tries to establish the 'true nature of justice' and then goes on to construct an ideal state that would be an embodiment of his understanding of justice. For Plato, justice was one of the four principles of virtue, the other three being temperance, wisdom, and courage. An ideal state would be the embodiment of justice, where every individual would be true to his nature, some men being philosophical and intellectual, and others good workers or artisans and so on. In a just state each individual would fulfil his duty diligently. (Needless to add, women hardly figure in Plato's scheme of things.) For Aristotle, justice lies in incorporating concerns of equality, proportionality and the maintenance of equilibrium in society. Thus, in him we find a shift away from the notion of hierarchy that informed the Platonic concept of justice.

Subsequent to the concern for justice displayed by Greek philosophy, there was a general lull on this subject. Either divinity and God were invoked, or the ideal of natural justice or else traditions and conventions, determined the ideas on justice. With the gradual secularization of life in Europe, thanks to a variety of changes ranging from the Renaissance to the Industrial Revolution, new ways of thinking about justice emerged. Justice came to be located as an idea firmly within the secular framework of the modern nation-state. What it meant and how it was to be maintained evoked different answers, but it was clear that justice was no longer seen as a religious principle or as based on traditional social practices. It was seen as a set of principles to be upheld by the state in order to make life and business well regulated.

Plato presented his account of justice more than 2,000 years ago, but even today some of the most interesting debates and discussions in politics, and more specifically in political theory, are around the question: 'what is justice?'.

The Issue of Distributive Justice

Politics is to a great extent about who gets what and why. In our country we know that school facilities, food, safe drinking water, health care and many such things are not available to all our citizens. What do you think is the basis on which this distribution is justified? The criteria commonly employed for distribution of goods and services are 'desert', merit and need. Justice is, thus, more often than not linked with distribution; it is a distributive concept.

The concept of desert (from the old French word *deserte,* meaning to deserve) refers to the actions of men and women that result in special treatment either in the form of rewards or in the form of punishments. It is to suggest that the rewards or punishments that a man or a woman receive, or is subjected to, are a consequence of his or her efforts and actions.

The criterion of merit is very similar, implying that the meritorious need to be rewarded. For instance, when a student fails an exam it is often said that she or he deserved the failure, but it is possible that the student could not attend classes and devote much time to studies because of various problems like an ailing family member or an alcoholic parent. Under such circumstances, can we still say that the student deserved to fail?

In other words, it is very difficult to isolate individual actions and efforts from what goes on in society, especially what the society considers desirable, valuable or meritorious. For instance, men and women might be working very hard at the various flyover construction sites in our cities, but the reward they get is far less than the reward a cricketer might get. Don't you think this has something to do with what our society considers to be more deserving of rewards and what is considered meritorious?

'Need' as a criterion suggests that people might differ in their capabilities as well as needs; the principle of justice based on need would argue that irrespective of people's capabilities their needs ought to be fulfilled. Imagine a situation where a *safai karmachari* (cleaner) with her family of seven children and old parents gets a four-bedroom flat and a neurosurgeon, on the other hand, with her two children and spouse gets a two-bedroom flat, based on the criterion of need.

If we lived in a world of abundant resources, then perhaps the question of justice would not have risen. Since we don't, the question of who should get what and why will always be an important one. Political theorists divide their answers to these questions into two broad categories—procedural and social. There are obviously many variations within these theories, but there are some main features that can be summarized. In procedural theories, demands of justice are satisfied if certain rules are followed. The outcomes of these procedures are not relevant to the evaluation of justice. Justice is only a property of individual behaviour and cannot be a feature of 'society'. Individuals are understood as autonomous and rational beings who make their own independent choices and are, therefore, responsible for the consequences of their actions.

In theories of social justice, justice is seen a feature of society, so evaluation is done in terms of not what an individual gets or does not get, but in terms of how just or unjust a society or state of affairs is according to some agreed upon criterion. Such theories would be far more likely to advocate the use of the state to uphold the principles of justice. For example, a society might consider it just to allow only a certain section of its people access to education; anyone else trying to get access would incur the wrath of the authorities.

Procedural Justice

The basic point that needs to be highlighted about procedural justice theories is that such theories do not make a distinction between production and distribution. This means that each individual is on his or her own and has entitlements that are individual in character and not dependent on any abstract principle of distribution that takes the whole society into account. This also implies that the state would have no authority to interfere in the matter of individual entitlements; in fact, it would be terribly unjust if the state was to do so. Based on a strong current of individualism these theories do not accept that societies have any 'ends' or purposes that need to be collectively strived for. This is, indeed, a very attractive idea and makes the individual very powerful, autonomous, and completely in control of his/her life, and also totally responsible for the successes or failures that s/he may encounter. But when we think closely about this idea we might feel a bit uncomfortable; it implies, for example, that cotton farmers in Andhra Pradesh are solely responsible for the hardships that they are facing, or that they ought to have worked harder.

Procedural theories of justice are more often than not based on a close association with the workings of market economy. It is believed that the market would, if not intervened with, make the best and most efficient use of resources. Any attempt to tamper with this would be unjust and detrimental to everyone. Besides, intervention would have to be based on some agreed upon principles of desert or need. This, in the opinion of procedural theorists, is not possible because in a free society there can be no general agreement about what constitutes needs or what is a just desert. While they would be concerned about those who cannot do well in the market, and might even accept that the state needs to step in to help, they would not accept that this has anything to do with justice.

Robert Nozick's theory of justice as explained in his book, *Anarchy, State and Utopia*, is a good example of the procedural theory of justice. The distinction that he makes between historical and end-state principles of justice is crucial to our understanding of his theory of justice. He argues that the historical principle holds that an individual's past actions determine the deserts s/he would be entitled to, and since actions are different so would be the entitlements to deserts. The end-state principle suggests that there would be a set of goals to which the distribution pattern should conform.

Nozick argues that individual property holdings are just if they are a consequence of fair acquisition or even transfer. This means that no fraud or force should have been used in the acquisition of the property. The idea is that at the heart of competitions, such as races, fairness is upheld if all contestants obey rules and there is no cheating, no one jumps the gun or indulges in substance abuse. Nozick allows for rectification if unfair practices have been followed in the acquisition of property. If, under these circumstances, some individuals are able to acquire and amass huge amounts of property without using force or fraud, Nozick would not allow for a redistribution of this property. By arguing in this vein, Nozick ensures that the state would have only a very limited role to play in redistribution. Individual liberty, Nozick argues, is thus safeguarded.

Nozick does not think of restrictions as being necessary so long as acquisitions are fair and exchanges are voluntary in nature. In other words, no acquisition or exchange must worsen the position of others. But this is indeed interpreted very narrowly. Nozick prohibits the appropriation of the total supply of something that is essential to life. The example that he gives illustrates this point effectively: no one should appropriate the only water hole in the desert and charge what he will. But this still leaves the possibility for the producer of a drug that cures a fatal disease to charge prohibitively, for nobody's condition is being worsened! A person afflicted by a fatal illness is in any case going to die, and by denying him/her a drug no new element of suffering has been introduced that worsens the individual's condition. By limiting the role of the state Nozick hopes to ensure individual autonomy. This, he believes, would help individuals take initiative and use their rationality effectively, creating conditions favourable for the protection of individual liberty. Thus, Nozick's theory of justice is a fierce and interesting defence of individual liberty.

John Rawls: Justice as Fairness

John Rawls' well-known book, *Theory of Justice*, presents a very strong defence of the idea of justice based on the basic tenets of procedural theory, i.e. justice requires a meticulous following of rules. Rawls' theory, however, takes care to respond to the most common criticism levelled against procedural theory—that despite the meticulous following of rules, unjust conditions might be created. In order to avoid this, Rawls suggests that under controlled conditions rational human beings would choose principles that would uphold ideas consistent with the basic idea of distributive justice.

Rawls insists that justice prevails only when every departure from equality can be rationally justified. Unlike in Nozick's entitlement theory where equality as an idea is conspicuous by its absence, Rawls's theory of justice is premised upon the need for equality. Rawls sets out his theory by placing individuals abstracted from their social and economic contexts behind what he calls the 'veil of ignorance'. Individuals behind this veil are unaware of who they are and what their interests, skills, needs and so on are. Why does Rawls do this? Because usually people are prevented from upholding just principles guided as they are by their selfish interests. So, imagine a group of people who do not know whether they are Dalit or Brahmin, Kuki or Naga, Muslim or Hindu and so on. Such a group of people will then not know which way the fault lines of discrimination run in their society. But in Rawls' hypothetical situation called the 'original position', these people would have an elementary knowledge of economics, psychology and what Rawls calls a 'sense of justice'. These people, Rawls suggests, would be self-interested but not egoists. They would have no particular vision of what constitutes the good life but would be interested in maximizing their primary good—liberty, opportunity, income, wealth and self-respect and, having no scope for envy, they would not be affected by the position of others. Rawls hoped this would enable them to pursue whatever conception of good they might discover to have, when the veil is removed. He also assumes that these hypothetical people would be conservative risk-takers and in a situation of uncertainty would obviously opt for the least disadvantageous outcome in any choice presented to them. Hence, they would choose those principles which would maximize the position of the worst-off, assuming that when the veil is removed, they themselves would turn out to be the worst off.

Such people, Rawls argues, would choose the following principles of justice:

1. Each person is to have an equal right to the most extensive liberty compatible with similar liberty to others.
2. Social and economic inequalities are to be arranged so that they are both:
   a) to the greatest benefit of the least advantaged, and
   b) attached to offices and positions open to all under conditions of fair equality and opportunity.

These principles are arranged by Rawls in a specific order and are subject to the priority rule. The first principle must always come before the second, and 2a) has to come before 2b). Thus, there is no risk of individual liberty being compromised for the liberty of others. It also ensures that any departure from the principle of equality brings maximum benefit to the least advantaged; in other words, inequalities should be so arranged that they benefit the worst-off.

In the Indian context, Rawls' fierce commitment to equality and the insistence that any departure from this principle can only be in the interest of justice is a familiar idea. The strong tradition of democratic politics with its roots in the national movement recognized that commitment to the ideals of equality, liberty and fraternity in the context of intense and deep-rooted social inequality called for some imaginative and creative political thinking.

Dr B. R. Ambedkar with his varied personal, educational, professional and political experiences provides us with insightful thinking on the subject of inequality and democracy. Despite the differences, the wide spectrum of groups that fought against colonialism in India were united by their commitment to the ideal of equality. This commitment, in the background of an elaborate and well-entrenched system of social inequalities, particularly in the form of caste, made it a rather difficult one.

After Independence when it was time for drafting the Constitution, Ambedkar, as the Chairperson of the Drafting Committee steered the Constitution in the direction of justice and equality. This was based on the fundamental assumption that systematic departures from norms of equality would have to be made in the pursuit of justice. These departures were justified on the grounds that it would guarantee against persistence of discrimination in subtle and indirect forms, and that it would promote integration and better utilization of talents and a more equitable distribution. Apart from all this, it would constitute a kind of historical reparation to offset centuries of deprivations faced by the lower castes in the past. Ambedkar argued that political democracy could not be sustained on the base of social inequality. Thus, the Indian Constitution permits the creation of an elaborate and diverse range of programmes that permit the departure from formal equality, for the purpose of favouring certain historically deprived groups.

The Constitution further bans discriminatory practices (caste-based) in government institutions. Apart from this is, of course, the whole policy of reservation of seats in legislative bodies, administration and educational institutions. All these together constitute the core of the constitutional commitment to compensatory discrimination. The beneficiaries of compensatory discrimination are three major groups consisting of the Scheduled Castes, the Scheduled Tribes and the Other Backward Classes. Preferences are of three basic types: 1) reservations to allot or facilitate access to resources and positions that are valued; 2) provision of services like scholarships, grants, loans and land allotments, health care, legal aid and so on; and 3) special protection schemes to prevent discriminatory economic and social practices that victimize the backward classes.

Thus, in its original conceptualization, these proposals and policies were seen as necessary extensions of the commitment to egalitarianism, where every member is seen as having equal stakes in the common resources of the Indian society. Thus, Ambedkar was suggesting that members of the Dalit and backward classes had long been denied their rights and independent India with its commitment to equality and freedom could not afford to ignore the claims being made by this section of its citizens.

Limitations of Rawls' Theory of Justice

C. B. Macpherson in his book *Democratic Theory: Essays in Retrieval* argues that Rawls' theory of justice is actually a rather elegant defence of what is essentially a liberal-democratic capitalist welfare state.

Rawls accepts that despite equality of opportunity and education, inequalities would remain because of the institution of the family. To illustrate this point, Rawls contrasts the difference between the son of a member of the entrepreneurial class and the son of an unskilled labourer. He argues that such inequalities create differences in expectations, providing incentives for the economy to become more efficient and generate greater material wealth, thus benefiting everyone (including those who are the worst off). Hence, Rawls would argue that not much is to be gained by making attempts to iron out such inequalities. It is such a defence of inequality that Macpherson finds inconsistent, given Rawls' initial commitment to the idea of equality. Rawls accepts the inevitability of class divisions based on income and wealth. Macpherson argues that such inequalities would adversely affect individual liberty by creating inequality of power in society.

Macpherson argues that Rawls does not really present a universal account of justice but an account that rationalizes liberal beliefs and values. Rawls admits that his theory is based on the existence of a particular kind of individual who is free and equal, and inhabits a pluralistic society that has no shared agreement about social institutions and ends, towards which they ought to work. His account, he argues, would in such a society provide stability and social unity. Thus, in Macpherson's opinion, far from being a universal account of justice applicable to all rational human-beings, Rawls' theory is culture-specific and appropriate only for liberal-democratic societies with a welfare orientation. Besides, the Rawlsian individual is hardly a stripped-down abstract individual; the rational, self-interested, individualistic and autonomous individual is too similar to the liberal conception of the individual to have any universal application.

Communitarian Critique

The main focus of the communitarian critique of Rawls is on the idea that people in the original position choose a set of principles that become the foundation of supposedly universal ideas of justice. Communitarians point out that individuals can only be identified as members of pre-existing social organizations. This means that whatever ideas men and women have, have come out of the society and community they belong to. Hence, their notions of what should be the distributive criterion will obviously emerge out of this context. For example, people in many communities believed that a part of their agricultural harvest belonged to the temple deity and to the priestly class. To us, in the present context, this would be unacceptable, but it obviously made sense to those people who lived in another time and another context.

Communitarians object to the idea that individuals abstracted from their social, economic and cultural contexts can make choices. They argue that such a 'stripped-down' individual will be unable to make choices. Since the Rawlsian veil of ignorance keeps individuals out of a real social context, communitarians ask the question of how the choices they make can ever be relevant in an actual social context. Communitarians argue that individuals are determined by their communitarian contexts and the choices they make are determined by their notion of what is good. This notion of the good is not in their opinion a consequence of individual rationality and determination but is created and held together by what the community—to which the individual belongs—thinks of as being the 'good'.

Michael Walzer in his book *Spheres of Justice* represents the communitarian case against Rawls. Walzer's basic point is that no system of justice can be evaluated as inherently just or unjust; evaluation is possible only on the basis of the social meanings attached to the goods at stake. The example that Walzer himself gives is of a society based on the caste system, where purity and pollution are determined by birth. Birth, thus, decides access to a variety of goods, e.g. water, land, education. Walzer argues that as long as all the members of the society share the social meanings of the caste system, justice would constitute being true to those meanings and upholding the principle of distribution that follows from it. Thus, the distribution of goods cannot be decided without understanding the specific meanings of those goods which are socially constructed and embedded in the community, its practices and institutions rather than in individual deeds and thoughts. Therefore, Walzer suggests that the goods that need to be distributed are social goods because their meaning and values are created socially. Justice, thus, can only be understood within a communal framework and not on the basis of abstract, universal principles. He is of the opinion that different social goods should be distributed for different reasons according to different procedures and by different agents. Needless to add, these differences would emerge out of the different understandings of the social goods themselves because of diverse and particular histories and cultures.

Feminist Critique

Susan Moller Okin in her book *Justice, Gender and the Family* points out that most grand and philosophical works on justice rarely consider the working of the family as being significant for any discussion on justice. Rawls is no different. The family is considered to be 'private' and justice as an idea has a bearing on the 'public' sphere. This assumption overlooks the fact that the family and its working is itself to a very great extent constituted by the 'public' world of laws and institutions and ideas of justice that constitute it. Think of the number of laws that govern our family lives—property, inheritance, divorce, adoption, and so on. Thus, the 'public' has a direct bearing on the 'private'. People's lives in the 'public' shapes, and is also shaped by their ways of participating in family life. For instance, unequal division of labour within the family creates obstacles for women in their lives outside the family and these inequalities are often supported by social traditions. Cooking, childcare and housekeeping are, for instance, supposed to be solely women's responsibilities, giving them very little time or energy and gradually even robbing them of a desire to enjoy an active life outside the family.

Okin argues that any theory of justice which is silent about the inequalities within the family is an incomplete one. If young people grow up within families where injustice is a norm and is rendered acceptable, masquerading as it does in the garb of either virtues like 'nobility', 'sacrifice' and 'patience' or nature, they can hardly be expected to acquire a sense of justice. Rawls is also guilty of this omission.

In Rawls' scheme it is only the heads of households—assumed to be men—who come together and agree to accept the principles of justice. Rawls accepts the family as the basic structure of society for which the principles of justice are being chosen. But he does not think it necessary to ponder about the injustices within the family.

Okin's suggestion while retaining the Rawlsian spirit is to deny people in the original position any knowledge of whether they are men or women and then insist that they undertake an evaluation of the family, for it is part of the basic structure of the society. This, she argues, will result in an evaluation of the injustices within the family and thus a truly humanist notion of justice could be created.

Some feminists argue that the model of a self-interested, autonomous, rational and individualistic person is a typically male conception and leaves little scope for values and practices like nurturing, caring, co-operation and empathy that are typically female qualities. Thus, they argue that female qualities are not represented in Rawls' original position. Yet another set of feminist arguments point out that Rawls' emphasis on impersonality, rationality and universality are based on male norms of moral reasoning; women's style of moral reasoning is different arising as it does out of considering the particular needs of each person. Therefore, the individual in the original position is a man and Rawls' theory can hence have little significance to women and specific situations and contexts. It would be worth debating whether men and women are essentially so different. Are all women always caring and full of empathy? Communal riots in our country have time and again shown us that this need not be the case. And are men never nurturing and caring?

Justice, Capabilities, and Freedom: Amartya Sen's Extension of John Rawls' Theory of Justice

The Rawlsian paradigm of justice assigns a central role to the achievement of liberty. Amartya Sen has certain reservations about this freedom-oriented evaluation of justice. In his opinion, the Rawlsian framework concentrates only on the means to freedom rather than on the extent of the freedom that a person actually has. Sen would like to describe his approach to justice as a capability-based one, wherein it is not just the access to primary goods but the extent of capabilities that each individual has to convert these primary goods into lives that they value living and that would determine freedom and ultimately uphold justice.

To explain this further, assume that there are two individuals both with access to the same set of primary goods. Does this ensure that both therefore enjoy the same amount of liberty? Sen's answer would be no. There could be various reasons like for example, physical limitations and challenges that impose restrictions on capabilities. So, despite similar access to primary goods there would be difference in the extent of capabilities to convert these into freedom. Sen clarifies that capability means a person's freedom to choose between alternative lives and there need be no unanimity about what would be considered a valued way of life.

Capability thus represents freedom, whereas the Rawlsian primary goods are just means to this freedom. Sen argues that equality of freedom to pursue our ends cannot be guaranteed by equal distribution of what Rawls describes as primary goods. Sen would want an examination of interpersonal variations in people's capabilities to pursue ends and objectives. People not only value different things as good but they also have varying capabilities to achieve freely the ends that they value. Rawls is sensitive to the first mentioned diversity. Sen would, however, like him to add to this a concern for variations in people's ability to convert resources into actual freedoms. Variations could be related to age, sex or genetic endowments. These variations influence people's abilities differently to build freedom in their lives, despite having the same primary resources.

End-State Theories

End-state theories of justice, i.e. theories that suggest a set of principles to control the process of exchange between individuals, can also be referred to as social justice theories. These theories require an evaluation of the society as whole, and not only of individual actions. Marxist theory is a good example of this approach. In his book, *Critique of the Gotha Programme*, Marx undertakes a detailed discussion of the concept of justice. He works with two types of concepts, one for the transitional socialist society and the other for the communist society that would no longer need the concept.

In the transitional socialist society justice would mean that each person should receive that which is in accordance with his or her labour contribution to the social product. Marx, however, was not satisfied with this contribution principle because it continued to regard people as workers only and did not acknowledge the fact that different workers vary both in talent and in need. Marx was dissatisfied with the contribution principle because it did not incorporate the crucial factor of needs.

In contrast, in communist society the principle would be from each according to his or her ability, to each according to his or her needs. This, of course, means that people would produce goods and services without the need for differential rewards and that they would be completely unaffected by what others get. This would clearly not be possible in conditions of scarcity and conflict between individuals; hence, material abundance is crucial for this principle to be upheld.

At the heart of the Marxist critique of justice is an objection to a community that has to be held together by a network of rights and principles of justice. For Rawls, justice is the first virtue of social institutions, but for Marx a truly good community would have no need for the concept of justice. Marx accepts that under circumstances of scarcity and conflict over goals, there would be a need for justice as a principle for operation of society. This would, however, inhibit the possibility of a higher form of community, where people would be spontaneously loving and cooperate with each other. Thus, justice is at best seen as an unavoidable but not very desirable necessity for societies flawed by conflict and scarcity. Marx advocates the abolition of private property as an essential step towards the creation of a cooperative and harmonious community. In Marx's opinion, the regime of private property that creates conditions for wage-labour in capitalism is both exploitative and alienating, and thus unjust.

Marx argued that labour is the source of value and that it is the worker who creates the immense wealth of capitalist society, but gets only a fraction of it as wage. This was unacceptable to Marx. Socialization of the production process is Marx's solution to this problem. This would, Marx argued, make it possible for workers to have an effective say in production, thus generating satisfaction for the worker and fulfilment of the most genuine human needs. From the Marxist perspective, pursuit of profits in a market-driven society can never be the basis for creating justice; it is only fulfilment of genuine human needs in conditions of unalienated labour that can be the basis for justice.

Thus, we see that the Marxist theory of justice, like most end-state theories, claims that certain ways of life constitute human perfection or excellence. Such ways of life should be promoted and other ways of life penalized. It is this privileging of one notion over others that lead critics to distrust it and suggest that these theories are potentially tyrannical in nature. Such theories, critics fear, would not hesitate to use the authority of the state to interfere and take away people's liberty on the pretext of upholding the perfect and just way of life. This is in sharp contrast to, say, Rawls' position; he tries to steer clear of favouring any one notion of the good life.

Feminist Accounts of Justice

One of the central debates within the feminist theory of justice revolves around the question of whether there is a specifically female way of moral reasoning distinct from the universal, objective and impersonal ethic of justice that much of mainstream political theory works with.

Carol Gilligan, for instance, argues that there are two distinct ethics correlating to two distinct conceptions of subjectivity: the abstract individual (as in Rawls) and the connected self (as in Gilligan and other feminist's works), manifested by men and women, respectively. They argue that women's morality is characterized by care, nurture, love, values and peace above all. This they would describe as an ethic based on care; and the impartial, objective and universal framework as the male ethic of justice. Nell Noddings demonstrates the difference between these two ethics by using the examples of Abraham and Ceres. Abraham was prepared to sacrifice his son for the sake of principles (neutral, universal, rational), whereas Ceres was prepared to sacrifice any principle for the sake of her child (specificity, love and subjectivity). This to Noddings is the essential difference between justice and care.

Many feminists are obviously troubled by this bifurcation. Catharine Mackinnon and Joan Tronto among many others have disputed this dichotomy and pointed out that such a dichotomy merely reaffirms the existing sexist stereotypes of women's traditional roles. After all, no one would like to believe that men are incapable of loving and nurturing. There is nothing inherent to women, which makes them incapable of rational, universal and objective sentiments. Feminists have argued that even if such a bifurcation is sensed today it has not always been the case and that this is a consequence of various changes that took place in Europe post-18th century. They seek to point out that this bifurcation is a cause for concern since both women's interconnectedness and men's autonomy are consequences of a largely unequal context. This generates very different and unequally valued sense of self. While a sense of interconnectedness surely needs to be valued it needs to be rounded-off by having an autonomous sense of self and should not necessarily be pitted against it.

The overwhelming majority of feminists would be keen to reconcile the two ethics. Susan Moller Okin's is one of the most articulate attempts to refashion the ethic of justice from a feminist standpoint. We have already discussed her point of view while examining Rawls' theory of justice. Most feminists today would suggest that an ethics of care could be made effective only if it is grounded in justice. They would rather see care and justice as complimentary to each other. In fact, feminist writers like Seyla Benhabib argue that the feminist theory of justice should work within a framework that acknowledges that every time we generalize the other (rational, impersonal, objective, universal way of thinking about people) we should remember that this other is also a concrete other (subjective, specific way of thinking about people). Thus, feminist theories of justice seek to reconcile care and justice.

Conclusion

In this chapter, we examined the liberal position on justice and the modifications within this position as envisaged by people like John Rawls. A critical look at Rawls' attempts to revise the standard liberal tenets led us to MacPherson's works. The communitarian and feminist criticism of Rawls was discussed next. Amartya Sen's very sympathetic account and further extension of the Rawlsian theory of justice might interest you enough to read his book *Inequality Re-examined*. We then moved towards an examination of the Marxist theory of justice. Interestingly, we found that Marx would like to not have to talk about justice because the need for such a discussion, according to him, was typical of societies characterized by conflict and scarcity. Finally, we took a brief look at feminist debates on the concept of justice.

What seems to emerge from the discussion on justice is that there can be no one uniform or universally acceptable definition of justice. Our understanding of justice would depend to a great measure on our understanding of the world around us and our opinion of how it is structured and how we would like to intervene to change it. Thus, it is a political concept and can be understood only politically.

Points for Discussion

1. The liberal position holds that no social or community practices can have such authority over the individual that he or she cannot evaluate and be detached from. In your opinion to what extent is this possible? Every year newspapers in our country report with a certain amount of disdain and horror the practice of mass child marriages that take place in some parts of Rajasthan. The parents of those small children obviously support and believe that it is a practice that is good for their children. What would you do if you were a parent in that context? Do remember that we don't get our notions of what is good and desirable out of nowhere.
2. Do you think that the controversy over the ban on turbans and headscarves in schools in France is just?
3. There could be conditions in society or situations in life when special provisions might be required. (a) Would making such special provisions be a violation of justice? (b) Can you think of any such situation that might require special provisions? (c) How will you defend the special provisions against the charge of being unjust? (d) The issue of reserving seats for students from certain socially and educationally backward communities in government-run educational institutions in our country is one possible example. Do you think this policy is unjust?
4. What would Nozick's response be to Vinobha Bhave's Bhoodan movement?

Reading List

Barry, N. P., *An Introduction to Modern Political Theory* (Basingstoke: Macmillan, 1992).

Kymlicka, Will, *Contemporary Political Philosophy*, Indian edition (New Delhi: Oxford University Press, 2005).

Macpherson, C. B., *Democratic Theory: Essays in Retrieval* (New York: Oxford University Press, 1973).

Marx, Karl, *Critique of the Gotha Programme*, 1875, full text with annotations available at http://www.econ.utah.edu/~ehrbar/gotha.pdf.

———, *The Marx-Engels Reader*, ed. Robert C. Tucker (New York: W. W. Norton and Co, 1978).

Nozick, Robert, *Anarchy, State and Utopia* (London: Basil Blackwell, 1981).

Okin, Susan Moller, *Justice, Gender and the Family* (New York: Basic Books, 1989).

Ramsay, Maureen, *What's Wrong with Liberalism: A Radical Critique of Liberal Philosophy*, new edited edn (London: Continuum, 2004).

Rawls, John, *A Theory of Justice* (London: Oxford University Press, 1972).

Walzer, Michael, *Spheres of Justice: A Defense of Pluralism and Equality* (New York: Basic Books, 1983).

CHAPTER 7

Rights

Papia Sengupta

Chapter Outlines

Introduction

That individuals have rights and the fact that rights mark important limits on what may be done to them by the state, or in the name of other conceptions, is now a familiar position in modern political philosophy.

When the founders of the United States stated in the Declaration of Independence (1776) that certain rights were inalienable, they were at the forefront of a moral movement that continues to exert a profound impact on society even today. Indeed, at the same time, the French were also developing their own equivalent, the Declaration of the Rights of Man and of the Citizen (1789). Thus, the two most influential political documents of the modern age take the notion of rights as the central concept upon which their political organizations are built.

This chapter attempts to give a comprehensive analysis of rights, kinds of rights, rights and duties, and different theories of rights. Recent developments and issues concerning rights are also discussed.

The interest in rights was not restricted to the 17th and 18th centuries only; the second half of the 19th century also witnessed a major resurgence of interest in the notion of human rights. Issues of rights play a central role in our political life. The civil rights movement from the 1960s onwards took rights as the cornerstone upon which the rebuilding of our society was to be based. More recently, issues about rights of women and disadvantaged minorities have been a matter of debate. With the increasing medical advancements, we are now discussing whether persons have a right to die, i.e. euthanasia. Discussions about using animals in research and testing are often phrased in terms of *animal rights*. Sexual choice is discussed in terms of *gay and lesbian rights*. Human rights have become a major concern in recent times. Thus, discourse about rights has become persuasive in our society. The language of rights has proved to be the most powerful language for moral change in the 20th and early 21st centuries.

The Idea of Rights

Now the question arises: what is a right? Simply speaking, a right is to get 'one's due', i.e. to get what is due to someone as a human, citizen, individual or as a member of a group, etc. To have a right, then, is to be entitled to do something or to have something done; for example, to vote, to speak, to avail of healthcare, etc. It is different from obligation, as Hobbes points out—on any occasion you have a choice whether or not to exercise your right. You are not obliged to do what you are entitled to do. For example, it is your right to vote, but you are not obliged to vote; you are free to exercise your choice, to vote or not to vote. While rights and obligations are not the same, they are still connected. Whenever you decide to do what you have a right to do, others have an obligation to let you do it.

But upon what grounds can the claim to have a right be justified? What is it that entitles me and obligates you? The right is conferred and the correlative obligation imposed by a law in a society of which you and I are both members and whose legal system we are both subjected to. But all rights are not legal in nature, moral rights for example. Thus, rights and their correlative obligations are essentially social in character. One has them as a member of a social group, be it a society or a nation. Rights need recognition from society and from the state. Rights, therefore, are claims which can be justified on legal, moral, ethical or human grounds.

A right must be justified in the first place as something I have as a member of some social group. Second, what I claim as a right must be something which is necessary for me if I am to play my proper part as a member. Third, my claim to have it as a right is justified only if I am able to and willing to respect the rights of the other members of the group.

Rights express a certain kind of relationship between two parties: the right-holder and the right-observers. Rights thus have two faces, depending on whether they are viewed from the perspective of the holder of the right or from those with whom the right-holder is interacting. From the standpoint of the right-holder, a right is permission to act, an entitlement 'to act, to exist. To enjoy, to demand'. But from the standpoint of the right-observers, the right usually imposes a correlative duty or obligation, as I mentioned earlier. This duty can be either negative (to refrain from interfering with the right-holder's exercise of the right) or positive (to assist in the successful exercise of the right). Finally, to have a right entails certain responsibilities. This brings us to the distinction between negative and positive rights.

Negative and Positive Rights

Negative rights are rights that entail non-interference from the society at large. For example, the right to liberty, life, property, etc. The right to life prevents others from killing me but it does not obligate them to do anything positive to assist me in living my life to the full or to live happily.

Positive rights are rights that impose obligations on other people or the state to do something for a fuller enjoyment of our rights. For example, the right to health, basic subsistence, etc. requires positive interference to do something. But negative rights restrict us from doing something. Negative rights entail only negative obligations of non-interference; positive rights entail positive obligations on the part of the right-observer to do something to assist in the right-holder's exercise of the right. Rights can be classified in various ways—moral, legal, human rights, etc. or civil, political, social rights. I will now discuss the difference between civil, political and social rights.

Civil, Political, and Social Rights

In contemporary political thought, the term 'civil rights' is indissolubly linked to the struggle for equality of African Americans during the 1950s and 1960s. The aim of that struggle was to secure the status of equal citizenship in a liberal democratic state. Civil rights are the basic legal rights a person must possess in order to have such a status. They are the rights that constitute free and equal citizenship and include personal, political, and economic rights. No contemporary thinker of any significance holds that such rights can be legitimately denied to a person on the basis of race, colour, sex, religion, national origin, or disability.

Until the middle of the 20th century, civil rights were usually distinguished from 'political rights'. The former included the rights to own property, the rights to make and enforce contracts, the right to legal recourse and the right to one's religion. Civil rights also covered freedom of speech and of the press; but they did not include the right to hold public office, vote, or to testify in court. The latter were political rights, reserved for adult males

The civil–political distinction was conceptually and morally unstable insofar as it was used to sort citizens into different categories. It was part of an ideology that classified women as citizens who were entitled to certain rights but not to the full panoply to which men were entitled. As that ideology broke down, the civil–political distinction began to unravel. The idea that a certain segment of the adult citizenry could legitimately possess one bundle of rights, while another segment would have to make do with an inferior bundle, became increasingly implausible. In the end, the civil–political distinction could not survive the cogency of the principle that all citizens of a liberal democracy were entitled, in Rawls' words, to 'a fully adequate scheme of equal basic liberties'.

The claims for which the American civil rights movement in the 1950s and 1960s initially fought belong to the first generation of civil rights claims. Those claims included the 18th-century set of civil rights—such as the right to legal recourse and to make and enforce contracts—but covered political rights as well. However, many thinkers and activists argued that these first-generation claims were too narrow to define the scope of free and equal citizenship. They contended that such citizenship could be realized only by honouring an additional set of claims, including rights to food, shelter, medical care and employment. This second generation (19th century) of economic 'welfare rights', they argued, helped to ensure that the political, economic and legal rights belonging to the first generation could be made effective in protecting the vital interests of citizens and were not simply paper guarantees.

Yet, some scholars have argued that these second-generation rights should not be subsumed under the category of civil rights. The traditional political and civil rights can be readily secured by legislation. Since the rights are for the most part rights against government interference the legislation needed had to do no more than restrain the executive's own arm. This is no longer the case when we turn to the 'right to work', the 'right to social security', and so forth.

The third generation of claims (20th century) has received considerable attention in recent years, what may be broadly termed 'rights of cultural membership'. These include language rights for members of cultural minorities, and the rights of indigenous peoples to preserve their cultural institutions and practices, and to exercise some measure of political autonomy. There is some overlap with the first-generation rights, such as that of religious liberty, but rights of cultural membership are broader and more controversial.

Another classification of rights can be made on the basis of legal and moral grounds. Let us now distinguish between legal and moral rights.

Legal Rights

Laws differ from ordinary life or moral discourse in that the truth of any legal statement depends ultimately on the acts of certain authorities. Whatever is legal or illegal is so because it was declared so by legal authorities. The ultimate touchstone, therefore, of all legal statements are the acts of these legal authorities. It is because courts have defined terms in a certain manner; whether these agree with the moral meaning is irrelevant.

Legal authorities used the term 'right' to refer to four different properties: the correlate of a legal duty (claim), the absence of duty (privilege or liberty), the capacity to change legal relations (power), and the protection against change in one's legal position (immunity).

Moral Rights

In ordinary language, we use the term 'right' in at least two ways; we say that someone has the right to something, and we also say that someone has a right to do certain things. In the first instance, the existence of the right concerns the behaviour of someone other than the right-holder, since to say that I have a right to something is to say that someone has the duty to act in a certain manner towards me. In the second instance, it is the right-holder's behaviour that is in question, and to say that he has a right to act in a particular way is to say that he is morally free to do so—that it is not wrong for him to do so. These two uses of the term 'right' correspond in part to Dworkin's (1977: 188) 'strong' and 'weak' senses of right, respectively.

The standard interpretation of a claim-right is that another person has the duty to act in a certain way with respect to the 'thing' to which the first person has a right. But does a right-to-something merely imply a duty in others or is it a package of normative advantages? Either way, the core idea of right appears to be that an object or interest protected by a duty has some things that are considered to be good, and to say that one has a right to such a thing means that one's interests in that thing deserves protection.

Not all goods or interests generate rights; it is only when there is a particularly important moral reason for protecting the good or interest in question that we speak of there being a right attached to it. This idea is expressed in Dworkin's (1977: 189–90) well-known claim that individual rights are political trumps held by individuals. He goes on to add that individuals have rights when, for some reason, a collective goal is not a sufficient justification for denying them what they wish, as individuals, to have or to do, or is not a sufficient justification for imposing some loss or injury upon them. The idea is also expressed in Raz's (1995: 166) claim that a right exists if an aspect of a single person's well-being is a sufficient reason for holding some other person or persons to be under a duty. Political theories will differ in their estimate of the importance of certain goods or interests for human beings, and therefore in their ascription of particular rights, but the central idea remains that of important interests of individuals protected against wider moral considerations. That is why, according to Hartney (1991), giving rights to the society would simply annihilate any competing individual rights. But he ignores the very important issue of individuals not as atomized entities but as culturally embedded, and the idea of 'good' as rooted in one's culture.

Theories of Rights

We will now discuss different theories associated with the idea of rights. Rights are not only of different kinds but there are various theories on the origin of rights. The first and the oldest theory of rights is the natural rights theory.

The Theory of Natural Rights

The most influential statement on natural rights was given by John Locke in his *Second Treatise on Civil Government* published in 1690 (repr. 1946). But before Locke, Thomas Hobbes had also propounded a theory of natural rights. Hobbes' idea of natural rights can be traced to his conception of the 'state of nature'. This state is the condition of human life in the absence of organized political authority and government, the natural condition of man in contrast to his artificial condition under a government. According to Hobbes (1946: 80–81), the right of nature or what he calls '*Jus Naturale*',

> is the liberty each man hath to use his power as he will himself for the preservation of his own nature, i.e. to say his own life, and consequently of doing anything which in his own judgment and reason he shall conceive to be the aptest means.

This liberty is a right to nature because each man has it in the state of nature. It is the only right anyone can have in the absence of a government. But this is not a worthy right because, as Hobbes (1946: 82) later points out, the state of nature is a condition of war where everyone is against everyone, and in which everyone is governed by his or her own reason. Thus, Hobbes concludes that the natural right of every man to everything must be given up as a necessary condition for the establishment of a government and to end the anarchy of the state of nature. All must agree to obey unconditionally one supreme authority. Hobbes, however, retains one natural right and that is the right to life. If the government orders a man to kill himself, he may resist.

John Locke (1946) also thinks of the state of nature as being the condition of human beings in the absence of government. But unlike Hobbes, he does not think that it is inherently a state of war. 'Men live together according to reason, without a common superior on earth with authority to judge between them are properly in a state of nature.'

According to Locke, in the state of nature men are in perfect freedom to order their actions and dispose of their possessions and persons as they think fit within the bounds of the law of nature, without asking leave or depending upon the will of any other man. He also adds that it is 'a state of equality, wherein all the power and jurisdiction is reciprocal, no one having more than the other'. But this natural freedom is not freedom to do as you like. It is freedom 'within the bounds of the law of nature'. The state of nature has a law of nature to govern it. This law teaches all humankind, who will consult it, that being all equal and independent, no one ought to harm another in his life, health, liberty or possessions.

Locke speaks of man as being born with a title to perfect freedom and an uncontrolled enjoyment of all the rights and privileges of the law of nature. But what are these rights and privileges? To this, Locke's answer is that every man has a natural right to his life and freedom of action to use his property as he thinks fit, provided that he does not interfere with any other man's enjoyment of the same conditions.

The theory of natural rights has been criticized by many thinkers, but the most vehement critics of this theory are the utilitarians.

The Utilitarian Theory of Rights

The utilitarian theory of rights was outlined by the English philosopher Jeremy Bentham (1748–1832). Bentham was dissatisfied with the aimless and 'unscientific' character of the legislation of his day and critical of the idea that significant and genuinely reforming legislation could be based on the traditional idea of 'rights'. He argued that lawmakers should use what he called the 'principle of utility' to construct morally sound legislation. By utility he meant that 'property in any object, whereby it tends to produce benefits, advantages, good or happiness or that which prevents the happening of mischief, pain, evil or unhappiness to the party whose interest is considered—if that party be the community; then the happiness of the community; if a particular individual then the happiness of the individual' (Burns and Harts 1970: 14).

Bentham defines the principle of utility as that which commands a state to maximize the utility of the community. The measure of a government is said to be dictated by the principle of utility when it takes care of the greatest happiness of the community, rather than the happiness of some people. He goes to the extent of bringing out a mathematical way of calculating utility to give an air of scientific authority.

Bentham's principle of utility has been persistently alluring to generations of politicians, policy makers and theorists ever since he promulgated it. It is not only simple, seemingly scientific, and can be given a mathematical formulation, but is also centrally concerned with what we may take to be the core of morality—human welfare. Yet, the principle of utility has been heavily criticized, so that over the years the advocates of that principle have felt the need to modify and redefine it to make it plausible. To appreciate these criticisms, consider the interesting theoretical assumptions built into the Benthamite principle of utility. First, Bentham takes it for granted that each of us can evaluate our own happiness. Second, he assumes that this evaluation can also be made by those who are determining policy in a state. Third, his principle assumes that this evaluation is quantitative, that is, happiness is something inside each of us that can be measured and represented by a single number, as if it were 'stuff' that came in degrees. Fourth, his principle assumes that the happiness of each person can be added to the happiness of any other person, allowing us not only to compare the happiness of persons but also to add their 'happinesses' together to get a sum total of 'happinesses'.

It was not long before these assumptions were attacked. Consider the third assumption, that the evaluation of happiness is purely a quantitative matter: can we really measure people's happiness, assuming that happiness is only one kind of thing that comes in degrees but does not differ in kind? Bentham insisted that happiness was not a word that denoted multiple experiences or feelings in a human being but only one kind of feeling—the feeling of pleasure. However, John Stuart Mill, himself a follower of utilitarianism, thought that this view was incorrect, since we intuitively think that experiences of 'pleasure' not only differ in quantity but also quality. Mill sympathized with critics of Bentham who contended that the idea that life has 'no higher end than pleasure' was 'utterly mean and grovelling'.

Many people who are attracted to the principle of utility have argued that we should not abandon Bentham's idea but only redesign it. They argue for a better way of identifying human welfare, such that it can be quantified, measured and aggregated. Moreover, contemporary utility theory, developed by John von Neumann, Oskar Morgenstern and Leonard Savage, has generated a way of doing something like 'measuring' the satisfaction of preferences, so that we come up with a number that accurately reflects how well a person has received what she wants, showing the intensity of those wants. However, these 'measurement numbers', as they stand, cannot be added together as the principle of utility requires.

Critics have argued that such an idea is wrong—and that expected utility theory is misused if it is seen as a source for the foundation of a notion of welfare that will be serviceable to the utilitarians. Such critics raised the technical issues about the nature of the 'measurement' of preferences that game theory gives. These sorts of problems have eroded the popularity of utilitarianism in our times. Yet, critics have argued that there are even more serious problems plaguing the theory, having to do with the kind of policy recommendation it would generate if its foundational assumptions could be better clarified and defended. Consider, for example, that the theory tells us to maximize total happiness. Now, if maximizing total happiness depended upon impoverishing some members of the society, the principle of utility would nonetheless tell us to do so. Yet, this intuitively strikes us as unfair.

Some people have actually put forward a moral theory called intuitionism. According to this view, we have fundamental moral ideas within us that are the source of our conceptions of justice and to which any adequate moral conception must answer. However, such a theory has not proven popular: first, it has no resources within it to systematize or interpret intuitions if they come to us in an inchoate form. Second, it has no theoretical resources to prioritize among intuitions or decide between them when they conflict. Third, and perhaps most important, given that many intuitions held by people reflect the prejudices, injustices and peculiarities of their culture, intuitionalism must be able to identify which intuitions should be morally relied upon—and yet it does not have the theoretical resources to do so. Hence, philosophers critical of utilitarianism have attempted to formulate alternatives to intuitionism. that could not only show the failure of the principle of utility in a way that relies less on intuition but also yield a satisfactory conception of justice based on reason. The most prominent of these attempts, by John Rawls, is the topic of our next section.

John Rawls on Rights

John Rawls' *A Theory of Justice* (1971) is the most influential contemporary work on rights. For Rawls, what is directly relevant for social ethics and justice is the individual's means to pursue their own ends to and to live whatever 'good life' they choose for themselves. Rawls' vision of the just state is deeply egalitarian in spirit. His argument makes use of the idea of a hypothetical social contract, applied not to the nature of the state's authority over the people but to the nature of justice. We are, says Rawls, to imagine ourselves in a contract situation in which we must agree with all those people who will live with us in a society based on the principles of justice that will govern it. He argues that any principle of justice that results from this hypothetical agreement process should be understood to be the best defensible conception of justice available to us.

Rawls also believes that the contract takes the individual seriously. He was greatly influenced by Kant, who seems to think that the idea of contract acknowledges the way in which people should be treated as 'ends' in themselves and not solely as 'means'. A social contract test of political policies is, in Kant's view, a way to secure that acknowledgement by hypothetically involving each member of the society in the assessment of those policies in a way that respects her interests and perspectives as an individual.

Rawls also believes that a contract test takes the individual seriously in a way utilitarianism does not. Rawls argues that in the utilitarian calculation the boundaries of the individuals are merged, and what is morally important about them—i.e. their welfare—is aggregated together. Instead of endorsing a moral reasoning procedure that explicitly conflates individuals, Rawls argues that an adequate theory of justice must morally respond to and preserve the 'distinction of persons'. Rawls' theory of justice as fairness consists of the two principles:

> **First principle:** 'Each person is to have an equal right to the most extensive liberty compatible with a similar liberty for others'.
>
> **Second principle:** 'Social and economic inequalities are to be arranged so that they are both (*a*) reasonably expected to be in everyone's advantage and in particular, to the advantage of the least well-off persons; and (*b*) attached to positions and offices open to all'.

Rawls' arguments have been attacked by many critics. There have been right-wing and left-wing attacks. On the right, critics have charged that Rawls has failed to acknowledge the proper role that effort, merit and responsibility should have in the distribution of resources. Why should people receive roughly equal allotments when some work harder than others, when some invest more wisely than others, or when some are lazy and fail to contribute effectively to the community? They claim that a system of distributive justice that ignores differences in effort undermines individual responsibility, promotes sloth and allows the lazy to free ride on the efforts of the industrious in a way that will likely lead to social unrest and eventual diminishment of the economic pool. Now, if it produces the latter results, Rawls' own theory would disallow that distribution, because in this situation giving more to the industrious is justified in order to increase the economic pool and to yield more for everyone. Hence, he would allow unequal distributions in order to forestall a drop in productivity. In contrast, he would not allow them if the economic pool were increased but the only people to benefit from the increase were the most advantaged.

Rawls' right-wing critics would object, however, if the more advantaged by virtue of creating those increases are allowed to enjoy their share of the increased economic pool even if that adds to societal inequality. On the left, critics have pointed to Rawls' willingness to depart from strict equality of holdings and some have wished for a conception of equality that focuses more on the equality of people's welfare than the equality of their resources. The critics from the left have also been troubled by his failure to incorporate more fully the idea of personal responsibility into his theory.

The Libertarian Theory of Rights

Shortly after the publication of Rawls' book, Robert Nozick published *Anarchy, State and Utopia* (1974), which is in some respect a libertarian reply to *A Theory of Justice*. Nozick argues against what he calls 'patterned' and 'end-state' conceptions of justice. The former are conceptions of justice that seek to implement a distributive scheme according to some patterning principle. The latter are conceptions that seek to attain a certain kind of *telos*, or goal, via a certain distribution of resources.

What is important in Nozick's view is the idea that each individual has certain rights and in particular, certain property rights that are 'absolute' in character in the sense that no amount of good accruing to the community generally or to other individuals can justify the infringement or overriding of these rights.

Nozick's ultimate concern is with the way end-state and patterned conceptions of justice interfere with liberty. Hence, he argues for a historical conception of justice, on which he bases the theory of rights. Nozick's particular version of historical principle is what he calls the 'entitlement theory of justice' which consists of three principles:

1. A person who acquires a holding in accordance with the principle of justice in acquisition is entitled to that holding.
2. A person who acquires a holding in accordance with the principle of justice in transfer from someone entitled to the holding is entitled to the holding.
3. No one is entitled to a holding except by repeated applications of (1) and (2).

In addition to these principles, Nozick also endorses a principle of rectification that would provide for the redressal of past injustices. But this conception of justice essentially entails the defence of the free market and the capitalist system. His argument is a way of defending the free market insofar as it realizes justice by respecting the liberty of the individual regardless of its effects on aggregate welfare and regardless of its economic implications.

There have been many criticisms of libertarian views in general and Nozick's version of libertarianism in particular—some of them passionate. The most obvious and popular criticism has been of the libertarian notion of rights: for why should we think that morality demands that we accord people such absolute rights? How could rights be thought to trump so decisively all considerations of others' welfare in the community? Moreover, what if the economy flourishes better if the state interfered in the market economy? Libertarians may not allow it, and yet most citizens and firms might actually want it and even demand it, insofar as they believe they will be better off with such governmental interference.

Human Rights

Human rights are international moral and legal norms that aspire to protect all people everywhere from severe political, legal and social abuses. Examples of human rights are the right to freedom of religion, the right to a fair trial when charged with a crime, the right not to be tortured and the right to engage in political activity. These rights exist in morality and in law at the national and international levels. They are addressed primarily to governments, requiring compliance and enforcement. The main source of the contemporary conception of human rights is the Universal Declaration of Human Rights (1948) and the many human rights documents and treaties that have followed in its wake.

The philosophy of human rights addresses questions about the existence, content, nature, universality and justification of human rights. The Universal Declaration of Human Rights (UDHR) sets out a list of over two dozen specific human rights that countries should respect and protect. We may group these specific rights into six or more families: (i) *security rights* that protect people against crimes such as murder, massacre, torture and rape; (ii) *liberty rights* that protect freedom in areas such as belief, expression, association, assembly and movement; (iii) *political rights* that protect the liberty to participate in politics through actions such as communicating, assembling, protesting, voting and serving in public office; (iv) *due process rights* that protect against abuses of the legal system such as imprisonment without trial, secret trials and excessive punishments; (v) *equality rights* that guarantee equal citizenship, equality before the law and non-discrimination; and (vi) *welfare rights* (or 'economic and social rights') that require the provision of education to all children and protections against severe poverty and starvation. Another family that might be included is *group rights*. The UDHR does not include group rights, but subsequent treaties do. Group rights include the protection of ethnic groups against genocide and the ownership by countries of their national territories and resources.

The general idea of human rights can be explained by setting out some defining features. It answers the question of what human rights are with a general description of the concept rather than a list of specific rights. Two people can have the same general idea of human rights even though they disagree about whether some particular rights are human rights.

Human rights are political norms dealing mainly with how people should be treated by their governments and institutions. They *are not ordinary moral norms applying mainly to interpersonal conduct* (such as prohibitions of lying and violence). As Thomas Pogge (2000) puts it, 'to engage human rights, conduct must be in some sense official'. But we must be careful here since some rights, such as rights against racial and sexual discrimination are primarily concerned to regulate private behaviour. Still, governments are directed in two ways by rights against discrimination. They forbid governments to discriminate in their actions and policies, and they impose duties on governments to prohibit and discourage both private and public forms of discrimination.

Not every question of social justice or wise governance is a human rights issue. For example, a country could have too much income inequality, inadequate provision for higher education, or no national parks without violating any human rights. Deciding which norms should be counted as human rights is a matter of some difficulty. And, there is continuing pressure to expand lists of human rights to include new areas. Many political movements would like to see their main concerns categorized as matters of human rights, since this would publicize, promote and legitimate their concerns at the international level. A possible result of this is 'human rights inflation', the devaluation of human rights caused by producing too much bad human rights currency.

Some Recent Debates on Rights

Communitarian Perspectives

Communitarians critique the earlier discussed notions of rights on the ground that they take the 'individual' as the unit for the distribution of resources. Communitarians argue that the 'individual' is not an abstract category but is deeply embedded in his/her culture. Thus, they assert that the 'community' or 'group' identity of an individual should be taken into account, rather than the 'individual'. For many communitarians, the problem with liberalism is not its emphasis on justice, nor its universalism, but rather its individualism. According to this criticism, liberals base their theories on notions of individual rights and personal freedom, but neglect the extent to which individual freedom and well-being are only possible within a community. Once we recognize the dependence of human beings on society, our obligations to sustain the common good of society are as weighty as our rights to individual liberty. The central argument of Michael Sandel's book, *Liberalism and the Limits of Justice* (1982: 183) is that liberalism rests on a series of mistaken metaphysical and meta-ethical views, for example, that claims of justice are absolute and universal; that we cannot know each other well enough to share common ends, and that we define our personal identity independently of socially given ends. Hence, communitarians argue, the liberal 'politics of rights' should be abandoned for a 'politics of common good'.

Many communitarians agree about the importance of rights and justice, but they claim that liberals misinterpret justice as an ahistorical and external criterion for criticizing the ways of life of every society. Utilitarians, liberals, egalitarians and libertarians may disagree about the content of justice, but they all seem to think that their preferred theory provides a standard that every society should live up to. They do not see it as a decisive objection that their theory may be in conflict with local beliefs—this is sometimes seen by liberals as the point of discussing justice—it provides a standpoint for questioning our beliefs and for ensuring that they are not local prejudices. As Dworkin (1985: 219) puts it,

> ... in the end political theory can make no contribution to how we govern ourselves except by struggling against all the impulses that drag us back into our own culture, towards generality and some reflective basis for deciding which of our traditional distinctions and discriminations are genuine and which are spurious.

Michael Walzer (1983) argues that this quest for a universal theory of rights is misguided. The only way to identify the requirements of rights and justice is to see how each particular community understands the value of social goods. A society is just if it acts in accordance with the shared understandings of its members, as embodied in its characteristic practices and institutions. Hence, the identifying principle of rights and justice is more a matter of cultural interpretation than of philosophical argument. Walzer asserts that the shared understandings in our society require 'complex equality', i.e. a system of distribution that does not try to equalize all goods, but rather seeks to ensure that inequalities in one 'sphere' do not permeate other spheres. However, he acknowledges that other societies do not share this understanding of justice and for some societies justice may involve virtually unlimited inequality in rights and goods.

Multicultural Perspectives on Rights

One of the central theoretical and practical conundrums of our age is the problem of reconciling the aspirations to political equality with the fact of social and cultural differences within liberal democratic states. The liberal democratic state is increasingly being challenged both by theorists of democratic equality and by political movements to recognize that the ideal of universal citizenship in which each person is treated with 'equal concern and respect' can no longer be easily identified with a programme of uniform rights. They assert that the ideal of universal citizenship is based on the conception of equality as 'difference-blindness', which multiculturalists argue is 'formal' and not 'real' in nature. Real equality, according to the theorists of multiculturalism, is ensured not through 'uniformity of treatment' but by keeping in mind their social and cultural location.

Many defenders of group rights for ethnic and national minorities insist that they are needed to ensure that all citizens are treated with genuine equality. According to this view, the accommodation of difference is the essence of true equality, and group-specific rights are needed to accommodate our differences. Proponents of individual rights respond that individual rights already allow for the accommodation of differences, and that true equality requires equal rights for each individual regardless of race or ethnicity. But some minority rights eliminate—rather than create—inequalities. Some groups are unfairly disadvantaged in the cultural marketplace, and political recognition and support rectify this disadvantage. Kymlicka (1989a, 1989b) gives the example of the national minorities, the viability of their societal cultures may be undermined by economic and political decisions made by the majority. They could be outbid or outvoted on resources and policies that are crucial to the survival of their societal cultures. The members of majority cultures do not face this problem. Given the importance of cultural membership, this is a significant inequality which becomes a serious injustice if not addressed. Any plausible theory of rights should recognize the fairness of protection for the minorities. Giving minority rights to members of minority cultures may eliminate the disadvantages faced by them. Group-differentiated rights—such as territorial autonomy, veto powers, guaranteed representation, land claims and language rights—can help rectify these disadvantages by alleviating the vulnerability of minority cultures to majority decisions. Given that it is important for minorities to preserve their culture and their differences, they demand special rights that are essential for preserving their culture. Is giving special rights to some people not against the idea of equality? Should all minorities be granted group-differentiated rights? What if by giving group-differentiated rights the minorities demand a separate state for themselves? What will happen to national integration? These are some important issues that come up, but which are beyond the scope of this discussion.

Although multiculturalism has found many supporters, there are problems within it regarding women's rights, since most cultures endorse and permit control over women by men. Also, multiculturalism would pose a challenge to the liberal notion of nation-state, i.e. it may lead to cessationist movements like the ones in Kashmir and the North-East in India, Tamils in Sri Lanka, etc. Either way, the apprehensions are well founded and deserve serious consideration. We need to examine whether communities should be given special rights to preserve their culture. Should they have the right to protect all prevalent practices? Are all existing practices crucial for preserving a particular way of life? Should there be some minimum conditions that all cultures must adhere to? These are important questions that need to be analysed further within the framework of multiculturalism—in this regard it is important to consider the issue of intra-group equality, too.

Multiculturalism has raised important questions about the status of minorities within the nation-state. They have revealed the other side of the so-called neutral politics of liberal democracies as being biased against minorities. Above all, it has compelled the liberal democracies to analyse the implications of their socio-cultural policies, to see if they discriminate against minorities. Multiculturalism, like postmodernism, has raised questions about universals. It has raised a finger on one standard, i.e. Anglo-American conception of rights, justice, equality, good life, value system and meanings. Multiculturalists say that a society with strong collective goals can be liberal, provided it is also capable of respecting diversity, especially when dealing with those who do not share its common goals, and also offer adequate safeguards for fundamental rights. There will undoubtedly be tensions and difficulties in pursuing such goals, but such a pursuit is not impossible. The sense of multiculturalism as it is debated today has a lot to do with the imposition of some cultures on others, what they intend to fight is forced assimilation.

As Bhikhu Parekh (2000) asserts, in multicultural societies, cultural communities generally demand various kinds of rights they think they need to maintain their collective identity. Some of these rights, usually called group, collective, or communal, are not easy to accommodate within liberal jurisprudence and raise difficult questions such as whether the concept of collective rights is logically coherent and what kind of collectivities may legitimately claim what kinds of rights.

Just as individual rights are those rights of which the individuals are the bearers, collective rights are those of which human collectivities are the bearers. Human collectivities are of several kinds, ranging from groups united by transient or long-term common interests to historical communities based on a shared way of life.

The Feminist Challenge

According to feminists, justice should be understood from a 'group' perspective, as groups or communities play a crucial role in shaping one's perspectives on justice. Feminists believe that social or political systems based on the individual perspective of justice are highly biased because they are shaped by the dominant individual male and not by women or other marginalized groups. Thus, such political and social systems of domination, such as that of men over women or of the privileged over marginalized groups, can distort society so severely that none of the theories of justice will prove acceptable unless these systems of oppression are overturned. The feminists argue that if women live in a society where they are not allowed to hold certain forms of property or vote or engage in certain occupations, then merely distributing resources in some kind of 'equal' fashion will not be enough to secure justice. Greater resources do not solve or ameliorate the fact that in such a society's women are partially mastered.

Susan Moller Okin's *Justice, Gender and the Family* (1989) offers both a critique and a reconstruction of Rawls' original position as an analytic tool used to define workable standards of justice for liberal democratic societies. She says that Rawls' own characterization of the original position, despite its occasional claims to gender neutrality, in fact contains many implicit assumptions that would tend to reinforce the current inequality of women in the gendered structure of social institutions. Rawls' characterization of parties to the original positions as heads of families and as member of the paid workforce suggests an implicit assumption that the parties are the male heads of relatively traditional families. Okin argues that the social structure of gender relations and the nature of family certainly raise issues of justice. In a society where domestic labour is performed mainly by women, women's inequality in other spheres is virtually assured. The equal value of political liberties is out of reach in a gender-structured society, because involvement is time consuming and women who bear responsibilities for domestic labour have little time for political activities as it imposes the constraint of a 'double workday' on them. Finally, the most important argument is that the primary goods for the social basis of self-esteem are less sure for girls than for boys. The consequences, Okin (1987: 107) contends, is that 'in a gender-structured society there is such a thing as the distant standpoint of women and … this standpoint cannot be adequately taken into account by male philosophers', whose moral reasoning abstracts from gender altogether.

Iris Marion Young (1989: 258) in her widely cited article argues that 'the ideal of universal citizenship' contains three meanings of universality: The first—universality as inclusion of all in full citizenship status and in participation in public life—this stands in tension with the other two meanings of universality, i.e. universality as a focus on the common good, defined in terms of what citizens share rather than what divides them; and universality as equal treatment, defined as same treatment without regard to group differences. Young says that a genuine commitment to universality in the first sense will require a conception of differentiated citizenship both with respect to deliberation about the common good and with respect to the allocation of rights. Young's critique is aimed directly at the republican tradition. She acknowledges that contemporary republicans emphasize on what citizens have in common. This undermines the differences between groups. Different social groups have different needs, cultures, histories, experiences and perceptions of social relations, which influence their interpretation of the meanings and consequences of policy proposals, and the form of their political reasoning. These differences in political interpretation are not merely or even primarily a result of differing or conflicting interests because groups have differing interpretations even when they seek to promote justice, and not merely their own self-regarding ends. Thus, a genuine commitment to the inclusion of all in public deliberation requires that differences be not suppressed but acknowledged and respected. The best way to do this is to establish special forms of representation for disadvantaged groups that ensure that these groups have the resources needed to organize themselves, and their perspectives are seriously considered in public decisions.

The attempt to realize an ideal of universal citizenship that finds the public embodying generality as opposed to particularity, commonness versus difference, will tend to exclude or put at a disadvantage some groups even when formally they have an equal citizenship status. The idea of the public as universal and the concomitant identification of particularity with privacy make homogeneity a requirement of public participation. All citizens should assume the same impartial general point of view. Young criticizes the view of universal citizenship on the grounds that societies have certain privileged groups and some oppressed groups, and in such a situation to leave behind particular affiliations and to adopt a general point of view would mean that the interests of the privileged will dominate. Thus, instead of a universal citizenship in the sense of this generality, Young proposes 'a group differentiated citizenship' and a heterogeneous public.

A liberal theory can accept special rights for a minority culture against the larger community so as to ensure equality of circumstances between them. But it will not justify special rights for a culture against its own members. Liberals are committed to supporting the right of individuals to decide for themselves which aspects of their cultural heritage are worthy passing on. Liberalism is committed to the view that individuals should have the freedom and capacity to question and possibly revise the traditional practices of their community should they come to see them as no longer worthy of their allegiance.

Conclusion

To sum up this discussion, there is no intrinsic reason to assign rights to individuals alone, for if individuals are incomplete without the cultural resources that communities provide them, individual rights are incomplete without community rights. But we cannot buy peace between the communities at the expense of individuals. Thus, we need to think of community rights as conditional rights. But these cultural rights should not override the core rights, i.e. the right to life, freedom, equality, and the right to assert rights.

Points for Discussion

1. A person is terminally ill, and is suffering from pain. There is no chance of recovery at any cost. Should the person have the right to die?
2. Do smokers have a moral obligation towards non-smokers to not smoke in public places even if it is not illegal to do so?
3. Two adults decide to get married against the wishes of their communities. Should they be allowed? In this situation which rights, i.e. individual or group rights should prevail?
4. Does the unborn child have rights?

Reading List

Burns, T. H. and H. L. A. Hart (eds), *Jeremy Bentham: An Introduction to the Principles of Morals and Legislation* (London: Athlone Press, 1970).

Daniels, Norman, *Reading Rawls* (New York: Basic Books, 1975).

Dworkin, Ronald, *Taking Rights Seriously* (London: Duckworth, 1977).

———, *A Matter of Principle* (Cambridge, MA: Harvard University Press, 1985).

Chandoke, Neera, *Beyond Secularism: The Rights of Religious Minorities* (New Delhi: Oxford University Press, 1999).

Gilligan, Carol, 'In a Different Voice', in Sandra Kemp and Judith Squires (eds), *Feminism* (Oxford, New York: Oxford University Press, 1997).

Hampton, Jean, *Political Philosophy: An Introduction* (Delhi: Oxford University Press, 1993).

Hartney, Michael, 'Some Confusions Concerning Collective Rights', *Canadian Journal of Jurisprudence*, 4(2), 1991: 293–314.

Hinman, Lawrence M., *Ethics: A Pluralistic Approach to Moral Theory* (Fort Worth: Harcourt, Brace, 1997).
Hobbes, Thomas, *Leviathan* (Oxford: Basil Blackwell, 1946), complete e-text available at http://ebooks.adelaide.edu.au/h/hobbes/thomas/h68l/
Kymlicka, Will, *Liberalism, Community and Culture* (Oxford: Oxford University Press, 1989a).
———, 'Liberal Individualism and Liberal Neutrality', *Ethics*, 99, 1989b: 883–905.
———, *Multicultural Citizenship: A Liberal Theory of Minority Rights* (Oxford: Clarendon, 1995).
Mill, John Stuart, 'Utilitarianism', in H. B. Acton (ed.), *Utilitarianism, Liberty and Representative Government* (New York: E. P. Dutton, 1972).
Nozick, Robert, *Anarchy, State and Utopia* (New York: Basic Books, 1974).
Okin, Susan Moller, 'Justice and Gender', *Philosophy and Public Affairs*, 16(1), 1987: 42–72.
———, *Justice, Gender and the Family* (New York: Basic Books, 1989).
Parekh, Bhikhu, *Rethinking Multiculturalism: Cultural Diversity and Political Theory* (Basingstoke: Macmillan, 2000).
Pogge, T., 'The International Significance of Human Rights', *Journal of Ethics*, 4, 2000: 45–69.
Rawls, John, *A Theory of Justice* (Cambridge, MA: Harvard University Press, 1971).
Raz, Joseph, 'Multiculturalism: A Liberal Perspective', in his *Ethics in Public Domain: Essays in the Morality of Law and Politics* (rev. ed.) (Oxford: Oxford University Press, 1995).
Sandel, Michael, *Liberalism and the Limits of Justice* (Cambridge: Cambridge University Press, 1982).
Sheth, D. L. and Gurpreet Mahajan (ed.), *Minority Identities and the Nation-State* (New Delhi: Oxford University Press, 1999).
Walzer, Michael, *Spheres of Justice: A Defence of Pluralism and Equality* (Oxford: Blackwell, 1983).
Young, Iris Marion, 'Politics and Group Difference: A Critique of the Ideal of Universal Citizenship', *Ethics*, 99, 1989: 250–74.
———, *Justice and the Politics of Difference* (Princeton, NJ: Princeton University Press, 1990).

CHAPTER 8

Democracy

Janaki Srinivasan

Chapter Outlines

Introduction

The concept of democracy is at the centre of fierce debates in political theory as well as in commonplace discussions on politics. This chapter examines the ways in which democracy has been conceptualized, defended and critiqued. In doing so, it discusses the evolution of democracy as a concept, the various criticisms levelled against the concept, followed by perspectives and debates in contemporary democratic theory. It concludes with some of the key debates which characterize democratic theory today.

Consider situations in your everyday life where you are part of a group and decisions have to be made for the group as a whole: whether it is a group of friends deciding if they should watch a movie or a family deciding where to go for a vacation. Suppose that among a group of ten friends, seven want to see a movie but three want to go for an art exhibition. What should the group decide to do? Consider another situation where a university class has been asked by their teacher to arrive at a convenient date for having a class debate. And here, in a class of thirty, everyone is agreed on a date except for five students. These five, however, have important and unavoidable reasons why that particular date is not convenient to them. What should the class do? Should it go by the decision of the majority? But doing so will deprive those five students from the chance to take part in the debate. Would that be a fair decision? Now, suppose the class has to decide on the topic of the debate. The number of opinions and suggestions made increase manifold and decision making becomes that much more difficult.

In all such situations of collective existence, there is a constant need to arrive at common decisions. Who takes these decisions and how? How do we judge whether these decisions are fair or the best possible? The idea of democracy provides one basis for making such judgements. A democratic decision is one that takes into account and reflects the wishes of the people who come under the purview of that decision. There are, of course, other ways to take decisions. A father can decide where the family will go for a vacation without taking the opinion of other family members, or a teacher can give no choice to the students on the topic or the date for the class debate. But advocates of democracy argue that a decision-making procedure which reflects a commitment of taking into equal consideration the preferences of members of the concerned group/s is a legitimate one. Democracy is, thus, both a method to arrive at collective decisions and a set of values and behaviour with which people approach decision making.

The Concept

How should a political community then arrive at collective decisions? In other words, who should rule? What should be the principle guiding government formation and what are the institutional arrangements required for this purpose? Democracy is now the universally accepted answer to this question, so much so that everyone—even military juntas, dictators and monarchs—claim to be democrats. The charge of being called 'undemocratic' is taken seriously now. However, this positive value accorded to democracy is recent in history; for a long time it was associated with 'mob-rule' and inefficient governments. The term democracy translates as 'rule by the people'. Who are the 'people' and how do they rule? On what matters? To what extent? Through what institutions? To secure which goals? Is this a desirable arrangement?

There are varied views on the nature, purpose, extent, effectiveness and desirability of democratic rule, as well as varied critiques on the practice of functioning democracies. Indeed, democracy is often called an 'adjectival concept' because of the endless number of 'types' or 'models' into which democracies are classified, for example; liberal, social, people's, direct and indirect, radical, associational, deliberative, strong and weak, procedural and substantive, pluralist and elitist ... the list goes on. Before we examine some of these debates, let us briefly discuss the concept and look at the various theories and types in the light of their differences and areas of consensus.

At the heart of all democratic theories is the concept of popular power. According to Anthony Arblaster (1994), it refers to a situation where power and authority ultimately rest with the people. A democratic government is contrasted with an authoritarian one where decisions are imposed on the people and exercised without their consent. Democracy ensures the accountability of those holding power to the people who are the ultimate source of that power. It is the *consent* of the people which makes government authority legitimate.

How is this consent to be given? The question of consent immediately connects with that of participation. How much participation is desirable? In a *direct* democracy, there is a high degree of participation as citizens collectively decide, often through mass meetings, on almost all major issues. In effect, people rule themselves. This form of democracy is associated with the classical Athenian model. In India, the *gram sabha* is such an institution of direct democracy as are a number of devices like *referendum*, *initiative* and *recall* practised in contemporary societies. In contrast, in an *indirect* or *representative democracy,* government functions through representatives who are chosen through popular elections. These representatives provide a link between the governments and the people and elections allow the people to control the action of the representatives and prevent abuse of power. Liberal democracy is a representative form of government. While these two methods are seen in opposition to each other, we shall see in the last section how contemporary debates on the question of participation seek to combine the two.

Democracy refers to a government based on political equality, i.e. consent is required of all the individuals who form part of the political community. It is informed by the belief that all people are equally capable of, and have a stake in making, collective decisions that shape their lives. In a democracy, no one person's opinion or interest is of more value than the other, hence the principle of 'one person one vote'. It is based on the idea of the equal moral worth of all individuals and against the exclusion of anyone from the political process. Thus, it is against hierarchy or inherited privileges and discrimination. Today, when we say 'the people' we usually refer to all adult citizens in a polity. This was not always so and a long struggle was waged by hitherto excluded groups demanding the right of suffrage.

From being initially restricted to the property-owning white men in Europe and America, eventually educated men, working-class white men, black men, and women (in that order) were subsequently recognized as full citizens with the right to vote and contest elections. Meanwhile, in the colonies of Asia and Africa, democratic struggles took on a specifically anti-colonial character and the peoples of colonies like India claimed the right of self-government as a people.

In a democracy it is assumed that there will be a diversity of opinions and interests on almost every matter of common concern. Indeed, this diversity is seen as its main strength and it calls for tolerance for all shades of opinion. A democratic society is also called an 'open society' where there is space for all voices, however unpopular or conventional they may be, to be heard. This requires a range of political freedoms like freedom of expression, association and movement among others, which are protected by the state. People must have access to information and be able to protest and freely criticize the government and others in order to make informed uncoerced choices and intervene in the decision-making process. Thus, the practice of democracy is unthinkable without rights.

But do these freedoms by themselves ensure that all voices are in fact heard, and heard equally? Equal distribution of political power, however, does not mean that everyone manages to have equal influence on the decision-making process. Is it the same for an influential industrialist and a poor farmer or a slum-dwelling labourer to have the right to vote? Do they have equal influence on policy making? For democracy to be effective, then those factors which discriminate against sections of people and hinder their effective intervention in collective decision making need to be addressed. The presence of structures of power that are sources of inequality in a society are an impediment to democracy. Equality, thus, is a condition of democracy and democratic societies are expected to devise arrangements which further equality.

What is the nature of a democratic decision? There has been much debate on this. As a conflict-resolution model, democracy is often identified with majority rule and this raises the problem of oppression of minorities. On the other hand, democracies are expected to arrive at a consensus. But in plural and complex societies that are also unequal, consensus is difficult to achieve.

We will see in the last section how these very issues of equality, participation, representation and diversity pose important questions and are the concerns of contemporary democratic theory. Before that we will now examine the two main models of democratic practice, namely, the direct participatory model and the liberal democratic models. Later, we examine some of the major critiques of democratic practice.

Direct Participatory Democracy

The most celebrated form of direct participatory democracy was the one practised in the Athenian city-state of ancient Greece during the 5th and 4th centuries B.C. Athenians prided themselves on the 'happy versatility' of citizens and their ability to perform all tasks of governance, i.e. in enacting, implementing and adjudicating of laws. They met in open assemblies to debate and deliberate on all matters and shared magisterial and judicial offices. All major decisions were made by the assembly to which all citizens belonged. Citizens were also meant to sit on juries and adjudicate on disputes. Offices were filled by either election or draw of lots and no officer was to enjoy perpetual tenure. The idea was to ensure that at least the short-term offices went to as many people as possible. What is remarkable in this model is that it ensured a high level of political accountability and political activity of the citizen.

Indeed, citizenship entailed participation; it was a sacred duty and the full-time occupation of the citizen. The purpose of political participation was the common good of the state. This common good was independent of and prior to individual interests and desires. It is when citizens set aside their private interests, completely identify with the community, and give it their best that common good can be achieved. The underlying philosophy was that there was a single, shared, substantive idea of good life for the whole community; the separation between state and society did not exist. Participation in the collective affairs of the community was considered important for the rational self-development of the citizens; it was the highest form of good life that they could hope to achieve, fulfil themselves, and live honourably.

Republican Rome shared some features of Athenian democracy, namely, the notion of popular participation in civic life, a strong sense of duty to the community, the idea of public good and civic virtue as being of higher value than private individual interests. This is also called civic republicanism.

Rousseau, an early critic of liberal democracy, was heavily inspired by this model. Writing in the 18th century, Rousseau was critical of electoral democracy and representative mechanisms which were emerging in various European states. For Rousseau, democracy was the way by which citizens could achieve freedom. By freedom he did not mean the absence of constraints on the individual's pursuit of self-interest. Instead, he articulated a positive notion of freedom. (See Chapter 4 on liberty for the distinction between negative and positive freedom.) Individuals are free only when they participate directly, actively and continuously in shaping the life of the community, especially in the making of laws. For him, law-making was an exercise of sovereignty—which cannot be transferred or represented by anyone else—and an expression of the will of the people.

For Rousseau, participation was essential for the self-development of the individual and democracy was a means of individual development, but not the pursuit of selfish interests.

Rousseau made a distinction between private will and what he called 'general will'. General will is not an aggregation of private will or interests of individual citizens. Instead, general will is that which emerges when people set aside their selfish interests and deliberate on the collective common good of the community. Freedom lies in obedience to the general will; by doing so they are obeying their own true nature. Rousseau goes to the extent of saying that people can be 'forced to be free', i.e. obey the general will.

Such conceptions of participatory self-governance, active citizenship and community life have been an attractive one for all those critical of liberal democracy. Socialists, feminists, radical and deliberative democrats have drawn on this legacy. However, the very conditions in which this model has been practised provides a note of caution. The successful operation of the Athenian democracy depended on a system of exclusivity and inequality. Only citizens were worthy of the good life and a majority of the population—women, slaves and resident aliens—were kept out of citizenship. Indeed, it was on the basis of their labour and economic activities that the free adult male could be freed for citizenship. Aristotle, even as he was critical of democracy, justified this denial of political equality to women and slaves both on the grounds of necessity and the latter's natural inferiority. (We shall examine Plato and Aristotle's critique of democracy in a later section.) Rousseau, too, explicitly kept out women from political participation. He argued that women were primarily meant to perform sexual and domestic roles and their public presence would be a distraction.

Rousseau did, however, consider a certain measure of economic equality essential for the exercise of citizenship. For any renewal of strong and active participation a society has to work out a balance between the satisfaction of material needs and political participation in a framework which treats all adults equally. A further point of debate is whether present societies can work with a single notion of common good which can be oppressive not just to individual freedom, as liberals fear, but also to the diverse groups and cultures which comprise most societies. In other words, a participatory system is seen to put pressure on attaining homogeneity. Rousseau's theory, as we observed, has totalitarian implications.

Liberal democracy

Today, when we talk of democracy, we often have what is known as liberal democracy in mind. It is the dominant form of democracy as most countries seen to practise this model in one form or the other. However, it is important to remember that liberal democracy is a product of a long history and it contains many strands.

Protective Democracy

For early liberals, democracy was meant to be protective, in the sense that it was meant to protect the rights of citizens and safeguard them from the tyranny of state power. The 'liberal' element in liberal democracy preceded the democratic element and has shaped its nature. Liberalism emerged in the context of the transition from feudalism to capitalism. In this process, the newly emerging bourgeoisie/middle class sought to put limits on the absolute powers of the monarchs and the feudal aristocracies in European states from the 16th century onwards. (See the chapters on Liberalism and the State.)

Underlying this challenge to absolute and unaccountable power is the new doctrine of individualism. According to this notion, all individuals are free and autonomous, masters of themselves, and makers of their own destiny. Individuals are primarily rational and self-interested beings, intent on pursuing their desires and goals. Each individual has his/her own preferences, values and goals, i.e. his/her own conception of a good life. What individuals require are the basic conditions to pursue these self-defined goals. Liberals identify these conditions as rights, namely, of life, liberty and property, which are fundamental and inviolable in nature. What binds individuals to each other is a common interest in protecting these rights which would allow them the maximum freedom for free exchange among themselves. The emergence of liberalism is linked to that of capitalism and market society. That is why property is understood as a fundamental right. An individual's property is considered an extension of the self and an individual is the master of his/her own self. According to liberal thinkers like Hobbes and Locke, individuals do not derive their identity from the community and are not bound to it by any sense of duty, nor do they see themselves as part of a hierarchical system or a divine plan. Thus, liberalism's lasting contribution to political thought is a radical notion of equality among human beings. This view on human nature meant a re-conceptualization of the role and purpose of government.

Liberals make a distinction between the state and civil society or the public and the private life of individuals. The public realm is the realm of politics; this is where they are bound to take collective decisions. The economy, family, associations, etc., are part of the civil society, the realm where individuals interact with each other in the pursuit of their interests. This is the realm of competition, conflict and co-operation among them. It is in order to resolve these conflicts that a regulated framework is required. Thus, the role of the government is to create and maintain a system of individual rights, and undertake activities to that end. The coercive power of the state is required to ensure that individuals in their interaction with each other in a civil society do not encroach on each other's rights. Governments were not meant to arrive at or promote a common good, since individuals do not share a substantive notion of good life. The state is a neutral arbiter; it is not supposed to interfere in the functioning of civil society.

At the same time, liberals share a deep fear that governments will abuse this power and encroach on these rights. Liberals were giving voice to the struggle by the bourgeoisie to unshackle the restrictions of feudal and aristocratic authority. In other words, there is need for a strong but limited government. Moreover, among free and equal individuals any institution of authority over them requires their consent, otherwise it will be illegitimate. Thus, there is need for a mechanism through which people can consent to a government and retain control over it to ensure the performance of the tasks entrusted to it and restrain it from exceeding its limits. This is where liberals turn to democracy as a solution.

Liberals advocate a representative democracy. The task of governance requires expertise, but those in power must be made accountable. Political participation is not considered a good in itself, like in Athenian democracy, but a means to control the government and ensure the protection of individual liberties. Through franchise and competitive elections, individuals choose representatives who then form governments on the majority principle. Political decisions can be made only by these representatives, because only they enjoy the consent of the people. This ultimate authority of the people is affirmed, and people can keep a check on the representatives through periodic elections. The powers and tasks of the government are defined through the constitution, especially by including within the provision of fundamental rights, and through the principle of rule of law and the presence of an independent judiciary (for example, the Bill of Rights in the U.S. Constitution and the Fundamental Rights in the Indian Constitution). The separation of powers among different branches of government is meant to provide a system of checks and balances, preventing the concentration of power.

Even though the model of representative democracy was based on the principle of equality, in early liberal democracies, franchise or political equality was in effect restricted to a few. They were more in the nature of oligarchies. Early liberals were as fearful of the 'tyranny of the masses' as they were of the tyranny of state power. Locke, James Mill, Madison and Montesquieu were all opposed to universal franchise. For example, John Locke, who was the first to articulate the key ideas of liberal democracy, restricted franchise to property owners, defended property as a 'natural' right as well as the unequal distribution of property, and modified his powerful notion of consent to mean 'active' consent of the propertied and 'tacit' consent of the rest. Even John Stuart Mill, who supported universal adult franchise and was among the first to support enfranchisement of women, sought to restrict the right to vote to those with basic educational qualifications and desired provisions for giving extra votes to educated and better qualified individuals. It was feared that if vested with political freedoms, the majority would not use their right to vote responsibly but would overturn the distribution of (unequal) property in society. In Indian courts, a series of cases came up after the adoption of the Constitution which challenged the land redistribution policies of the government as being violations of the fundamental right to property. Understood as popular rule without the restrictions of individual rights, democracy, thus, becomes a threat to liberty. There is a conflict between the 'liberal' and 'democratic' components.

It was in the aftermath of the French and the American Revolutions that popular democratic struggles emerged. The 19th and 20th centuries were marked by increasing and often violent struggles by the working class, African Americans, and women, demanding the extension of suffrage on the basis of the very ideas of individualism that had been invoked by the propertied male to win freedom from aristocracies and monarchies. The implicit radical potential of the notion of individualism, rights and equality was realized by these struggles. It is only with this acceptance of universal adult franchise that liberal democracy acquired its current form.

John Stuart Mill and Developmental Democracy

Predominantly, liberal democracy is concerned with the protection of individual rights and prevention of abuse of power. Participation in this context is of value because it allows the individual to put forward his/her interests and keep a check on the activities of those in positions of power. It is of no intrinsic value in terms of the self-development of the individual. James Mill controversially claimed that since individuals find political activity a distraction from the pursuit of self-interest, franchise need not be extended to those whose interests are subsumed under those of others. Not only did he exclude women in this way but also men under the age of 40, whose fathers could represent their interests.

The views of John Stuart Mill, known as the best advocate of liberal representative democracy, present a contrast to this. For Mill, a representative system must create maximum space for people to take part in the functioning of the government and not restrict their involvement by merely allowing them to vote. He considered participation important because it develops the confidence of the people in their ability to govern themselves. Mill, thus, understood democracy as a system which allows for the development of an individual's personality. It develops the intellectual talents of people and is the best condition for liberty to flourish. Participation makes informed and intelligent debate possible. It is through thorough debate and discussion, where there is space for rational persuasion of each other, that the best argument emerges and this helps in solving the problems affecting the whole community. This is why he regarded the parliament as the forum where all kinds of opinion should find a space and be vigorously debated. Mill considers a measure of socio-economic equality as necessary for democracy and liberty to be actualized. Despite his insistence on the value of participation, he was sceptical of the capability of every citizen to govern and considered governance a task requiring expertise. He sought to balance this by recommending maximum participation at the local level so that people get educated in the task of governance. In the next section, we shall see how he suggested institutional measures to counter the ills of democracy.

Policy Making and the Pluralist View

Decision making in a liberal democracy is an outcome of the aggregation of individual preferences or choices. In a protective model, these choices are aggregated over the choice of government personnel and not over the activities of the government. That is, the vote and electoral processes allow people to choose or reject a representative or a political party but not to determine what policies the government should undertake. This is because protective democracy offers minimal scope to government activity.

However, as the functions and activities of the government increased, the focus turned to the policy-making process itself. Utilitarian thinkers like Bentham and James Mill propounded the principle of 'greatest happiness of the greatest number' (see the chapter on liberty) as the basis of determining functions of the government. While they advocated minimal government and free market, they did make space for selective state intervention in the economy for welfare activities like education and wage reforms. But the idea that government policies must reflect the aggregate choices of the majority became important for liberal democracies. The welfare state model of liberalism assigns more tasks to the government in the economy and these tasks, like the provisions for social security, education, regulation of industry and making employment opportunities available, are justified in the name of democracy. John Rawls, for example, justifies extensive intervention in the economy to provide equality of opportunity to all (for more details see chapter on justice), but most liberals are sceptical of extensive redistribution of wealth.

How do people influence policy? The pluralist theory provides an answer. The pluralist view, associated with the work of Robert Dahl, is a specifically American understanding of political processes, but still has relevance for understanding liberal democratic practice in general. Power, according to Dahl, is the capacity to influence ... the process and outcome of decision-making. People form groups and associations based on their specific interests; so in any society there will be a wide variety of interest groups. Interest or pressure groups are the mechanisms that people adopt in order to advance their interest, promote their causes and achieve preferred policy outcomes. For example, *kisan sabhas*, teachers' and students' unions, women's organizations, trade unions, associations of industries like FICCI or CII in India. The policy making arena is like the market, where different groups pursue their interests and the outcomes are not pre-determined, but a balance is achieved out of conflicts; through a sort of an 'invisible hand' mechanism. Political decision making is a complicated process and involves bargaining between various actors. In the process, people use a wide range of means at their disposal like economic and social position, education, organization skills, reputation, religion, etc. Unlike elitist and Marxist views, pluralists understand power as not concentrated in a particular class, but as spread throughout society.

It is a democracy that provides opportunities for everyone to articulate interests, mobilize support and seek representation. A vigorous interest group activity keeps the wielders of political power in check. Democracy here is identified with certain institutional mechanisms and procedures, representative institutions, accountability of executive to elected assemblies, basic liberties for all including the freedom of expression and organization and an independent judiciary. As long as these procedures are followed, a system can be referred to as being democratic. This is also called procedural democracy as distinguished from a substantive democracy. The latter is concerned with the attainment of certain ends, like equality or justice.

The chief merit of the pluralist analysis is that all modern democracies do have a plurality of forces struggling and competing for their interests. However, procedural democracy is compatible with the results which are always skewed in favour of particular interests and groups. Social and economic inequalities reduce the opportunity of disadvantaged groups to influence policy outcomes. Thus, an agricultural landless labourer's collective effort cannot hope to match CII or FICCI either in resources or in influence. In his later writing, Dahl does acknowledge the fact that inequalities can be debilitating and consistently leave certain groups out of the political process, despite the formal freedoms of a democracy, in which every citizen has the right to participate in the decision-making process. Thus, there are structural and ideological constraints which prevent democracies from operating as an open, equal marketplace of competing interests. In this process, the existence of democratic procedures and its openness to conflicting views, interests and methods of influence is valuable for a democracy, but the outcomes are liable to be undemocratic.

Thus, in the liberal view, the aim of democracy is to aggregate individual choices and preferences in the best possible way. This aggregation of choices could be restricted to the choice of government (by voting for a representative who usually belongs to a political party) or should constitute a mechanism of policy making. In the first view, the role of democracy is to basically provide a defence against arbitrary and unaccountable government through elections and constitutional government. In the second view, democracy has a more direct link with choosing and influencing the activities of the government. This is usually done through a wide range of interest groups, political parties and pressure groups.

Today, liberal democracy is both at a moment of triumph and crisis. On the one hand, the collapse of the communist bloc, introduction of liberal democratic institutions in the former communist countries as well as the military intervention of the USA in West Asia to introduce democratic regimes signal its near universal acceptance as the only practical model of democracy. Indeed, the key ideas and institutions of liberal democracy like representative governments, rule of law, individual rights, electoral competition and multi-party system have become central to any conception of democracy. Francis Fukuyama in his 'end of history' thesis argues that there is no credible alternative to liberal democracy. On the other hand, liberal democracy continues to be subjected to a scathing critique by socialists, feminists, multiculturalists and deliberative democrats for not being democratic enough and these critiques have sharpened in the context of globalization. They observe how the form of liberal democracy currently advocated is minimalist or what Benjamin Barber calls a 'weak democracy' emphasizing elections and a choice of political parties. Before we examine these critiques, let us look at some of the common objections to democracy.

Objections to Democracy

Critics of democracy can be classified into two groups—those who are dissatisfied with a particular kind of democratic practice and seek to deepen it and those who are critical of the democratic principle as such. We have observed how the positive value attached to democracy is a recent one in history. The very principle of popular power continues to be subjected to trenchant critiques. Let us examine the main objections to democracy.

A key objection to democracy is that it produces incompetent and inefficient governments. In his critique of Athenian democracy, Plato argues that governance is a matter of skill and expertise and therefore should be left to experts. Human beings are by nature fundamentally unequal. However, democracy presumes that everyone can handle complex matters of governance and is, therefore, based on a false understanding of human nature. Thereby, it substitutes ignorance and incompetence for excellence and expertise. Because it allows non-experts to rule, democracy is an irrational form of government. He recommended a strict division of tasks depending on one's ability. Matters of the state would thereby be left to a particular class of people who by nature and training were most fit to rule—whom he called 'philosopher-kings'. To rule meant ensuring that everybody else performed tasks they were most fit for.

A distinction is made here between popular rule and public interest, whereby governments are prevented from functioning in public interest and taking strong purposive action due to the compulsions of democracy. In India, for example, democracy is often blamed for the ills afflicting the country. Common middle-class assessments blame the government for following 'populist' policies (and not 'correct' or 'rational' policies), like providing slum-dwellers with ration cards because of the compulsion to seek votes. A deep fear and distrust of the 'masses' runs through the history of democracy. Aristotle in his classification of governments placed democracy as an 'impure' system where the multitude rule in their own interest.

As already observed, early liberals were sceptical of mass suffrage and considered political equality a threat to liberty. Constitutionalism and an elaborate system of checks and balances were devised to prevent majoritarianism. Writing in the 19th century in the context of the emerging democratic society in Europe and America, Tocqueville coined the phrase 'tyranny of the majority' to describe the threat that democracy posed to minorities and individual liberty. He particularly feared its cultural repercussions. Since the cultural standards of the majority are dominant, general morals, manners and creativity are debased in a democracy. For example, when Bollywood films are discussed, a distinction is often made between films for the 'masses' and those for the 'classes', or between 'popular' and 'art' films.

Even J. S. Mill for all his defence of democracy and political participation considered majoritarianism and mediocre government as the biggest weaknesses of democracy. Not only does majoritarianism exclude minority voices but it lowers the standards of the government. Subsequently, people with a lower level of intelligence perform the most important task of legislation and administration. Mill suggested a number of institutional mechanisms to counter these ills. Through proportional representation, minorities can obtain a place in the legislative assembly and, through plural voting, educated and intellectually superior individuals can have more say in the choice of representatives. He was particularly concerned about the opinion of minorities the experts and the geniuses—who get sidelined when the majority principle is applied. Majority rule has a tendency to promote uniformity and conformity, whereas the main catalysts of progress are the non-conformist geniuses. This system of plural voting, in fact, violates the basic democratic principle of political equality. He also recommended a separation of the tasks of government, wherein the all-important task of law formulation would be done by an expert constitutional committee, and the administrative tasks were to be carried out by a skilled bureaucracy. The task of the representative assembly was to debate and deliberate on the legislation and to monitor the functioning of the government.

Mill's philosophy, thus, combines a value for participation and equality (which is unique among liberal thinkers) with elitism, where governance is seen as the task of the educated and the experts. Moreover, despite his egalitarianism, he did not recommend representative governments for colonies like India. Democracy was possible only in 'civilized' countries and not in 'barbaric' ones and, therefore, despotic rule was suitable till the time the people of the colonies were ready and capable of democracy.

While Plato and Mill draw attention to the dangers of majority rule, elite theorists consider a functioning democracy impossible because of the inevitability of concentration of power. While Mill and Plato among others are elitist in their views, elitist theory is attributed to a specific critique developed by Pareto, Mosca, Mills and Michels about the inevitability of elite rule. Classical elite theorists like Pareto and Mosca say that political power in every society has always been in the hands of a minority, the elite, which has ruled over the majority in its own interest. These elite manage to dominate because they possess exceptional skills, especially the psychological attributes and political skills of manipulation, and coercion. They are far better organized than the masses and also possess qualities which are considered valuable and hence use it to justify their privileged position in the society. C. Wright Mills' study of the American political system refers to a 'power elite' which dominated executive power and members of this class were closely knit, sharing the same background and common values. Thus, they dispute the pluralist contention that power is widely distributed in society. In his study of socialist parties, Michels noted how despite socialist principles, the actual working of the decision-making process tended to concentrate power in the leadership due to bureaucratization and centralization. Not only did the leaders not consult the working-class members, the decisions taken were often contrary to their interests. This led Michels to postulate an 'iron law of oligarchy' which applied to all organizations resulting in undemocratic outcomes.

In India, we note the wide prevalence of dynastic rule and the involvement of all members of a family in politics. This phenomenon is observed in almost all countries and is an evidence of the tendency of concentration of power among a few who have access to the political system.

The merit of these critiques lies insofar as they expose the myths of democratic practice by exposing who actually wields power. But in considering this concentration of power as inevitable, these critiques affirm a belief in the natural inequality among human beings, and are pessimistic in nature.

In this view, the value of democracy, given the inevitability of elite rule, is that it allows people to choose among the elites. Joseph Schumpeter in his influential work *Capitalism, Socialism and Democracy* puts up a model of competitive elitism as the most workable one in modern industrial societies. He has a low opinion of the ability of people to develop an informed opinion on key issues and opines that it is better to let experts rule. Passive citizenship is good for governance. The only role that people have is in the selection of the government among rival competing political elites through voting. Democracy, thus, performs the crucial function of legitimating a government. The unanswered question is one of how people who are incapable of reflecting on key issues can make an informed choice among political groups.

Perspectives on Democracy

Let us now examine those perspectives on democracy that affirm it as an ideal but critique its practice. Since liberal democracy has been the dominant form of democratic practice in modern times, critics who seek a deepening of democracy begin with an assessment of liberal democracy and develop their alternative with reference to it.

Socialist View

Socialists share the elitist view that even in a democracy, political power is used to protect and advance the interests of a minority. While elitists attribute psychological, social and economic attributes to the elite which allow them to dominate; for socialists, the power of the minority derives from their economic class position, that is, their control over the means of production. The inequality then is not 'natural' but a product of specific social and economic arrangements. The capitalist market economy produces systemic inequality. All strands of socialism draw attention to the incompatibility between democracy that is based on political equality, and capitalism which is based on the right to private property and market economy. In a market economy people have unequal access to economic resources and this also is the source of unequal access to knowledge and information. Thus, the existence of private property and the unequal distribution of wealth is the source of socio-economic inequality in society and this prevents most people from effectively exercising their political freedoms. In a market economy most people neither have the time nor the resources for more political involvement.

Marxists challenge the liberal conception of the state as a neutral body. The state insofar as it is committed to securing the right to private property is deeply implicated in civil society. There are two strands of thinking about political power in the writings of Marx and Engels. In the first instance, the state and its agencies are the instruments of dominant class interest. As Marx declared in *The Communist Manifesto* (1848), 'the executive of the modern state is but a committee for managing the common affairs of the whole bourgeoisie'. In the second instance, Marx and Engels talk about the 'relative autonomy of the state' from the dominant class. The practice of parliamentary democracy and the compulsions of elections do lead governments to respond to some demands of the working class majority. Many liberal democracies do undertake policies to correct the uneven outcomes of the market, like restrictions on wealth, employment guarantees, etc. But for Marxists this is at best a short-term measure because the state cannot go against the long-term interests of capital. This is why, for Marxists, the vote cannot be used to transform the system, because any welfare policies will be corrective at best and will not address the structural reasons of inequality. The ability of the governments to undertake welfare policies is constrained by the constitution.

Marxists acknowledge the emancipatory potential of liberalism because it rejects hierarchy and affirms the equal moral worth of all individuals. However, the liberal distinction between the state and the civil society, or the public and the private marks the economy out as the private realm of freedom and therefore, out of the purview of political decision making. The socio-economic divisions generated in civil society render the political equality guaranteed by the state ineffective. A democracy which does not tackle the inequities of class power is inadequate at best and a sham at worst. As against the fear of people like Tocqueville that democracy can lead to the tyranny of the masses, Marxists fear that it will not. The ideological and cultural hegemony of bourgeois values secure the consent of the working classes. This includes telling the poor that the reasons for poverty are because they are not hard-working enough. (See Chapter 9 on power for the concept of hegemony.) Liberal democracy and its institutions thus provide an ideological facade of equality and thereby act as a legitimizing shell for capitalism. While democracy provides the 'road to socialism' it is incompatible with capitalism.

Marxists and socialists are further critical of the nature of individualistic rights which are the corner stone of liberal democracy. Marx terms these the rights of the egoistic man, separated from his community and perceiving everyone else as a competitor and a threat. The socialist aim is a situation where the free development of each is compatible with the free development of all. Thus, they endorse a more participatory democracy where democracy extends to the management of all collective affairs, including the workplace. The idea of a cooperative without the divisions of owner and wage labour informs socialist conceptions of economic democracy.

Communist countries seek to achieve socialist aims through a revolutionary break and they advocate a model of people's democracy where a single party—the communist party—assumes leadership and directs the country in its transition to socialism. Social democracy, on the other hand, seeks to reconcile socialist aims and liberal democratic institutions. It perceives the establishment of socialism as a longer gradual process in which electoral democracy can be used to correct the injustices of capitalism. This is to be done by extensive regulation of the economy, provision of employment and educational opportunities including affirmative action and social security measures. We shall elaborate on social democracy in the next section.

Marxists have usually ignored the concentration of power in the party and the state. The experience of one-party communist states, the distortions of the communist bloc in Eastern Europe and the fall of USSR have led to a reappraisal of democracy within Marxist thought. The debate had usually been structured as prioritizing between political freedom and economic freedom. Contemporary thinkers on the left, on the other hand, affirm that socialism and the attainment of economic equality do not necessitate giving up the gains of liberal democracy, and particularly those of individual rights. What is needed is a deepening of democracy which can both tackle inequalities and allow more participation. They also draw attention to the rise of corporate power and the unaccountable nature of international financial organizations that dominate world economy. They understand neo-liberal globalization as posing the biggest threat to democracy in present times.

Indian Debates on Democracy

In India and the rest of the Third World, democratic ideas emerged as part of anti-colonial struggles which claimed that colonial rule was a violation of the principle of self-determination and that the people had a democratic right to self-rule. These movements further claimed that the backwardness of their countries was because of colonial exploitation wherein the resources of the colonies were used not for the benefit of its people but for those of the colonizer. With independence all Third World countries had to address the need for rapid economic development and social transformation. The possibility and desirability of democracy and the nature of democratic arrangements were debated in this context. The Indian Independence movement was inspired by socialist ideas and impressed by the achievements of the Soviet Union. Thus, socialist analysis was sought to be applied to understand Indian problems. In this section, we will examine the views of two thinkers, Jawaharlal Nehru and

Ram Manohar Lohia, both of whom sought to adapt socialism to the Indian context, and see how their understanding of socialism had an impact on their approach towards democracy.

Jawaharlal Nehru is credited for the strong foundation of India's constitutional and democratic institutional traditions. He was influenced both by the liberal democratic traditions of the 19th century and the Fabian socialism of the early 20th century. At the same time, he was also impressed by the rapid economic transformation achieved by the Soviet Union. His views on democracy reflect all these influences.

He considered democracy a peaceful way to achieve the goals of individual freedom and social justice. For Nehru, the well-being of the individual was of principal value and the highest goal of the society and the state. His thought reflected respect for the freedom and dignity of the individual and the need to allow all individuals to grow and develop their potential. He had faith in the power of debate and discussion in the pursuit of truth and the possibility to educate and persuade people through rational means to think in terms of common interests. This required free public discussion, tolerance for differing points of view and dissent. He advocated the institutional framework of liberal democracy for India, i.e. fundamental political and civil rights of the individual, freedom of the press, secularism in terms of the separation of religion and the state, rule of law, parliamentary government and an independent judiciary.

Nehru shared the socialist critique of capitalism. He defined equality not just in terms of political equality but as equal opportunity for all and progressive economic equality. He recognized that in the context of economic inequalities the democratic machinery can be hijacked by the ruling class. As he said, equality before law cannot make a millionaire and a pauper equal. Democracy can flourish only in the context of social and economic equality. So, political democracy can be of value only if it can be used to achieve what he called economic democracy. This meant active involvement of the state in the economy and he advocated a state-led economic development programme through the device of planning as well as redistributive mechanisms like land reforms. While he admired the prosperity and equitable redistribution of wealth achieved by the Soviet Union, he was critical of communism because it had a tendency to become authoritarian, violent and to suppress political dissent. He did consider that political liberties slow the pace of growth and achieve lesser redistribution, but he preferred slower growth and lesser equity to the sacrifice of political liberties.

In this way democracy was to make possible both economic justice and individual freedom. Thus, Nehru advocates a model of social democracy. Democracy in the international scenario was another area of concern for him and the policy of non-alignment was formulated in order to secure independence in foreign affairs and equality in international forums, especially for weaker countries.

Lohia's views are significantly different from Nehru's. He is critical of both communism and Nehru's democratic socialism. Both, according to him, understand socialism as involving only a transformation of capitalist relations of production. That is, they are concerned primarily with redistributive mechanisms. However, the inequalities of capitalism lie not just in its production relations but in its technology. Capitalism specifically requires large-scale industrialization and a centralized production process. In the political domain, this requires a centralized state apparatus. Thus, capitalism has a tendency towards centralization of power and this makes it authoritarian. Nehruvian socialism was nothing but state capitalism with some welfare features. While Nehru recognized the tendency towards centralization, he considered the provision of fundamental rights and universal franchise as guarantees of the freedoms of the individual. Lohia considered electoral and parliamentary mechanisms as important but inadequate to achieve either the active involvement of the people or in achieving social transformation. Lohia, thus, drew attention to the way communist states concentrated power in the state apparatus.

Socialist transformation can be achieved only with the active participation and struggles of the people. Democracy involves people taking control over their lives. It is a process of empowerment. This means preventing the concentration of power and energizing the civil society's constant struggles against oppressive social and cultural injustices. Lohia advocated a two-pronged strategy to tackle centralization and concentration of power decentralization of political power through the four-pillar framework and decentralization of the economic production process through the small-unit machine. Use of the latter along with appropriate technology would help technology address the specific needs of Indian society. This meant rejecting a singular model of economic development based on the experience of the Western capitalist countries. With the four-pillar framework, the sovereign power of the state would be constitutionally diffused into four levels—namely, village, district, province, and the Centre. Areas like the army or core industries would come under the Centre, smaller industries under the district, and agriculture under the village level. What is significant about this decentralization was that it was meant to be decentralization not just in executive powers but in the legislative and planning process, too. This would ensure decision making by the smallest of communities in human activities like production, ownership, administration and education. Lohia was particularly concerned about the interlinked structures of caste and gender oppression that characterized Indian society. Empowerment of this majority and making them take an active and effective part in the affairs of the country required decentralization.

Lohia's views assume importance because there is a renewed focus on participation and decentralization as a way to tackle bureaucratization and centralization of power. We will look at this issue in the last section.

Feminist View

Feminists have further critiqued the liberal distinction between the public and the private. They characterize relations between men and women as one of unequal power relations. In the sphere of the family and the household, the division of labour is unequal as the bulk of the child-rearing and household tasks is done by women. Further, these tasks are devalued and not considered productive enough to constitute paid labour. Thus, the domestic arena is a site of unequal power structures and is, therefore, an arena of democratization. In liberal theory, the family is part of the private sphere and hence kept out of politics and therefore, out of democratization. This is one dimension of the feminist slogan 'the personal is political'. The other dimension is that this gendered division of labour and power in the private sphere is linked to the unequal distribution of political status and power in the public sphere. In Western countries, which have the longest history of democracy, women were the last category to get the right to vote. Switzerland, for instance, enfranchised women as late as 1971. Most political thinkers explicitly excluded women from the category of citizenship on the grounds of their natural inferiority and incapability. Despite formal political equality, women continue to be grossly underrepresented in political institutions and decision-making structures. In India, for example, the proportion of women in the Lok Sabha has never exceeded 12 per cent.

Further, political equality has been undermined on the grounds of sexual, social and economic inequality. Thus, specific policies are required to enhance participation and representation and deliver equality, for instance, redistribution of domestic work (both through sharing and through public provisions for childcare) and electoral reforms. In India, the proposal to reserve 33 per cent seats for women in the Parliament and the Legislative Assemblies is a proposal of the latter kind.

Feminists, however, note that the measures to ensure substantive equality for women have to be of a distinctive kind; they have to incorporate a notion of difference. Typically, democratic theory understands equality as the removal of differences. So, formal political equality recognizes no difference among people and socio-economic equality understands difference as a disadvantage, and seeks to remove them. But the idea of disadvantage is based on a notion of comparison which is always based on a particular standard. The concept of the individual that is central to liberalism is that of an independent, rational, self-interested person. Understanding differences between men and women solely as a disadvantage is to adhere to a male norm. For example, politics has always been construed as a male domain and women politicians have to prove they are 'tough' and 'strong' according to this standard. At the level of policy too, for example, pregnancy is understood as a disease or illness because it is the male body which is the standard of normality. Understanding differences as disadvantages has meant that democratic theory has been insensitive to the realities of women's lives. Using a particular norm as the standard and imposing it on others is an act of discrimination. This disadvantages women as a group. Thus, feminists contend that there is a gender bias in the democratic theory itself. In order to ensure substantive equality, democracy has to think in terms of recognizing and accommodating differences.

Like the deliberative democrats (see next section), feminists have also been critical of liberal democracies for taking people's preferences as given and for the restrictive view it has of participation. If interests and preferences are taken as given, then democratic decision making will simply reproduce the status quo. Unequal power structures sustain themselves through ideologies and socialization. Thus, for women, the process of democracy is also a process of empowerment, where they become aware of exploitation, gain confidence, and seek to transform their conditions. This, however, calls for a more active and participatory democratic practice.

Deliberative View

In contemporary political theory, a key idea is that of deliberative democracy. It is associated with people like David Miller, J. Drysek and Joshua Cohen, among others. Liberal democracy views decision making as an outcome of aggregating the preferences of individuals. In this sense, it is believed that people's preferences and interests are formed independently and the political process only negotiates between the conflicting interests. Deliberative democrats, on the other hand, believe that people's preferences are formed *during* the political process and not prior to it. Democracy, then, is a process of arriving at an agreed upon judgement or a consensus. Such an agreement is an outcome of deliberation, i.e. a process where people try to persuade each other through the give-and-take of rational arguments. In this way, people become aware of information and perspectives that they are previously unaware of and then they can question each other's views. In this process, preferences or interests get transformed to reflect a common agreement. Deliberation, thus, reinvents a participatory model of democracy and the key idea is that of a dialogue. Through open participation and unlimited discourse, a better argument emerges. But this needs what Habermas calls 'an ideal speech situation', i.e. a situation where free and equal participants are able to communicate with each other without discrepancies of power and constraints of particular circumstances. There is an inherent danger of preferring certain dominant forms of communication and knowledge as more authoritative. Moreover, deliberative democrats hope for a consensus which is difficult, if not impossible to achieve in diverse and complex societies.

Key Debates in Democratic Theory

In this section, we briefly discuss those issues which have emerged as areas of debate in contemporary democratic theory.

Democracy and Difference

Historically, democracy has been a movement that has aimed at the removal of differences. It was assumed that equal political rights and recognition of citizenship would counter the discrimination people faced on account of differences on the grounds of caste, race, ethnicity, and gender. This idea of eliminating differences in consideration of equality has been important for emancipatory politics because it affirms the idea of equal moral worth of all individuals. We have seen how feminists consider that a substantial notion of equality must incorporate a notion of difference.

On the notion of difference, feminists are joined by multiculturalists who argue that in culturally plural societies, treating all differences among people as a disadvantage is to use the dominant group's culture as a norm. Most contemporary societies are culturally diverse and are composed of many communities, for example, immigrants, indigenous people, racial minorities. India itself is multireligious, multilingual, multicultural, and also has *adivasi* communities. Not only are communities socially and culturally different, they are often in relations of domination and subordination with each other. Further, liberal democracies claim to be neutral with respect to conceptions of good life and leave these to individual choice. However, the laws and practices of a country reflect the cultural bias of the majority. Feminists and multiculturalists say that liberalism, which values the abstract self-interested individual, is itself a particular notion of the good life. For an *adivasi* group, where property is common, the insistence on private property is alien.

Liberalism values diversity, but in terms of opinions it recognizes diversity only at the individual level. But an individual's identity is formed in a cultural context, and ignoring or devaluing the culture is discriminatory both to the individual and to the group. Thus, a commitment to the equal worth of all individuals means equal respect to their culture and equal treatment of all groups. It is only when this diversity is valued and respected that people can develop their capacities and contribute to collective life meaningfully.

Not recognizing the differences among groups is to ignore the diversity of the ways of life and experiences among people. Such a democracy assimilates and evaluates everyone, keeping the culture of the privileged groups as the standard. Those not conforming to this standard either have to lose their identity to assimilate or get marked out as the 'other'. Ignoring the specificity of a minority group is to marginalize it.

Democracy involves equality in setting standards, too. Thus, according to the late Professor Iris Marion Young of the University of Chicago, asserting the value of group differences provides a standpoint to both point out that the norm presented as universal is culturally specific, and criticize them by presenting an alternative. Some feminists say that care and nurture, which women have been associated with, are desirable values for everyone. Tribal communities and forest-dwellers compare their harmonious co-existence with the environment to the destructive industrialization which is presented as 'development'.

As democracies are concerned with equality, it must have procedures and mechanisms which recognize difference. Iris Marion Young recommends procedures that ensure additional representation for all oppressed groups, affirmative action and public funding to promote the self-organization of groups, consultation with the groups on policy matters affecting them and a veto power over specific policy decisions which directly affect the group. The meaning of representation in this context requires that a democratic polity must be representative of the diversity within it. Will Kymlicka recommends self-governance rights for indigenous peoples and cultural rights for ethnic groups. The Scheduled Tribes and other Traditional Forest Dwellers (Recognition of Forest Right) Bill, 2005, passed in the Lok Sabha in December 2005, likewise proposes that forest-dwellers have a right to the forest and mineral resources.

These proposals, however, raise significant issues. There is a danger of freezing identities and privileging a particular identity of an individual over the other identities s/he may have. Further, there is the question of internal democracy in the groups. Whose views are to be seen as representative of the group? In India, for example, in the debate over the uniform civil code, personal laws of religious communities are sought to be replaced on the lines of which ignores the differences among communities. However, all personal laws are discriminatory to women. The right of a group to maintain its identity conflicts with the equal rights of women within the group.

Thus, the recognition of difference is both a requirement of and poses important issues for democratic theory.

Representation and Participation

Most practising democracies are indirect or representative in nature. However, what does it mean to represent? Are representatives meant to be delegates, i.e. give voice to the wishes of their electors? In territorial constituencies, however, the process of amalgamating the interests of a diverse electorate is a challenge. J. S. Mill rejects the idea that representatives are delegates because that would tie them down to the preferences of the electorate. Instead, he says, representatives must be free to act according to their own judgement. However, they are meant to act on behalf of the people and not merely reflect their views. In that case, what kind of control can people hope to have over their representatives? The other view of representation is that people mandate a person or a political party to carry out a specific set of policies, and thus direct the government. But in most countries the election manifestos tend to be very general in nature and are not concrete policy documents. Moreover, elections are fought and won on a variety of grounds as political parties try to incorporate all sections. Political parties, which are the main players in an electoral system, themselves constitute the political elite and are often deliberatively vague about policies. Elections are media-orchestrated events. Besides, in most countries either a first past the post (FPTP/FPP) or a proportional system of election is followed. In the former system in particular, the victorious party that forms the government has most often not secured the majority of votes. There is, hence, a mismatch between the number of seats won and the percentage of vote secured by the party. Thus, an election, which is the main vehicle of representation, is an inadequate mechanism to convert people's views into policy directives.

All these developments have meant a renewed attention to participation. Even in order to ensure that there is a check on representatives, and to prevent abuse of power (protective democracy), there is need for more active citizen involvement. The remedy for bureaucratization, corruption, centralization, lack of transparency, and accountability is sought in participation. In that sense, the traditional line dividing a direct and indirect democracy is being redrawn. The recent Right to Information Act, which seeks to make government functioning open, is one such initiative in India. Critics of centralized government also advocate decentralization through local self-government institutions like *panchayats*.

The main objection to participation has been that it is difficult to make it work in a large and diverse society. However, the advancement of technology, the spread of the reach of the media and the Internet, devices like the *jan sunvai* or public hearing, devolution of powers to local bodies wherever possible, and involvement of citizen groups like resident welfare associations, make increased participation possible. The point being made is that both representative and participatory mechanisms can be combined.

Democracy and Development

Indian democracy has often been analysed as a miracle because it has survived in the context of widespread inequality, poverty and unemployment. Democracy is often blamed for the slow rate of development achieved by India. We often hear popular calls for a 'strong political leadership' or even a 'dictator' who can lead the country towards economic growth. Democracy here is seen as a luxury that poor countries cannot afford. It is also seen as an impediment to development and so suspension of democratic rights or political freedoms is desirable. This is popularly known as the 'Lee Thesis' attributed to Lee Kuan Yew, the former Prime Minister of Singapore, who held that the denial of political and civil liberties and a measure of authoritarianism is advantageous to economic growth. The notion that democracy slows growth is popular and we saw how communist regimes made it a choice between political freedom and economic rights.

Amartya Sen contests this thesis and says that it is not supported by satisfactory empirical evidence. He further argues that in poor societies, democracy has both an instrumental and a constructive role to play in promoting development. In a democracy where the rulers have to face the electorate, there is an incentive to listen to the needs of the people. Political freedoms and civil rights, a free press, the presence of opposition parties—all of these mean that the actions of the government are subject to the evaluation and criticism of society and that has a direct impact on the political fortunes of those in power. Democracy, thus, plays an instrumental role in promoting the economic needs of the people. Additionally, he argues that democratic arrangements play a constructive role in the sense that they even allow for the conceptualization of what constitutes economic needs. Democracies create a set of opportunities, and through open debate, discussion and dissenting opinions, people get involved in formulating their needs and priorities.

This view is important because there are contending views on what constitutes development. The idea that economic growth constitutes development is contested not just by those critical of the way the benefits of growth are concerned by the powerful but also by environmentalists. Movements like the Narmada Bachao Andolan contest the claims of benefits that high-level industrialization and multipurpose river projects are supposed to bring. Many tribal and local communities claim the right to use natural resources in a way that is beneficial to the community. They contest the notion that there is a single model of development which is applicable to all. Social and environmental movements assert the need to formulate alternative, people-centred, sustainable models of development. If by development one means improvement of living conditions, then the precise mode of development to be adopted by a society is a matter of democratic decision making.

The Scope of Democracy

Socialist, feminist and multicultural critiques as well as anti-race and anti-caste movements draw attention to the presence of various structures of power and inequity in society. Since these power structures affect the way people exercise their political freedoms and their ability to influence collective decisions, removal of these structures becomes a concern for democracy. That is, a democratic society is the basis for democratic political arrangements. Chantal Mouffe and Ernesto Laclau identify the task of radical democracy as a struggle against all modes of oppression and subordination in society by fully realizing the ideals of liberty and equality for all. As the concept of equality expands from formal equality to include equality of opportunity and equal treatment of culturally diverse communities, thus requiring a notion of difference, the scope of democracy will widen.

Democracy, conceived in this form, is of relevance to all spheres of human collective life, be it the family, association, workplace, community or the nation. Within the framework of the nation-state, the agenda of deepening democracy involves enhancing participation and the devolution of power to regional and local levels. However, the principle of democracy is relevant beyond the level of the nation-state as well. Our globalized world is characterized by a high degree of interdependence among nation-states due to changes in production, communication, and trade. International financial agencies like the International Monetary Fund and World Bank, and transnational corporations, are powerful players in the world economy and exercise much influence over Third World states. They are not subject to any transparent system of accountability. On the other hand, many pressing issues like environmental protection and human security require co-operation among states, and on issues like violation of human rights and peace, international intervention in nation-states is required. The current UN system and international organizations like the World Trade Organization are skewed in favour of the most powerful states. These underline the need for effective and democratic global systems of governance. David Held suggests a cosmopolitan model of democracy as a way to respond to these changes and democratize the global system. It envisages setting up political, legal, administrative and regulatory institutions at global and regional levels, which would help create methods to ensure transparency and accountability in international government and non-government institutions; secure world-wide consultation and referenda on certain issues; and enforce peace and human rights within nation-states. This model of democracy is not meant to be an alternative to the nation-state but a system that complements democracy at the national and local levels.

Conclusion

Everybody's for democracy in principle. It's only in practice that the thing gives rise to stiff objections.

—Noam Chomsky

The history of political theory is witness to divergent views on the desirability of democracy as well as its nature and extent. These differences emerge from what one expects democracy to achieve. In this chapter, we examined the key ways in which democracy is understood and the dilemmas faced when it is sought to be applied.

Points for Discussion

1. Movements for self-determination exist in many parts of the world. Can democratic principles be applied to resolve them, and how?
2. Is it possible to combine the political participation valued in the classical model with equality of all individuals in the community? What sort of changes in the life of the society and the arrangement of its activities would be required for this purpose?
3. World War I was fought to make the world safe for democracy. Similarly, today we face a situation where the US leads an attempt to introduce democratic regimes in many parts of the world. Given this situation, do you think democracy can be imposed from above?
4. In your opinion how can the conflict between the cultural rights of a community and the equal rights of women be democratically resolved, as in the case of the Uniform Civil Code in India?

Reading List

Arblaster, Anthony, *Democracy: Concepts in the Social Sciences* (New York: Open University Press, 1994).

Carter, April and Geoffrey Stokes, *Democratic Theory Today: Challenges for the 21st Century* (Cambridge: Polity Press, 2002).

Cunningham, Frank, *Theories of Democracy: A Critical Introduction* (London, New York: Routledge, 2002).

Elstub, Stephen, 'Democracy', in Iain Mackenzie (ed.), *Political Concepts: A Reader and Guide* (Edinburgh: University of Edinburgh Press, 2005).

Held, David (ed.), *Prospects of Democracy: North, South, East, West* (London: Polity Press, 1993).

———, *Models of Democracy* (Cambridge: Polity Press, 1996).

Mahajan, Gurpreet (ed.), *Democracy, Difference and Social Justice* (Delhi: Oxford University Press, 1998).

Marx, Karl, *Communist Manisfesto*, first pub. 1848 (London: Penguin, 2002), entire text with study guides and questions available at http://www.marxists.org/archive/marx/works/1848/communist-manifesto/index.htm

Parekh, Bhikhu, 'The Cultural Particularity of Liberal Democracy', *Political Studies*, XL, Special Issue, 1992.

Phillips, Anne, *Engendering Democracy* (Cambridge: Polity Press, 1991).

CHAPTER 9

Citizenship

Anupama Roy

Chapter Outlines

Introduction

The form and substance of citizenship in each historical period reflect the dominant configuration of socio-economic and political forces of each historical period. The specificity of citizenship in each historical period can be understood by seeking answers to questions like—Who are the citizens? Who are excluded from citizenship and what is the process/basis of exclusion? What is the nature of citizenship? Is it a legal status indicating entitlements or does it also involve active participation in political life? What kind of relationship between the individual and the religious-cultural community is envisaged in the rights and responsibilities of citizenship? What are the avenues of participation towards building a responsible citizenship? Answers to such questions would give us an insight into the manner in which the notion of citizenship has evolved historically, and grasp the complexities of contemporary debates. Contemporary debates on citizenship raise questions around notions of equality and rights, issues of individual, group and community rights, active and passive citizenship and the relationship between, and relative primacy of, rights and duties.

What do we mean by Citizenship?

More often than not, citizenship is seen in terms of a legal/formal status—having a specific nationality, holding a passport, and deriving from this status, entitlements and claims, rights guaranteed by the constitution, as well as specific duties and responsibilities which the constitution may lay down. The idea of citizenship, however, goes beyond the legal-formal framework to denote substantive membership in the political community. The commonly accepted definition of citizenship by T.H. Marshall in *Citizenship and Social Class* (1950) as 'full and equal membership in a political community' holds the promise of equality and integration within the political community. While citizenship may be identified with an ideal condition of equality, it may actually remain elusive and fettered, as societies are always marked by hierarchies of class, caste, sex, race, and religion, rather than equality of status and belonging. Equality and integration as constitutive elements of citizenship give it, however, its unique character as a momentum concept—citizenship's internal logic that demands that its benefits necessarily become progressively more universal and egalitarian (Hoffman 1997: 71–72). Citizenship may then be seen as a condition that is continually evolving and changing. At different moments in history, 'becoming a citizen' has involved either an extension of the status to more persons, or a liberatory dismantling of hitherto existing structures of oppression.

The constituent elements of citizenship have been uncertain and often contradictory, making it difficult to outline a precise notion of citizenship. There are divergent responses, for example, to questions pertaining to whether rights or duties are the defining elements of citizenship, or whether the arena of politics or state activities is its rightful domain as opposed to the spheres of culture, economy, and society. Again, there is no consensus on whether citizenship is only a status or a measure of activity, or what is of primary significance for citizenship—the autonomy of the individual or the community and the societal contexts that shape the needs of the individual. Even on questions pertaining to the legitimate unit of citizenship identity, viz., the nation-state, or the global civil society, there is a lock of consensus. In order to understand why these contradictions co-exist in the conceptual framework of citizenship, it is important to see them in terms of historically emergent strands. It is important, moreover, to explore these various strands in their specific historical contexts, keeping in mind, however, that at each historical moment the earlier strands co-existed, keeping alive the tensions and uncertainties over the form and content of citizenship.

Historical Development of the Concept of Citizenship

The word 'citizenship' is derived from the Latin *civis* and its Greek equivalent *polites*, which means member of the *polis* or city. The manner in which citizenship is understood today as a system of equal rights, as opposed to privileges ascribed by conditions of birth, took roots in the French Revolution (which started in 1789). With the development of capitalism and liberalism, the idea of the citizen as an individual bearing rights irrespective of her/his class, race, gender, ethnicity, etc., became further entrenched. Since the 1980s, globalization and multiculturalism have provided the contexts within which this notion of citizenship has been challenged. Thus, the development of ideas that surround the concept of citizenship can be attributed to four broad historical periods: (*a*) classical Graeco-Roman period (4th century B.C. onwards); (*b*) late medieval and early modern period including the period of the French and American Revolutions; (*c*) the developments in the 19th century corresponding to the growing influence of liberalism and capitalism; and (*d*) the contests over the form and substance of citizenship in the late 20th century, with an increasing preoccupation with multiculturalism and community rights. Two dominant strands or traditions of rights and citizenship can be seen to have developed over these periods: civic republicanism, characterized by the ideas of common good, public spirit, political participation and civic virtue; and liberal citizenship with an emphasis on individual rights and private interests. The Marxists and feminists have criticized both these traditions as exclusionary and have suggested radical changes in the theory and practice of citizenship. Similarly, cultural pluralists, radical pluralists and civil society theorists have offered alternative ways of thinking about citizenship and rights.

The Classical Period and Civic Republican Citizenship: Civic Virtue, Freedom and Active Citizenship

The term *civic republican* denotes a constitutional government founded on principles of sharing of power to prevent arbitrary authority, and the involvement of citizens in public affairs to the mutual benefit of the individual and the community. The Greek republics or city-states, Athens and Sparta, were exponents of the classical institution of citizenship that we identify with the civic republican tradition. Athens and Sparta were based on opposing political principles—Sparta on stern authoritarianism and Athens on democracy. But they were both exponents of the principles of classical citizenship as public service and civic duties. If Athens required commitment from her citizens for ready participation in governmental and juridical functions, for Sparta, civic duty involved selfless devotion of her citizen-soldiers. In *Politics*, Aristotle explicates what citizenship should ideally be and what the conditions are, in which such an ideal may be realized.

In its earliest forms in the Greek republics or city-states, citizenship was an expression of the inherent centrality of the political element in human nature, and remained the primary organizing principle of human life. Greek republics like Athens and Sparta were closely knit, self-governing political communities characterized by small populations and minimum social differentiation. The organization of the republic was based on familiarity and trust, principles of active political participation, the prioritization of the public and political aspects of life, and the primacy of the identity of man as citizen. The idea of citizenship around which the city-states were organized may be seen as manifesting the conditions in which human beings may, following the Aristotelian dictum, realize their natural selves. In its classical formulation, therefore—as a binding force in the community and as the means by which human beings could be in touch with their true nature—citizenship emerged as 'a framework for securing freedom for citizens'. This notion of citizenship as the means as well as the state or condition of freedom, has been an enduring element of citizenship since classical times.

An important element of citizenship as a means and condition of freedom was participation in civic life. Greek citizens were described by Aristotle as 'all who share in the civic life of ruling and being ruled in turn'. While the idea of participation in the act of ruling continues to be a significant component of active citizenship—zealously cherished by those who espouse citizenship as a civic ideal—in the context of classical Greece, not everyone could share in the civic life, which consisted of the ruling and the ruled. Citizenship was limited to those having the *capacity* to participate in the process of governance and was confined to 'free native-born men', excluding women, children, slaves and resident aliens. In the ultimate analysis, citizens constituted only a small part of the population, whose participation in public life was made possible by the exclusion and subordination of the private sphere of the family and economic life, and by the existence of slaves, who were responsible for performing the principal economic functions. Thus, the classical notion of citizenship, while handing down the legacy of citizenship as a 'realm' of freedom and participation, also spelt its association with privileges and exclusion.

The Greek idea of citizenship as active participation was modified during the time of Roman Imperialism, dictated by the need to hold together a large and heterogeneous empire. Even as fresh grounds of inclusion were added to meet the need of integrating a diverse population into the Roman Empire, a gradation within the framework of citizenship was introduced. While within the *polis* there existed only one kind of citizenship, whereby all citizens enjoyed equal privileges of participation and governance in a manifestation of what may be called 'imperial inclusiveness', the idea of citizenship was modified by the introduction of a passive notion of citizenship as a legal status. The introduction of this element brought large numbers of people, ethnically different from Romans, within the purview of Roman influence by extending to them the protection of a uniform set of laws. Subsequently, citizenship could now be imagined not solely as participation in the making and implementing of laws (as was the case in the Greek tradition), but also as a legal status involving certain rights and equal protection of the law. The new element of citizenship as legal status, while making possible a degree of inclusiveness (i.e. including non-Romans to Roman citizenship), also added a hierarchy of status by introducing the second-class category of *civitas sine suffragio* (citizenship without franchise, i.e. legal but not political rights). Moreover, women and the (chiefly rural) lower classes continued to be denied the status of citizens. The characteristics of a citizen, however, remained marked in a way that citizenship ideally denoted activity or manifested the potential or capacity for activity. Citizens were required thus to develop qualities of 'civic virtue', a term derived from the Latin word *virtus,* which meant 'manliness' in the sense of performing military duty, patriotism, and devotion to duty and the law.

The Late Medieval and Early Modern Periods: Legal Protection of Liberty and Passive Citizenship

Around the 16th century, the notion of citizenship as a legal status seemed to have become dominant. The aim of absolutist states to impose their authority over heterogeneous populations provided the context in which a citizen came to be defined by Jean Bodin (1945), the 16th-century jurist, as 'one who enjoys the common liberty and protection of authority'. In this view, the citizen was, unlike the Greek citizen, not himself an authority, but following the Roman tradition, someone who was under the protection of the state. Unlike the Greek and Roman traditions, however, citizenship was primarily a passive idea. Citizenship in this period did not stand for common (shared) public responsibilities and civic virtues. Instead, the notion of 'common liberty' became the primary concern of citizenship. This concern embodied a 'passive' or 'negative' notion of citizenship, involving claims for 'security' or protection that was to be provided by the authorities. For the early modern liberals what was to be protected was one's physical life (as in Hobbes), the family and home (as in Bodin and Montesquieu), or conscience and property (as in Locke). The principle of liberty thus established the primacy of the private and the familial world. The protection of authority was needed primarily to preserve this domain. Again, unlike the classical idea of citizenship, citizens were not political people. The political community was not the predominant core of their lives but rather the outer framework, in which each citizen enjoyed the liberty of private pleasures and pursuits of happiness and, as mentioned earlier, the protection and security of the (private/familial) domain in which these pleasures were realized. Thus, in this period the principle of imperial inclusiveness seems to have brought about a passive notion of citizenship as a legal status.

A nostalgia for citizenship as activity, as in classical Greece and Rome, with an emphasis on civic virtue and public duty persisted, however. Alongside the notion of citizenship as a status that guaranteed the enjoyment of liberty, the emphasis on public responsibilities and civic virtue remained influential as an ideal. Machiavelli, for example, praised the ideal of 'civic virtue' in classical republicanism. He firmly believed that men had to be kept constantly alert to their performance of civic obligations, which could be achieved by education, religion, and a fear of consequences in case of dereliction of citizenship duties. For Machiavelli, not only was good citizenship essential for a secure state and republican government, citizenship was possible only in a republic. Machiavelli's citizens, however, had to be made of sterner stuff and tougher moral fibre than their classical counterparts, equipped with 'courage, fortitude, audacity, skill and civic spirit'—the latter meaning spirited action. Montesquieu likewise argued that a state based on the principle of popular participation, as distinct from other forms of government, depends on its stability on the civic virtue of its citizens. For Rousseau, civic virtue and participation were the necessary elements of citizenship. He saw the 'general will' as citizens contributing without thought of personal advantage to political decisions. It may be pointed out that all the thinkers of this period looked at 'civic virtue' as an ideal to be pursued, and lamented the lack of citizenship qualities in their own social-political contexts. Machiavelli, for example, lamented the fact that few of the Italian states of the 16th century displayed the qualities of the ancient republics and even fewer men, the qualities of virtue. Most thinkers of this period (16th–18th centuries), including Rousseau and Montesquieu, whose ideas influenced the American and French Revolutions, favoured the revival of the civic ideals of the classical republican tradition, which had been sidetracked by pursuits of private pleasures and personal interests.

It was this strand of civic republicanism, a feature of classical tradition and remained an elusive ideal in the medieval and early modern periods, that was revived by the French Revolution in 1789. The French Revolution was a revolt against the passive citizenship of the early modern times. It attempted to resurrect the republican ideals of participation against the claims of the empire and the monarchical state. Apart from attempting to transform the apolitical lives of the citizens, the French revolutionary tradition introduced an important element to citizenship that changed the way in which rights were incorporated into the notion of citizenship. In fact, the manner in which citizenship is understood today as a system of horizontal (equal) rights as against the hierarchical (feudal) system of privileges, has its roots in the doctrines of the French Revolution. The French Revolution and the 'Declaration of the Rights of Man and of the Citizen' gave rise to the notion of the citizen as a 'free and autonomous individual', participating in making decisions that all had agreed to obey. Thus, the conception of the citizen established by the French Revolution combined the classical connotation of citizenship as civic participation with modern liberal individualism.

The revival of civic republicanism, and its association with the idea of the citizen as an autonomous and rational individual was due to nationalism, which was a powerful force that redefined the form of socio-political solidarity and paved the way for a more democratic notion of citizenship. Generally understood, nationalism refers to the self-definition and self-consciousness of the 'nation' or 'a people' as a unified entity. An expression of solidarity or interconnectedness among people and a recognition by others of this solidarity are integral to nationalism. In other words, nationalism involves (*a*) the self-awareness by a people that they constitute a nation; (*b*) the consciousness that there is something about them as a nation that makes them different from other nations; and (*c*) that there is a larger imperative from which the self-definition as a nation derives. The definition of nationalism by Anthony Smith (1983) as 'an ideological movement, for the attainment and maintenance of self-government and independence on behalf of a group, some of whose members conceive it to constitute an actual or potential nation like others' captures the essence of nationalism, which he sums up in the phrase 'ideal of independence'. The aspiration for solidarity and sovereignty implies, argues Smith, that the group should be free from external interference and internal divisions to frame its own rules and set up its own institutions, in accordance with its needs and 'character'. The group is self-determining, because its individuality gives it laws that are peculiar to it. Only the assembly of all the citizens of the community acting in concert can make laws for the community; no section, no individual, and no outsider can legislate.

The 19th and 20th Centuries: Capitalism, Liberalism and Universal Citizenship

With the development of capitalist market relations and the growing influence of liberalism in the 19th century, the combination of the two traditions—civic republicanism and liberal individualism—proved tenuous. The idea of citizens as individuals with private and conflicting rather than a commonality of interests gradually gained precedence. A much less demanding liberal citizenship involving a loosely committed relationship to the state took over, held in place by a set of civic rights honoured by the state, which in turn interfered as little as possible in the citizen's life. The emergence of a market economy and an influential bourgeoisie was accompanied by the dismantling of the existing (feudal and quasi-feudal) socio-economic structures that had fettered individual initiative and autonomy with their emphasis on personal subservience and entrenched social and economic hierarchies. The idea of citizenship that emerged in this context was characterized, according to Derek Heater (1990), by individual rights and individual mobility across social class—made possible by the idea of equality among citizens and the replacement of a localized civil society by an all-encompassing national political community.

T. H. Marshall: Equal and Universal Citizenship

T. H. Marshall, in his influential account of the growth of citizenship in England, states that the concept developed in a peculiar relationship of conflict and collusion with capitalism. Marshall's widely accepted definition of citizens as 'free and equal members of a political community' comes primarily from the study of citizenship as a process of expanding equality against the inequality of social class, the latter being an integral element of capitalist society. In *Citizenship and Social Class* (1950), Marshall distinguishes three strands or bundles of rights constituting citizenship, viz., civil, political and social. Civil rights, defined by Marshall as 'rights necessary for individual freedom', include freedoms of speech, movement, conscience, the rights to equality before the law, and the right to own property. These were 'negative' rights in the sense that they limited or checked the exercise of government power. Political rights, viz., the right to vote, the right to stand for elections and the right to hold public office, provided the individual with the opportunity to participate in political life. The provision of political rights required the development of universal suffrage, political equality, and democratic government. Social rights, argued Marshall, guaranteed the individual a minimum social status and provided the basis for the exercise of both civil and political rights. These were 'positive' rights 'to live the life of a civilized being according to the standards prevailing in society'. These standards of life and the social heritage of society are realized through active intervention by the state in the form of social services (the welfare state) and the educational system. Each of these three strands has, he suggests, a distinct history confined to a particular century—civil to the 18th, political to the 19th, and social to the 20th—and corresponds with the development of specific state structures—the judiciary, parliamentary institutions of governance, and the educational system and the welfare state, respectively.

The elements of equality and universality are emphasized by those espousing the virtues of liberal citizenship. Marshall's definition of citizenship as 'full and equal membership in a political community' is seen as encapsulating the two promises that modern citizenship makes: (*a*) a 'horizontal *camaraderie*' or equality, as opposed to hierarchical inequalities among members of the political community, and (*b*) the promise of 'integration' whereby the expanding circle of citizenship gradually brings into its fold various excluded and marginalized sections of the population. This membership is thus also the expression of an identity, of a sense of belonging to the political community that is the nation-state, and assures a share in a common (national) culture and social heritage.

Citizenship's promise of equality is, moreover, premised on effacing or masking ascriptive and hierarchical inequalities of culture, caste, gender, ethnicity, etc. For example, the provision of equal rights by state, or equal protection by the state to its citizens, irrespective of class, caste, gender, race etc., has at its core the idea of a neutral state. This basically means that for the liberal state the citizen is like an individual wearing a mask, so that attributes of class, caste, gender race, etc., are not visible. Logically, then, all citizens appear the same to the state and it would therefore treat everyone equally by applying uniform standards, so that irrespective of whether a person is an upper-caste man or a Dalit woman, they possess the same rights and are protected by the state in the same manner and measure.

Limits of Liberal Citizenship: Uniformity and Generality

The notion of equality proposed in liberal citizenship has been seen both as the basis of its achievements, as well as the source of its limitations. As far as achievement is concerned, it holds out the promise of including all persons irrespective of their caste, class, gender, race, and religion, as citizens—in other words, *generalizing citizenship across social structure*. The promise of inclusion involves the assurance that all persons are equal before the law and, therefore, no person or group is legally privileged, and that the state shall not discriminate among persons on the basis of any of these differences. The provision of citizenship in this manner, in terms of *uniform application of same rules*, disregards, however, the differential situation of persons across classes to exercise the rights or legal capacities that constitute citizenship. This basically means that, in effect, the status of citizenship will not be available equally to all. Those disadvantaged by class, caste, race, gender, etc., will be unable to participate in the community of citizenship in which they have legal membership. The disability is a double one because in such circumstances citizenship rights that are only formal cannot influence the conditions that render the possession of citizenship ineffective, if not worthless.

Critics of liberal citizenship including those on the left, the feminists, communitarians, multiculturalists, etc., have pointed to the contradictions and ambivalences that surround citizenship's relationship with capitalism. While Marxist and feminist critiques will be examined later, it is important to point out that even within liberalism these ambivalences and the limits they put on citizenship's potential as a 'momentum concept' have been visited at various points in time. Marshall himself located the roots of this contradiction and its potential for conflict in future, in the element of citizenship that assured to each citizen 'equal social worth, not merely of equal rights', which would guarantee to citizens an equality of status—'a minimum supply of certain essential goods and services' (Marshall 1950: 24).

These contradictory impulses were addressed by John Rawls in the 1970s (*A Theory of Justice*, 1971) and then again in the 1990s (*Political Liberalism,* 1993). Generally speaking, Rawls' citizens are free and equal members of a constitutional democracy, each with his/her distinctive conception of the good. To pursue these goods, they need the same primary goods, i.e. the same basic rights, liberties, and opportunities as well as the same all-purpose means such as income and wealth and some social basis of self-respect. In order to ensure that the same primary goods are available to all, they agree on a conception of justice that states that 'all social primary goods—liberty and opportunity, income and wealth, and the bases of self-respect—are to be distributed equally, unless an unequal distribution of any or all of these goods is to the advantage of the least favoured'. Rawls' two principles of justice provide the framework within which a liberal democratic citizenship could now unfold, viz., (*a*) 'a fully adequate scheme of equal basic rights and liberties', and (*b*) equal opportunity combined with the most clearly distinguishable feature of Rawls' approach of justice as fairness, *'the difference principle'*, viz., that 'social and economic inequalities' would be acceptable only insofar as they operate 'to the greatest benefit of the least advantaged members of society' (quoted in Shafir 1998: 7).

The Search for Alternatives

Marxist Critique of Bourgeois Citizenship

It is generally pointed out that for Marx the claims of liberal citizenship to equality and freedom were incompatible with capitalism. The explanation for this incompatibility has been sought in Marx's interpretation of the modern state as a bourgeois state, as a manifestation and guardian of bourgeois interests, incapable of delivering the promises of equal citizenship. 'Equal right' in a capitalist society is a bourgeois right consisting only in the application of an equal/uniform standard. This works out in effect as 'a right of inequality in its content', since with the application of an equal standard, people's (unequal) location in a hierarchized society, their needs, social contexts, relationships, etc., are ignored. Such rights, moreover, are embedded in the notion of 'alienated', 'isolated'. 'circumscribed' and 'egoistic' individuals. Marx's treatment of citizenship and rights is, however, more nuanced and differentiated. As pointed out by Amy Bartholomew (1990), in his work *On the Jewish Question*, Marx, distinguished 'the 'rights of man' from the 'rights of citizens', directing his criticism of rights primarily towards the 'rights of man' or the so-called natural rights.

Marx rejects the 'rights of man', viz., freedom of religion, equality, liberty, security and private property, embodied in the French and American declaration of rights. None of these rights, he argued, went 'beyond the egoistic man ... that is as an individual separated from the community....' The only bond that they admit between people is one deriving from necessity, need and private interest. These rights, therefore, not only reflect but also constitute competitive, egoistic and atomistic individuals who view the community and others as potential enemies. None of these rights, he points out, addresses or embraces communal or social concerns, human sociality or the species being. Marx had a different view of citizens' rights, and political participation in general. Citizens' rights in Marx's schema included political and civil rights, and rights of democratic participation. Marx is appreciative of citizen's rights because they could be exercised by individuals only as members of a community, and their content was 'participation in the community life', in the 'political life of the community', and the 'life of the state'. They are, moreover, embedded in the political life of the community, and envisage an individual without egoistic boundaries. Marx was supportive of citizens' or political rights, both in terms of restricting the freedom of the state and in providing the participatory rights that encouraged some kind of collective action. He supported freedom of speech, dissent, and organization as well as universal franchise because he admitted the possibility of achieving socialist transformation through the vote. Marx's criticisms of rights can, therefore, be better understood as pertaining to the actually existing 'rights of man' (e.g. right to liberty, which he argued emerged from and contributed to a particular form of individualism—bourgeois individualism), and were 'wholly preoccupied with his private interest and acting in accordance with his private caprice'.

Feminism and Citizenship

As discussed above, the idea of 'general' and 'uniform' citizenship has been criticized by Marxists for overlooking the inequalities that exist in real life. Feminists have shown how the idea of citizenship has been especially inimical to women. Feminists of all strands have criticized the dominant conceptions of citizenship on two counts. They argue, first of all, that citizenship is gender-blind. By focusing on uniform and equal application, it fails to take cognizance of the fact that modern societies are steeped in patriarchal traditions, which make for male domination and privileges. Equality in such conditions remains a façade and the inequality of women is sustained by policies that work within the framework of formal equality. Second, most historical conceptualizations of citizenship have thrived on the division between members and non-members. The discursive practices surrounding the notion of citizenship have produced dichotomies where the space for citizenship became increasingly identified with male and public activities. The universality and generality demanded by citizenship required that concerns around particular contexts of caste, class, race and gender be removed from the public domain and be relegated to the private. While the public/private distinction was essential for the assertion of the liberal notion of citizen as the autonomous individual, it also led to the identification of the private with the domestic, which played an important role in the exclusion and subordination of women. Thus, feminists have argued that both the ancient and modern concepts of citizenship have been inimical to women, either excluding them from citizenship altogether as in the classical tradition, or integrating them indirectly as citizen-consorts, as in the French revolutionary tradition. Modern citizenship, while not entirely excluding women, incorporated them on the basis of their socially useful and dependent roles as mothers and wives, thereby placing them outside the sphere of politics, and distancing them from resources and opportunities like education, property, etc., which equip individuals for political participation.

Feminists have taken different routes to overcome their exclusion from the political community. One strand has focused on political participation, viewing citizenship as an aspect of public/political activity and as embodying the transformative potential of democracy. They have argued for women's inclusion in the public sphere as equals, laying emphasis on revitalizing/democratizing the public sphere through communication, speech, and action (which are seen as empowering), and through alliances for a shared common objective. Thus, it is the exercise of rights in the political sphere which is seen as crucial to the full development of women's citizenship as part of what Rian Voet (1998) calls 'an active and sex-equal citizenship'.

A second major strand of feminism is, however, sceptical of what is felt to be a merely 'add women' approach, which while looking for avenues of inclusion into the public sphere, does not question its 'maleness'. This view approaches citizenship from the vantage point of what women do in the private realm. Questioning the patriarchal state, it argues for the inclusion of women's specific functions into the public realm of citizenship, hoping thereby to promote the suppressed private side of the public/private divide into the realm of democratic politics. This has led to two distinct lines of argument: the personal is political, which implies a continuity of power between the state and the so-called private domains, and submits them both to the norms of justice and equality of the public realm; and maternal citizenship, which advocates that women should value their particular skills and interests, rather than merely enter the bastions of male-defined politics on its terms. By emphasizing the 'public' role, maternalists like Carol Gilligan (1982), Jean Elshtain (1981) and Sara Ruddick (1989) feel that the degradation of the 'private' role, the domestic, becomes unavoidable. They would prefer to see the dismantling of citizenship based on male personalities, and the development of new notions based on female characteristics of love and compassion.

New Contexts and Changing Concerns: Multiculturalism and Globalization

Differentiated and Multicultural Citizenship

Contemporary debates on citizenship and rights have questioned the idea that the citizen can enjoy rights independent of the contexts to which s/he belongs. A significant terrain of contention has opened up since the 1980s in citizenship theory, with multiculturalism, plurality, diversity and difference having become significant terms of reference for re-theorizing citizenship. This contest pertains in effect to the unmasking of those differences that were earlier seen as irrelevant to citizenship. There is a growing effort to redefine citizenship by giving due importance to cultural differences among individuals and striking a balance between the numerous religious, ethnic, and linguistic identities while constructing a common political identity of the citizen of the nation. Notions of multiculturalism and minority rights have been invoked in contemporary times as democratic values, whereby cultural communities can lay claims to inherent rights and negotiate fair terms of inclusion in the national political space. This influential strand within citizenship theory has sought to invest in multiculturalism as the core element of democratic citizenship that cherishes cultural diversity and envisages a society in which different communities forge a common identity while retaining their cultural provenance.

The case for a *differentiated citizenship* was put forth by theorists who felt that the common rights of citizenship, originally defined by (and for) white men in a class-differentiated society, could not accommodate the needs of large numbers of ethnic, religious and linguistic groups, who feel excluded from the 'common' rights to citizenship. They emphasized that instead of masking these differences in the allocation of rights, effort must be made to take account of the specificity of the different circumstances of citizens. An increasing number of theorists argue that different groups can be accommodated into common citizenship only by adopting what Iris Marion Young (1989) calls 'differentiated citizenship', which means that members of certain groups should be accommodated not only as individuals but also through their group, and their rights would partially depend upon their group membership. Young argues against a society where some groups are privileged while others are oppressed, insisting that as citizens, persons should leave behind their particular affiliations and experiences and adopt a general point of view. Reinforcing the perspective and interests of the privileged will tend to dominate this unified public, marginalizing or silencing those of other groups.

Seeking to redefine the principle of equality, to make it compatible with the 'multicultural present', Will Kymlicka (1996) provides a framework of representation and membership that accommodates cultural and group differences in a way that a person's group membership and membership in a cultural community is not of any disadvantage to her. Moreover, he also seeks to find a meeting ground between cultural communities, the right to self-preservation, and rights to individuals as defined in terms of civil and political rights.

Kymlicka suggests the following ways in which the demands of national minorities and ethnic groups may be accommodated within a framework of democratic citizenship: (*a*) By protecting the common rights of all citizens, which basically means the protection of civil and political rights of individuals; freedom of association, religion, speech, mobility and political organization for protecting group difference. (*b*) By accommodating cultural diversity through special legal and constitutional measures, with members of specific groups being guaranteed special rights, or as Young (1990) would call them, group-specific or group-differentiated rights.

Kymlicka identifies three forms of group-differentiated rights: (i) self-government rights, (ii) poly-ethnic rights, and (iii) special representation rights.

Self-government rights recognize some kind of political autonomy or territorial jurisdiction of national minorities, which they claim were not relinquished by their (often involuntary) incorporation into the larger state. Such rights may be manifest in federal structures where the boundaries of federal sub-units give some autonomy.

Poly-ethnic rights concern themselves with specific rights of immigrant communities and represent a challenge to the Anglo-conformity model, which assumes that they should abandon all aspects of their ethnic heritage and be assimilated to existing cultural norms and practices. At first, such rights may take the form of demanding the right to express their peculiarities and differences without fear of prejudice or discrimination in the mainstream society. Ethnic groups have, however, expanded this right demanding positive action in the form of protection, preservation, and nurture from the state to root out discrimination and preserve their existence as distinct entities. Some ethnic and religious minorities have also demanded various forms of public funding of their cultural functions—funding of ethnic associations, magazines and festivals. The most controversial demands have perhaps been those that demand exception from laws and regulations that disadvantage them given their religious practices, for example, Jews and Muslims in Britain have sought exemption from Sunday closing, Jews in the United States have sought to wear the *yarmulka* during military service, Muslim girls in France and Britain have asked for exemption from the school dress code—to be allowed to wear the *hijab* or *chadors*.

Special representation rights have evoked interest amongst national and ethnic groups, as well as non-ethnic categories—women, the poor and the disabled. This basically translates into democratizing the structures of the state by making it more representative, for example, making legislatures more representative by including members of ethnic and racial minorities and women, the poor, disabled, etc. Defence of these rights has come both on the basis of rectification of oppression and also for providing opportunities for self-determination.

The arguments made in favour of multiculturalism are, thus, not only for the correction of 'historical wrongs', or even the removal of discrimination. The commitment to sustain the community is primarily rooted in the belief that communities have much to offer the political community. The investment in diversity is also based on the assumption that every culture has valuable elements that can be shared and learned from. This assumption immediately opens up possibilities of conceiving the political community as a shared public space where equality is a significant norm. An important contribution of multiculturalism to the theory of citizenship has thus been that it has altered the way in which the political community has been thought of. Far from being a homogeneous whole, the political community is seen as heterogeneous. Moreover, this heterogeneity is seen as valuable for a democratic public space. Yet, in its enthusiasm to establish the primacy of the community and the idea of the individual-in-community, multiculturalism runs into the danger of denying the individual the right of critical and creative membership in the community and overlooks the hierarchies and oppressions that communities themselves sustain and promote. By focusing disproportionately on the preservation of community, it leads to arguments favouring not only the protection of the community from external constraints, but also the acknowledgement of its right to apply internal restraints. By empowering the community to apply internal restraints, it preserves structures of authority that work to the detriment of individual freedom. Moreover, by acknowledging the community's power to apply internal restraints, it seems to subscribe to the notion that the rights and freedoms of *all* individuals do not matter. In other words, within such a framework, the rights of individuals who belong to minority communities appear to be dispensable.

Return of Civic Republicanism: Civic Virtue and Good Citizenship

Alongside the recognition of cultural contexts for the formulation of citizen's rights, the republican ideals of 'civic virtue' and 'good citizenship' have also been revived in various ideological strands. The ideal of good citizenship defined by civic virtue, patriotism, and participatory citizenship, as discussed earlier, emerged in classical antiquity, and was revived as an ideal in Renaissance Italy, 18th century America, and France. From the late 18th century the civic republican tradition gave way to the liberal. The revival of civic republicanism or 'neo-republicanism' has come about in the non-liberal as well as liberal articulations of citizenship, taking different forms depending on the specific ideological tradition in which it is placed. By and large the revival has been attributed either to the implications the liberal 'style' of citizenship has had for social relations, or the intrinsic values of civic republicanism itself.

Broadly, two strands of 'neo-republicanism' may be identified. One strand exhibits disillusionment with the 'thin democracy' that liberal citizenship has generated over the years, manifested in political apathy and passivity. While theorists on the Left would like to roll back passivity by enabling and 'empowering' citizens through democratic participation, radical pluralists like Chantal Mouffe (1992) believe that a relation of 'democratic equivalence' may be established through political participation and the articulation of difference. These notions of active citizenship conform to the distinction between civil society and political society, where civil society is an extra-political arena in which individuals enter in order to articulate their purely private concerns. On the other hand, political society is generated whenever individuals communicate not their purely private concerns but rather matters of shared importance, in order to influence or make demands on the state.

A different articulation of active citizenship is found in Michael Walzer's works. Acknowledging the plurality of social life, Walzer proposes that citizenship provides a common binding principle. Citizenship as a binding principle makes itself manifest in civil society, 'the setting of settings' (Walzer 1989), which provides the space where individuals as part of diverse social groups are trained in civility and self-restraint. It is in this articulation of public life, in the shared forum of participation of diverse groups, that individuals think of a common good beyond their own conceptions of the good life. Critical of the growing numbers of people who are 'radically disengaged' or 'passive clients of the state', Walzer is equally uncomfortable with political participation as the only form of active citizenship. He places faith in the idea of 'critical associationalism', which is based on the belief that in the modern world the density of associational life and the activities and understandings that go with it need to be recaptured and relearned, and proposes that participation in voluntary organizations of the civil society—churches, families, ethnic associations, voluntary groups, schools—inculcate the civic virtues that bind citizens in mutual obligation.

On the other hand, another strand represented by communitarian theorists such as Alisdair MacIntyre (1981), Amitai Etzioni (1995), and Michael Sandel (1982) blame the passivity of liberal citizenship for the disintegration of social bonds and the rise in anomie and alienation in modern societies. Broadly speaking, this strand, like those discussed earlier, extracts from the republican tradition the focus on community and duty. Yet, it is distinct from them, since it omits from its programme direct political participation and the republican concern for freedom. Moreover, in their quest for ways to a 'restored sense of neighbourhood', and even a 'national togetherness', they are intolerant of the political and plural diversity that the other strands of theorizing espouse. MacIntyre and Sandel represent, therefore, the growing strand of social and political conservatism, which dismisses the idea of the 'unencumbered self', but rejects all forms of pluralities, arguing that the 'politics of right' should be replaced by a 'politics of common good'. We may recall that in Marshall's formulation, social rights constituted the third phase of the evolution of rights, coinciding with the development of the welfare state, and instrumental in integrating the poor, migrants, and racial minorities into the fold of citizenship. Theorists of the 'New Right', however, see social rights as promoting passivity and a culture of dependency among the poor. Working within a framework of common good and common obligation of all citizens, they argue for a workfare programme instead of a welfare programme, cutting back the safety net of the poor, and tying welfare benefits to work responsibilities. Unlike the civil society theorists, who argue for the enhancement of responsible citizenship through participation in institutions of civil society, the New Right sees the market, characterized by free trade, deregulation, tax-cuts, the weakening of trade unions, and the tightening of unemployment benefits, as the 'school' where citizenship 'virtues' of initiative, self-reliance, and self-sufficiency are learned.

Globalization, World Citizenship and Human Rights

An influential strand of citizenship theorists argues that an increasingly globalized, interdependent and interconnected world, marked by transnational movement of populations and multicultural national populations one can no longer talk of citizenship in terms of membership in a territorially limited *nation-state*, the hitherto uncontested unit of membership. They propose the delinking of the relationship between citizenship and the nation-state, replacing it with global/world citizenship with its basis in human rights. Yasemin Soysal (1994), for example, argues that globalization has brought in a 'new and more universal' concept of citizenship that has 'universal personhood' rather than 'national be-longing' as its core principle. Universal personhood delinks legal rights from citizenship status and national belonging and is reflected in the status of guest workers in Europe, who have lived in Europe for years without ever acquiring citizenship, primarily because the countries of residence assured their legal and social rights. These assurances, feels Soysal, are further augmented by the global system of human rights law, the United Nations network, regional governance, etc., that have ushered in the idea of a global civil society. The assurances guaranteed by membership of this global civil society make the securities of nation-state membership redundant. Much of this assurance, it is argued, has emanated from the high degree of agreement on the need for human rights, and the recognition that violations of human rights have global ramifications, and their protection must, therefore, involve transnational efforts.

The emphasis on world citizenship with human rights at its core is, however, riddled with contradictions. Despite the increased role envisaged for a transnational network and cooperation, human rights by themselves are not able to ensure the development of participatory networks essential for safeguarding rights. In the case of Soysal's guest workers, for example, the denial of political rights, even when social and civil rights are assured, deprives them of a right to participate in the formulation and implementation of policies, which may impact their social entitlements and civil liberties. Moreover, the emphasis on human rights and the world citizen is counterbalanced by a simultaneous lament of a 'crisis in citizenship' which is addressed with the invocation of stringent immigration laws, the fortification/reinforcement of national and regional boundaries, and emphasizing 'descent' and 'blood ties' in the consideration for citizenship. Moreover, human rights, like 'citizens', are almost always articulated in abstract and universalistic, i.e. context-free terms, masking the diversity and historicity of citizenship and rights. The idea of human rights as the replacement for citizenship rights can be retained only when citizenship is construed in passive terms, and rights themselves are detached and distanced from the social and political structures that sustain them, and the specific struggles that produce them.

Conclusion

The significance of contemporary debates on citizenship lies in their admission that the political community is complex, hierarchical, and culturally and ideologically plural. Even the fact that they envisage a public sphere beyond the boundaries of the nation-state is important, since it gives an analytical framework to understand the politics of a heterogeneous public. This assures, as Iris Marion Young (1990) puts it, that (*a*) 'no persons, actions or aspects of a person's life [may] be forced into privacy; and (*b*) no social institutions or practices [may] be excluded *a priori* from being a proper subject for public discussion and expression' (Young 1990: 120, 178). The significance accorded to the contextualized self too, is crucial in building a substantive notion of citizenship. The idea of the individual as a part of the community, bound to other individuals not by necessity or private interest, but by community or social concerns, is an important aspect of such a formulation. At the same time, the notion of community and what constitutes common concerns must be worked out continually through processes of interaction and dialogue. It is through a concerted effort at the retrieval of the political as an interactive public space that collective energies can be congealed into shared bonds of citizenship. What is required therefore, is not the essentialization of community/cultural identities into compartments that exclude dialogue, but to see how economic, social and political factors, constitute the life experiences of people within and across communities.

Points for Discussion

1. While legal and political rights were being won in Europe, colonization was proceeding in many parts of the world. Do you think Marshall's evolutionary threefold typology of citizenship rights hold true for other societies?
2. Do you think positive discrimination in the form of reservation of seats in recruitment or in political representation can be understood within the framework of differentiated citizenship?
3. The practice of citizenship in the contemporary world has seen simultaneous and contradictory trends towards both transnational citizenship and fortification of nation-state boundaries and sovereignty. Do you agree? Identify such patterns in state practices in India and abroad.
4. The manner in which individual, group and community rights figure in the Constitution, manifests the ways in which the different strands of citizenship have sought to address the limits of liberal rights. Discuss.

Reading List

Bartholomew, Amy, 'Should a Marxist Believe in Marx on Rights?' *Socialist Register*, 1990: 244–64, http://socialistregister.com/socialistregister.com/files/SR_1990_Bartholomew.pdf

Bodin, Jean, *Method for the Easy Comprehension of History*, trans. Beatrice Reynolds (New York: Columbia University Press, 1945[1566]).

Elshtain, Jean Bethke, *Public Man, Private Woman: Women in Social and Political Thought* (Princeton, NJ: Princeton University Press, 1981).

Etzioni, Amitai, *The Spirit of Community: Rights Responsibilities and the Communitarian Agenda* (London: Fontana, 1995).

Faulks, Keith, *Citizenship* (London and New York: Routledge, 2000).

Gilligan, Carol, *In a Different Voice: Psychological Theory and Moral Development* (Harvard: Harvard University Press, 1982).

Heater, Derek, *Citizenship: The Civic Ideal in World History*, Politics and Education (London: Orient Longman, 1990).

———, *What Is Citizenship?* (Cambridge: Polity Press, 1999).

Kymlicka, Will, *Multicultural Citizenship: A Liberal Theory of Minority Rights* (Oxford: Clarendon Press, 1996).

Kymlicka, Will and Wayne Norman, 'The Return of the Citizen', *Ethics*, 104(January), 1994.

MacIntyre, Alisdair, *After Virtue* (Notre Dame: University of Notre Dame Press, 1981).

Marshall, T. H., *Citizenship and Social Class* (Cambridge, UK: Cambridge University Press, 1950).

Marshall, T. H. and Tom Bottomore (eds), *Citizenship and Social Class* (London: Pluto Press, 1992).

Mouffe, Chantal (ed.), *Dimensions of Radical Democracy* (London: Verso, 1992).

Ruddick, Sara, *Maternal Thinking: Towards a Politics of Peace* (Boston: Beacon Press, 1989).

Sandel, Michael, *Liberalism and the Limits of Justice* (Cambridge: Cambridge University Press, 1982).

Shafir, Gershon, *The Citizenship Debates: A Reader* (Minnesota: University of Minnesota Press, Minneapolis, 1998).

Smith, Anthony D., *Theories of Nationalism* (London: Duckworth, 1983).

Soysal, Yasemin, *Limits of Citizenship* (Chicago: University of Chicago Press, 1994).

Voet, Rian, *Feminism and Citizenship* (London: Sage, 1998).

Walzer, Michael, 'Citizenship', in Terence Ball, James Farr and Russel L. Hanson (eds), *Political Innovation and Conceptual Change* (Cambridge: Cambridge University Press, 1989).

Young, Iris Marion, *Justice and the Politics of Difference* (Princeton, NJ: Princeton University Press, 1990).

Yuval-Davis, Nira, 'Women, Citizenship and Difference', *Feminist Review*, 57(1), 1997: 4–27.

CHAPTER 10

Power

Nivedita Menon

Chapter Outlines

Introduction

This chapter begins with an overview of the debates centred on the different conceptions of power, which leads to the idea that power is an 'essentially contested' concept. This is followed by the consideration of power in different forms—as exploitation, as legitimate power and authority, and as hegemony. Thereafter, feminist theories of power are briefly discussed. The chapter concludes with Foucault's conception of power, which marks a radical break with the earlier notions.

Conceptions of Power

Power in ordinary usage is understood as an ability, strength, or capacity; for instance, in the term 'electric power'. In social and political theory, however, power refers to the ability to do things and the capacity to produce effects *within social interaction*. In this sense, power is a type of behaviour and specifically derives from the existence of social relationships and organized social interactions.

The most well-known definition of power is given by Robert Dahl—'A has power over B to the extent that A can get B to do something which B would not otherwise do.' This definition assumes two things about power:

(*a*) power is an attribute of *individuals* which is exercised over other individuals, and
(*b*) power is domination over others, that is, power is used to make others do what one wants, against their own will.

But both these assumptions are challenged by other theorists. There are those, for example, who locate power at the *collective* level, and attribute it to collectivities and structures. Marxist theory views power as distributed unequally in a class-divided society, such as a capitalist society, where the ruling classes own the means of production and exercise power over the working class, which owns no property, but produces surplus value through its labour power that is appropriated by the capitalists. Similarly, feminist theorists understand power as located within structures of patriarchy, which ensures that there is a systematic domination of women by men. In both analyses, power is seen as located within structures, and individuals derive power from their location within a structure.

The second assumption is challenged by theorists who view power not simply as domination; that is, not only as *power over* but as *power to*—power as an enhanced capacity emerging from collective action. This view is associated with Hannah Arendt, who theorizes power as enabling and generated when people communicate and act together in a shared enterprise. In this sense, having power is the basis of being able to act as a morally responsible human being.

Power as *power to* can be understood in a different way, too. Renowned sociologist Talcott Parsons developed an account of political power, which treated it as the analogue of money in economic systems. That is to say, he thought of power as something that circulates in society the way money does. In this sense, just as the possession of money enables the capacity to secure economic goods and services, so the possession of power enables the capacity to secure the performance of political obligations. Just as money circulates, so does power. Parsons, thus, emphasized on both the *facilitative* dimension of power—that is, its capacity to get things done—as well as its *systemic* character, that it is a property of the entire social system, not merely of individuals.

In view of the debates on the notions of 'power', Steven Lukes suggests that power is an 'essentially contested' concept. This notion was first outlined by W. B. Gallie. The argument is that there are concepts, the very description of which are value laden. For example, when you term something as an 'art' or when you refer to a 'democracy', you are not merely objectively describing it, you are ascribing a value to it. That is, non-art and non-democracy are implicitly devalued in this description. William Connolly points out that when we describe something we 'characterize a situation from the vantage point of certain interests, purposes and standards'. That is, any description, however value-free it may appear, is subjective to the extent that it has embedded in it the intention with which the thing is described. In that sense, every description is made with some interest or purpose in mind, and assumes some standard. Thus, when you describe something as a 'lever', you are ruling out other descriptions of the thing as a piece of wood or iron, or when you refer to a *tulsi* leaf, for example, as a 'medicine', you are ruling out its description as a green leaf. Similarly, when you describe a woman as 'tall' you have a standard of height in mind. This means that to choose one description as more appropriate over another depends on the purpose which the description is to be put to. Values are involved in choosing the 'correct' description. The choice is not made in a vacuum, nor is it dependent on some inherent objective quality that the concept possesses.

According to Lukes, there are three dimensions of political power, which explains why he considers power to be an essentially contested concept.

(*a*) At the most explicit level, power may be exercised to ensure that a more powerful set of interests prevails over others. This is closest to the view of power, as expressed by Dahl, which we began with.

(*b*) Less obviously, power may be exercised to ensure that certain issues and options never come up for debate at all. That is, power can shape the setting of the agenda for debate itself, and exclude certain issues from the beginning. This view of power is put forward by Peter Bachrach and Morton Baratz. They argue that if political theorists look for power only at the explicit level, they will remain unaware that even in situations of apparent equality among participants, power may already have been exercised. That is, power may have been used to prevent the articulation of certain demands and views. These demands and views then never reach the public domain, which can as a result appear to be homogeneous and equal.

(*c*) Steven Lukes goes even further and presents what he considers to be the most radical view of power. The second view still depends on observable conflict, but Lukes argues that power should be understood as structural, and working in various ways to shape the very perceptions of people. Power can work in a way that what people consider to be in their interest is, in fact, what is desired by those in power—people's real interests are hidden from them. In this view, power should be assumed to be operating even when there is no apparent conflict. This view is closest to the Marxist view of power.

Why Lukes calls power an essentially contested concept is because whether we agree that the second and third dimensions also express power relations will depend on our over-all understanding of politics, morality, and ethics. That is, you might disagree that the third dimension can be recognized at all as power, because you believe that society is plural and equitable, that everybody has the opportunity to be powerful, and that there is no hidden dimension that hides from people what is in their best interests. Thus, Lukes suggests that since people differ in their understanding of how society functions, and what is just or un-just, equitable or not, we will not be able to arrive at a mutually and rationally agreed-upon notion of what power is. It is in this sense that power is an 'essentially contested concept'.

Power as Exploitation

Exploitation is a specifically Marxist understanding of power. In any society in which technological advancements have made possible the production of a surplus—when more is produced than the minimum need for survival of the population—this surplus is appropriated by or taken over by one section of the population. *Exploitation* occurs when the surplus produced by one section of the population is controlled by another section.

In the Marxist understanding of history, society develops through several modes of production. In such a situation, exploitation takes place in specific ways. Under capitalism, exploitation takes the form of extraction of surplus value from the working class mainly by the industrial capitalists, but other fractions of the ruling class also share in this appropriation of the surplus.

Capitalism differs from other non-capitalist modes of production in that exploitation can take place without the direct intervention of force. Thus, exploitation is hidden from the participants by the language of the contract, in which every individual is equal. In a capitalist society, the myth of free and equal exchange between equal partners to the contract is perpetuated by law and the state, through *juridical equality* (which implies that everybody is equal under law). For Marxists, this is a fiction because freedom of contract, equality before the law and the right to vote are all severely restricted in the absence of economic democracy. To quote a saying in 19th century England, 'Everyone is free to sleep under the bridges of London, from the King to the pauper'—the point being that the king would never have to sleep under the bridges, and the pauper does not have the corresponding right to sleep in a palace!

In the previous modes of production, exploitation was transparent. For example, the peasant had to give a part of the crop produced to the landlord, or work for a fixed number of days in the landlord's fields. If the peasant did not do so, the landlord would use force to extract what was expected. Such modes of exploitation continue even today in many parts of our country. The modes of extraction of surplus value involved force, which can be referred to as *extra-economic coercion*.

Under capitalism, however, the coercion is purely through *economic* means—since the contract involves a wage paid in exchange for the labour performed, the exchange is seen to be equal. In the Marxist understanding, however, the surplus produced by labour far exceeds the wage paid for it in exchange and is appropriated by the capitalist. This appropriation is *exploitation*.

Authority, Legitimacy and Hegemony

When rules are complied with or obeyed, it suggests that it has the consent of the citizens; that they affirm a belief in legality. Such a system is assumed to be *legitimate*, and power that is complied with because it has legitimacy is termed *authority*.

Max Weber's discussion of authority is the classic one. He distinguished between three kinds of authority—*rational-legal, traditional*, and *charismatic*.

Rational-legal authority is characteristic of the modern industrial bureaucratic state. Here, those who occupy positions of power, exercise their power and are obeyed on the basis of impersonal rules that can be justified on rational grounds. Thus, when you stop at a signal from the traffic police, you are not obeying that particular person, but what s/he represents—the rules of traffic in an urban society, where the absence of such rules would spell chaos.

Traditional authority exists because of historical and cultural reasons. Instances of traditional authority are those vested in tribal chiefs and religious leaders.

Charismatic authority exists because of some personal quality possessed by an individual who may not have either modern official status or traditional authority. Jesus, Mohammed, Hitler and Gandhi would all be examples of those wielding such authority.

Weber presented these types of authority as 'ideal types', that is, theoretical devices to help in social analysis, rather than as descriptions of empirical reality. So, no one institution or individual in authority exemplifies one type entirely—charismatic authority often draws on tradition; rational-legal authority and charismatic authority may go together, and so on.

A related distinction is between *de facto* and *de jure* authority. The latter refers to the authority that has legal sanction, while the former refers to the person or institutions actually exercising power. This is best exemplified in the situation of *coup d'etat* in which an elected government is overthrown by the military. Here, the deposed government represents the *de jure* authority while *de facto* authority is exemplified in the military dictator and the army.

However, David Held is one of those who questions the equation of *obedience to a system* with *legitimacy*. Held points out that the reason or ground for obedience is not necessarily *normative agreement* amongst everyone about what a society as a collective should do. Only in this case can we say that obedience to rules proves that the system has legitimacy. Held argues that, in fact, the reasons for obedience to rules can be varied—people may obey because of *coercion*, because they do not question *tradition*, or simply because of *apathy*.

We have already seen how the Marxist concept of exploitation offers a similar challenge to the idea that obedience to a system proves that it is legitimate. It provides an alternative understanding of how obedience to power is enforced through legal codes. Economic compulsion is an important medium of ensuring obedience—modern capitalism has created a mass of propertyless wage workers who have no option but to sell their labour to owners of capital in order to survive. This ensures conformance and obedience to rules.

Another dimension of legitimacy is provided by the notion of *hegemony*. This concept was developed by the Marxist theorist Antonio Gramsci. Hegemony is the control of society by purely cultural means. Thus, he distinguished between the repressive function of state power on the one hand, and the ability of the ruling class to control society by generating consent on the other. In this understanding, power is not exercised only through 'coercion', but is complemented by the 'direction' provided by the ruling classes. Thus, the consent of the ruled is a crucial part of the power exercised through hegemony.

In this understanding, therefore, the state has a wider, more organic meaning than the simpler Marxist understanding of the state as a coercive apparatus serving the interests of the ruling classes. The state in Gramsci's sense is understood as an equilibrium between 'political society' (the coercive apparatus) and 'civil society'. (Located therein are a multiplicity of private associations, both 'natural' and 'contractual'—such as the family, Church, schools, and so on. These generate a web of social relations and ideas that create and re-create the hegemony of the dominant class, which, in Marxist understanding, is the class that owns the means of production.) Thus, in Gramsci's view, ideology does not simply reflect or mirror class interest. But a dominant hegemonic ideology provides a coherent systematic worldview that influences the entire population. A whole complex of institutions, public and private, legitimize bourgeois dominance, rendering its values universal.

A striking illustration of hegemony is provided by the following example by Gramsci. When we look at a map of the world we know immediately which direction is North and which is South. We understand this to be a simple physical fact of nature. Gramsci illustrates this understanding with Bertrand Russell's statement that though we could not think of the cities of London or Edinburgh without the existence of man on earth, we could still think of the existence of two points in space, one to the North and one to the South, where Edinburgh and London now are.

Gramsci's objection to this common sense understanding is that locating fixed points on the globe as north/south or east/west is not a fact of nature but a convention or a 'historico-cultural construction'. He puts it like this: 'What would north–south or east–west mean without man? *They are real relationships* and yet they would not exist without man and without the development of civilization. Obviously, east and west are arbitrary and conventional, that is, they are historical constructions, *since outside real history every point on the earth is east and west at the same time.*'

Is this not true, that since the earth is roughly spherical, every point on it is simultaneously east and west, north and south? But we always look at the globe or a map only from a particular direction or angle. This is, in fact, the viewpoint of the European imperialist nation-states. That is why West Asia is the 'Middle East' (even to people in India for whom it is on their immediate West) or Australia is 'Down Under' (but if we look at the globe from the perspective of Australia, it is the rest of the world which is underneath!) Through this illustration, Gramsci shows us that east and west are historically constructed conventions reflecting power relations—the 'world-wide hegemony' of 'the European cultured classes', whose point of view was naturalized across the globe. Such a point of view that reflects and is produced by power relations and is made to appear natural and innocent of power—this is how hegemony operates to produce consent.

Feminist Theories of Power

Feminism is a political viewpoint that holds that the oppression and subjugation of women is not simply a matter of individual behaviour, or individual strength and weakness. Rather, a category of human beings called 'women' are systematically dominated, subjugated, and denied equal access to resources through the structural operation of patriarchal ideology. *Patriarchy* is a key category in feminist analyses of power, and refers to an overarching system of male dominance operating at every level—economic, political, and cultural. An understanding of patriarchy enables us to see that power or powerlessness cannot be explained in terms of individuals alone.

Under patriarchy, it is possible that individual women may have some power, but it would be strictly within the limits set by patriarchal rules. Thus, in the South Asian context, for example, women as mothers-in-law may have some power, but not as daughters, wives or sisters (of men). Note also that women in this understanding are defined entirely in terms of their relationship to men. Single women are, thus, invisible and disempowered.

Patriarchy is not understood to be a single homogeneous structure, rather feminist scholars now think in terms of patriarchies—differentiated over historical epochs, geographical regions, and cultural communities. In addition, patriarchy overlaps and interacts with other systems of oppression—on the basis of class, caste, imperialism, race, etc.—and produces specific effects. Thus, a white woman in the USA is affected by patriarchy differently from a Dalit woman in India, and feminist scholarship and politics attempts to negotiate these differences in complex ways.

It is also important to note that there is not one feminist analysis of power; feminists coming from varied political traditions analyse the sources of patriarchy differently. Liberal feminists would try to show the deficiencies of liberal conceptions of liberty, equality, and justice to the extent that they do not take into account gender, while Marxist feminists would produce a critique of the gender-blindness of class analysis. Radical feminists hold gender to be the primary category of analysis, and argue that all later forms of power imitate the original power relationship of men over women. At the same time, liberal feminists would have a critique of Marxist analyses, and Marxist feminists of liberal philosophy—there are more debates within feminism than there are between feminists and non-feminists.

Foucault on Power

Michel Foucault radically reconceptualized the notion of power. According to him, power is not *repressive*—that is, in the modern era, power does not operate by preventing us from doing what we want. Rather, Foucault sees power as *productive*—power produces identity and subjectivity. Further, power does not emanate from a single source, whether the state or the ruling classes. Power is conceptualized by Foucault as *capillary*—flowing throughout the system like blood in the capillaries of our body. At first glance, then, there may appear to be similarities between Arendt's understanding of power as *power to*, and Parson's conception of power *flowing* like money through the system. But both terms—*productive* and *capillary*—have entirely different meanings in Foucault's conception of power. In his understanding the identities produced by power are ways of controlling through naming, and this control is exercised in a variety of locations, in our everyday lives. How does this happen?

Through the mechanisms of what Foucault calls 'governmentality' (also see Chapter 11), we are produced as the subjects of governance. By governmentality he refers to the increasing homogenization and organization of society in modern times—through a huge bureaucratic machinery that evolves endless ways of classifying people. This *subject* is created and *subjected* to classification and surveillance through all sorts of things we take for granted—identity cards, passports and so on—through which we can be tracked, and in which we have to state who we are—Indian/Pakistani, Hindu/Muslim, educated/illiterate, etc. But we are also produced as subjects by discourses of medicine (healthy/sick), psychiatry (sane/insane), biology (male/female) and by legal discourses that judge your identity on the basis of the authority of these discourses. So, the mechanisms of governmentality are not located at the level of 'government' in a narrow sense, but operate through a variety of dis-courses. Governmentality operates through *normalization*, by which Foucault means the processes through which every individual is made to conform to the dominant norm.

Note the pun on the word 'subject', which means both the independent actor or agent, the thinking person ('I' as Subject) as well as that which is ruled (for example, the 'subject' of a monarch). What this means is that the moment you are produced as *subject* you are also *subjected to* the mechanisms of governmentality.

Thus, when asked—'Who are you'?—which is a question about your identity, every single answer you can possibly give is the result of different systems of classification that you don't think about, but which are produced by the mechanisms of governmentality. Take one possible answer, which appears to be 'purely biological', that is, natural—I am a man, or I am a woman. This identity is, in fact, produced by the language of the biomedical sciences, which use the notions of chromosomes, hormones, and organs to determine what you are. However, there is enough evidence to show that no human being fits exactly a two-sex model—this is the reason that 'gender verification tests', which were commonly conducted for the Olympic games, were suspended in 2000. It emerged after years of conducting the tests that atypical chromosomal variations are so common that it is impossible to judge femininity and masculinity on the basis of chromosomes. Similar evidence is available for hormones too, that every human being has both kinds of hormones in their bodies, and large numbers of bodies cannot be rigidly classified as either male or female on the basis of hormones. But whenever such cases are encountered, medical dis-courses are brought into play to treat them as diseased, treated, and made 'normal'. This rigid classification of all bodies as belonging to one or the other sex means that a large range of bodies are rendered invisible. We have no language to refer to trans-gendered people (He? She?), and babies that are born with no clearly determined sex are made to undergo invasive surgery.

This subjection through the production of governable identities is even more obvious when we think of identities based on race, caste, religion and so on.

Thus, the construction of *subjectivity* by those who tell us the 'truth' of about who we are—doctors, psychologists, the law—is at the same time a *subjection to* the power they exercise.

Hence the concept of 'power/knowledge' in Foucault; he does not simply mean that knowledge is power. Rather, he means that knowledge is already a function of power relations—knowledge is produced and gained in order to be put to certain use; in order to achieve power. 'Far from preventing knowledge, power produces it', he says. Understanding power as being merely repressive means failing to see that what needs to be explained—how the knowledge required for controlling the human body and labour have emerged. Foucault's study of history is intended to show that the human body could have been constituted as labour-power only if there were a technology or knowledge of the body that made it possible to organize and subjugate bodies into useful and docile roles. Further, this subjugation is not imposed by one class on another—it permeates and characterizes all aspects of society.

Power is not a thing or substance, it is not embodied in an institution or a group of people—power is exercised as a technique. The only way it can be identified is when it is exercised by some people over others. This is why, for Foucault, an important indication of the existence of power is a display of resistance to it. 'At the very heart of the power relation-ship, and constantly provoking it, are the recalcitrance of the will and the intransigence of freedom.' It is clear, then, that while at first glance Foucault's understanding of power might appear to offer no way out, in fact, he suggests quite the reverse—that wherever there is power, there is the possibility of resistance.

In Foucault's understanding, there are three types of struggles against power:

(*a*) Against ethnic/social/religious domination—typical of feudal societies.
(*b*) Against exploitation (which separates individuals from what they produce)—typical of 19th century capitalist societies.
(*c*) Against forms of 'subjection' (meaning both 'to be a subject' and 'to be subjected to'). In this kind of struggle, the attempt should be to promote new forms of subjectivity through the refusal of the kind of identity and individualization linked to the state and to governmentality.

At each stage, of course, the earlier forms of struggle continue alongside the new ones.

Conclusion

To conclude this discussion of the various debates around the idea of power, it can be argued that political theory cannot be restricted to the study of institutions of the state or to the laying down of norms of public behaviour. Such an understanding must be complemented by an awareness of how power operates to produce both institutions, as well as apparently universal and neutral norms. In short, an awareness of power must inform the theorizing of politics.

Points for Discussion

1. Do you think power is an 'essentially contested concept'? Do you agree with the argument that all concepts in political theory are essentially contested?
2. Discuss the idea of legitimate power. How does the concept of hegemony complicate the notion of legitimacy?
3. How would you relate the Marxist conception of exploitation to Steven Lukes' view of power?
4. How does Foucault's conception of power as productive and capillary differ from earlier conceptions of power both as repressive as well as power as 'power to', in the sense in which Hannah Arendt and Talcott Parsons used the term?
5. How would you relate the feminist conceptualization of patriarchy to the concept of hegemony?
6. A 'map projection' is a way of projecting the three-dimensional spherical earth on to a flat two-dimensional surface, such as the page of an atlas. Search the Internet for Peter's Projection, which is a map projection that produces a completely different map of the world than the one which we are accustomed to, which is called Mercator's Projection. How would you relate the issues raised by the debate over Peter's Projection to the discussion on hegemony above?

Reading List

Arendt, Hannah, 'What Is Authority', in *Between Past and Future* (London: Faber, 1961).

Barnes, Barry, 'Power', in Richard Bellamy (ed.), *Theories and Concepts of Politics* (Manchester, UK: Manchester University Press, 1993).

Bottomore, Tom (ed.), *A Dictionary of Marxist Thought* (Oxford: Blackwell Publishing, 1991).

Connolly, William, *The Terms of Political Discourse* (Oxford: Martin Robertson, 1983).

Dahl, Robert, *A Preface to Democratic Theory* (Chicago: University of Chicago Press, 1956).

Foucault, Michel, 'Power, Right, Truth', in Colin Gordon (ed.), *Power/Knowledge* (Brighton: Harvester, 1980).

———, 'Truth and Juridical Forms', James D. Faubion (ed.), *Essential Works of Foucault 1954–1984* (London: Penguin Books, 2000).

Held, David, 'Power and Legitimacy', in *Political Theory and the Modern State: Essays on State, Power and Democracy* (Stanford: Stanford University Press, 1989).

Hoy, David Couzens (ed.), 'Power, Repression, Progress', in *Foucault: A Critical Reader* (Oxford: Basil Blackwell, 1986).

Lukes, Steven, *Power A Radical View*, second edn (Basingstoke, UK: Palgrave Macmillan, 2005).

CHAPTER 11

Sovereignty

Krishna Menon

Chapter Outlines

Introduction

National and international politics today is dominated by the notion of sovereignty and contests over it. The debate also reflects the changing contours of the relationship between the state and civil society. Sovereignty according to its defendants, both in theory and in practice, aims at establishing order and clarity in what they describe as a turbulent and incoherent world. It is one of the central ideas of modernity and its antecedents can be traced back to changes that took place in Western history and politics around the 16th century A.D.

This chapter discusses the historical evolution of the concept of sovereignty and an attempt is made to locate it within the history and politics of Europe. It also looks at some significant theoretical formulations that shape our understanding of sovereignty, ranging from Bodin to Hobbes to Austin. The last section engages with the more contemporary debates questioning the validity of the concept of sovereignty in the context of a rapidly changing world economy and politics.

Historical Evolution of Sovereignty

The concept of sovereignty is relatively new, although in contemporary discourse it has an almost universal usage. In earlier civilizations, sovereignty would have meant little. Tribal communities in Africa, for instance, were primarily organized around the ties of lineage and kinship. China had a multi-state system with a very fluid relationship between the monarch and the feudal lords. Again, medieval Europe was certainly not divided into sovereign states. To understand sovereignty, therefore, we need to look at a particular set of social and economic conditions specific to Europe.

In medieval Europe, both the rulers and the ruled were governed by universal laws supposedly derived from the authority of God and the society was a patchwork of various overlapping political loyalties and allegiances that cut across geographically interwoven jurisdictions and political enclaves. In this maze, it was the Church that provided an overarching, organizational, and moral framework transcending both legal and political boundaries. Feudal Europe knew no difference between the domestic and external spheres of organization, nor was there any dividing line between the public and the private.

By the end of the 15th century, Europe comprised some 500 more or less independent political units. But this order was clearly in decline. A new set of social and economic conditions were emerging characterized by increasing trade. The manufacturing class was gaining in strength, and was supported by increasingly centralized monarchies. These, along with competent civil servants and hired armies, began to levy royal taxes, and individuals now no longer owed their allegiance to the overlord and their village.

The end of the 16th century saw further changes; the Renaissance led to a secularization of life and a corresponding decline in the authority of the Church. Reformation, counter-reformation and the wars of religion further facilitated the acceptance of a secular state. Papal sovereignty was undermined and this prepared the way for secular absolutism. The bloody Thirty Years' War came to an end with the Treaty of Westphalia in 1648. This led to the recognition of a religious stalemate in Europe. The economic practices of the new trading and manufacturing classes on the one hand, and the power of new science and technology on the other, effectively undermined the authority of the Church.

The decentralized political arrangements that characterized Europe, now replaced by the Westphalian state system, became a thing of the past. The latter came to be characterized by territorially bound sovereign states; each with its own centralized administration and a monopoly over the legitimate use of violence. A new form of political control and relocation of population and reorganization of territory facilitated the expansion of trade and growth of industry. The new form of state based on the notion of sovereignty redefined the idea of private property; it came to be understood as the right to exclude others from the possession of a commodity, be it land, labour or capital. Private and public spheres of life came to be demarcated very strongly. The royal court became the supreme authority in the public sphere and paternal authority took on this role within the family, thereby consolidating patriarchy. Laws supporting paternal authority and inheritance in the male line thus dovetailed into a new form of sovereign state.

The feudal state in Europe was replaced by the absolutist state based on the notion of absolute sovereignty, wherein the king/queen was believed to have absolute right over their domain, and acquisition of new territories was simply a matter of extending sovereignty. This later became the instrument through which colonial expansion was carried out.

Theories of Sovereignty

The sovereign state system in Europe emerged as a response to specific historical circumstances. By the 16th century, the Church in Europe was beginning to lose control over the state and societal structures since these were moving in a secular direction for a variety of reasons, some of which have already been discussed. Expanding avenues of trade, new forms of manufacturing industries, new developments in art, culture, philosophy, and, of course, a systematic expansion of scientific and technological base accompanied by a challenge of doctrinaire religion were the main components of the new cultural and political milieu of which the idea of sovereignty is a product.

There are two sides of sovereignty, internal and external. Internally, the state is considered to be sovereign and has supreme authority within its borders. This implies that no higher authority exists internally above the state to take any coercive or any other action. In its external dimension it implies that no state can interfere or dictate terms to any other state.

Feudal laws were undermined by Roman law, which was based on the simple but fundamental principle that a political community had the inherent power to exact unlimited obedience from its citizens. Machiavelli, writing in 1513–14, clearly revived Roman law.

He defined the state as an organization of force that ensures security of persons and property. However, it was Bodin and later Hobbes who articulated more sharply the contemporary understanding of sovereignty.

The theory of sovereignty typically conceives of the state as a structure with absolute power and authority in the society. In this formulation it has to address three separate but closely related issues: (*a*) the limits of sovereignty; (*b*) the location of sovereignty; and (*c*) the question of the relationship between state, sovereignty, and civil society. We find various answers to these questions; let us begin by considering Bodin's analysis.

Bodin's answers are to be found in *De la Republique* (1577). According to his basic thesis, a central authority should wield unlimited power. In the context of the deeply divided politics of France, this seemed the only way out. Such a centralized authority was advocated to steer France away from 'disorder' and hopefully create greater security and order. Such a power, he argued, should be endowed with sovereignty, that is, the supreme power over citizens and subjects unrestrained by law and unlimited in extension and duration. Bodin, however, accepted that the laws of God and nature on the one hand, and the customary laws of the land on the other, would limit the sovereign. There is even room in his conception for a pluralist view of the community consisting of associations like the family, church, market and the guild. These, he believed, would have their own life and organization. How this would be reconciled with his absolute notion of sovereignty is a question that remains unanswered.

The next set of answers to the questions on sovereignty come from Hobbes in his book, *The Leviathan* (1651). The backdrop of this book was the civil war in England. Hobbes did away with every limitation on sovereignty by insisting that every right of the people (except for the right to self-preservation) has to be given unto the sovereign. He suggested a contract in which individuals would agree to give up all their rights to the sovereign. The consequence of such a universal surrender of rights by people would be a 'multitude united in one Person'—a Leviathan. In Hobbes' formulation there would thus be no distinction between the society and the state as also between the state and the government. Groups in the community existed so long as they were sanctioned by the sovereign and allowed to exist.

According to Hobbes, human beings are basically selfish and competitive by nature. In order to demonstrate the need for an all-powerful state, he describes a hypothetical situation without the state—a 'state of nature'—where intensely selfish and competitive people would be fearful and distrustful of each other and life would become, to quote Hobbes, 'nasty, brutish and short'. Thus, life in the state of nature would be no better than a constant state of war, and individuals in this state, though free and equal, would be gripped by perpetual feelings of insecurity. The only way out would be to voluntarily give up their conditions of equality and autonomy to create a sovereign with absolute powers. This sovereign would guarantee protection to all by enforcing laws. No authority, religious or moral, should limit the sovereign. Nor would religion or natural and customary law have any force unless they are consented to by the sovereign. Hobbes, thus, responded to both the anarchy within England and to the need for security and order felt by the emerging trading classes by arguing for an absolute sovereign who would be beyond challenge.

Political absolutism was revised by Locke's framework that was based on a reinterpretation of natural law as a claim to innate, inalienable rights inherent in each individual. The primary purpose of the state and society for Locke was the protection of these individual rights. Locke argued that governments are held in trust by the people and derive legitimacy from their consent, given only in return for adequate protection of individual rights. Or else, the government would lose its authority to rule. Sovereign power, Locke seems to imply, finally rested in the people. Hence, he argued that state power needed to be circumscribed by devices such as representative government and a constitutional framework. He was clearly uncomfortable with the idea of absolute sovereignty and articulated the scepticism of the now stronger English bourgeoisie vis-à-vis an unchallenged sovereign. His writings represented the desires of this class for greater freedom and autonomy, which would be possible only if the state's sovereignty could be kept in check and the state made accountable.

This discomfort with handing over sovereign powers to the state while claiming that people have the ultimate sovereignty is referred to as the 'paradox of sovereignty' by James Buchanan. Jean Hampton (1988) refers to this dilemma and illustrates it with the example of babysitters who are hired to supervise a group of unruly children and then it turns out that the former are themselves unruly, making the supervision useless. The relationship between the citizens and the modern nation-state is somewhat like this: political institutions are created because people cannot govern themselves, but the assumption of the political regime that is created thereafter is that it is the people who rule. In such a situation, what really is the point of creating a sovereign state that is expected to rule? Of course, the answer provided by conventional political theory is that this relationship between the citizens and the modern nation state is based on the idea of tacit consent. Jean Hampton is, however, not entirely persuaded by this and prefers to use the term 'convention consent', which she says is the consent extended to a sovereign nation-state, but not sufficient to extend moral legitimacy in full. Authority exercised by elected office holders would be acceptable only if the basis of the exercise of such an authority is rational and moral, or else, Hampton argues that 'convention consent' to the regime would not be extended.

Rousseau in his book *Social Contract* (1762) begins with the assumption of a community of citizens united by a commitment to collective good, distinct from the private interests of its members. This collective good was characterized as the general will, and it endowed the state with absolute power over all its members.

Taking the arguments on sovereignty to a new direction, Rousseau argued that all individuals in the political community should be involved in law making. Thus, it would be the people themselves who would be the sovereign authority, making the laws by which they are governed. Hence, in Rousseau's scheme of affairs, there was no distinction between the state and the community or between the government and the people. Rousseau, like Hobbes, held that state sovereignty would be unlimited and indivisible, but unlike Hobbes, Rousseau does not distinguish between the state and the body politic, thus reducing the government to a mere commission.

While appearing to agree on several issues, Hobbes and Rousseau also say completely different things, and it would be interesting to evaluate them as representing two opposing ends of the debate on sovereignty. A criticism common to both would be the potentially tyrannical implications of their projects. In Hobbes' framework, the state was accorded an all-powerful position with respect to the community, but according to Rousseau, it was the community that was accorded a similar status vis-à-vis the individual.

Many questions remained unresolved. Once the sovereign made laws, were the citizens ever entitled to disobey these laws? Was the basis of law, moral authority or did it rest on the state's sovereign coercive power? These unanswered questions led to the enunciation of a fairly simple framework within the notion of sovereignty generally known as the legal theory of sovereignty. John Austin, the English utilitarian philosopher best represents it. For Austin, the state was a legal order in which a clearly determinate authority would be the ultimate source of power and be habitually obeyed while the sovereign state would be immune to the command of others. This sovereign would have unlimited authority, and the moral worth of the laws would be irrelevant. All that matters would be the effectiveness of the laws. Laws are conceptualized as the command of the sovereign, who would be responsible for formulating all laws, direct as well as indirect.

Pluralist critics like Laski have tried to limit the monistic assumptions of the legal theory of sovereignty advanced by Austin by pointing that laws do not emanate from a single source as the command of the sovereign. Rather, laws are to be seen as an expression of the multiple associations that make up the community. Pluralists, in keeping with their democratic orientation, argue that no law can be above the scrutiny of the individual citizen who has a moral obligation to obey only those laws that are in keeping with the tenets of justice.

Despite over three centuries of theoretical engagement with the notion of sovereignty, it still remains a contested concept. The location of sovereignty is a keenly debated question. The monistic position has been criticized for being unsuitable for the requirements of a democratic polity. Most of the theories that have been examined so far have conceived sovereignty as an attribute of the state and have ignored its relationship with the civil society. The other drawback of these theories is that they tend to be divorced from the historical context from which they actually emerge. Because of this the theories appear un-real and as an exercise in abstraction.

One theoretical presentation that stands apart is, however, Marx's. For him, the claims of the sovereign state representing the general interests of the society had to be seen as an illusion that masks the reality of a state that expresses the will of private property. Marx disagreed with the view that the sovereign state represented public power and public will. According to him, it is a structure representing particular interests, economic processes, and institutions.

This brings us to a discussion on the important function of a sovereign state which are as follows:

The most obvious function of the modern state endowed with sovereignty would be the organization of physical space. Sovereignty is exercised within a clearly defined territory.

This, in turn, reinforces the territorial conception of community. This function is linked with the economic responsibilities of the modern state. Besides, the sovereign state is also charged with the responsibility of securing an organized market, defend private property, and the resulting property relations. Such a sovereign state is also responsible for levying taxes and erecting a legal order that would facilitate all these activities.

The sovereign state in Europe also became the vehicle for cementing cultural identities within the framework of a state, thus creating a nation-state. National sovereignty came to be seen as the defining principle of political organization and the world as consisting of political units, i.e. each state with supreme authority enjoying allegiance of its citizens and possessing unlimited powers within its territory and over its resources. This idea was initially applied only to the European context, but eventually societies in Asia and Africa also began to articulate similar claims. Today, of course, it is an idea inscribed in the United Nations Charter. In fact, today we live in a world where all sovereign states are considered to be equal and independent of outside authority in matters of control of territory and population. Territorial integrity and legal equality are considered to be the hallmark of sovereign states.

The state system continues to perform two other very vital functions: military protection and legitimation. But nuclear weapons, especially since their proliferation, have been able to overcome the notion of the sovereign nation-state to a great extent, especially in the context of the fear of these weapons falling into the hands of non-state actors and groups. It is true that national borders are no longer defensive.

Critics of the concept of sovereignty point to the emergence of federal and decentralized governance patterns that have emerged in most states, accompanied by an elaborate system of checks and balances. They wonder where the concept of sovereignty can be located internally under such circumstances. Externally, they point to numerous international laws and organizations that have considerably limited the sovereignty of the states. Besides these questions is, of course, the whole issue of compatibility between the democratic ethos that most nation-states seek to uphold and the absolutist claims of the concept of sovereignty.

Charles R. Beitz draws our attention to the issues that emerge while applying the concept of sovereignty in the context of international affairs. In the modern context, sovereignty has a dual reference: first, to the constitution of political and legal authority within the boundaries of the state; and second, with reference to the state in relation to the other states and agents in the international environment. Beitz is of the opinion that this duality emerged primarily in the context of the European states, quest for effective independence from the Pope. Several problems, however, emerge in the context of external sovereignty, for instance, disagreements about the nature and character of international law and the extent to which it could be binding on states is fairly common. In the face of increasing economic interdependence and political integration, the concept of external sovereignty does appear to be of limited applicability. The concept of external sovereignty seems further limited when applied to the context of disputes about rights and duties of states and their citizens with respect to the rest of the world.

As a normative ideal, the idea of external sovereignty advocates a world political system organized into separate states which recognize each other's political independence and respect each other's rights to conduct their internal affairs without deliberate outside interference. In an increasingly integrated and functionally complex international system the application of the idea of external sovereignty is problematic. An example that Beitz gives should illustrate the nature of the problem effectively: intervention by State A (on the basis of the concurrence of some recognized international agency) in the affairs of State B (on the basis of the latter's violation of internationally accepted norms of human rights and dignity). This immediately raises the possibility of State B objecting to the intervention on the grounds that it has domestic jurisdiction over which it has sovereign powers.

Beitz identifies four possible responses to this dilemma:

(*a*) One extreme point of reaction would be to deny the consideration of any ethical or moral principles when it comes to the pursuit of national interest undertaken by a sovereign state.

(*b*) The second would be what Beitz has characterized as the cosmopolitical response, seen in the writings of Leo Tolstoy and others. They argue that there is a need, under all circumstances, to uphold cosmopolitical morality even if it conflicts with narrow sectional definitions of domestic welfare.

(*c*) The third position accepts the hypothetical possibility of such a conflict but denies its possibility in reality. This response is built on the argument that an international convention of respect for the sovereignty of states is the best way of ensuring respect for the rights, entitlements, and dignity of the individual citizens of the state.

(*d*) At the other end of the spectrum is the communitarian position that argues against global standards of social value and worth. According to them, the determination of what is good or how a human being ought to be treated cannot be the result of global, universal values. Instead, they recommend referring to the values held in esteem by consensus within a particular community. Such a position is not to be misunderstood as advocating national chauvinism; it should not descend into an obtuse and complacent position but should be open to self-criticism and correction. Despite this, however, the truth is that conflict over morality in the context of international affairs are bound to emerge and have a bearing on the issue of sovereignty.

The Changing World and the Concept of Sovereignty

In the world that we live in, most of the functions that the sovereign state is expected to perform are being subjected to new limitations and considerations. Economic functions have, by far, been the most important, and it is these that have undergone a major transformation. National economies are no longer insulated spaces and have become very interdependent; processes of production, exchange, circulation, and consumption are all inter-linked. Technological changes and the increasing integration of international finances have further facilitated this process. Transnational corporations are the most significant agents of these new changes. Immanuel Wallerstein describes this as a new stage in the development of the 'world system' whose defining characteristic is the transnational scope of capital.

Wallerstein argues that a 'world economy' has been in the making for some time now, running parallel to the growth of capitalism and the formation of the modern state. In the earlier stages of the development of capitalism, national economies and nation states were decisive in the internationalization of economic activity. In the contemporary world, however, systemic interaction seems to have acquired a dynamic of its own. Wallerstein visualizes the world system as universal, and by virtue of its universality and regularity, he argues, it exercises a constraining influence on all the subsystems, including the nation states.

We cannot understand the functions performed by the states purely in terms of requirements of global economic integration. The fact is that individual states and the state system as a whole retain a degree of autonomy, although it might fall short of the attributes of a sovereign state. It would not be wrong to say that there are, in fact, two competing systems in today's world: the global market on the one hand, and the sovereign state system on the other.

Paul Hirst examines more closely the issue of sovereignty in the context of a rapidly changing world characterized by many as a globalized world. Hirst wishes to make a distinction between an internationalized economy and a globalized economy. In the former system, companies continue to trade from their bases in distinct national settings; whereas in the latter, national policies are redundant. In fact, the state itself is so because it is understood that the global market forces would provide governance and solution to all the problems.

Hirst argues that what we are witnessing today is a highly internationalized economic system. In such a system national policies remain viable and in fact, are essential so as to preserve the distinct national styles and strengths of the economies. Thus, from this perspective the nation-state and its most defining characteristic—sovereignty—remain essential and relevant.

Those who see the contemporary world as a globalized economy argue that it is only the global market and transnational companies that have relevance and it is to them that the task of governance should be handed over. They contend that global market forces will replace the need for any form of public governance and thus the rationale for the state and by that implication of its sovereignty is undermined.

Hirst suggests that a world economy with a high degree of international trade and investment is not necessarily a globalized economy. In such a system, he observes, nation-states and forms of international regulation created and sustained by nation-states have a crucial role to play especially in providing governance of the economy. So long as nation-states remain important, sovereignty would remain relevant, although he suggests that its role and manifestation have altered.

The internationalized economy as Hirst describes, has mechanisms of international governance and needs re-regulation; he argues that for all this to happen, the role of the nation-state is pivotal. Nation-states, therefore, have sovereignty but not in the sense of being the sole governing power able to impose outcomes on all dimensions of policy within a territory, but as loci from which forms of governance can be proposed, legitimated and monitored. Nation-states continue to have sovereignty, albeit of a changed nature, because now they are one class of power and political agency, extending from the world to the local level.

The nation-state's centrality over determining the relationship of population to its territory remains sovereign more or else in its earlier form. People are still identified by the boundaries of the nation-state within which they live, and so its territorial limits continue to determine citizenship. It is only the very highly skilled and educated and the very impoverished, who are desperate to flee their poverty, who are able to move. For the bulk of the people such mobility is really not an option, although there is tremendous mobility of finance and greater integration of communication, information and entertainment.

Hirst maintains that states remain sovereign not in the sense of being all-powerful and omni-competent within their fixed territories, but are sovereign because they police the borders and can claim to represent the people within the borders more so if the system is a credible democracy. In the changed scenario that Hirst is drawing our attention to, sovereignty is definitely ceded to supra-state agencies created by the nation-states themselves. However, even as the nation-state is doing so it is also acquiring new roles in the context of legitimating and supporting the authorities that they have created by grants of sovereignty that the states have themselves made.

Thus, sovereignty in this changed context is of significance as a distinguishing characteristic of the nation-state because the state now has a legitimate role in transferring power or sanctioning new powers to agencies both 'above' and 'below' it. This happens when the state determines along with other states, the creation of new international agencies and bodies to re-regulate trade, investment and other related issues—thus, the state uses its sovereignty to create agencies above it. Similarly, through constitutional ordering within its own territory, it restructures the relationship of power and authority between central, regional, and local governments. Thus, it uses its sovereignty to determine the re-ordering of power and authority below it.

Hirst, thus, senses a paradox: the more the world economy has been internationalized (as opposed to globalized), the greater is the need for the sovereign nation-state, understood not in its traditional guise of undisputed sovereign power, but as an agency that by virtue of its sovereignty can guarantee the stability of the global economy.

The shift towards world government is cited by many as a vital reason for the erosion of state sovereignty. The example cited more often than not is the emergence of the European Union (EU). While this is an interesting development that is bound to have a strong impact on the state system, the capacity of the EU to coordinate and mobilize military forces and the potential of its members remains rather limited. This is very clear from the EU's response to the wars in Yugoslavia in the early 1990s.

The other challenge to the sovereign state system comes from the development of what is often referred to as a global civil society. A rather amorphous concept, it probably refers to a range of new social movements and public opinion that cut across national boundaries, and work through international non-governmental organizations. Bodies such as Amnesty International, International Greenpeace and even the International Football Federation (FIFA) are apt illustrations. Needless to say, it would be a mistake to exaggerate the influence of these bodies.

Conclusion

In the context of a rapidly changing world, sovereignty seems to have become a redundant notion. It is important to remember at this point that the concept of state and sovereignty are rooted in a particular historical and socio-political context. The re-evaluation of the concept of sovereignty emerges from the needs of an altered context. Sovereignty has acquired all the dimensions of a framework that we might refer to as a totalizing discourse not allowing space for other ways of conceptualizing the state and civil society and the arrangements of power through social institutions.

In the existing framework, sovereignty has come to be seen as necessary and natural. To challenge the concept of sovereignty means to challenge one of the foundational truths of our times. Power has systematically been centralized within state structures and there is acceptance of this as a natural fact. Ironically, even those who oppose existing oppressive states or seek secession are merely hoping to create their own state structures in the future rather than thinking of any alternative ways of social arrangements.

Points for Discussion

1. If sovereignty is unique to the modern nation-state then how did states prior to the modern nation-state assert themselves? For instance, how did the state system in ancient India evolve and assert its authority?
2. Imagine a country in the neighbourhood in the grip of a horrible natural calamity. What should the role of our armed forces be? Would our country be guilty of violating the principle of sovereignty if our army were to march into the neighbouring country with humanitarian relief and aid?
3. All of us depend on the Internet for communication, leisure, information and entertainment. Sitting in our country it is possible to chat with our friends and family living far away. The Indian state has very little control over our forays into the Internet. What implications do you think all this has for the concept of sovereignty and the position of the modern nation-state?
4. Satellite radio and television have changed our entertainment patterns and our tastes in cinema, fashion, music and so on. Nation-states no longer have a monopoly over questions of culture and identity. What do you think is the future for the nation-state in this context?
5. Terrorism and nuclear proliferation have threatened the idea of a sovereign nation-state like nothing else has. Discuss.

Reading List

Hampton, Jean, *Hobbes and the Social Contract Tradition* (Cambridge, UK: Cambridge University Press, 1988).

Held, David, *Political Theory Today* (Cambridge, UK: Polity Press, 1989).

Hinsley, F. H., *Sovereignty* (Cambridge, UK: Cambridge University Press, 1986).

Wolff, Jonathan, *Introduction to Political Philosophy* (Oxford and New York: Oxford University Press, 1996).

CHAPTER 12

The State

Swaha Das

Chapter Outlines

Introduction

The ubiquity and the power of the state shapes the conditions within which we lead our lives. Our interaction with the state begins much before we gain awareness of it. The registration of our birth, travel on roads, the police, board exams and certificates, voter identity cards and passports—these are a few instances of our routine encounters with the state, which point to the pervasiveness of the modern state in our daily lives. The state compels us to do certain things, and to refrain from doing others. Besides, it aims to provide us with basic protection against an attack on ourselves and our possessions, and also restrains and regiments us in several ways. It provides us with a wide range of benefits: health care, education, roads, telephone, parks, movies, etc. Christopher Morris, pointing to the omnipresence of the state in our lives, says in an adaptation of Leon Trotsky's quip about war: 'You may not be interested in the state, but the state is certainly interested in you.'

What is the State?

Most of us are members of a state and live within the borders of one. Statehood today refers not merely to a set of institutions, but also to a body of attitudes, practices and codes of behaviour that we follow consciously and willingly at times, and unconsciously and unwillingly at other times. These codes of behaviour could encompass obedience of state laws, obligatory voting in elections, compulsory military training, or conscription. Some political thinkers maintain that the state is the most important concern of modern political theory. Concepts that we study in political theory—rights, democracy, equality, liberty—are based on the relationship between state and those living within it. For this reason we need to be familiar with the idea and functions of the state.

Any discussion about the state would refer to the actual functioning of the institutions of the state, as well as to what the state is obliged to do. It is often assumed that the state refers to the government, but as we shall see in the course of this chapter, the state and the government are not coincidental. Modern political thinkers of different political persuasions would agree with Max Weber, the German sociologist, that the one common element of all modern states is the monopoly over the legitimate use of force within a common territory. Weber also stresses on three more important elements: territoriality, monopoly of the means of physical violence, and legitimacy.

What does legitimacy mean? Legitimacy is derived from the Latin verb *legitimare*, which means to legitimate, and signifies rightfulness in a broad sense. It confers a binding or authoritative character on an order, thus transforming power into authority. (See Chapter 9 for the difference between power and authority.) The state has the authority to ensure that its laws are obeyed and the power to punish those who disobey. Authority may be of various kinds, but here we are concerned with the question of political authority, that of the state over us. For robber instance, can have the power to harm us, and yet have no authority because his power is neither legally nor morally rightful. What gives the state this right to rule over us, and why are we obliged to obey the state? This is a problem that has preoccupied several political thinkers, and is known as *political obligation*.

An obligation is a duty to act in a particular way. Political obligation necessitates obedience to the laws of the state. We are often made to accept the laws of the state as binding on us, be it the traffic rules or the laws regarding marriage, trade, and property. We obey more the state because it promotes our happiness than any alternative political organization. Alternatively, we could justify political obligation on the grounds that we ourselves have consented to the state on the basis of a social contract, and it is this very reason that binds us to obey the laws of the state. We shall examine these later in the chapter, but for now, let us return to our discussion on the state.

The Montevideo Convention on Rights and Duties of States in 1933 put forth what is widely regarded as the classic legal definition of the state. According to it, states must possess the following a permanent population, a defined territory, and a government capable of maintaining effective control over the corresponding territory and of conducting international relations with other states. Recognition by other states was often seen to be crucial because it implied acceptance into the international community. However, these definitions are not absolute. For instance, international law does not necessitate settled boundaries or frontiers to accord recognition to the state.

One of the most important things to remember is that when we talk about the state, we are referring to a whole gamut of different organized institutions that are connected to one another and enjoy some cohesion. That is, the state is organizationally highly differentiated as well as centralized. Thus, it is not a monolithic structure; it consists of a set of institutions and organizations. The three arms of the modern state are the judiciary, the executive, and the legislature—each different, but with a certain level of cohesion with each other. The different arms of the state exercise the authority that they have, not on their own behalf, but on the basics of the authority they are entitled to as part of the state. The government refers to the administrative organ of the state and is constrained by the constitution of the state. The government may change but the state persists. This is the reason why the American governments are called administrations—the Clinton administration, the Reagan administration, etc.

The Modern State

Before getting on with the discussion on the modern state, let us briefly look at its conceptual history. In political theory, questions are often raised as what concepts like state, liberty, equality, justice and so on mean. A particular concept could have several different, sometimes overlapping conceptions. Conceptual history tries to examine the different meanings that a concept has had over the ages. Therefore, the question that needs to be asked is, did the word 'state' mean the same thing to people in other ages and times as it does to us right now? Conceptual history suggests that words may not change, but their significance does, depending on historical and social contexts. One could cite several examples. For instance, the words patriot, revolution, and rights, have all had different meanings in different times. As Quentin Skinner, a historian of political thought tells us, when we read some of the classic texts and come across the word state, we need to understand the meaning of the word according to what it meant at the time the text was written.

Thus, how we interpret and evaluate the state as a concept depends on the values that are derived from the political, cultural, religious, and economic contexts of a particular time. The word 'state' derives from the Latin word *stare* (to stand) and more specifically from *status* (a standing or condition). Clearly, we need to think how this relates to the function or the role of the state today. Did the state always mean the same set of institutions as it does now?

In this chapter, when we use the word 'state', it refers to the modern state, a form of political organization that could be said to have evolved in early modern Europe, and was transmitted primarily through colonialism to other parts of the world. Thus, the modern state and the modern system of states have not been permanent and universal features of human history. Further, we can say that the trajectory of the development of the state in other parts of the world has been very different from that in Europe.

Many political philosophers point out that the idea of the modern state could be traced to the late medieval ages, especially in the writings of Nicolo Machiavelli, who is often credited with first using the concept of the state—*stato*—to refer to a territorial sovereign government in his work *Il Principe* or *The Prince*, which was published in 1532. Skinner points out that Machiavelli's use of the word *lo stato* was different from the use of the word 'state' in modern times. When he used the word for the first time, it did not have the impersonal standing as it does now. Rather, the state then meant that it was *someone's* state: the prince's or the monarch's.

Machiavelli's treatise was intended as a guide to the ruler for the maintenance of political power. It attained infamy for advising the prince to do whatever is necessary to maintain power. What is important for us here is that when Machiavelli talks about political power, he begins and ends with one individual: the prince, who is the sovereign. So, the state meant the prince's state. In Western political theory, it is with Hobbes that the theorization of power moves on to an abstract, non-human entity, the modern sovereign state.

What is distinctive about the modern state in terms of its difference from earlier kingships is the distinction between the rulers, and the office and institutions they occupy. Thus, the modern state is characterized by its impersonal standing. The current holders of power in the government do not constitute the state. The state exists before they come to power and continues to be there after they leave. It aims to gain autonomy from the contending parties or groups that come to hold political power. It is for this reason that the state is said to be abstracted from the power holders. The modern state is a public order distinct from and located above both the ruler and the ruled.

The emergence of the modern state in Europe is linked to the differentiation of various spheres of people's lives. It identifies the political sphere, and is at its apex. It is concerned only with the political aspects of the lives of the people living within it, though it is debatable what the realm of the political is. Is the political concerned only with formal institutions of power? The distinction between civil society and the state is based on the recognition that individuals who are subject to the power of the state also have capacities and interests of a non-political nature. In the 14th and 15th centuries, political power was held by several different sources. These included the Church, the king, and the feudal lords. There was no clear differentiation of political functions. The same set of political functions: declaration of war, collection of taxes, etc., could be performed by different sources of authority. The Church and the king had their own armies and they both had the power to declare war. The Peace of Westphalia at the end of the Thirty Years War in 1648 concluded a series of religious wars among the main European powers, and led to an undermining of the power of the Church, giving the king authority over his own realm. It led to the strengthening of a new conception of international law based on the principle that all states have an equal right to self-determination. The earlier dispersed political authority was replaced by what would eventually lead to centralized modern authority, and the state came to be the source of political authority. David Held identifies the following features of the Westphalian model:

1. The world consists of, and is divided by, sovereign states that recognize no superior authority.
2. The processes of law-making, the settlement of disputes, and law enforcement are largely in the hands of individual states.
3. International law is oriented towards the establishment of minimal rules of co-existence; the creation of enduring relationships is an aim, but only to the extent that it allows state objectives to be met.
4. Responsibility for wrongful acts across the border is a 'private matter' concerning only those affected.
5. All states are regarded as equal before the law, but legal rules do not take account of asymmetries of power.
6. Differences among states are often settled by force; the principle of effective power holds sway. Virtually no legal fetters exist to curb the resort to force; international legal standards afford only minimal protection.
7. The collective priority of all states should be to minimize the impediments to state freedom.

Sovereignty refers to the state being the ultimate source of political authority within the territory under its jurisdiction. There are two aspects of sovereignty—internal and external. Internal sovereignty refers to the fact that within its boundaries, there are no authorities higher than the state. The state is supreme, and a citizen cannot appeal against the state to any other authority. The state has the right to make binding decisions upon its citizens and upon those who enter its territory.

External sovereignty of the state refers to the recognition that other states accord to a particular state, and the acceptance that the state can speak for its citizens in international affairs. External sovereignty implies the autonomy and independence of the state in the international sphere. The sovereignty of the state can be challenged in many ways; the state might surreptitiously lose its sovereignty despite having voluntarily entered into international treaties, or other states might intervene in the affairs of the state on the grounds of a deemed violation of human rights, the possession of weapons of mass destruction, etc.

The state's monopoly over the legitimate use of coercion is reflected in the institutions of the armed forces, the paramilitary forces, and the police. These the reflect the immense power that the state has over people's lives. Imprisonment, death penalty, declaration of war—all these involve the use of violence, and only the state is entitled to the legitimate use of these powers. That is why the state is said to have a monopoly over the legitimate use of violence. The coercive institutions help to maintain the supremacy or the sovereignty of the state, and to ensure the observance of laws and the maintenance of order when these are considered to be infringed.

The modern state is territorially based. This means that the state exercises its authority within its territorial borders which are acknowledged by other states. This acknowledgement distinguishes the state from other forms of political organizations, where governance is over people rather than over land, and people allegiances are not territorially determined. So, one's rights and duties depend on one's place in the hierarchical social order within a tribe or clan or other forms of ethnic organization. For instance, in India, one's location in the hierarchical structure of the caste system still tends to determine one's rights and duties.

The modern state has no authority outside its borders, and no other state possesses authority within another state's borders. Within the boundaries of the state, there is a single system of governance, distinct from others that operate externally. The territorial foundations of the state distinguish it from other types of organizations and associations, which could be religious. The demands for statehood by groups are often for the recognition of the claim to territory. One of the most tragic, poignant, and complex struggles over the claim to territory in the recent past has been the Palestine–Israeli conflict. The Palestinian struggle for statehood could be a struggle for the recognition of the claim to land.

What the State is Not: Civil Society and the Nation

The state is distinct from the civil society. The former represents coercion, while the latter is said to be based on voluntary participation. Do you think it is desirable that the two spheres be kept distinct? States vary in the amount of independence that they permit to other social institutions. This determines the nature of the state as totalitarian or liberal. A state that seeks to fuse the distinction between its sphere of activity and that of the society is called a totalitarian state, because it seeks to intervene in the totality of human life. A totalitarian state might supervise what books you read, what your political views are, and even what careers you opt for.

The distinction between the nation and the state is particularly important in view of the struggles by many nations for statehood. When we talk about international relations, we are actually referring to inter-state relations. A nation could be defined as community feeling among people who recognize that they are distinct from other communities and wish to control their own affairs. This distinction could be based on their possession of a common language, religion, political values and attitudes, a sense of having done things together in the past, and a desire to do things together in the future. The entire population in same states share this feeling, giving rise to the term 'nation-state'. However, this is not the case with all the states in the world today. So, the nation and the state do not coincide. There are people who feel part of the same nation, and are spread across different states. The Kurdish people, for instance, are spread across Iran, Iraq, Syria, and Turkey and consider themselves to be a nation. A question that concerns contemporary political philosophers is whether all the people who consider themselves to be nations can demand statehood and whether they are entitled to statehood. (See Chapter 17 for a detailed discussion on these issues.)

Justifying the State

Justifying the state has often involved imagining a situation without one common institution protecting our lives and property and punishing us for transgressions. Whether such a situation is desirable or not is dependent on our views on human nature.

Human Nature

The necessity, or otherwise, of the state is often based on beliefs concerning human nature. While one could not automatically move from a premise about human nature to a theory of the state, there is usually some kind of relationship between human nature and the structure of political arrangements. One could even say that those who have argued for a strong centralizing tendency in the state, and those who have argued for greater powers of the state are usually those who view human nature with distrust. Thomas Hobbes viewed human beings as naturally selfish and went on to argue that the necessary solution to this problem was absolute sovereignty. Gandhi had a much more optimistic and generous view of human nature, and believed that though human beings were a combination of good and bad qualities, they could become good and act responsibly even in the absence of the coercive apparatus of the state.

The anarchist response to the state was that the state was an unnecessary evil that curtailed the human spirit by imposing externally devised rules and regulations on it. The only laws that human beings should admit to are those that they have made for themselves. The anarchists could be said to believe in a theory of society without state rule. Peter Kropotkin, the Russian anarchist believed in the supreme goodness of human nature, and said that any divergence from that goodness was due to the insidious influence of state authority and exploitative capitalism. He believed that any external authority was corrupt by definition.

The State of Nature and the Social Contract

Imagine a situation without the existence of a government, without a defined territory over which the government operated and without a centralized authority having a monopoly over the legitimate use of coercion. A situation in the absence of the state is called the state of nature. This is a situation where the laws that operate are natural laws, that is, laws not made by human beings, but which could be intuited by human reasoning. For Hobbes, given his assumption of human nature as selfish, the state of nature was a state of war of all against all. Each person is on his own, in the sense that there is no higher authority with the power to command people's obedience, or with the responsibility of protecting their interests or possessions. Given this situation, it is most likely that people would opt for some form of centralized political authority. The issue then was regarding the kind of political authority that individuals in a state of nature would agree to.

Hobbes argued that this kind of a situation necessitated the setting up of a common power to protect us from one another and from external threat. This implied that the state emerged from a contract that individuals in a state of nature consented to in order to protect themselves from one another and from external threat. The social contract argument asserts that the state emerged from our individual consent, and only our consent can bind us to obedience. This brings us back to the question of political obligation. We are bound to obey the laws of the state most of the time because it has emerged from our consent, which is voluntarily given. John Locke, Jean-Jacques Rousseau, and Immanuel Kant used the concept of the social contract and came up with different answers on what the government is obligated to do and what the citizens are obliged to obey.

The social contract is not a historical event. Critics of the social contract have argued that since it is fictitious, it has no moral or political force. To this, Kant replied that the idea of the contract is important even if no actual contract exists. He put forth the idea that if an arrangement is such that free individuals could not have agreed to it, then it is unjust.

Let us take an example. Would any free individual have agreed to be a slave or to be considered an untouchable? Since it seems highly unlikely that any free, sane individual would agree to this proposition, the institutions of slavery and untouchability are unjust. The social contract argument bases political obligation on our consent to the state. This consent could be expressed or it could be tacit.

Utilitarianism

We can argue that the state is justified because of its utility in bringing about greater happiness to a greater number of people than any alternative political arrangement. We would then be concurring with utilitarianism, which has two basic claims: first, that human happiness and well-being are important; and second, that we assess an act purely by its consequences. This is why utilitarianism is a form of consequentialism. Early utilitarian philosophers like Jeremy Bentham and James Mill believed that the consequences one should consider were the happiness and unhappiness that one's actions would cause. If we put the two claims together, we could say that utilitarianism aims at bringing about a state of affairs that results in the greatest happiness of the greatest number. For the utilitarian, the state is justified on the grounds that it brings about greater and more happiness than any alternative political arrangement.

The justification of the state in this case is based on its utility, and not on consent as the social contract argument would assert. Sometimes, the greatest happiness of the greatest number could be that the number matters, and not each individual. There could be instances wherein unqualified utilitarianism would lead to a situation where the greatest happiness of the greatest number is based on the sacrifice of an individual's rights. Liberalism would, however, find the above instance unacceptable. It would base its claim on the state showing equal respect to every individual and respecting each individual's rights.

The Neutral State: Liberalism

The Indian Constitution is characterized as liberal since it recognizes that the individual citizen is entitled to equal rights and to equality before law. Liberals believe that the state is a neutral arbiter between different competing interests and stands to realize what is called the common good in society. The neutrality of the state is linked to the idea of the moral equality of individuals, which could be based on any of the following grounds: their ability to think, feel, or make choices. The emphasis here is on capacity or ability, and not the actual exercise. So, even if we do not actually exercise these capacities right now, we do possess them as individuals. This makes the liberals argue that individuals are entitled to equal respect from the state. Respect for an individual implies respect for his/her ability to make choices, as well as for the choices. Some might argue that individuals differ in their intellectual prowess, in their possession of wealth and strength of character. Given these differences, should they be entitled to equal respect from the state? Liberals would respond by saying that these are not sufficient grounds for the state to treat an individual as inferior to others. Citizens are entitled to equal respect and concern from the state because the state is committed to respect the moral equality of citizens, which means non-discrimination and impartiality at the very first level. The state should not arbitrarily discriminate in its treatment of one citizen against other.

Liberals believe that the state should seek to ensure that each individual has the freedom to exercise his/her choice. The best state of affairs, according to them, is the set of rules or the framework that would best ensure that the government treats its citizens with equal respect, and not impose any conception of what good life is. Thus, for liberals, the state is concerned with rules that would enable individuals to pursue their own ideas of what they think is good life, so long as the freedom of others is not infringed upon.

What do you think the entitlement to equal respect and consideration implies? According to Ronald Dworkin, liberal equality could have two implications: first, equal distribution of certain goods and opportunities. One instance of this could be the principle of one person, one vote. Another example could be the equality of opportunity. The second conception of liberal equality would challenge the identical distribution to all concerned without taking into account what their needs are and what kind of situation they find themselves in. Liberals are divided on the extent of state obligations. Should it be concerned only with the maintenance of law and order or should it also be concerned with redistribution of resources, and with the welfare of its citizens—should the state be a welfare state? Should the state attempt to reserve seats in educational institutions and in employment for individuals who come from deprived groups, groups that have suffered systemic discrimination in the past? Does this violate the liberal state's commitment to treat its citizens as entitled to equal respect and concern, or is in consonance with this principle? On what grounds do liberals justify these provisions? (See Chapters 3–6 for further discussion on these issues.)

The Class State: Marxism

The liberal view of the state as a neutral arbiter among conflicting interests is challenged by Marxists. Marxism offers a method of evaluating the idea and practice of the state in its day-to-day affairs. To understand their view of the state, it is important that we begin by explaining the materialist conception of history or historical materialism, which assumes that human history progresses through contradictions or 'dialectics' at the level of the production of goods in society.

Karl Marx and his collaborator Friedrich Engels borrowed the concept of the dialectical method from the German philosopher, G. W. Friedrich Hegel. For the ancient Greeks, the dialectic was a form of argumentation through question and answer, and thus, an argumentative technique involving contradiction. Hegel maintained that history was the development and conflict of abstract principles that included cultures, religions, and philosophies. There was always tension between the present state of affairs and what it was becoming; thus, every state of affairs contained within itself the seeds of its own destruction and transformation to a higher stage. Each successive stage was a progress beyond those that had preceded and contained elements from them. This could be represented by the 'thesis' which is opposed by the 'antithesis', which consequently produced a new 'synthesis'. Marx took up the concept of the dialectic, but instead of abstract principles, he focused on the changing economic base of the society—and the social classes to which it gave rise. For Marx, conflicts between these classes were the causes of the changes taking place in human history.

Historical materialism maintains that the key to changes in society lies in the way human beings produce goods in common. Production is the real foundation or the 'base' of society. History is the record of increasingly sophisticated ways of producing goods. Developments in production lead to a change in the economic structure which, in turn, leads to changes in the 'superstructure', that is, political, religious, legal, and philosophical realms, accordingly. Production itself has two aspects: the material and the social. The former refers to the technology and tools used in the process of production and the latter to property relations, and to the division of society into two classes: those who own the means of production—land and the instruments of production—and those who are the direct producers: slaves, peasants, or wage labourers. The exploitation of the direct producers by the owners of the means of production leads to conflicts between the two classes. The economic structure, therefore, determines whether the state exists and if so, what kind of state it is.

Marx's ideas of the state developed as a critique of Hegel's political philosophy. According to Hegel, the entire process of human history was the progress of the absolute 'Spirit' towards self-realization, that is, towards a determinant endpoint. In his *Philosophy of Right* (1821), he portrayed the state as an ethical ideal and the highest expression of human freedom, which was realized as human beings acted in accordance with their reason. Human beings were truly free when they realized that instead of allowing the forces of history to control them, they could take control of themselves. If they saw themselves as independent beings with conflicting wills, they would regard other human beings as alienated from them. This, in turn, would hamper their own freedom. Their recognition of the common ability to reason in other human beings would resolve this problem. If a community could be built on the basis of this common ability to reason, it would be acceptable to every human being as an expression of his or her own rational will and not as something outside oneself. The coincidence of duty and self-interest would lead to the realization of their nature as rational beings. According to Hegel, the state is the community that secures freedom and integration for the individual.

Hegel maintained that there are three moments of social existence: the family, civil society, and the state. These three spheres of social existence are different spheres of ethical development in which individual self-determination is realized in larger ethical communities. Within the family, a 'particular altruism' prevails, encouraging people to set aside their own interests for the good of their relatives. This, however, does not happen in a civil society. While the family is constituted by sacrifice and unity, civil society is the sphere of 'universal egoism', that is, ethical life in competition. Here, individuals place their own interests before those of others, and behave selfishly and instrumentally towards others, though in this very process they form a system of complete interdependence wherein their livelihood, happiness and legal status are interwoven with one another. However, civil society cannot provide people with a self-determined ethical life because of its inability to produce freedom and integration. (See Chapter 13 for more on Hegel's views). Thus, an ethical sphere higher than both the family and civil society must be found for the realization of human freedom.

The state, according to Hegel, is the ethical sphere of universality, freedom and integration. The state is founded on freedom instead of coercion and so it is the final realization of the 'Spirit' in history. Its strength rests not on force but on its ability to organize rights, freedom, and welfare into a coherent whole. Hegel challenged the social contract argument, saying that it was based on the arbitrary will of the individuals. It is wrong to say that the foundation of the state is something at the option of all its members. Instead, he maintained that it is not up to the individual to separate himself from the state, because we are all citizens of the state by birth. The state reconciles individual freedom with the values of the community and in the realization of the community each individual would find his/her own fulfilment while simultaneously contributing to the well-being of the whole.

Marx, on the other hand, maintained that it was illusory to hold that the state had a universal character that could harmonize the discordant elements of civil society. According to him, as long as the society is divided into classes on the basis of the ownership of the means of production, there would be a dominant class and an exploited class, and the state would conduct its business in a manner conducive to the interests of the dominant class. We can find in Marx's writings two kinds of theories of the capitalist state. One that is most often quoted from the *Communist Manifesto* (1848) says, 'the executive of the modern state is but a committee for managing the common affairs of the whole bourgeoisie'. Here, the state is the instrument of the ruling class and is subordinate to the capitalist class. If it is the instrument of a particular class, its neutrality and impartiality is then under question.

Marx put forth a second view of the state in *The Eighteenth Brumaire of Louis Bonaparte* (1852) where he examined the revolutionary events in France from 1848 to 1851. What emerges from this examination is the 'relative autonomy of the state'. This referred to the capability of the state to impose its will upon society. This was because Bonapartism was an opportunistic and populist alliance between part of the bourgeoisie and part of the proletariat to secure legitimacy for the regime. This represented the autonomy that the state may achieve when class forces in society are precisely balanced. Marx's emphasis here is on the capability of the state to impose its will. What distinguishes this view from the one expressed above is that the state is not referred to only as an instrument of the dominant class. Nevertheless, it is important to remember that the autonomy of the state is only relative and not absolute. While appearing to mediate between competing class interests, the state keeps the class structure intact. The state is not a neutral arbiter, but acts to maintain the division of society into classes. We notice that the abstraction and the independence of the state from partisan interests are challenged in the Marxist view of the state.

With the overthrow of capitalism, the capitalist state would also be overthrown, and in its place, the proletariat, that is, the working class, would take over the reins of the state and establish its dictatorship. This would be marked by the working class exercising the kind of hegemony that the bourgeoisie had exercised, leaving the actual task of governance to others. Marx identified a form of government whereby the working class would actually govern and fulfil many of the tasks hitherto performed by the state. The socialist state would try to create the conditions for the eventual transition to a stateless and classless society.

Marx affirmed his view of the state as an instrument by which the economically dominant class could repress and subdue the other classes. All states, then, are examples of class dictatorships. The purpose of the dictatorship of the proletariat is to safeguard the gains of the revolution and prevent a counter-revolution by the bourgeoisie.

Marx challenged the necessity and the endurance of the state. Liberalism does not challenge the endurance of the state. By associating the state with the class system, Marx believed that the abolition of the latter would lead to a withering away of the former. Can you imagine the state 'withering away'? It is not very clear what Marx exactly meant by the withering away of the state and this has provided other Marxist writers with further scope to elaborate the analysis of state power.

So far, we have seen that Marxism focused on the coercive role of the state—the state is essentially the institution whereby a dominant exploiting class imposes and defends its power and privileges against the class/classes that it dominates and exploits. The Italian Marxist, Antonio Gramsci, introduced into Marxist thought the idea that it is not just through open coercion that the domination of the ruling class is secured. This is also elicited through ideological manipulation. According to Gramsci, the state is force plus consent, or hegemony and coercion, in which civil society provides consent and political society organizes force. Hegemony refers to the ability of the dominant class to secure the consent of those it dominates. It is a process through which the bourgeoisie maintains its dominant position in the society. The system of education, the mass media—these are part of what could be called the ideological state apparatus.

Louis Althusser, a French Marxist, further developed the idea of the ideological state apparatus. Althusser wrote that the capitalist state has two distinct but related coercive instruments to secure the stability and the continual reproduction of the capitalist mode of production. This includes the repressive state apparatuses—law courts, police, army, and other state functionaries. These rely on violence in the sense that if one fails to comply with the directives of the state then some form of sanction is imposed against the person in the form of fines, imprisonment, and so on. On the other hand, ideological state apparatuses function not by force but by ideology. These include areas where we acquire and exercise our individual rights and freedom, such as the family, trade unions, the media, and the church, but it is primarily the education system that assumes the role of the dominant ideological state apparatus.

The Marxist evaluation of the state inspired many movements that sought to change the nature of the existing state. The Russian Revolution of 1917 and the Chinese Revolution of 1949 were attempts at overthrowing the existing political structures and creating in their place an alternative and fairer form of political organization.

The Patriarchal State: Feminism

Feminist theory includes within it a wide range of perspectives, and has thus, engendered different attitudes towards state power. Liberal feminists generally subscribe to a belief in the state's basic neutrality. The denial of legal and political equality to women would imply that the laws of the state are biased in favour of men. Yet, it is possible to rectify these laws by the intervention of the state. They, therefore, see the state as capable of playing a role in promoting equality between men and women. This is evident in many campaigns—for instance, the demand for the reservation of seats in parliament for women, the extension of welfare schemes for women—all these are instances of liberal feminism's belief in the basic neutrality of the state and the possibility of appealing to the state to remove legal and political inequality between the sexes.

Radical feminists believe that the power of the state is a reflection of the patriarchal nature of society. They question the idea of the basic neutrality of the state, for they view the state as a reflection of patriarchal values in society. For radical feminists, the origin and roots of the disparity between men and women lies within the family, in the organization of labour within the family. The state is an instrument of male power. Catherine MacKinnon has argued that in a liberal state, it is through law that women's subordination and silence are maintained. In an unequal society, the definition of the 'normal' status of women is determined by the application of male values and practices. Thus, radical feminism criticizes the view of the state as impartial and neutral.

Feminist theories have sometimes led to a redefinition of what is political. The term 'the personal is political' contains within it several implications.

Governmentality: Foucault on the State

As discussed earlier, the government is the administrative apparatus of the state. However, according to Michel Foucault, the French philosopher, the state is the result of the practices of the government. Foucault was interested in how modernity was marked by the emergence of a broader field of government of human conduct—of the self, of the family, of institutions and of the body. He maintained that the state is the result of this tendency towards the government of conduct. So, rather than saying that the state is the condition for the existence of government, he turned around saying that the state flows from this modern practice of *ordering life* into structures, something that was not common in the Middle Ages. Foucault saw governmentality as a rationale of governing that takes the form of a series of mundane, daily practices of social ordering. (See Chapter 9 for further discussion on Foucault.)

Recent Debates: Challenges to the Sovereignty of the State

Globalization

Globalization is the process through which events and decisions in one part of the world have come to affect people in another part of the world. It has led to a greater inter-locking of different parts of the world. It has often been claimed that globalization poses challenges to the sovereignty of the state. Globalization is a multi-dimensional process, and includes the economic, cultural, and political aspects of life. The economic aspect refers to the emergence of an interlocking global economy and the worldwide spread of capitalism. The indicators of economic globalization are the growing power of multinational corporations, the internationalization of production, and the flow of financial capital between countries. It has become increasingly difficult, and perhaps impossible, for any country to regulate the international flow of capital, thus making it difficult for individual states to manage economic life. States have also found it difficult to regulate multinational companies for they can easily relocate production and investment.

Political globalization is reflected in the growing importance of international bodies like the United Nations (UN), the European Union (EU), and the World Trade Organization (WTO). The membership of the EU threatens state power, as many decisions on matters like monetary policy and defence are made by European institutions rather than by the member-states themselves. It is for these reasons that it is often said that globalization has challenged the sovereignty of the state.

The above stated case has been challenged by several authors and commentators who point that we should investigate the ways in which the state's role is changing as a result of globalization. According to them, there is the possibility of states adapting themselves to the transformations in international society, in the form of 'pooled sovereignty'—the idea that states that would be weak and ineffective acting independently could acquire greater influence by working together with other states through the vehicle of international or regional institutions. Others believe that globalization is itself driven by the state. States are themselves the authors of globalization by promoting and shaping the nature and pace of globalization. Trade agreements and regionalization are instances of this. Political elites in different countries often use globalization as an ideological device to make the move towards market reforms appear inevitable and irresistible. States are now more concerned about their role as actors in global markets to protect national economic well-being, and are entrepreneurial. They are less concerned with political sovereignty and security than they were earlier. Moreover, as Michael Mann (1997) argues, we need to make distinctions between states to understand the changing role of the state. Globalization will affect a powerful European state differently from a vulnerable country in South America or Africa. Some states might become stronger and more powerful, while others weaker.

Therefore, globalization could have different consequences for different states. As states differ in the degree of international power, they can assume the role of agents of globalization as well as become its passive victims. Thus, the impact of globalization on state sovereignty is much more complex than what the 'end of the state' thesis allows for.

The Imported State and its Consequences

As discussed earlier in the chapter, the modern state emerged and evolved in Europe. Through colonialism, it was transplanted in Africa, Asia, Australia, and the Americas. The development of the state in these areas has been along a trajectory different from that in Europe. Independent India inherited a state structure that colonialism had introduced. It did not evolve organically from the people. It could be argued that this structure of the state was imposed on the people from the top. When the state tried to penetrate into a pre-modern, traditional world by bringing different spheres of life under its supervision and control—it could be the abolition of child marriages, the registration of births, the abolition of the practice of untouchability—it was sometimes met with violence by the state and/or by those who tried to resist the growing powers of the state. This has often led to a loss of the meaning of state authority for the people governed by it, thus straining relations between the government and those governed by it.

Manoranjan Mohanty (2000) points to the emergence of two streams of critiques of the Indian state in the 1960s and the 1970s. These include, first, the rise of revolutionary politics and the Naxalite movement, and second, mass movements like the Chhatra Yuva Sangharsh Vahini in Bihar in 1974–75 to which Jayaprakash Narayan provided inspiration and impetus. The Naxalite movement sought to demonstrate the semi-colonial and semi-feudal nature of the Indian state, which was itself seen as an institution of violence. The Jayaprakash Narayan movement offered a critique of state power from the vantage point of civil society.

The monopoly of the state over the legitimate use of violence could be challenged by the establishment of parallel governments, particularly in the context of the emergence of the demand and the struggle for statehood by different groups. For instance, many of these groups might set up what are termed parallel governments (claiming for themselves the power to levy and collect taxes), and create a rival centre of coercion and force, challenging the monopoly of the state over the use of legitimate violence. The transplantation of the state and the consequent Westernization of the political order are held responsible for this state of affairs. The recent attempts at state-building in Iraq and Afghanistan are often considered to be attempts to import the Western model of the state into a terrain socially and politically not suited for this kind of transmigration. It is a matter of great debate how fruitful such exercises at state-building would be.

Thus, the state represents not merely a set of institutions, but rather a set of ideas and attitudes. What is the meaning of the state representing a set of ideas and attitudes? The state is an abstract entity, as are the other concepts like democracy, liberty, equality, etc. The defining feature of the modern state is the standard of abstraction from the regime that it is expected to uphold. Feminists hold that the state is patriarchal in nature, while according to Marxists it upholds the interests of the dominant section. Various critiques of the liberal view of the state point to the inability or the unwillingness of the state to abstract itself from the dominant sections of the society.

The modern state might share one or more but not all of its defining features with other associations and organizations. Does the state exhaust the possibility of our imagining alternative forms of political organization? Given the role of the state, sometimes benevolent, but always coercive, there have been many images of alternative forms. However, a paradox emerges: while the authority of the state is constantly questioned and challenged, there are also several demands made on the state to confer full-fledged rights and entitlements on citizens, to confer ever more recognition to more institutions, and a growing demand from the international community to address development problems effectively.

Points for Discussion

1. Sometimes, one could say that the appeal to individual conscience is a valid claim against state authority. This raises the question: when is it imperative to disobey the laws of the state? Mohandas Gandhi, John Rawls, and Ronald Dworkin have addressed the question of civil disobedience. Do you think that we are obliged to obey all laws of the state at all times?
2. Imagine the security checking at the airport, at the metro station and the powers of the guards posted at these places to examine your baggage—many of the rules and laws are made in the light of a distrust of human nature. If all human beings were generous, fair and just, would we need the police or the army?
3. Based on our discussion of liberal equality, we notice that people often find themselves in situations that are not of their own making and these act as constraints on their choices. Ram wants to study, but his parents cannot afford to send him to school. Should the state aim to rectify this situation by providing him with subsidized schooling, or set-up schools that charge no fees from their students?

Reading List

Anderson, Perry, *Lineages of the Absolutist State* (London: Verso, 1979).

Badie, Bertrand, *The Imported State: The Westernization of the Political Order* (Stanford, CA: Stanford University Press, 2000).

Ball, Terence, *Transforming Political Discourse: Political Theory and Critical Conceptual History* (Oxford: Basil Blackwell, 1988).

Gill, Graeme, *The Nature and Development of the Modern State* (Hampshire: Palgrave Macmillan, 2003).

Hansen, Thomas Blom and Finn Stepputat (eds), *States of Imagination: Ethnographic Explorations of the Postcolonial State* (Durham: Duke University Press, 2001).

Held, David, Anthony McGrew, David Goldblatt and Jonathan Perraton, *Global Transformations: Politics, Economics and Culture* (Cambridge: Polity Press, 1999).

King, Roger and Gavin Kendall, *The State, Democracy and Globalization* (Hampshire: Palgrave Macmillan, 2004).

Mackinnon, Catherine, *Toward a Feminist Theory of the State* (Cambridge, MA: Harvard University Press, 1989).

Mann, Michael, 'Has Globalization Ended the Rise and Rise of the Nation-State?' *Review of International Political Economy*, 4(3), 1997.

Mohanty, Manoranjan, *Contemporary Indian Political Theory* (New Delhi: Samskriti, 2000).

Poggi, Gianfranco, 'The Nature of the Modern State', in Malcolm Waters (ed.), *Modernity: Critical Concepts*, Volume III (London: Routledge, 1999).

Skinner, Quentin, 'The State', in Robert E. Goodin and Philip Pettit (eds), *Contemporary Political Philosophy: An Anthology* (Oxford: Blackwell Publishers Ltd., 1998).

Sorenson, Georg, *The Transformation of the State: Beyond the Myth of Retreat* (Hampshire: Palgrave Macmillan, 2004).

CHAPTER 13

Civil Society

Mohinder Singh

Chapter Outlines

Introduction

These days, we often come across the term 'civil society' in newspapers or in television programmes, or in a public meeting. For example, we read a newspaper report that a 'civil society organization' submitted a memorandum to the chief minister of Delhi highlighting the problem of homeless children in the city. Or a newspaper report with information on a conference of 'civil society organizations' that adopted a resolution demanding that a right to shelter be included in the Constitution as a fundamental right. There are other occasions when we confront the term 'civil society'. It has been estimated that Canada has more than a million civil society organizations. Similarly, India is said to have around two million such organizations (Mitra 2001). So, this brings us to the question, what does the term 'civil society' mean? What does it refer to? Why are certain kinds of organizations performing certain functions referred to as 'civil society organizations?' What should an organization do to be called a 'civil society organization'? Which are the organizations and institutions that are not included in 'civil society'? In this chapter, we shall try to find an answer to these and other similar questions.

Like many other concepts of political theory, the meaning of the term civil society has undergone several changes in its history and there is no consensus in the meaning of civil society among its contemporary users and proponents. However, one thing that is common to the various meanings of the term is the idea that social life is differentiated into various spheres and civil society is one among them. Civil society, thus, describes an aspect of social life and not the whole of it. At the very outset, therefore, it must be clarified that the meaning of the term civil society is different from that of society. In its contemporary usage—whatever the specific connotations of that usage might be—civil society is one among many spheres of the larger society along with family, economy, politics, etc. The concept of society, therefore, is much broader in scope than that of civil society. Society, according to Louis Dumont, can be defined as an organization into which we are born, to which we involuntarily belong and from where we get all our ideas and education. Society in this way is an all-purpose organization (Dumont 1986).

Civil society, on the other hand, can be understood as a collective entity that springs from society and exists for specific and limited purposes. The purposes, limits and scope of the domain of civil society vary from one conception to another. Yet, there seems to exist, in the contemporary usage of the term civil society, some basic attributes of the latter on which the differing conceptions tend to agree. What are these attributes? First, one of the most important attributes is that the domain of civil society is separate and independent from that of the *state*. Second, the domain of civil society is made up of *voluntary associations* and some involuntary associations and groups in society, such as family and caste, are not part of it (Bhargava 2005: 14). But, as stated earlier, the contemporary meaning of the term 'civil society' has a long history to which we now turn.

It is held that the first articulations of the concept took place in the 17th and 18th centuries in Europe. At that time, the concept was part of the economic and political liberalism that arose with John Locke and was elaborated in the writings of the thinkers of the Scottish

Enlightenment: David Hume, Adam Smith, and Adam Ferguson, albeit with a different meaning. The concept then found a significant place in the writings of Georg Hegel and Karl Marx in the 19th century. The concept went into disuse for a long time after this, only to appear in theoretical and practical usage towards the end of the Cold War. It then gained immense popularity after the end of the Cold War in both the academic and political worlds. After its newly acquired prominence in East Europe, it gradually acquired popularity in the political discourses of the West and the Third World. The revival of the concept of civil society in East Europe had taken place on the assumption that it was an important part of the heritage of Western democratic theory. However, if we study the history of concept of civil society in Western political theory, we find that it has gone through many changes in meanings.

Historical Evolution of the Idea of Civil Society

The idea of civil society evolved with the emergence of the modern age in Western Europe. As discussed earlier, the basic idea underlying the concept of civil society is the existence of differentiation in social life. This means that different institutions perform different functions in society according to the principle of functional specialization. Modern societies are more differentiated than the earlier societies which results in clear separation of different spheres of family, economy, civil society, and state. Pre-modern societies were less differentiated than modern ones in the sense that many functions (necessary for social existence) were performed by one or a few institution(s). For example, in tribal societies, kinship performed many social, cultural, political and economic functions. In the Middle Ages, feudal bonds performed many of those functions. Similarly, in India, caste performed, and in many areas still performs, multiple social, political, and economic functions. In many other societies monarchs performed multiple functions related to the economic, cultural, and political life of the members. At the same time, there were societies the members of which thought themselves to be so fully integrated with the whole that they could not even imagine what it meant to stand in opposition to the patriarch, matriarch, or head of that particular society. The idea of differentiation of various spheres of social life, along with the idea of civil society, is connected to the story of modern Western political theory.

Civil society in early Liberal Political Theory

The first articulation of the concept of civil society took place in the liberal political theory of the 17th century. In the ancient European political theories—Greek and Roman—the idea of political life was all comprehensive. No other sphere of society was expected to play any political role other than the state. In medieval Europe, however, the political sphere was considered as one among many spheres. The realm that provided most competition to the state was the Church. There were two sources of authority: the Church and political authority. At the same time, the relationship between the two authorities was unstable, prone to quarrel with regard to their respective spheres of competence (Taylor 2003). Ideas of modern state and civil society originated against the background of medieval Christendom with its dual source of authority. The story of their origins can be divided into two stages. During the first phase there was a long ideological-political battle on behalf of the institution of the state and against the claims of the Church. In the second phase, we see a struggle against the state's authority and for the rights and liberties of individuals. It is in the second phase that we can locate the historical origin of the modern idea of civil society as a space for the articulation of political interest of individuals against the authority of the state. This component is at the core of the concept of civil society and has remained there from its inception to its latest connotations.

The first phase begins with the historical events of Renaissance and the Reformation. These historical movements proved to have far-reaching consequences. Along with the new political theories of the 16th and 17th centuries these movements led to the strengthening of the claims of the state against the internationalism of the Roman Catholic Church, leading to the emergence of a powerful modern state with a new idea of sovereignty. In the 17th century, the specifically modern order was elaborated in the political theory, particularly in the writings of Thomas Hobbes and Jean Bodin, that elaborated the idea of a strong state with absolute sovereignty as its chief attribute. The political theory of Hobbes imagined public space as divided into two sharply separate domains: a domain of political authority or state and a subordinate domain of individual subjects. Gradually, during the second stage, in the 18th and 19th centuries, political theory started questioning the state's monopoly of power by articulating the concepts of individual rights and liberties.

In the first phase, the Reformation played a very important role in the emergence of the modern state by dividing the European Christendom into Catholic and Protestant Churches. The Protestant Church supported the independence of the state from the dominance of the Roman Catholic Church. But more importantly, the Reformation also facilitated the emergence of the doctrine of secularism. This doctrine specified that the spheres of the Church and the state ought to be separate with their own well-defined arenas of competence. With this separation, religion and morality were relegated to the sphere of the private concerns of individuals, whereas the state's main obligations became law, order, and security. In other words, by freeing itself from the interference of the religious authorities and placing itself above the quarrelling religious denominations, state monopolized political power.

Another important source for the modern ideas of state and civil society is the tradition of natural law in political theory. The modern natural law theorists imagined society to be composed of individuals. In their doctrine of natural law, individuals are given priority over society and are seen as self-sufficient, as the repository of reason, and as prior to and independent of society. Natural law theories derived the authority and legitimacy of the state from the qualities of man as an autonomous being independent of any social or political attachment. In a revolutionary transformation, these theories replaced the earlier basis of political authority, based on the thesis of the divine origin of the king's powers, with a new one. The political authority of the sovereign was no longer seen as flowing from God as its divine source. The natural law theorist began to explain it without recourse to any divine source. The starting point of the new theoretical speculation became the individual, and the state was regarded as a union of individuals. This was the beginning of the two poles of liberal political theory: the state and the individual. The revolutionary import of this shift in the argument lay in the fact that the source of political authority now was located within the society itself. It is on this basis that later on, in the second stage, the arbitrary powers of the state would be questioned (von Gierke 1987). These theoretical developments taking place in the early modern age proved to be important first steps towards the evolution of the contemporary concept of civil society. One of the most important early articulations of the natural law doctrine is to be found in the 17th century works of John Locke.

John Locke's Concept of Civil Society

John Locke contrasts the concept of civil society with the state of nature (Locke 2002: 1–59). The state of nature, according to Locke, is a hypothetical condition of human beings prior to the foundation of political or civil society. Locke refers to it as the state of nature because in the absence of any positive legal and political authority, the only force that guides human beings is the law of nature. In other words, it is a 'state all men are naturally in'. According to Locke, in this condition there is freedom and equality amongst the members of a species who share the same *human* nature. This condition is governed by the laws of nature that guide human beings regarding fundamental rules of right and wrong. All human beings have been endowed with the faculty of reason with which they can recognize and follow the law of nature. The state of nature is a condition 'of perfect freedom' where man can live within the limits set by the law of nature. Everybody is independent of the will of the other. It is also a state of equality, where no one has more rights than the other. Each man has the 'executive power' of punishing the transgressor of the law of nature. Locke's state of nature is a peaceful condition of human living where rational and free men respect each other's freedom.

Gradually, due to some reasons, men in the state of nature decide to get out of it and establish a civil society to get over the problem of the absence of any common judge to interpret the law of nature in specific situations. As stated earlier, each man in the state of nature has the 'executive power' as far as the law of nature is concerned. But in the absence of a common judge their judgments are fairly erratic and they are far from being impartial in their assessment of the rights and wrongs in conflicts between themselves and others. At some stage in history, according to John Locke, human societies grow to become richer and there is a division between people with considerable amount of property and those without, mainly because the invention of money makes the amassing of infinite amount of property possible. With the emergence of a propertied class in society the chances of potential conflicts among people in the state of nature become very high. And because of this, *civil* society is established as an alternative to and a remedy for these problems. The important thing for the present purpose is that Locke's conception of civil society is not that of a sphere separate from the political sphere of the state. Civil society provides a stable set of positive standing laws, impartial judges, and a coercive apparatus for enforcing those laws.

In Locke's schema, the concept of civil society also works as a standard with which to judge the existing political orders of his time. The main thrust of Locke's political philosophy is against the absolutism of political power. He did not approve of the existing absolutist monarchies prevailing at that time in France and other states of Europe. Locke was also critical of the monarch's monopoly of power in England and was in favour of a constitutional monarchy. The concentration of power in one place, e.g. in the hands of the monarch, placed the subjects in a condition of disadvantage. This arrangement did not provide the subjects with effective means of restraining the political authority and holding it responsible for its actions. Such a state, for Locke, is no better than the state of nature. It does not fulfil the requirements of a civil or political society. What we observe here is the normative charge of Locke's concept of civil society. In other words, Locke uses the concept of civil society to judge actually existing states. Authoritarian or despotic regimes do not qualify to the status of *civil*. In Locke's conception, subjects have legitimate right to revolt against the despotic and tyrannical rulers.

Already in Locke's political theory one can observe the emergence of the idea of political authority that can be legitimately challenged if it tends to take a turn towards despotism and which fails to uphold the trust of the subjects. With this idea begins the second stage of our story, wherein the main emphasis is on questioning the state's monopoly of power. With Locke, political theory already adopts a critical posture towards the absolutism of the state. Historically, this was also a period when most of the European states were ruled by powerful monarchs. They were known as absolutist states. These states faced a further challenge from the political theories of the 18th century, a period of intellectual growth known as the Enlightenment. Locke, thus, became the spiritual father of the Enlightenment's struggle against absolutist states.

Rise of Political Economy and the Enlightenment Concept of Civil Society

The Enlightenment concept of civil society is closely linked to the emergence of the sphere of economy by the end of the 18th century. In the wake of the Industrial Revolution, institutions of capitalist political economy had acquired a very important place in the social life of countries in Western Europe (particularly, England) and the United States. One of the important features of capitalism was the establishment of an independent sphere of economy with laws of its own. The term 'economy', derived from the Greek word *oikos* (household) originally meant household management, but came to acquire a new meaning around this time. In its new meaning, it referred to the intermediate sphere of commercial and production activities spatially situated between the family and the state. Economy, earlier confined to the private domain of the household, came out in the public sphere and sought independence from the domestic sphere as well as from state control. Unlike the earlier agriculture-based feudal society, production in the new capitalist economy was fundamentally geared towards trade, commerce and exchange of goods in the market. The social functions of production and distribution of things, employment of labour in production became privatized. In other words, these functions came to be performed more and more by non-political means under the legal conditions of free, uncoerced exchange in the market. In contrast to pre-modern practices, the distribution of various resources and labour in society did not take place by direction of political authority, hereditary duty, tradition, or religious obligation, but through the mechanisms of free exchange in the open market.

Thinkers of the Scottish Enlightenment, such as David Hume, Adam Ferguson, and Adam Smith, reflected on the significance of these developments and constructed theories about them. Smith developed his influential theory of political economy in which he argued that the processes of economy are governed by laws of their own and must be kept free from the control of the state. He conceptualized the state as a *laissez faire* state, with its functions being restricted to law and order, defence, currency, and communication.

The concept of civil society, as distinct from the state, emerged with this new idea of 'political economy'. According to the new concept, commerce is the source for civility and refinement in 'civil society' since it links completely anonymous individuals in the market-place. On the other hand, the state could legitimately monopolize the spheres of law and justice, its tasks reduced narrowly to the maintenance of peace, order, and security. Thus, according to Scottish Enlightenment thought, civil society is a name given to modern commercebased society, which is a product of capitalist political economy. In this conception, the sphere of civil society is clearly demarcated from that of political society or state. This development marks a concrete step forward from Locke's conception of civil society in which this separation is not clearly worked out. At the same time, the ethical foundations of civil society were located in the philosophy of individualism which the thinkers of Enlightenment inherited from 17th century thought, particularly from Locke. Individuals were seen as autonomous social actors pursuing their private interests in the civil society where they were not driven purely by the motives of selfish interests. They were also seen as sociable in nature with sympathy and affection, dependent on each other for their needs. These attributes provide psychological and moral foundations for the idea of civil society as a space for the social interaction of private individuals.

Historically, the development of an independent economic sphere played an important role in the gradual emergence in new practices of politics, particularly the institutions of representative democracy. As a result of the gradual dominance of the capitalist economy, a new class of people was created that did not have any significant political role to play but was playing a leading role in the new economy and had acquired social prestige and wealth—a class of merchants, bankers, and businessmen. There were other sections of the middle strata working in the offices of the state—bureaucrats and people involved in the legal profession—that had gained social influence and prestige but resented the lack of any political role. These classes, collectively called *bürger* or bourgeois, played an increasingly important role in the politics of 18th and 19th century Europe. However, they faced a peculiar historical predicament. Although they bore the financial burdens of the state, they were not allowed to participate in political decision making, which was the monopoly of the monarchs and the feudal classes.

With the spread of new ideas of freedom, equality, and the rule of law, the bourgeois opposed the claims of the absolutist state and called for limiting their powers. These were expressed in the form of various open and underground movements, created various public spaces and took various forms such as clubs, coffeehouses, salons, library societies, and literary societies (Koselleck 1988: 66). Initially, all these spaces took the form of 'social' entities without any overt political intention of challenging the established order. This way, they could provide the critique of the absolutist order thereby cutting the sinews of its legitimacy without posing any direct challenge to the existing power arrangement. New means of communication and representation through newspapers, books, reviews, etc., also helped in the formation of 'public opinion'. These were the spaces of early civil society, where political issues were discussed outside that of the state and often in direct opposition to it.

In the 19th century, the role of various public associations as a bulwark against the tyranny of the state and for the defence of the freedom of individuals was emphasized by Alexis de Tocqueville in his book *Democracy in America*. Tocqueville noticed that democratic governments tend to promote equality in society. But more importantly, he also noticed that the democratic advancement of equality might pose a threat to the liberty of the citizens. He argued that in democratic countries, old status-based social hierarchies and old forms of social solidarity tended to gradually disappear and there is a general passion for equality. Gradually, society gets polarized with a powerful centralized state on the one hand, and isolated individuals on the other. According to Tocqueville, social conditions of isolated families would promote the despotic tendencies of the state, if not checked by other social mechanisms. In such a situation, the only institutions that could prevent democracies from becoming despotic were associations freely created by the independent initiative of the individuals. For Tocqueville, political parties, churches, literary and scientific societies, and professional and recreational groups were the examples of such associations. These associations, interposed between individual families and the all-powerful state, could perform significant functions. First, they could perform an educative function by helping citizens cultivate civic virtues and democratic values, which, in turn, could help citizens think beyond their narrow private interests. In this way they would create bonds of solidarity among citizens. Second, these associations could also provide a guarantee against the abuse of power by the state authorities. Thus, they would tend to make the state authorities accountable to the citizenry.

Critiques of the Enlightenment Concept of Civil Society

In the 19th century, two powerful critiques of the Enlightenment concept of civil society appeared in the philosophies of Hegel and Marx. As already discussed, civil society was seen as a self-contained arena with internal laws and a mechanism of its own. Thinkers of the Enlightenment placed their hope in the functioning of morality in the realm of civil society. The task of the state, on the other hand, was to maintain law and order from above. The individuals in the civil society were supposed to perform dual roles. They were individuals of a market economy trying to maximize their own self-interests. On the other hand, they were also supposed to play the role of citizens caring for the general interest of the whole society from time to time. Both Hegel and Marx criticized this split between morality and legality, and tried to overcome this opposition in their own ways.

Hegel's Concept of Civil Society

Like the 18th century Enlightenment thinkers, Hegel also conceptualized civil society as a sphere consisting of people involved in the market (*bürgerliche Gesellschaft*: the society of city folks). Thus, civil society in Hegel's system comprised an economic system where formally free and equal individuals could engage in work and trade. Apart from that, it also included those civil institutions needed to keep such a system going; institutions like markets, courts and an administration of justice, and business corporations. Civil society for Hegel was a 'system of needs' where individuals pursued their freely chosen economic goals. It was also a system of mutual inter-dependence of individuals where exchange was the main medium of need fulfilment. The only thing about civil society that was problematic for Hegel was that each individual was concerned with his own interests and no one cared about the whole. It was a sphere where individuals' particular interests clashed.

Critique of Civil Society and the Role of the State Modern society, according to Hegel, is divided into three separate domains: family, civil society, and state. The three institutions are organized on three different principles. In Hegel's formulation, family is the domain of private life based on love and trust, where there is no space for individual egos. In contrast, both civil society and state are spheres of individuals' 'public' activities. Civil society is the sphere of pursuit of private or sectional interests in an open market. The state, on the other hand, makes its appearance in order to overcome the problems created by modern civil society. Its justification is based on Hegel's critique of civil or bourgeois society.

Civil society, according to Hegel, is based on the principle of unrestrained individual egoism. Hence, it leads to hitherto unknown divisions that need to be overcome. The freedom available to individuals here is only partial. Complete freedom, according to Hegel, also demands unity. The institutions of civil society only provide partial space for self-determination of individuals and the freedom they offer is somehow formal and empty. There are needs and desires, both natural and socially accepted, for which there is space in civil society. Civil society also directs people to choose efficient means to achieve our goals. The only restriction on the freedom of individuals is that they respect the similar freedom of others. But the same separation that had liberated persons from their traditional social roles also creates problems of its own. The form of sociability available in civil society creates divisions. There is division among individuals because of the principle of competitiveness in the economy. There is disunity brought about by the emergence of sectional and partial interests because of social and economic inequalities. In other words, a society organized on the principles of gain and profit left to its own rules would produce grave evils. Hegel finds the thread that could provide unity missing in civil society. Modern society, therefore, needs another form of sociability to overcome the problems arising from civil society. In Hegel's schema this function is performed by the state.

These divisions mentioned above, can be overcome by the state as a larger community transcending civil society. However, Hegel is critical of the liberal theory of the state prevalent at that time, according to which the state's functions ought to be minimal and limited to the protection of individual liberty and property. The state, for Hegel, is a 'non-minimal political sphere' transcending civil society. The basis of the state, according to Hegel, lies in individuals' need to live in *solidarity* with others in a community. He did not visualize the state as an institution merely for the protection of self-interest. State, according to him, is a sphere where human beings do not enter in their capacity as private individuals with self-interest, but as citizens concerned about the general interests of the whole community.

Civil Society in the Marxist Tradition: Karl Marx and Antonio Gramsci

Agreeing with Hegel, Karl Marx too claimed that the basic political contradiction in modern society is between 'man as citizen' and 'man as private individual' (Femia, 2001: 135). This split between private individual and citizen in modern society was criticized by Jean Jacques Rousseau in the 18th century and the idea had had a significant influence on the course of the French Revolution. Rousseau had argued that for the construction of a political community of citizens the pre-eminence of private or sectional interests needed to be checked. This idea continued in Marx's writings on civil society and capitalist political economy. But Marx did not understand the state–civil society relation in the same way as Hegel. Contradicting Hegel, Marx argued that state cannot stand above civil society to protect universal interests against the private interests articulated in civil society. The modern state, according to Marx, was neither independent of nor neutral towards the particular interests of civil society. On the contrary, state for Marx was deeply embedded in civil society. Accordingly, to understand the nature of the state it is necessary to understand the nature of civil society. For Marx, civil society included within its sphere the whole of pre-state economic and social life. The true nature of civil society can be understood by analysing the nature of political economy.

There may be formal equality in civil society but it in itself is divided into classes. Because of this division there is inequality among the members of civil society. The state, according to Marx, is an instrument of the domination of capitalist class, the owner of the means of production, over the working classes. The capitalist class subordinates the general interests that the state is supposed to protect, to its own class interests. Hence, political life is subordinated to economic life in civil society which, for Marx, is an obvious fact that even the bourgeois political theorists accept. According to Marx, because of private property and the general prevalence of selfish interests, life in a modern civil society is essentially unsocial and the modern state has its foundations in this unsocial life. So, instead of the state controlling the civil society, it is, in fact, the civil society that is the determining element. For Hegel, on the other hand, the existence of classes does not prevent the unification of the community at the level of the superior ethical order of the state. Marx argued that it is an illusion to believe that it is possible for individuals to periodically set aside their selfish, egoistic interests and participate in political affairs as public-spirited citizens. The prevalence of such illusions also provides a deceitful cover that hides the real identity between the interests pursued in the economic and the political spheres. According to Marx, without abolishing the capitalist civil society—which meant the abolition of capitalist relations of production—true citizenship and true political life is not possible. As long as capitalist relations of production exist, the political sphere will always be marked by narrow private interests. Only a working-class revolution can establish conditions free from the tyranny of particular interests.

In the first half of the 20th century, the Italian Marxist thinker, Antonio Gramsci, enriched the concept of civil society to a great extent. Retaining Marx's idea of class war, he focused as much on the question of war as on class. He understood politics as a kind of war and used metaphors from military warfare to explain its many processes. But unlike in military warfare, in politics the battles are not limited to the use of sheer force. Although force is used as well, the battle in the field of ideas is more important. Civil society, for Gramsci, is a space where this battle for the control of ideas takes place. According to him, the dominance of the ruling classes is not maintained solely on the basis of their control of the coercive apparatus of the state, namely, the police and the army. They also need to acquire a dominant intellectual and moral leadership in civil society.

In Gramsci's view, exploitative class relations of capitalist society have to be made to appear right and proper in order to establish the legitimacy of the ruling exploitative class. In other words, the ruling classes need to create a false perception among the working classes of their own social situation. Since human beings define themselves in terms of ideals and values, the ruling classes need to control those institutions where ideas, ideals, and values are formed. This function, according to Gramsci's conception, is performed by the various institutions of civil society. These civil society institutions are churches, parties, trade unions, universities, the press, publishing houses, and voluntary associations of all kinds. By disseminating the ideology of the dominant class, these institutions ensure its cultural and moral supremacy over the subordinate classes. In this way, the ruling class obtains the consent of the latter for their own subordination. Gramsci used the term 'hegemony' to describe all the processes through which the dominant class attained this intellectual and moral leadership. Through the concept of hegemony, he also emphasized that the ruling classes rely more on the institutions of civil society than those of the state for obtaining the consent of the subordinated. The coercive apparatus of the state is used only where 'spontaneous consent has failed'. The concept of hegemony had a strategic importance in Gramsci's own political practice. He argued that in order to properly fight the revolutionary battle for the working classes and peasantry, communist parties in different countries need to contest the hegemony of the ruling classes in civil society.

Contemporary Revival of the Concept of Civil Society

As already discussed in the beginning of this chapter, the revival of the concept of civil society took place in East European countries. This revival was related to people's struggle against the authoritarian communist states in some of the East European countries, particularly Poland. Against the dictatorial regime in Poland, people wanted to seek freedom under the state. So, they started a movement named Solidarity, which invoked the model of civil society from the Western countries as an independent sphere of freedom against the state. Similar movements started in other countries of Eastern Europe like Czechoslovakia and Hungary. Intellectuals and political activists presented the image of an unrepressed civil society to mobilize citizens against oppressive states and reclaim the sphere of privacy in social life. During these movements, dissident leaders and activists began to assert their rights to free speech and free association to carve out a public space for their political activities. Such movements saw the utility of the concept of civil society in its anti-statist charge. Their leaders and supporters used the concept of civil society in opposition to the party state that existed in these countries. The main reason for this kind of reaction against the authority of the state was that communist countries over-extended the legal jurisdiction and effective control of state institutions, such as bureaucracy, over nearly all spheres of social life. After the collapse of this kind of state, encouragement to the institutions of 'civil society', outside the legal jurisdiction of the state, was considered necessary for safeguarding the freedom of citizens.

At about the same time, the idea of civil society was also gaining prominence in Western Europe and the United States, though due to entirely different reasons from the ones in Eastern Europe. The former were facing a crisis of political apathy and lack of political participation among citizens after World War II and a decline in the membership of political parties, trade unions, and other voluntary associations. Similarly, the participation of citizens in elections had steadily declined, as was evident from low electoral turnouts in most Western countries. The notion of civil society was sought to be revived in order to resurrect the structures of civic solidarity among citizens. There was a marked emphasis on the role of voluntary associations in the new avatar of civil society, thus underscoring the contemporary relevance of Tocqueville's political thought.

One of the important contributions to the contemporary revival of civil society in the West has been made by Robert Putnam. Putnam emphasized the Tocquevillian concern for the role that civil society associations played in the creation of solidarity among citizens. In his research, he showed that the quality of political life and the performance of political institutions are directly affected by the quality of civic engagement in a particular society. He also showed that democracies function better in regions where there are long-standing traditions of civic engagements that are defined by indicators such as voting, political participation, newspaper readership, and participation in various voluntary associations. He further argued that norms and values of civic engagement are found in communities with a substantial stock of social capital. Social capital refers to those features of social life that make coordinated and efficient social action possible. It also refers to social networks and the norms of reciprocity and trustworthiness that arise from interaction among individuals. In that sense, it is closely linked to what we in everyday parlance call 'civic sense' or 'civic virtue'. The important point to highlight here is that social capital is not a function of individuals taken singularly, but of the connections between them. It includes such values as mutual trust, cooperation, and a shared sense of responsibility. These values make trustworthy dialogue among the members of society possible and help in the creation of social networks that are necessary for a well-coordinated political action. Participation in civic associations aids the development of cooperation, a sense of shared responsibility for collective endeavours and a means of engaging with the institutions of a political system.

Civil Society in the Post-Colonial Context

In Third World countries, too, the concept of civil society was revived during the 1980s the 1990s. Soon after the concept of civil society acquired popularity in Europe, it was revived in many countries of the Third World, particularly in the Latin American countries. Beginning in 1964 and till the late 1970s, many Latin American countries—including Brazil, Argentina, Peru, Chile, and Uruguay—came under authoritarian dictatorships. These regimes established political and economic domination by a tiny elite within the concerned countries. They also effectively excluded large masses of people from the process of decision making by banning elections and suppressing the rights and liberties of people that are a necessary condition for political participation. A simmering discontent was present in these countries as the military regimes were extremely repressive. They did not pursue policies that could cater to the economic and social demands of the lower and middle classes of the society. By the early 1980s, most of these regimes were faced with economic and political crises because of increasing foreign debt and popular discontent. Soon, various kinds of associations—later called civil society associations—were formed, particularly in Latin American countries, to press for the extension of civil and political rights. Like in East Europe, here too, the idea of civil society was invoked as a sphere of freedom against the authoritarian state.

The popularity of the concept of civil society is related not only to the democratic struggle against authoritarianism, it also shows a decreasing faith in the capacity of the state to cater to peoples' needs and aspirations. In other words, the resurgence of the concept also indicates the failure of most of the post-colonial states to carry out economic and political development in these societies. Most of the newly independent states in the Asian, African, and Latin American countries failed to meet the expectations and aspirations of the people. These states were neither capable of attaining high economic growth nor were they able to institutionalize democratic politics. The crisis of state led to a questioning of the very ideas of political and economic development that had dominated political discourse so far.

The challenge to the existing models of development appeared in the decades of the 1980s and 1990s in the form of new social movements. They were new in the sense that they carved out an oppositional political space distinct from traditional political parties and pressure groups. They were also new in the more important sense that many of these movements questioned the models of development that had been pursued by the developing countries. In India, we can think of the Narmada Bachao Andolan (NBA) and the Chipko Movement as examples of such movements. The NBA, for example, questioned the sustainability of big development projects like the Sardar Sarovar Dam on the Narmada River on ecological grounds, and has also been struggling for the rights of the local people displaced by the dam. It also criticized the project for over-centralization of the decision-making structure in which there was no participation of those directly affected by it. These and many such movements have created awareness about economic development through various traditionally non-political channels and have been successful in changing public opinion to some extent.

Recently, we have seen a spate of non-governmental organizations (NGOs), funded by various international agencies, taking up these issues. These organizations work in a wide range of important social areas like education, health, human rights, ecological aspect of development, gender bias in development policies, rights of people affected by development projects, minority rights and transparency in governance. These organizations seek to stay aloof from party politics and use methods like public interest litigations (PILs) in courts, lobbying with political leaders and legislators, campaigning in the mass media and working directly with people. In the last decade, various NGOs and other independent organizations have got together to form a worldwide organization called the World Social Forum (WSF) to coordinate their agendas and activities. However, there are different ideological positions among different NGOs on important economic and political issues. For example, there is an important debate on the role of the state in economic development and liberalization of the economy. It is an important issue given the fact that one of the important sources of support to the contemporary revival of the idea of civil society is the neo-liberal economic doctrine. The neo-liberal doctrine is supported by the World Trade Organization (WTO), the World Bank and the International Monetary Fund (IMF). According to this doctrine, the old welfare functions of the state need to be dismantled and developmental work should be carried out by various civil society organizations.

Modernity and Civil Society in Post-Colonial States: Critical Issues

The application of the contemporary concepts of civil society for understanding and analysing the politics and society of the post-colonial societies poses unique problems. Such problems arise basically because these societies have their own historical logic and at the same time they have been irreversibly affected by Western modernity. The connotations of the concept of civil society are different in different countries of the Third World. These depend on the particular cultural contexts in which the concept is invoked. In this context, there is a need to be sensitive to the particular intellectual and cultural traditions of a given society (Kaviraj 2001: 306–07).

In the post-colonial set-up, the historical context of the emergence of civil society in most Third World countries is very different from that of the West. The main reason for this is that most of these societies did not experience the reign of an all-powerful sovereign state of the absolutist kind discussed earlier in this chapter. In most colonized countries, as Sudipta Kaviraj argues in the case of India, society had an organizing principle independent of the state. The state authority did not usually interfere in its functioning and, traditionally, could not be as authoritarian as the historical absolutist state in Europe. The colonial states, on the other hand, were driven by the ideology of sovereign power and with that they tried to establish control over these societies. The beginning of a civil society-like sphere in the colonial context can be traced historically to nationalist struggles against colonial regimes. A brief discussion of the concept of civil society in Indian history will help us understand better the problems involved with the institution of civil society in the post-colonial context.

In India, like in other erstwhile colonized countries, modern political institutions did not originate solely out of civil society's own historical dynamics. They were also a result of the colonial encounter. The colonial state introduced modern institutions necessary for its own functioning, like a centralized legal system, unified administration, census for counting population groups, elected legislative assemblies (initially with restricted franchise), and modern English education. Modern education gradually produced a section of people in the society that came in contact with European political ideas and concepts. Through Bentham, Rousseau and Mill, the ideas of liberty, democracy and equality became known. Under the influence of the new ideas, the English-educated classes became critical of some of the liberty and equality-hindering practices of their own culture. Gradually, they became critical of the colonial state.

By the beginning of the 20th century, leaders of the nationalist movement had already begun to think in terms of the right to self-governance. Gradually, this political demand took the shape of a movement for complete independence from colonial rule. A great part of nationalist politics was conducted in the vocabulary of Western political theory, but not all of it. The main problem was that the majority of the people of India, largely untouched by modern education, were not conversant with this vocabulary. If we compare this situation with the situation in European history, we can say that modern ideas like democracy, rights, freedom, and civil society needed to be translated in the local idioms of peoples' languages. In other words, political concepts grown in the soil of individualism did not match the social situation of this society. A modern civil society based on the ideals of freedom, equality, and citizenship instead became a hope and a goal of the dominant section of the nationalist leadership favouring modernization.

Soon after Independence, a leading group of political leaders, particularly those who shared Jawaharlal Nehru's modernist vision, believed that with the spread of modern education and scientific ideas, with the new industrialized economy and secular political institutions, Indian society would be able to break away from its traditional practices and modern civil society would emerge. Modernization theories in social sciences, too, had placed hope in the modernizing capacities of the newly independent state. At the same time, modernization theories had also presented the political culture of Western European countries and North America as a model and goal for the societies of the developing countries. Gradually, there was a realization in the social sciences as well as in political theory that the political cultures of Third World societies had presented them with unfamiliar and unexpected elements (Kaviraj 2001).

As already discussed, the idea of civil society was closely linked to liberal individualist thought in the early Modern Age. To recapitulate, civil society in Western political theory is understood as a space for associations, membership to which is based on the criteria of rational interests of the individual citizens. Associations with membership based on *traditional* criteria do not have any place in this neat model of civil society. As some observers have noted, beginning in the late 19th century, there have been both kinds of associations in India, associations based on modern individualism as well as those based on purely traditional identities like caste and religion. The spread of modern ideas through English education was slow. Initially, politics in this sense was basically an elite affair. Gradually, the modern forms of politics reached the masses in urban and rural areas. The very idea of association-based politics of interest articulation and bargaining was definitely a modern form of politics. So, the interaction of modern political institutions and traditional elements of Indian society produced new kinds of political organizations and activities. Some scholars termed such phenomena as the 'modernity of tradition' as it contained politics of associations based on traditional identities such as caste (Rudolph and Rudolph 1967).

From the above discussion, it is clear that the concept of civil society has a normative charge when it is presented by liberal and modernization theories as an essential condition for the modernization of society and polity. For a post-colonial country like India, civil society is presented as an ideal to be achieved. Such a predicament poses a problem for the application of the concept. The problem is as follows: If we take too broad a view and include all kinds of associations based on caste, religion, and other traditional identities, the concept tends to lose its normative appeal. Such a civil society will be far from the normative ideal that refers to a sphere of political activities, situated between the institutions of state and family, carried out by the rational and modernized citizenry. If, on the other hand, we take a narrow view of civil society which restricts its scope only to modern associations, there is a risk of limiting civil society to the urban and the elite. Therefore, it seems that the idea of civil society based on associational form of politics is gaining popularity in contemporary times primarily in urban areas. The fact that regional translations of the term 'civil society' have still not become prevalent in regional political discourses also indicates the inherent limitations on the use of this concept. Presently, it seems, the usage is restricted to English-speaking sections of the population. In addition, some important critics of the concept have also found it difficult to fix the ideological content of civil society. If civil society consists of associational life per se, then nothing can prevent us from including the associations of all ideological hues: patriarchal forces alongside feminist groups; religious fundamentalists alongside reformists; social groups supporting liberalization of economy alongside those opposing it (Chandhoke 2003; Seligman 1992).

Conclusion

We have seen that the concept of civil society has undergone many changes in its meaning. The concept of civil society made its historical journey beginning with Locke's political theory in the early Modern Age, went through various mutations in meaning via Enlightenment thinkers—Hegel, Marx, Tocqueville and Gramsci—until it was rediscovered as a useful category of social theory in the decades of the 1980s and 1990s. We have also observed that the current meaning attributed to civil society is a recent historical phenomenon. In this conception, civil society is considered as one sphere among many in social life. In its current usage, the domain of civil society is clearly demarcated from the domain of state and it consists of a network of voluntary associations. So far, there seems to be an agreement among the contemporary users of the concept, but there are considerable differences when we raise the question regarding the type of groups and associations that should be included within the scope of the concept. According to one view, civil society is to be located basically in the sphere of the economy. This view seeks to defend the freedoms available in the market economy against the encroachments by the state. An alternative view, on the other hand, finds the location of civil society in the space that is independent of both the state and the economy. According to this view, civil society is constituted by voluntary associations, groups, and movements that are products of the free exchange of ideas in a democratic framework and that also seek to keep a permanent check on the powers of the state in the interest of citizens' freedom (Cohen and Arato 1994; Khilnani 2001:13–14). In the latter version, civil society also acquires normative dimensions as it becomes a state of affairs that is desirable for the sake of democracy and freedom.

Points for Discussion

1. As we have seen in this chapter, the term 'civil society' has had many different meanings from its use in the 17th century to the present times. How has the meaning changed from its definitions in John Locke's political theory and the theory of the 18th century political economists, to its usage in the last two decades?

2. When an activist of the People's Union for Civil Liberties (PUCL) was arrested by the Chhattisgarh government, *Tehelka* news reporter Shivam Vij wrote in its 21 October 2007 edition: 'The war on Maoists in Chhattisgarh is beginning to turn on *civil society*' (emphasis added). Try to think about the connection between the two.
3. In the same paper, a columnist had written: 'For too long, the idea of civil society in India had been abdicated to the NGO sector—deemed a professional activity meant for others.' What do you think are the dangers of abdicating the idea of civil society to the NGO sector?

Reading List

Bhargava, Rajeev and Helmut Reifeld (eds), *Civil Society, Public Sphere, and Citizenship: Dialogues and Perceptions* (New Delhi: Sage Publications, 2005).

Chandhoke, Neera, *State and Civil Society: Explorations in Political Theory* (New Delhi: Sage Publications, 1995).

———, 'The "Civil" and the "Political" in Civil Society', in Carolyn M. Elliot (ed.), *Civil Society and Democracy: A Reader* (New Delhi: Oxford University Press, 2003).

Cohen, Jean and Andrew Arato, *Civil Society and Political Theory* (Cambridge: MIT Press, 1994).

Dumont, Louis, *Essays on Individualism: Modern Ideology in Anthropological Perspective* (Chicago and London: The University of Chicago Press, 1986).

Elliot, Carolyn M. (ed.), *Civil Society and Democracy: A Reader* (New Delhi: Oxford University Press, 2003).

Femia, Joseph, 'Civil Society and the Marxist Tradition', in Sudipta Kaviraj and Sunil Khilnani (eds), *Civil Society: History and Possibilities* (Cambridge University Press, 2001).

von Gierke, Otto, *Political Theories of the Middle Age* (Cambridge and New York: Cambridge University Press, 1987).

Kaviraj, Sudipta, 'In Search of Civil Society', in Sudipta Kaviraj and Sunil Khilnani (eds), *Civil Society: History and Possibilities* (Cambridge: Cambridge University Press, 2001).

Kaviraj, Sudipta and Sunil Khilnani (eds), *Civil Society: History and Possibilities* (Cambridge: Cambridge University Press, 2001).

Keane, John (ed.), *Democracy and Civil Society* (London: Verso, 1988).

Khilnani, Sunil, 'The Development of Civil Society', in Sudipta Kaviraj and Sunil Khilnani (eds), *Civil Society: History and Possibilities* (Cambridge: Cambridge University Press, 2001).

Koselleck, Reinhart, *Critique and Crisis: Enlightenment and the Pathogenesis of Modern Society* (Oxford and New York: Berg, 1988).

Kumar, Krishan, 'Civil Society: An Inquiry into the Usefulness of an Historical Term', *British Journal of Sociology*, 44(3), 1993.

Locke, John, *The Second Treatise of Government* (New York: Dover Publications, 2002).

Mitra, Amit, 'Civil Society, Globalization and Sustainable Development', http://www.indiaseminar.com/2001/507, 27 November 2001.

Rudolph and Rudolph, *Modernity of Tradition: Political Development in India* (Chicago: The University of Chicago Press, 1967).

Seligman, Adam B., *The Idea of Civil Society* (Princeton: Princeton University Press, 1992).

Taylor, Charles, 'Modes of Civil Society', in Carolyn M. Elliot (ed.), *Civil Society and Democracy: A Reader* (New Delhi: Oxford University Press, 2003).

de Tocqueville, Alexis, *Democracy in America* (both Volume 1 and 2 ed. by Richard D. Heffener) (New York: Mentor Books, New American Library, 1956).

CHAPTER 14

Property

Mohinder Singh

Chapter Outlines

Introduction

Like with most concepts in political theory, the meaning of the concept of property is not constant. It has changed over time according to the evolution of the institution of property in history and according to the way different societies have evaluated the uses of this institution. In its broadest sense, the concept of property refers to exclusive ownership of a thing or objects of value. But the practices of property differ from one society to another. In common parlance, we sometimes identify things themselves as property. These things may be concrete material things like a piece of land, a house, a car, etc. We sometimes see advertisements for sale of things like a house, a plot of land, a shop as property for sale. What constitutes property here, is the enforceable legal claim of persons or groups to things, not the things themselves. Property, thus, refers to a legal relation between persons with respect to specific things—material or abstract—things such as copyright. Therefore, for the institution of property to exist, there has to be some legal authority to enforce property as a legitimate claim. For example, I own a bag which I somehow lost at a railway station. The bag is now lying at the lost property counter. The bag is not with me but it is still my property insofar as I can rightfully claim it as mine, and insofar as this claim is legally recognized. Property, therefore, is not merely something I am able to take, occupy, or possess. I must be entitled to possess it legitimately. Hence, property is necessarily relational and is possible only in a legally organized community of people.

Property does not only refer to private property. Private property is only one of the various forms of property. Other forms of property are common property and public or state property. Private property is a right with a private individual, a family, a corporation, or a group, which excludes others from the use, consumption, or enjoyment of things owned privately. In this sense, property rights grant the owner an exclusive power to decide what will happen to a particular thing or resource. In the case of common property, on the other hand, access and utility are not limited to an individual and his/her family but are shared commonly by many people, a community or a village. Public or state property refers to those things controlled by the state for public purposes: transport, railways, historical monuments, public parks, etc.

The Extent and Limits of Property Rights

As we mentioned above, legal recognition is necessary for the institution of property. Legally, property is recognized as property right or the right of ownership. Property rights, however, are never absolute. There are always some restrictions placed on the use of our property. For example, you may not be allowed to blow the horn of your car, near a hospital, although the car is your property. These rights are restricted by legal systems in order to protect the rights and freedoms of other persons. The American philosopher Robert Nozick (1974: 171) gives an example of one such restriction: 'My property rights in my knife allow me to leave it where I will, but not in your chest.' These are obvious restrictions on people's right to the use of their property. The precise extent of ownership rights, however, depend on their definition by a given legal system. The commonly recognized elements of ownership are right to possess, right to use, right to transfer, right to bequeath, right to exclude others, right to manage, and right to income and capital from one's property.

The Concept of Property in Political Theory

The concept of property can be approached from a legal, sociological, economic, or philosophical perspective. In this chapter, our focus is on the concept of property in the history of political theory, and we shall briefly discuss some of the most influential arguments regarding property. Traditionally, political theories have investigated the idea of property as part of their integrated vision of an ideal human life. Instead of providing a focused investigation of a particular idea or institution, they have dealt with it in terms of its place in their overall vision of the ideal organization of political life. In their approaches, traditional political theories have contained empirical as well as normative statements. In other words, they have not only described the existing institutions and practices related to property but also prescribed the best and the ideal possibilities. At the same time, the bulk of the debate in the history of political theory has been around the problems of private property. With respect to private property, two kinds of arguments have been given: arguments for the moral justification of private property and political arguments as to how property ownership affects public spirit, virtue, citizens' behaviour, political ethics, etc. In a particular theory, we can find a version of either of the two arguments or a combination of both. We shall now discuss the notion of property as represented in some of the most important political theories.

Property in Ancient and Medieval Political Thought

The political thought of Plato and Aristotle in ancient Greece was developed in close connection with their ethics. The central question they were concerned with was: what are the conditions for a good life for man? Greek life was communally lived and was organized around the city-state (*polis*). A life lived in isolation from the city-state was not considered a properly *human* life. It was through the city-state that a good life for man could be possible. Man, for Plato and Aristotle, was essentially a political animal. Since they were concerned with the truly good and happy life for man, and because properly designed political arrangements could enable the pursuit of that good life, it was imperative for them to determine the true nature and functions of the state. Citizens would be unable to lead the good life if the state they lived in were a bad state. With respect to property, their main concern was the ideal property arrangements necessary for the good ethical life of the citizens.

In his *Republic,* Plato argued that private possessions tend to make human beings selfish. Therefore, in the ideal state described in the *Republic*, private property is prohibited for the rulers. Plato argued that if the rulers were allowed private ownership of property, they would start amassing property and would primarily be interested in pursuing their self-interest instead of taking care of all the citizens of the state. On the other hand, if whatever belonged to the guardians belonged to them in common, it would encourage a feeling of public spiritedness among the rulers and that would be an ideal condition of harmonious living together. To summarize, Plato criticized private ownership of property for the rulers because it induces selfishness and destroys public spiritedness among citizens. In other words, private ownership is a hindrance to the unity and harmony of the state, whereas ownership in common enhances them. So, to avoid social divisiveness and to ensure harmony, Plato advocated collective ownership as the ideal.

Aristotle criticized Plato's argument for the abolition of private property on many grounds. First, disputes and quarrels would not necessarily end because those who hold property in common tend to have more disputes than those who own privately. Therefore, Plato's scheme is not a guarantee of harmony in the state. Second, Aristotle takes Plato to task for this argument that '… all men saying "mine" and "not mine" at the same instant of time' is a sign of perfect unity of a state (Aristotle 2001: 1262a). Aristotle argues that least care is bestowed on things belonging to many in common. In such situations, everybody is more inclined to neglect the duty which they expect others to perform. In this way, things owned in common will be neglected by everybody. By saying that all persons caring for common things does not necessarily translate into each person caring for them, Aristotle has produced an argument which is used very frequently by the opponents of common ownership. Third, Aristotle says that there are both good and bad effects of private property. While the bad effects of private property can be removed without abolishing it, mainly through education, the good effects cannot be rescued without it. According to Aristotle, private ownership can promote virtues like prudence and responsibility: '[W]hen everyone has a distinct interest, men will not complain of one another, and they will make more progress, because every one will be attending to his own business' (Aristotle 2001).

Interestingly, Aristotle also says that without private property, some virtues like friendship and generosity cannot be developed. So, property owned individually provides us with the opportunity to be helpful and generous towards others—activities that give great satisfaction and joy to us. The Platonic abolition of private property would, according to Aristotle, produce morally worse results than its existence. Aristotle considers ownership of property to be a source of pleasure and happiness. And a state where the rulers are deprived of this happiness cannot be a happy state.

Although Aristotle defends private property, he is not in favour of endless accumulation of property. In fact, he does not approve of one-sided attention given to the accumulation of wealth. In other words, property for Aristotle is not an end, rather a means to an end. The desirable end for Aristotle is a virtuous and good political life spent in the company of fellow citizens. In itself, property has no great value. Moreover, caring for property is a private matter to be handled by the master of the household. For an ideal political organization, he recognized a need to provide the citizens training, through education, not to desire excessive wealth.

The political thought of the Middle Ages shared with Aristotle the idea that property cannot be an end of human life but only a means. The political thought of the Middle Ages was dominated by the Christian worldview. The Christian idea of the end or purpose of human life was very different from that of Aristotle's. Unlike the Greeks, the Christian worldview did not value active political life very highly. True happiness, according to this worldview, is possible only in the everlasting life of the other world. In this world, only imperfect happiness can be achieved. Saint Thomas Aquinas, the most influential Christian thinker of the Middle Ages, rejected seeking earthly glory, honour, wealth, power, sensory pleasure, etc., as desirable goals of human life. The best life for human beings, he felt, is a life devoted to spiritual activities. For leading this kind of life, human beings need property as a necessary means to such a life. The most important ethical consideration for Aquinas is that the use of property should be made subservient to the higher goal of life. Like Aristotle, Aquinas too justified private possessions only to the extent that things are used as a *means* for leading a virtuous life.

Modernity and the Concept of Property

Before the rise of the modern age, the main form of property was land, and commerce was not a very highly valued activity. As we have seen in the section on Aristotle and Aquinas, there were significant moral constraints on the accumulation of property. Medieval ethical and political theories and the medieval Church had put enormous ethical constraints on the activity of money earning. Practices like usury, so essential for commercial activity, were considered sinful and banned. With the emergence of the modern age, commercial activity gained a prominent place in society. The modern era is usually identified with the rise of capitalism, a system of production where production of things takes place largely for commerce and money plays a very crucial role in commercial exchange. The preeminence of business and commerce in the modern age would not have been possible without a struggle against the prevalent medieval moral and religious values. In the struggle at the level of ideas, modern political theories played a very important role. They attempt to overcome traditional moral constraints.

Modern political theory played a big role in undermining the ancient and medieval doctrines of society and politics. First of all, political theory itself underwent significant transformations. The most important change that took place in political theory was the separation of ethics and politics. In the 16th and 17th centuries, the writings of thinkers such as Niccolo Machiavelli, Thomas More, Jean Bodin, Thomas Hobbes and John Locke attempted to shake off the ethical baggage inherited from classical and medieval doctrines of politics. For the new thinkers, the most important task of political authority was not that of caring about the good and virtuous life of the citizens. It was to provide conditions of security under which citizens could live a peaceful and economically secure life. The emphasis of the new political theory was on security, particularly economic security. Gradually, economic concerns started to acquire the centre-stage in political thinking in place of the ethical. Along with these changes, another important aspect of the new political thought was that it provided justification for a commercial, capitalist form of property as against the feudal form of property. In the following section, we shall study one of the most influential doctrines of property in the early modern political theory developed by John Locke in the 17th century.

John Locke on Property

John Locke provided a very strong moral justification of private property in *Two Treatises of Government* (1967). The core idea of Locke's theory of property is that people are entitled to own as property whatever they produce by their own labour and initiative. Locke argues that in the state of nature, nature and its resources have been given by God to humankind in common. Thus, originally, no one has any private property. At the same time, human beings have a natural right to self-preservation and consequently to things necessary for self-preservation. After describing these conditions, Locke gives a peculiar argument that the fruits of nature, though given in common, *must be appropriated* before being of any use to any particular man. For example, in the case of literally a fruit, Locke is very clear as to *when* the fruit begins to be a person's: "When he digested? Or when he ate? Or when he boiled? Or when brought them home? Or when he pickt them up? And 'tis plain, if the first gathering made them not his, nothing else would" (Locke 1967: 288).

For something to become someone's private property, therefore, it is necessary that he removes it from the common and makes it his own. Such an appropriation by removal from the common can create an exclusive right to property if such a removal, according to Locke, can satisfy three conditions. These are moral conditions that limit the right to property in the state of nature (For Locke's concept of 'natural rights', see Chapter 6 of this volume). First, one can make something their property by removing it out of the common only if they have 'mixed [their] labour with it' and joined to it something that is their own. Locke argued that in applying labour to something, some part of what that person owns gets mixed with the object in such a way as to exclude the common right of other people to own it and to make that thing his/her own property. Locke's example: a pitcher of water taken from the flowing river can turn some quantity of the flowing unowned water into someone's exclusive property. The second condition Locke puts on the right to appropriate is that 'enough, and as good' must be left in common for others to appropriate. No one has the right to appropriate in such a way that the situation of others is worsened by the act of appropriation. This proviso was given in order to make sure that others' situation is not worsened by someone's appropriation of some portion of the wealth given to all in common. The third condition is that one can legitimately appropriate only as much as one can use and consume before it spoils or decays.

Soon afterwards, in the same section of the book, Locke overcomes all the conditions he sets for the appropriation of the resources of nature as private property. The condition that one's own labour has to be expended in order to acquire something as private property is overcome if it is possible to buy and sell labour legitimately. The meaning of this provision in Locke's political theory is that if I buy someone's labour, I am also entitled to the product of that labour. For example, if I own some amount of cotton and the machinery to manufacture textile from it, but I employ another person or persons to work on the machines to produce textile, I am entitled to the manufactured textile. The assumption here is that transfer of labour also implies transfer of the labourer's entitlement to the things produced by him. Similarly, Locke argues that the other two limitations are no more valid once money as a medium of exchange has been invented. Since natural things of human use such as grains, meat or clothes, etc., are likely to rot or decay after some time, it is foolish as well as dishonest to hoard up more than one can use before they decay. But with money, either in the form of metal coins or paper notes, there is no such risk. Therefore, one can legitimately accumulate as much money as one can.

But how is the stipulation that 'enough, and as good' must be left for others for their own use, overcome with the use of money? It is here that Locke underscores the importance of land as property. Land as property can become significantly superior to other natural resources only if it is privately owned. As we saw for the argument relating to labour getting 'mixed up' with objects, you can be a legitimate owner of land if you cultivate it with your own labour. By tilling and cultivating the owned land, you can get much more produce from it than would be available if the land remained in an abandoned state. Therefore, Locke says, by appropriating the land, far from reducing the total share of human beings, a rational and industrious appropriator actually adds to it by generating new resources and opportunities for work. The produce from the land owes its existence to human labour. The introduction of money, on the other hand, facilitates trade and commerce among individuals and communities.

The private appropriator of land can, in the modern era, produce not merely for consumption but for trade. Therefore, even if some people appropriate as much land as not to leave enough for others, the greater productivity of the appropriated land compensates for the lack of land available to others. A strong assumption behind this argument is that the increase in the whole product will be distributed to the benefit of those left without any or enough land. Private accumulation in a society where trade and commerce flourish actually increases the amount left for others by increasing the general level of prosperity. The conclusion of this crucial argument of Locke's is that even bare subsistence, at the standard prevailing in a society where all land is appropriated is better than the standard of any member of society where land is not appropriated and fully utilized.

In Locke's theory the contribution of human labour is evaluated very highly whereas natural resources are considered almost worthless. Thus, Locke's justification of private appropriation rests on two basic arguments. First is that one's labour is one's own property and second is that before being privately and exclusively appropriated, resources of nature are valueless. At the same time Locke's justification of private property is a justification of the capitalist form of property because it is under capitalism that production basically takes place for the purpose of exchange; the exchange of commodities. (Macpherson 1967) It is on the basis of the assumed superiority of the capitalist farming and production for trade that Locke justified the British colonist's occupation of lands belonging to the American Indians. Locke argued that the American Indians did not know how to fully utilize the land; hence the land was justly available for appropriation.

The Utilitarian Justification of Private Property

According to Locke, the chief function of the government is to guarantee the protection of individuals' natural rights and to secure conditions under which they can peacefully enjoy their properties. However, Locke's concept of natural rights entails that the institution of property existed prior to and without the government. The institutions of civil society and government originated in order to make property secure. Locke's natural rights theory of property was severely criticized by the utilitarian thinkers. The utilitarians have two main arguments regarding property. First, in contrast to the natural rights doctrine, utilitarians defend private ownership on the ground of its enormous utility. And second, they argue that the institution of property cannot exist without the prior existence of legal and political authority of the government. Let us elaborate the utilitarian arguments in more detail.

Modern utilitarianism has its origins in the ideas of the 18th and 19th century British thinkers, such as, David Hume, Jeremy Bentham, James Mill, and John Stuart Mill. The tradition continued in the ideas of important thinkers like Henry Sidgwick, R. M. Hare, and J. J. C. Smart. Utilitarianism is the name given to that branch of ethical and political theory which judges the rightness of acts and decisions of individuals and institutions by their capacity to promote the happiness of those affected by them. According to Bentham, human beings naturally tend to seek pleasure and avoid pain. The happiness of an individual can be defined by a calculation of these two basic elements, and it is calculable. Happiness, according to Bentham, is to be understood as presence of pleasure and absence of pain, and unhappiness as absence of pleasure and presence of pain. According to utilitarian ethical theory, the acts which promote happiness are right and those which produce the opposite are wrong. Bentham also believed that it was possible to assess, indeed calculate pleasures and pains of an individual according to the duration, intensity, and propinquity of the sensations of pleasure or pain. It is, therefore, possible to make a judgement on the acts and policies of institutions according to such a calculation. So, an act is right if it produces a situation in which the happiness of a maximum number of people is ensured. In other words, an act is right if the net balance of pleasure over pain of those affected is greater. The governments and the limit to the governments' sphere of activity have to be justified by reference to the principle of utility, i.e. by reference to the greatest happiness of the greatest number. This is the earliest and a crude form of modern utilitarianism, rejected by almost all the later utilitarians, and replaced by more sophisticated versions. Bentham's views on what constituted the individual's pleasure were criticized by his successor John Stuart Mill who introduced the distinction between higher-order pleasure and lower-order pleasure. In the 20th century, the utilitarians have replaced pleasure with individuals' rational preferences. However, despite disputes within utilitarianism on what is to be counted as legitimate preference of individuals, the basic idea has remained the same. The basic idea of the utilitarian political theory is that it is possible to gather information regarding the sum-total of all the utilities in a society. The goodness of institutions can be judged by looking at what they do with respect to this sum total of utilities.

The utilitarians reject the Lockean view that there could be any pre-legal and pre-political natural rights, including the right to property. They place great value on legal-political institutions and reject rights in the imaginary pre-political state of nature as nonsense. On the question of property, the utilitarians maintain that the right to property is meaningless in the absence of positive legal institutions to enforce the right. Property is a creation of law and is impossible without the coercive institutional apparatus of the government. Even in the presence of institutions the important questions are: what kind of right to property do utilitarians defend? And on what grounds? The utilitarians maintain that individuals should have a right to exclusive private property. Existence of this right is obviously defended on the ground that it is compatible with the principle of utility.

Human beings do not live from moment to moment. Rather, they plan their lives with future material security in mind. Expectations from the future are an important part of their happiness and a sense of well-being. Security in expectations leads to peace of mind and promotion of happiness. Frustrated expectations, on the other hand, are a major source of hindrance to happiness or a source of unhappiness. If I sow today, I expect to reap tomorrow. If someone else reaps what I have sown, it leads to frustration, insecurity, and ultimately to unhappiness. On the other hand, insecurity in possession, use and control over goods makes an individual's achievement of happiness impossible. From the above assumptions, the utilitarians conclude that a system of property rights is necessary if individuals are to achieve some degree of happiness.

Another important utilitarian argument in favour of the right to property is the incentive argument. Utilitarians argue that labour is a painful activity and human beings would not happily like to engage in it. Therefore, an individual reward is necessary to overcome the natural disinclination towards labour. By guaranteeing the security of rewards through a system of rightful ownership human beings will have the incentive to work. But also, and more importantly, it is a system of private property that creates incentives for individuals to work harder. Imagine a situation where you are working collectively with some people and the rewards of the work are to be shared equally. You will not get any extra benefit even if you were to work harder than everybody else. In other words, you do not have the incentive and consequently no motivation for working more. But if there is individual entitlement to the rewards of labour, you have the necessary motivation to work more.

Since the increased wealth due to extra individual effort adds to the total wealth of the society, the utilitarian argues, that private property rights are not only beneficial for the concerned individual; they also increase the social utility. Therefore, if governments want to promote the overall happiness of people they should encourage productivity by protecting individuals' property rights. Similarly, no government should take away property some people are expected to possess and enjoy. Taking both the security argument and the incentive argument together, utilitarianism justifies private property because such an arrangement not only contributes to our happiness but also improves our ability to make use of the things of the world and of our own abilities.

Utilitarians argue further that legal institutions are necessary for enforcing property rights. They assume that there is a scarcity of goods in the world, and that human beings have innumerable wants. Given the way human nature is (Utilitarians have a bleak view of human nature), there are high chances of conflict and violence. The need for institutions arise from the need to control potentially violent situations. It is the task of institutions to create conditions in which individuals can peacefully enjoy the fruits of their labour and can predict others' conduct in order to plan their own activities. In other words, institutions are necessary for creating the stable conditions necessary for the security of individuals' expectations. The opposite conditions—the insecurity of possession and use—make happiness impossible.

Karl Marx's Critique of Private Property

The historical context of the natural rights and the Utilitarian doctrines of property was that of the emergence and expansion of capitalism in Europe. The basic feature of the capitalist mode of production is that production in society takes place for the market. In the market, one commodity is exchanged for another through the medium of money. With the Industrial Revolution in the 18th century, the capitalists started to invest more and more capital in large-scale production in modern factories. The growth of industrial capitalism engendered, on the one hand, large-scale accumulation of wealth in the hands of the capitalist class, and on the other, an impoverished working class. The condition of industrial labourers in Europe in the 19th century was very poor. The working conditions in the early capitalist factory were very harsh. The working hours were long and the wages were at the subsistence level. As a result, the 19th century capitalism was ridden with extreme social and economic inequalities. Karl Marx's critique of private property needs to be understood against this historical background.

Karl Marx advocated the abolition of private property. By private property, Marx refers to the private ownership of the means of production. His analysis is historical. He focuses on the specific historical capitalist form of private property arrangements and methods of production. Marx specifies abolition of private property as an essential condition for the establishment of communism, an ideal society imagined by him. However, he does not advocate abolition of all kinds of property rights, but only capitalist private property, or in other words, private property as capital. Marx, in other words, is not hostile to the idea of individuals owning some amount of property necessary for their basic needs.

Marx's first arguments against private property appear as a critique of Hegel's defence of private property. Hegel believed that possession of property is essential for the realization of man's personality. Against Hegel, Marx argues that private property in the capitalist form is not a realization but a negation of personality. Marx believed that human beings under the conditions of the capitalist mode of production were not able to master the world through their ownership of property. On the contrary, the forces of market decide what happens to human beings in the world. They are not the true owners of their own selves, nor can they fully realize their own will under such conditions. Marx argued that only after the abolition of the capitalist mode of production can human beings truly master the world.

This argument of Marx against private property can also be understood in comparison with Locke's. The main point of Locke's justification of property is that private property is something that is produced by the application of someone's labour. Locke was able to overcome this limitation with the provision that labour could be bought and sold legitimately and the product of labour belonged to someone who had bought the labour. So, where there is a labour market, the producer of a product may not have control over the product of his labour. This 'lack of control' is one of the points in Marx's critique of private property and wage-labour arrangement in a market economy. Marx's analysis tried to show that there is no real freedom or choice for those who labour and who own no property. They must either work by selling their labour or starve. Marx also showed that capitalism had historically eliminated those systems of production where individual producers could own the means of their production. The elimination of such systems of production was a historical precondition for the emergence of the capitalist mode of production.

According to Marx, the capitalist mode of production is based on the monopolization of the means of production by a small class of people, the capitalist class. The majority of the labourers are those who own no means of production. This happened through a two-fold process in the European history during the transition from the feudal to the capitalist mode of production. On the one hand, large number of peasants and small-scale producers are deprived of their means of production leading to the emergence of a class of labourers who have nothing but their 'labour power' to sell in order to survive. On the other hand, all means of production get concentrated in the hands of a class of capitalists with the help of the legal mechanism of private property rights. Marx names this process 'primitive accumulation.' The capitalists' ownership of the means of production makes sure that labourers sell their labour to the capitalists since they themselves have nothing to work with or work upon, i.e. instruments of production, raw material, etc.

Thus, the main method of acquiring property under capitalism is through the appropriation of the products of labour. How, according to Marx, does this appropriation take place? Marx argued that labour was the creator of value of things. The worker, who produces, therefore, should be entitled to the whole product of his labour. In reality, and because the worker does not own the means of production, he only gets a portion of the labour expended for the production of a specific thing in the form of wage. The wages that are given to the workers are sufficient only to fulfil the subsistence needs of the worker and his family. Marx attempts to show through his analysis of the dynamics of capitalist production that the source of profit in capitalist production is the unpaid labour of the worker. According to him what the worker gets in the form of wages is only a fraction of the value he produces in a particular period of time. The remaining value created by the labour of the worker is appropriated by the capitalist. Marx refers to the latter as surplus value, which is shown to be the source of profit for the capitalist. But for Marx, the appropriation of surplus value, since its source is unpaid labour, amounts to exploitation of the workers. In this way, he argues that capitalist private property in founded upon exploitation.

Another ground of Marx's critique of capitalist private property is his theory of alienation worked out in his early work, *Economic and Philosophical Manuscripts* (1844). Marx argues that in the capitalist mode of production and under the regime of private property, various kinds of alienation or estrangement take place. This means a process of becoming strange or foreign to oneself. Alienation is the effect of property relations under capitalism. Marx's starting point is what he considers as the 'actual' economic fact. This, according to Marx, is that the more the labourer produces, the poorer he becomes. This is because under capitalism, wage labour does not create property for the labourer; it creates capital.

Marx describes three kinds of alienation or estrangement that workers go through under capitalism.

- According to Marx, production in human societies always involves an interaction between human labour and nature. In all productive activities—be it agriculture or craftsmanship or industrial production—human beings work upon nature with the help of certain tools, implements, or machines. While working on nature, their labour gets embodied in the objects they produce or create. Through such productive and creative activities man's labour gets realized. The producers, therefore, have a special relationship with the products of their labour. They find something of their own—their labour—in such things. But under capitalist relations of production, i.e. under the conditions of wage-labour, where workers, by agreeing to sell their labour, produce for others, and where the products of their labour are taken away from them, the relationship between worker and the product of his/her labour changes completely.
- The second kind of alienation results because the capitalist production is organized in such a way that workers conceive their work as nothing but sheer drudgery. In the assembly-line factory production, work is repetitive, monotonous and stressful. It does not involve the creativity of the workers because work is extremely fragmented. Fragmentation means that labourers do not get to produce a complete product the way artisans used to in pre-modern artisan production. Working under such conditions, i.e. in big modern industries does not lead to the 'free' development of the worker's personality but 'mortifies his body and ruins his mind'. The worker does not enjoy the activity of working and feels happy when he/she is not working. The worker, therefore, feels alienated from the activity of working.
- Very closely related to the second kind of alienation is the alienation from the species being. According to Marx, every animal species has a specific 'species character.' Man has a specific 'species character' that distinguishes him from other animals: free, conscious activity. What does free, conscious activity mean, and how does it distinguish human beings from other animals? According to Marx, 'Milton produced *Paradise Lost* for the same reason that a silkworm produces silk. It was an activity of *his* nature.' The reason may be the same and it may lie in the essential

nature of each species, but the activities themselves are very different. An animal's life activities are at one with itself. It does not distinguish the animal from itself. Human beings, on the other hand, direct and control their activity consciously and with freedom. Under the condition of capitalist production, where workers find their work repulsive, they relate to it in a non-human way. In other words, human life under capitalism is reduced to the level of animals, separating human beings from their very human essence. As a result of all these alienations human beings get alienated from each other. Marx, therefore, argues that only after the abolition of private ownership will human beings achieve full humanity and true freedom. This, Marx believed, could be achieved with the social control of production.

Developments in the 20th Century: Socialism, Welfarism, Libertarianism

The Socialist idea, indirectly affected the 20th-century politics in many ways. Within the capitalist economies, strongly organized trade unions fought for the rights of the workers under the banner of Socialism and gained important victories. In these countries, important welfare schemes were implemented to mitigate the bad effects of capitalism on the workers. Most of the developed capitalist countries and many developing countries implemented social welfare policies particularly after the World War II. The main components of these policies were taxation on property and transfer of basic industries, and basic public amenities like health and education to state control. These schemes led to the substantial improvement of the condition of the working class, particularly in the developed countries of Europe and North America.

State welfare schemes also found strong theoretical support from the 20th-century developments in utilitarianism as well as from the influential John Rawls' theory of justice. Rawls argued that the policies of redistribution of resources should be judged on the basis of their impact on the least advantaged sections of society. The utilitarians, on the other hand, advocated those policies of redistribution which enhanced the overall utility of the maximum number of people in a society. These theories faced strong criticisms from the libertarian thinkers like Friedrich von Hayek, Milton Friedman, Ayn Rand, and Robert Nozick. The libertarians argued that justice does not demand any particular distribution pattern. They believed that any outcome arrived at by separate just actions of individuals could be called 'just'. Robert Nozick advanced this version of libertarianism in his book *Anarchy, State, and Utopia* (1974).

Robert Nozick's Entitlement Defence of Private Property

Robert Nozick revived the Lockean idea that individuals are absolute owners of their talents, and capacities. He used this argument to justify private ownership. Nozick's theory of property is known as the theory of historical entitlement. Like Locke, Nozick also favours individual property rights and starts from the position that individuals are the owners of their own selves and have certain basic rights and duties, in particular, rights not to be harmed in life and liberty. Each human being is the morally rightful owner of his own person and powers. Consequently, he is free to use those powers as he wishes, provided that he does not employ them aggressively against others. He may not harm others; he may not be forced to harm others. He should also not be forced to help them, as is done in case of the redistribution system of the welfare state.

According to Nozick's theory, individuals obtain absolute control over objects through historical processes. This means that they may retain or transfer the ownership of these objects only at their own discretion. All compulsory transferences, therefore, constitute an infringement of rights. Similarly, any coercive regulation of owned objects infringes on the right of the owner. Further, Nozick's theory elaborates on procedures by which individuals may justly acquire titles to particular resources. It is a historical principle of justice in that it too holds that 'past circumstances or actions or people can create differential entitlements. This principle requires not that the size of shares be proportioned to past action, but that particular items are acquired by particular procedures' (Nozick 1974: 155). The entitlement theory connects individuals with particular holdings acquired by particular procedures. Nozick's entitlement theory has the following components:

1. The theory of just acquisition of holdings: This component tells us under what condition a person is entitled to something taken from the state of nature. According to Nozick, if a person has acquired a holding according to the principle of just acquisition of holdings, then this person is legitimately entitled to it.
2. The theory of just transfer of holdings: This component specifies the ways in which persons can justly transfer their holdings. According to Nozick, market transactions, charity, and barter are examples of legitimate means of transfer; theft, extortions, and taxation are examples of unjust means of taking of someone's property. This component of Nozick's entitlement theory states that if a person acquires a holding in accordance with the principle of justice in transfer from someone else who is justly entitled to that holding, can legitimately become the owner of that holding.
3. The theory of rectification: This component describes a procedure through which the effects of past injustices may be rectified or corrected. According to this component, if a person owns some holding according to the principle of rectification, s/he is justly entitled to that holding.
4. No one is legitimately entitled to a holding except by following the above-mentioned procedures (Nozick 1974: 150–53).

Distribution of property is to be defended or criticized, according to Nozick, not in the light of consideration of needs or rewards for effort, or the like, but by reference to information about the whole past history of the objects in the distribution. With respect to a given item of property, we have to obtain the required historical information regarding the origins of that item. In other words, we have to know whether its owner acquired it justly in the first place according to principle 1 (original appropriation of a previously unowned object), principle 2 (just transfer of a previously justly owned object), or principle 3 (property accruing to someone as a result of rectification of unjust ownership). The legitimacy of an entitlement, thus, depends on originally just appropriation and subsequently just transfer, except where the holding is a result of rectification of some past unjust appropriation or transfer.

Now, the most important point is to specify how a person can legitimately acquire property originally. Nozick begins by considering the procedures specified in Locke's theory of property. Locke's procedures as discussed above say that a title is acquired by mixing labour with unowned objects, provided that 'enough and as good' is left for others. Nozick does not assign much importance to the means of acquiring property, as a matter of fact, he provides a critique of Locke's labour-mixing argument. Nozick takes Locke's 'enough and as good' proviso more seriously and uses it as an important qualifying condition for a legitimate appropriation of property.

Nozick argues that others' liberty is not violated as long as 'enough and as good' is left in common for others. If A appropriates some natural object but there remains enough unappropriated for others to do anything they might have done before A's appropriation, then the appropriation has not violated any rights. Each person has as much a liberty as before. The 'crucial point' for Nozick is, 'whether an appropriation of an unowned object worsens the situation of others' (Nozick 1974: 175). If the position of others no longer at liberty to use the thing is worsened by a certain act of appropriation, that act is not justified. One has to be sure that 'enough and as good' is left for others.

Locke and Nozick differ on the interpretation of this condition. Nozick thinks that in certain circumstances loss of liberty by others due to appropriation of some hitherto unowned object can be legitimately compensated. If appropriation and enclosure leave no further land or resources to appropriate and the propertyless have lost the right to use the resources appropriated, it will be justified if their overall position is not worsened (if the opportunities gained through others' appropriations at least compensate for the liberties lost). Nozick thinks it is enough and as good to compensate others with equivalent opportunities and resources, and not necessary for either exactly the same or nearly similar sort of items to be there as existed before appropriation. Nozick's argument has been criticized on the ground that it allows the comparison of only two situations, those of no ownership and those with private ownership. G. A. Cohen argues that he does not take into account other alternatives like joint ownership of resources. This alternative, however, does not go against Nozick's ideal of self-ownership of individuals (Cohen 1985: 95).

Gender and Property Rights: Feminist Perspectives on the Concept of Property

In the 20th century, the feminist movement highlighted the inequality between men and women and provided a powerful critique of it. Feminist thought developed a very important perspective on social reality by focusing on the experiences of women in society as well as on the impact of different theories and practices on women's lives. One of the most important feminist arguments is that the distribution of resources in a particular society is strongly affected by the prevailing gender relations in that particular society. The resulting iniquitous distribution, in turn, consolidates and perpetuates the gender bias against women. Feminist scholars have argued that an important condition of the subjugation of women throughout history has been the denial of access to resources of income, such as land. Because of the prevailing patterns of male ownership and control of such resources, the status of women has been one of dependence on men. This dependent status is then legitimized by means of ideologies which claimed that the subordinate status of women has a grounding in the order of nature. Political theory—both modern and pre-modern—has played an important role in the production of such ideologies. Contemporary feminist thought has critically analysed many important texts of political theory—those of Aristotle, Rousseau, Locke and others—from this standpoint (Freedman 2002: 26–30). As an example of this mode of feminist criticism, we shall briefly discuss Carole Pateman's critique of early modern social contract theory.

According to Carole Pateman, modern political theory, beginning with the works of Hobbes and Locke, seeks to define the spheres of society and politics in a special way. Social and the political spheres gain their meaning from what they exclude as much as from what they include. One of the exclusions that takes place in this strategy is that of familial and kinship relation. Society, or the space for 'social' activities, has no space for particularistic or ascriptive ties. It is a space where free and equal individuals interact and transact their businesses. This understanding of the social sphere, Pateman claims, leads to the exclusion of women from it. [Pateman, 1987] How does this exclusion happen?

Pateman questions the belief that the 'individual' in modern political theory includes both men and women, and hence is gender neutral. She, in fact, shows that the 'individual' in modern political theory is masculine. According to her, Locke's concept of individual in *Two Treatises of Government* excludes women because he does not allow equality between men and women. Locke argues that women are 'naturally' subject to men because the subjection of wife to husband has 'a foundation in nature'. Therefore, this being a given, women can be neither free nor equal to men in such a conception of society. Although, historically, Locke's political theory challenged various feudal inequalities of hierarchies and status, it fails to challenge inequality present in the family, as the family is excluded from the social space. Pateman argues that although Locke's political theory was presented ostensibly as an argument against Robert Filmer's defence of patriarchal power, it ended up justifying a new, modern form of patriarchy.

The individuals in Locke's political theory, who go out in the society and are the owners of private property and bearers of rights—the citizens—according to Pateman, are the men who are heads of households. They represent women and children in the public social sphere. Women, on the contrary, remained confined to the private, non-political sphere without property and rights. The division between public and private maintained by this theory is based on patriarchal assumptions. It is men, as heads of households, who enter into the original social contract that created the political state. As a result, while men acquired full citizenship of the body politic, women were reduced to a subordinate position in it. For a long time later modern democracies denied women many civil rights, most importantly, the right to vote, on the grounds that they were represented in the political realm by their husbands (Freedman 2002: 26–30). The subordinate position of women in the public sphere, however, is a function of their position of dependence in the private sphere of family because of the lack of independent source of income or independent access to property.

Thus, the institution of family comes under the critical scrutiny of feminist thought. From this standpoint the question of distribution of property within the family is a crucial question, because it is on this distribution that the status of women as social beings and as citizens depends. As Pateman's critique showed, political theory has traditionally been reluctant to consider the sphere of the family from the point of view of equality and justice. In the context of South Asia, Bina Agarwal's work has criticized such attitudes in the formulation and implementation of government policies. Agarwal's article, 'Gender and Command over Property' (1994), is a critical investigation of the development policies of many South Asian countries in the second half of the 20th century and questions their underlying assumptions from a feminist perspective. She also raises the much-ignored question of inequality between man and woman within the household. Agarwal argues that when such policies undertake the distribution or redistribution of various resources, particularly land, they give ownership title to the heads of the families, who are usually men. Agarwal criticizes the basic assumption of such distributive policies that the sphere of the household is equitable and a just distribution of resources takes place there in irrespective of gender. Since family is not a sphere of equality and justice, such development policies cannot be gender neutral. They ignore the intra-household gender relations. In her investigation, Agarwal shows that in the land redistribution policies followed in India, Sri Lanka, and Pakistan in the decades of the 1950s and 1960s, titles were granted only to men, and not to women independently.

Another important issue raised by Agarwal is the distinction between ownership and control. She argues that even if gender equality is guaranteed in legal ownership of property, it does not lead to *de facto* scontrol over it. There is a big gap between legal and practical situations. Because of traditional prejudices and actually existing power relationships, most of the South Asian women face difficulties in exercising their legal right in landed property. Therefore, hurdles against women gaining control over resources occur not only at the legal level but at the social and cultural levels as well (Agarwal 1994: 159–61). As already discussed, the underlying assumptions of political theory and of the development practices of the welfare state are deeply problematic from the point of view of gender relationship. Contemporary feminist scholarship has criticized this gender order based on the idea of male as the family head with a single source of family income as patriarchal and anachronistic.

Points for Discussion

1. What are the basic differences in Locke's justification of private property and that of the utilitarian justification?
2. In your opinion, how will it affect the structure of family if individuals are considered units of society for land distribution rather than family?
3. In Locke's argument regarding private property, what difference does the introduction of money make?
4. According to Marx, how does private ownership of means of production in capitalist society produce alienation?
5. Try to find out the recent changes related to inheritance of family property made through a parliamentary legislation in India. Try to relate them to the feminist critique of gender inequality.

Reading List

Agarwal, Bina, 'Gender and Command over Property: A Critical Gap in Economic Analysis and Policy in South Asia', *World Development*, 22(10), 1994: 1455–78.

Aristotle, 'Politics', in Richard McKeon (ed.), *The Basic Works of Aristotle* (New York: The Modern Library, 2001).

Becker, Lawrence C., *Property Rights: Philosophical Foundations* (London: Routledge and Kegan Paul, 1977).

Cohen, G. A., 'Nozick on Appropriation', *New Left Review*, 150, 1985.

Freedman, Jane, *Feminism* (New Delhi: Viva Books, 2002).

Locke, John, *Two Treatises of Government* (Cambridge: Cambridge University Press, 1967).

Macpherson, C. B., 'Political Theory of Property', in C.B. Macpherson (ed.), *Democratic Theory* (Oxford: Clarendon Press, 1973).

———, *Political Theory of Possessive Individualism* (Oxford: Clarendon Press, 1967).

Marx, Karl, *Economic and Philosophical Manuscripts*, 1844. Entire text available online at http://www.marxists.org/archieve/marx/works/1844/manuscripts/preface.htm

Nozick, Robert, *Anarchy, State, and Utopia* (New York: Basic Books, 1974).

Parel, Anthony and Thomas Flanagan (eds), *Theories of Property: Aristotle to the Present* (Ontario: Wilfrid Laurier University Press, 1979).

Pateman, Carole, 'Feminist Critiques of Public/Private Dichotomy', in A. Philips (ed.), *Feminism and Equality* (Oxford: Blackwell, 1987).

———, *The Sexual Contract* (Cambridge: Polity Press, 1988).

Reeve, Andrew, *Property* (London: Macmillan, 1986).

Ryan, Alan, *Property and Political Theory* (Oxford: Blackwell, 1984).

———, *Property* (Milton Keynes: The Open University Press, 1987).

CHAPTER 15

Gender

Nivedita Menon

Chapter Outlines

Introduction

One of the key contributions of feminist theory is the creation of a distinction between 'sex' and 'gender'; a distinction that has subsequently been developed differently by various strands of feminist thought. This chapter begins with this basic distinction that is made, and its significance. This is followed by a brief discussion on how the rigid male/female opposition is specific to modernity and to Western cultures. Thereby, the four different ways in which the sex/gender distinction has been complicated by different kinds of feminist theory is looked at. The chapter concludes with a brief look at an emerging field in feminist theory—the study of masculinity, how it is constructed, and its implications for men in patriarchal society.

Sex is to Nature as Gender is to Culture

The initial move was to use the term *sex* to refer to the *biological* differences between men and women, while *gender* indicated the vast range of *cultural* meanings attached to that basic difference. This distinction is important for feminism to make because the subordination of women has been fundamentally justified on the grounds of the biological differences between men and women. The philosophical reasoning which legitimizes various forms of oppression as natural and inescapable, because the oppression that arises supposedly from natural and therefore unchangeable factors, is called biological determinism. Racism is a good example of this, as is the caste system, because both ideologies are based on the assumption that certain groups of people are superior by birth, and that they are born with characteristics such as greater intelligence and special skills that justify their power in society. Biological determinism has also been one of the most important legitimizing mechanisms of women's oppression over the centuries. The challenge to biological determinism is, therefore, crucial for feminist politics.

Feminist anthropologists, particularly Margaret Mead, have demonstrated that the understanding of masculinity and femininity varies across cultures. In other words, not only do different societies identify a certain set of characteristics as feminine and another set as masculine, but also, these characteristics are not the same across different cultures. Thus, feminists have argued that there is no necessary correlation between the biology of men and women and the qualities that are thought to be masculine and feminine. Rather, it is child-rearing practices that try to establish and perpetuate certain differences between the sexes. That is, from childhood, boys and girls are trained in appropriate, gender-specific forms of behaviour, play, dress and so on. This training is continuous and most of the time subtle, but when necessary, can involve punishments to bring about conformity. So, feminists argue that sex-specific qualities (for example, bravery and confidence as 'masculine' and sensitivity and shyness as 'feminine') and the value that society attributes to them, are produced by a range of institutions and beliefs that socialize boys and girls differently. As Simone de Beauvoir puts it, 'One is not born, but is made a woman.'

In addition, societies generally value 'masculine' characteristics more highly than 'feminine' while at the same time ensuring that men and women who do not conform to these characteristics are continuously disciplined into 'appropriate' behaviour. For instance, a man who expresses sorrow publicly by crying would be humiliated by the taunt, '*Auraton jaise ro rahe ho?*' (Why are you crying like a woman?) And who does not remember that stirring line of Subhadra Kumari Chauhan—'*Khoob ladi mardani, woh to Jhansi wali rani thi*' (bravely she fought, the Rani of Jhansi/She fought like a man). What does this line mean? Even when it is a woman who has shown bravery, it still cannot be understood as a 'feminine' quality—bravery is still seen as a masculine virtue, no matter how many women or how few men display it.

There is nothing 'natural' about the sexual division of labour. The fact that men and women perform different kinds of work both within the family and outside has little to do with biology and more to do with ideological assumptions. Only the actual process of pregnancy is biological, all the other work within the home that women must do—cooking, cleaning, looking after children and so on (in other words, the whole range of work we may call 'domestic labour')—can equally be done by men. But this work is considered to be 'women's work'. This sexual division of labour extends even to the 'public' arena of paid work, and again, this has nothing to do with 'sex' (biology) and everything to do with 'gender' (culture). Certain kinds of work are considered to be 'women's work', and other kinds, men's; but more important is the fact that whatever work women do gets lower wages and is less valued. For example, nursing and teaching (particularly at lower levels) are predominantly female professions and are also comparatively ill-paid in relation to other white-collar jobs which the middle classes take up. Feminists point out that this 'feminization' of teaching and nursing is because such work is seen as an extension of the nurturing work that women do within the home. So, while on the one hand women are supposed to be physically weak and unfit for heavy manual labour, that is precisely what they are made to do both in the home and outside—carry heavy loads of water and firewood, grind corn, transplant paddy, and carry headloads in mining and construction work. But when the manual work that women do is mechanized, making it both lighter and better-paid, then it is men who receive training to use the new machinery and women are edged out. This happens not only in factories, but even with work that was traditionally done by women within the community; for example, when electrically operated flour mills replace hand-pounding of grain, or machine-made nylon fishing nets replace the nets traditionally handmade by women, it is men who are trained to take over these jobs, and women are forced to move into even lower-paid and more arduous manual work.

It is, thus, clear that the present subordination of women arises, not from the unchangeable biological differences (sex), but from social and cultural values, ideologies and institutions that ensure the material and ideological subordination of women (gender). Thus, feminists question sex-differentiated work, the sexual division of labour, and more fundamentally, questions of sexuality and reproduction, as issues to be extricated from the realm of 'biology'—which is understood to be natural and unchangeable. The feminist agenda is to relocate these issues in the realm of the 'political', which suggests that they can and must be transformed.

Male/Female in the Non-West

In this context, it is interesting to note that some scholars are of the opinion that the strictly bipolar model of masculinity/femininity and the devaluing of the feminine are characteristic only of modern Western civilization. Even in Western culture, the two-sex model was entrenched by law and the state only with the advent of modernity. Anne Fausto-Sterling (2002: 469) points out that in Europe it was only by the end of the Middle Ages that biological hermaphrodites (people born with one testis and one ovary) were compelled to choose an established gender role and stay with it. The penalty for transgression, she says, was often death. Until this period, people's sex was not necessarily fixed strictly into a two-sex model. Fausto-Sterling, therefore, argues that sex is 'a vast, infinitely malleable continuum' that defies the constraints of all fixed categories.

Pre-modern Indian cultures, too, had greater space for a variety of sexual identities—eunuchs, for example, had a socially acknowledged status in Indian society that they have lost in contemporary times. Again, the Sufi and Bhakti traditions drew upon notions of androgyny and often rejected the two-sex model. Take, for instance, this poem by a 12th-century Shaivite poet, Basavanna, who wrote in Kannada (Ramanujan 1973: 29).

Look here, dear fellow,
I wear these men's clothes only for you.
Sometimes I am man,
Sometimes I am woman...

Another Shivabhakta, Devara Dasimayya, writing two centuries earlier, wrote (ibid: 110)

If they see breasts and long hair coming,
They call it woman,
If beard and whiskers
They call it man.
But look, the self that hovers in between
Is neither man nor woman...

Such examples would be found in all Indian languages. In this context, a thought-provoking argument is made by Ashis Nandy (1983). He notes that pre-colonial Indian cultures accorded greater value to femininity. It was with the coming of colonialism that the Western valorization of masculinity became the norm. Nationalists, too, then played into this understanding, and tried to resist the deriding of Indian culture as 'effeminate' by claiming to be as 'masculine' as the colonial masters—the ideology of revolutionaries for example, was very masculinist. According to Nandy, Gandhi was unique in attempting to focus on 'feminine' rather than 'masculine' qualities as having the power to resist colonialism—that is, he emphasized spiritual and moral courage over aggression and violence (Nandy 1983).

Developments in the Sex/Gender Distinction in Feminist Theory

The distinction between 'sex' and 'gender' has been made more complex by feminist scholars over the years. Although the distinction continues to be broadly accepted by all feminists, the initial understanding that 'sex' is related to nature while 'gender' is related to culture has been reworked considerably. Broadly, we can discern four main ways in which the sex/gender distinction has been further developed in feminist theory.

First, scholars like Alison Jaggar (1983) argue that 'sex' and 'gender' are dialectically and inseparably related and that the conceptual distinction that earlier feminists established between the two is not sustainable beyond a point. In this understanding, human biology is constituted by a complex interaction between the human body, the physical environment and the state of development of technology and society. Thus, as Jaggar puts it, 'the hand is as much the product of labour as the tool of labour' (Jaggar 1983: 109–10). What is meant here is that two processes are involved: human intervention changes the external environment and simultaneously, changes in the external environment shape and change the human body. This is true in two senses. One, in a long-term evolutionary sense, over the millenia. That is, human bodies have evolved differently in different parts of the globe, due to differences in diet, climate, and nature of work performed.

Again, in a more short-term sense, it is now recognized that neurophysiology and hormonal balances are affected by social factors like anxiety, physical labour, level and kind of social interaction, just as much as social interaction is affected by people's neuro-physiology and hormonal balances. For instance, certain chemical changes in the body may produce certain symptoms of stress that can be treated by drugs. But equally, high stress levels can, in fact, be the reason for higher chemical imbalances, and it may be possible to restore the body's balance only by changing the conditions in which it lives.

Consider this passage from Dorothy Dinnerstein (1976: 22):

> ... humans are by nature unnatural. We do not yet walk 'naturally' on our hind legs, for example. Such ills as fallen arches, lower back pain, and hernias testify that the body has not adapted itself completely to the upright posture. Yet this unnatural posture, forced on the unwilling body by the project of tool-using, is precisely what has made possible the development of important aspects of our 'nature'—the hand and the brain, and the complex system of skills, language and social arrangements which were both effects and causes of hand and brain. Man-made and physiological structures have thus come to interpenetrate so thoroughly that we are what we have made ourselves, and we must continue to make ourselves as long as we exist at all.

When we apply the understanding that biology and culture are interrelated, to the sex/gender distinction, the relevant implication is that women's bodies have been shaped by social restrictions and by norms of beauty. That is, the 'body' has been formed as much by 'culture' as by 'nature'. For instance, the rapid improvements in women's athletic records over the past two decades is an indication that social norms had shaped biology and restricted women's physical development. Feminist anthropologists have also pointed out that in some ethnic groups there is little physical differentiation between men and women. In short, we must consider that there are two equally powerful factors at work—one, there is a range of interrelated ways in which society produces sex differences, and two, sex differences structure society in particular ways.

'Sex', in this view, is not an unchanging base upon which society constructs 'gender' meanings, but rather, sex itself has been affected by various factors external to it. There is no clear and unchanging line between nature and culture.

A second kind of rethinking of sex/gender has come from radical feminism, which argues that feminists must not underplay the biological difference between the sexes and attribute all difference to 'culture' alone. To do so is to accept male civilization's devaluing of the female reproductive role. This is a criticism of the liberal feminist understanding that in an ideal world, men and women would be more or less alike. They claim that on the contrary, patriarchal social values have denigrated 'feminine' qualities and that it is the task of feminism to recover these qualities, and this difference between men and women, as valuable. Their position on the sex/gender distinction is that there are certain differences between men and women that arise from their different biological reproductive roles, and therefore, women are more sensitive, instinctive and closer to nature. Radical feminists such as Susan Griffin and Andrea Dworkin, for example, believe that women's reproductive biology, the process of gestation and the experience of mothering, fundamentally affects their relationship to the external world. Women are according to this understanding, closer to nature and share in nature's qualities of fecundity, nurturing and instinct. These qualities have been rejected by patriarchal society but feminists should accept and revalue these qualities.

Carol Gilligan's book, *In a Different Voice* (1993) is a significant example of this viewpoint. Using a psychoanalytical point of view, she argues that because the primary caregiver in childhood is invariably a woman (the mother)—given the sexual division of labour—the process by which men and women come to adulthood is different. Boys move into adulthood learning to differentiate from the mother, while girls do so by identifying with her. That is, in a sex-differentiated society, while all infants identify with the mother, gradually boys learn that they are 'different' while girls learn that they are the 'same' as their mother. This results, Gilligan argues, in women having a more subjective, relational way of engaging with the world, while men have a more objective mode. Women relate to others, while men learn to separate themselves. This explains, for example, the difference in the nature of male and female friendships. Gilligan's focus in this work is the difference in the ways men and women take moral decisions, and she comes to the conclusion that women are less influenced by normative notions of what is right and wrong, and more by other factors like empathy, concern, and sensitivity to another's predicament. Men, on the other hand, tend to take moral decisions based on well-accepted notions of what society thinks is right and wrong. Thus, Gilligan concludes that the basic categories of Western moral philosophy—rationality, autonomy and justice—are drawn from and reflect the male experience of the world. The female experience is invisible here. To deny difference is, therefore, to agree with the patriarchal negation of femininity as worthless.

Third, a more recent feminist position takes the opposite view from that of radical feminists. While radical feminists argue that the sex/gender distinction underplays sex differences, the school of post-modern feminist thought holds that it over-emphasizes the biological body. Judith Butler (1990: 6), for instance, argues that if 'gender' is symbolic of the cultural meanings that the sexed body takes on, then gender cannot be said to follow from 'sex' in any one way. According to her, 'gender' is not the cultural inscription of meaning on a pre-given 'sex', rather, gender as a way of thinking and as a concept, produces the category of biological sex. Butler, thus, suggests a 'radical discontinuity' between sexed bodies and culturally constructed genders.

Butler further uses the term *heterosexual matrix* to designate the grid produced by institutions, practices and discourses, looking through which it appears to be 'a fact of nature' that all human bodies possess one of the two fixed sexual identities, with each experiencing sexual desire only for the 'opposite sex'. From this viewpoint, the removal of this grid or heterosexual matrix will reveal that sexuality and human bodies are fluid and have no necessary fixed sexual identity or orientation. The characteristic feature of this position is that it holds that the category of 'woman' does not exist prior to the thinking about it. Gender is something that is constructed through relations of power, and through a series of norms and constraints that regulate what will be recognized as a 'male' body and a 'female' body. Through such norms, a wide range of bodies are rendered invisible and/or illegitimate, for instance, infants born with no clear determining sexual characteristics, or eunuchs, or men and women who choose not to follow the dress norms prescribed for their gender. All these are either marginalized, criminalized or forced to fit into the existing two-sex model in some way or the other. Most modern languages have no way of speaking of a human who does not fit into either sex. What this means is that language forces 'reality' into certain pre-given patterns and prevents certain possibilities from being realized.

One of the most powerful languages determining 'sex' is that of the biomedical sciences and feminist scientists have thoroughly criticized it. Feminist scientists such as Ruth Bleier and Evelyn Fox Keller have argued that a rigid sex/gender distinction restricts biological sex—that is, sex defined as anatomical, hormonal or chromosomal—as something to be studied by the biomedical sciences, while gender is to be studied by the social sciences. Such an understanding takes for granted that while cultural notions of gender may change, the body remains as an unchanging biological reality that needs no further explanation. These scientists argue that on the contrary, our perceptions and interpretations of the body are mediated through language, and biomedical sciences function as a major provider of this language.

A startling study in the United States of intersexed infants (babies born with both ovarian and testicular tissue or in whom the sex organs are ambiguous) showed that medical decisions to assign one sex or the other were made on cultural assumptions rather than on any existing biological features. Thus, a baby might be made into a female but then still require hormonal therapy all her life to make her stay 'female'. In other words, male and female are not only culturally different, they are not even biologically stable features at all times (Kessler 1994).

Alison Jaggar discusses a similar study of children whose sex had been incorrectly assigned at birth due to such ambiguity—when the 'real' sex of the child emerged at a later stage, both the parents and medical practitioners decided on surgery to confirm the sex attributed at birth. This was invariably preferred to simply accepting that the child's sex was different from that attributed at birth. In other words, surgical intervention to change 'sex' was thought to be easier than eradicating years of cultural 'gender' conditioning.

Nelly Oudshoorn's (1994) work shows that scientists have understood 'sex' in different ways over centuries—from the ancient Greeks until the late 18th century, male and female bodies were understood by medical texts to be fundamentally similar. This 'one-sex' model of humanity, with the woman as a lesser version of the male body, dominated biomedical discourse for thousands of years. In the 18th century, biomedical discourse began to emphasize differences between the sexes rather than similarities. Every part of the human body was sexualized, and physiological 'facts' (for example, smaller brain size) were used to prove the lesser intelligence of women, their passive nature and so on. The feminine 'essence' that supposedly differentiated women from men, was sought to be located in different parts of the body—in the 18th century, the uterus was thought to be the seat of femaleness, in the 19th century, it was the ovaries. By the 20th century, the essence of femininity was understood to be located in chemical substances called hormones.

The hormonal conception of the body is now one of the dominant modes of thinking about the root of sexual differences. What Oudshoorn points out is that the hormonal conception of the body, in fact, allows for the possibility of breaking out of the tyranny of the binary sex-difference model. If bodies can have both female and male hormones, then maleness and femaleness are not restricted to one kind of body alone. However, the biomedical sciences have preferred increasingly, to portray the female, but not the male, as a body completely controlled by hormones. In this process, a clear nexus has emerged between the medical profession and a huge, multi-billion dollar pharmaceutical industry. 'Disorders' in women—such as the ageing of the skin, depression, menstrual irregularities—are prescribed hormonal therapy. Such drugs are expensive, but even more disturbing is the fact that it is in the interest of the pharmaceutical industry that natural processes such as ageing are treated as diseases. Moreover, depression, which has social causes, is treated with drugs as if it were a purely physiological problem. If women can be made to feel that looking old is 'unfeminine' or that their depression arises, not from their being undervalued and overworked, but from something inside themselves, then the profits of multinational drug companies are assured.

Therefore, the post-modern feminist position rejects the idea that scientific facts about the body simply exist to be discovered. Rather, scientific facts are deeply embedded in society and culture. 'Sex' itself is constructed by human practices.

A fourth kind of rethinking of the sex/gender distinction comes from locating 'gender' in a grid of identities—caste, class, race, and religion. This would mean that the biological category of 'woman' does not necessarily have shared interests, life-situations, or goals. This kind of understanding has arisen from the political practice of women's movements all over the world, which has increasingly revealed that 'women' do not exist as a pre-existing subject which can simply be mobilized by the women's movement. That is, women identify themselves not only, and not even primarily, in terms of their gender, but as black, or muslim, or Dalit, or peasant. So in many cases, women may be easily mobilized in terms of their religion, for example, than by the women's movement.

In the case of India, a good example of this is the debate over the uniform civil code. All religious communities have their own personal laws which discriminate against women on matters of marriage, divorce, inheritance, and guardianship of children. A demand for a uniform civil code that would give all women equal rights as citizens has, therefore, been made by the women's movement since 1937. However, in the growing atmosphere of communalism since the 1980s, and the insecurity felt by religious minorities, most sections of the women's movement have gradually shifted to the opinion that the position of women should be improved by reforms within personal laws, rather than by forcing communities to obey to the legislation passed by the state. The state no longer has the legitimacy it had in the immediate post-Independence years, its role in communal violence is increasingly suspect, and it cannot be seen simply as an agent of progressive social change. Thus, what was a simple feminist demand that all *women* should have equal rights has been considerably transformed by the politics of *religious* identity.

Further, all politically active women do not necessarily act as feminists—they may well be representing interests and structures of power which feminist politics in India has sought to struggle against. Thus, we find women active in right-wing politics and in anti-lower caste movements like the agitation against the Mandal Commission report. In other words, in this understanding, the feminist sex/gender distinction must take into account other modes of constituting identity. Depending on the context, even as feminists, we may have to privilege caste or class identity over gender in some cases, just as we expect Marxists or Dalit activists to privilege gender over class and caste in some contexts.

Masculinity

A significant body of scholarship that has emerged in recent years is around the construction of 'masculinity'. While feminist scholarship on gender has focused on the construction of femininity and the female body, it has increasingly begun to be felt that it is equally crucial to expose the mechanisms by which the parallel construct of masculinity is sustained under patriarchy. It is, therefore, necessary to understand how this construct empowers men, how it restricts and disempowers those men who cannot or do not obey the rules, or meet the expectations of masculine behaviour—for example, old men, or homosexuals. The operation of masculine norms and the discourse of masculinity also 'feminizes' powerless men as a way of rendering them inferior—working class or poor men, Dalit men, and so on.

Thus, the original sex/gender distinction made by feminists has been made considerably more complex by the theory and practice of feminist politics. This distinction, thus, continues to be crucial for any feminist understanding of the subordination of women.

Points for Discussion

1. What do you understand by sexual division of labour? Do you think it has any implications for citizenship rights of women?
2. Do you think it is liberating or constraining to believe that 'gender'—both masculinity and femininity— is the product of particular social, cultural and economic formations? Explain why.
3. Use the Internet and interviews with appropriate people to explore the ways in which non-Western and pre-modern cultures have blurred the sharp distinction between 'male' and 'female'. Can you think of contemporary practices that are still prevalent that do this? (You must use your imagination to think of what kind of people around you could have this kind of information.)
4. Imagine you had a three-year-old son whom you took to the doctor for some reason, and discovered that the child was more female than male. Would you prefer to now come to terms with the fact that you have a daughter, inform everybody, change the way you dress and think of your child, or would you prefer surgical intervention to retain your 'son' as a son? Does the latter option seem easier, and why? What does this tell us about the supposedly unchangeable 'natural' category of biology and, conversely, about the supposedly changeable category of 'culture'?

Reading List

Barrett, Michele, *Women's Oppression Today* (London: Verso, 1988).

Butler, Judith, *Gender Trouble* (New York and London: Routledge, 1990).

De Beauvoir, Simone, *The Second Sex* (London: Picador, 1988).

Dinnerstein, Dorothy, *The Mermaid and the Minotaur: Sexual Arrangements and Human Malaise* (New York: Harper and Row, 1976).

Fausto-Sterling, Anne, 'The Five Sexes: Why Male and Female Are Not Enough', in Christine L. Williams and Arlene Stein (eds), *Sexuality and Gender* (Oxford: Blackwell, 2002).

Gilligan, Carol, *In a Different Voice: Psychology and Women's Development* (Harvard: Harvard University Press, 1993).

Jaggar, Alison, *Feminist Politics and Human Nature* (Brighton: Harvester Press, 1983).

Kessler, Suzanne J., 'The Medical Construction of Gender: Case Management of Intersexed Infants', in Anne C. Hermann and Abigail Stewart (eds), *Theorizing Feminism* (Basil Blackwell, 1994).

Oudshoorn, Nelly, *Beyond the Natural Body. An Archaeology of Sex Hormones* (London: Routledge, 1994).

Ramanujan, A. K., *Speaking of Siva* (English trans.) (Harmondsworth: Penguin, 1973).

Tharu, Susie and Tejaswini Niranjana, 'Problems for a Contemporary Theory of Gender', in Nivedita Menon (ed.), *Gender and Politics* (Delhi: Oxford University Press, 1999).

Whitehead, Stephen M., *Men and Masculinities* (Cambridge: Polity Press, 2002).

PART III

Ideologies

CHAPTER 16

Liberalism

Ashok Acharya

Chapter Outlines

Introduction

Liberalism, like socialism, fascism, or nationalism, is a political ideology. A political ideology explains our social reality, interprets it in a certain way, evolves a set of interrelated principles, contests the nature of the political, and prescribes appropriate action. There is, however, a closed and rigid structure to ideology that does not leave much room for flexibility of interpretations or contestations of received ideas. Both in prescribing a set of beliefs and in setting an agenda for action, an ideology may not provide much space for creative interpretation that one may find, for instance, in various ethical debates carried out in contemporary political theory. Some variants of liberalism display this but in a minimal way. Since liberalism also attests to, in a loose sense, a set of dispositions and a way of life sustained by reason and human values, it is in many ways more flexible than an ideology. Indeed, liberalism itself offers an intellectual climate and platform, made possible by its commitments to freedom and toleration, for other ideologies to exist and function. As Alan Ryan makes it clear, '(w)hatever liberalism involves, it certainly includes toleration and an antipathy to closing ranks around any system of beliefs' (Ryan 1993: 292).

A Brief History

Liberalism has a longer history than most political ideologies. It has primarily evolved out of sustained struggles against hierarchically organized social and political relations. In many ways, liberalism captures the ideological map of various political struggles that human beings have witnessed, roughly in the last 300 years. However, some claim that its roots go back further in history. Ancient Greece, we are told, kindled the first spark of self-rule and has inspired generations of liberals. However, liberty for the ancients was different from liberty for the moderns. Benjamin Constant, a forerunner of liberalism, held that liberty for the ancients 'consisted in an active and constant participation in collective power', whereas for the moderns it consisted in 'peaceful enjoyment and private independence'. Whereas the ancients drew their happiness from an active engagement in collective life within the political community for which they were prepared to make sacrifices, individuals in the modern world are 'lost in the multitude' and unsure of their influence in collective decision making. The happiness of the modern individual derives more from the comforts gained through civilizational progress, commerce, and communication than finding fulfilment in collective projects (Constant 1988: 316). Constant offers us a powerful diagnosis of modernity, but the contrast he draws between ancient and modern liberty pleads the impossibility of resurrecting the liberal project from ancient roots.

In some ways, the earliest liberals were the Protestant reformers who challenged religious hierarchy and orthodoxy in the Church during the 16th century. The Protestant reformers repudiated the authority of the clergy in interpreting a 'true' religion that sought to establish a direct communion between human beings and God. In creatively interpreting this true religion, freed from the grip of the priests and resting instead on the volition of the believers, the Reformation produced grounds for discovering the autonomy of the individual—a fundamental moral resource for later developments in liberal theory.

If the authority of the priests could be questioned, how could the kings' power be spared? The competence of ordinary people to choose their own path to salvation soon transformed into the ability to judge temporal or secular matters. This coincided with calling into question the divine right of monarchs and aristocratic privileges of feudal lords in the early modern period. Much later, the spirit of liberalism expressed political struggles against all forms of absolute authority, including regimes of oppression as varied as fascist, communist, and autocratic.

Liberalism is usually divided into two phases: the classical and the modern. How do we distinguish between the two, who were the representative voices of each, and what are their distinctive features? Let us examine them individually.

Classical Liberalism

Classical liberalism is usually associated with the work of John Locke, besides Adam Smith and Thomas Paine, and other 20th-century thinkers such as Friedrich von Hayek, Robert Nozick, and Milton Friedman. Its chief distinguishing ideas are those of limited government, the rule of law, the inviolability of private property, the freedom to enter into, and maintain, contracts, and finally, the acceptance by individuals of their own fates. In its 20th-century variant, classical liberalism as defended by Hayek, Nozick, and Friedman is distrustful of progressive doctrines, including those inspired by democratic means, values such as distributive justice and all political arrangements, including the welfare state, where the government acquires more power than required.

It is to the credit of John Locke, however, that liberalism holds out one of its most influential ideas: that the aim and justification of government is to protect the life, liberty, and property of its citizens. These are natural rights constituted in, and protected by, natural law, which are antecedent to political society. Locke believed that the appropriate means by which the government can provide this protection is a system of justice defined and made possible by law. All citizens are equally subject to the authority of the government, and citizens find it reasonable to accept the authority because each is guaranteed the rights of life, liberty, and property. Legitimate authority safeguards these rights and in the Lockean scheme, it is perfectly justifiable to oppose political authority if it transgresses these inviolable rights. What is particularly appealing in Locke's thinking is the idea that a government must be able to justify its authority to its citizens. This justification rests on the protection of the rights of the citizens that the system of justice upholds more than what could be hoped for under a different arrangement.

Modern Liberalism

Modern liberalism is best illustrated in the views of John Stuart Mill, besides those of Kant, Green, and Hobhouse. In very distinct ways, modern liberalism establishes an affirmative relationship between liberty (especially, the positive variant) and human progress. The modern liberal believes man to be 'a progressive being' with an unlimited potential for self-development, one which does not jeopardize a similar potential in others. It seeks to qualify the sanctity of private property by admitting the necessity of addressing certain social and economic ills that can be remedied by the state. In attempting to do so, it does concede more functions to the state than allowed for by the classical alternative. This approach lays down and justifies, the value of distributive justice and experiments such as the welfare state. It hopes for more from the perfectibility of human beings and the liberal state, sustained by reason and conviction in progress. The idea that both human beings and society can be perfected by the use of reason was brought home most forcefully by the Enlightenment. Jeremy Waldron (1993: 43) makes this point most poignantly.

> The Enlightenment was characterized by a burgeoning confidence in the human ability to make sense of the world, to grasp its regularities and fundamental principles, to predict its future, and to manipulate its powers for the benefit of mankind. After millennia of ignorance, terror, and superstition, cowering before forces it could neither understand nor control, mankind faced the prospect of being able to at last build a *human* world, a world in which it might feel safely and securely at home.

Liberalism generally believes in the ability of individuals to make meaningful choices and to be responsible for them. The importance that liberalism attributes to individuals received the most robust intellectual defence from Immanuel Kant who, influenced by Rousseau, formulated the clearest case for individual autonomy. Kantian autonomy may be understood as the condition in which individuals are free from external determination such as coercion, threat or manipulation in taking actions to implement one's choices. In making such choices, an individual is also to be free from internal influences such as passions or prejudices and, instead, be guided by reason, understood in the final analysis as conformity to unversalizable principles. Kant held that all human beings are equal in their capacity for autonomy, that this capacity explains an individual's moral responsibility and human dignity, and that morality requires that we respect everyone capable of autonomy. He thus expressed the idea that individuals are entitled to equal respect, hindrance to which is the denial of universal morality.

John Stuart Mill further reinforced liberalism by arguing that it is morally impermissible to interfere with the actions of individuals even if they are motivated by irrational or emotive considerations, provided the actions in question do not harm others. As Mill argues, liberalism is opposed to the coercion of even non-autonomous actions, so long as such actions are compatible with the autonomous existence of others. Disagreeing with Bentham's utilitarianism, Mill opposed paternalistic interference intended to benefit individuals. This opposition is based on the liberal belief that individuals know best what is good for them, and even if they are mistaken about this, it is better to allow them to make such mistakes than impose an alien view about what is in their best interests. Governments must adhere to the requirement of not imposing what they think is best for their citizens. This would promote, as Mill hoped and justified, a diversity of ways of life.

What links both traditions—classical and modern—is an opposition to absolute power, a distrust of political authority, and a whole-hearted affirmation of the values of freedom and autonomy of individuals.

Contemporary Liberalism

Locke, Kant, and Mill have been the three most important thinkers who shaped the modern liberal tradition. Contemporary liberalism owes much to them. However, if one has to single out one important political philosopher of the 20th century whose influence has been the most profound in liberal thinking, it is John Rawls. Two monumental treatises written by Rawls—*A Theory of Justice* (1971) and *Political Liberalism* (1993)—have set the contemporary terms of debate and discussion on liberalism and its values. Rawls revived the social contract tradition of Locke, Rousseau, and Kant, both redeployed and deepened Mill's vindication of liberty in a free society, and argued against conventional judgements, especially those of utilitarianism, that treated individuals as means towards attaining the collective good. A liberal state, according to Rawls, must not only guarantee that all its citizens have an equality of fundamental liberty rights, such as voting, and freedom of speech, religion and association; it must also ensure that those who are least well-off are assured as good a life as possible. Rawls asserts that freedom should never be sacrificed on the grounds of an increase in material well-being. This is why he gives priority to the equal enjoyment of liberty (the liberty principle) over the principle that requires the welfare of the least well-off to be taken care of (the difference principle). Overall, Rawls holds out an account of egalitarian liberalism that is hospitable to redistributive experiments of the liberal state.

A central trait of Rawls' liberalism is its political view that citizens are entitled to live in accordance with their own freely chosen values or ends. Individuals are entitled to their own conceptions of what constitutes a good life. A conception of the good is supposed to be internally determined by the individual and not imposed from the outside by the larger society or the state. The state is required to be neutral among the many conceptions of good that individuals choose. Neither can the state nor the larger society pass judgements on how to lead a good life, which religion one must adopt, or the values one must live by. A primary ambition of Rawls' work is to free the idea of what is right and just from the idea of what is good or advantageous for an individual and in giving primacy to the former over the latter—*the priority of the right over the good*. This allows Rawls to depart from the utlitiarian tradition by insisting, as he rightly does, that the Utilitarian conception of good—say, the greatest good of the greatest number—overrides both the moral separateness of persons and their self-determining capacities.

Instead, he offers an account of rights that people have, defined by the principles of justice, that is substantially independent of particular notions of good, which are bound to be disputable. A paradigm case where notions of good may prove contentious is religious controversy. No two persons belonging to two different religions will ever agree on fundamental issues of faith. Moral disagreements on what gives value to life will persist in a free society and reasonable people will set these aside to evolve rules of social cooperation. But the requirement to evolve rules of social cooperation on the basis of a shared agreement flies in the face of deep and persistent moral disagreements that divide a society on the bases of caste, community, religion, ethnicity, language and other markers of identity. How can we expect them to bury their differences? This is a central problem in Rawlsian liberalism and in spite of his best efforts in later works, Rawls has not been successfully able to defend his version of liberalism from the attack of communitarians such as Alasdair MacIntyre, Charles Taylor, Michael Sandel, and Michael Walzer. The communitarians would criticize Rawls, and the tradition of liberalism associated with him, for overlooking the fact that people's identities are constituted in large part by their membership in different communities, for underestimating the significance of shared values, and for wrongfully asserting the virtues of individualism and universalism that are either hollow or impossible to achieve. Defenders of the Rawlsian version of liberalism have usually responded by upholding the worth of individual autonomy (that allows individuals the freedom to change and shape their lives), the unattractiveness of the idea that a state must use coercion to keep the community united, and a political morality that rises above the bias of particular contexts.

The liberal–communitarian debate has evoked a rich body of scholarly literature in recent times. The debate in its various forms has enriched liberalism in a number of ways. Contemporary liberals are now less averse to address questions of identity and cultural pluralism. Whereas in the past it was commonplace for liberal theory and practice to neglect or override claims of cultural difference made by identity groups in a plural society, most versions of liberalism now exhibit moral sensitivity to issues of diversity. Debating the principles of liberalism in diverse societies has now come to mean endorsing *multicultural* values that have implications for citizenship, the rights of groups, majority–minority relations, moral obligations to protect and preserve cultures, and so on.

Responding to these challenges has meant undertaking the task of broadening and enriching the conceptual repertoire of liberalism. If liberalism in its earlier phase crystallized around the values of freedom and a minimal state, the constellation of liberal values would now include a range of diverse but interconnected concepts: freedom, rights, equality, distributive justice, and pluralism. This raises the question of what constitutes the theoretical foundations of liberalism.

The Foundations of Liberalism

Liberalism does not have a monolithic tradition. Some claim that there are not one, but several liberalisms. An effort to discover a common core of liberalism is hence likely to be futile and counterproductive. The richness of liberalism lies in being able to draw upon multiple sources, including those from rival ways of thinking. This being a given, it may be difficult to agree on a set of values that lie at the core of liberalism. Yet, liberals try delineating a common set of values and consider this enterprise well worth their effort. John Gray (1998), for instance, suggests that what is common to all variants of the liberal tradition is a distinctive modern conception of man and society, which has several elements to it. In asserting the moral primacy of the person against the claims of any social collectivity, liberalism is *individualist*. It purports to be *egalitarian* by conferring on all individuals the same moral status. In affirming the moral unity of the human species, liberalism is *universalist*. Finally, it is *meliorist* in pronouncing that social institutions and political arrangements are improvable (Gray 1998: xii). Is Gray's analysis persuasive? Gray's interpretation, it might be said, blots out some significant transformations that liberalism has undergone in the recent past. For instance, an insistence on viewing liberalism as essentially individualist fails to notice and take stock of the various ways in which liberal values have come to roost in and negotiate with dissimilar values in different contexts. The argument here is that there is no one way of claiming what a distinctive liberal way of life is. Moreover, this argument cuts into liberal claims of universalism (that we has already been discussed above) in the context of the communitarian critique of Rawlsian liberalism.

Instead of harping on the common features of different strands of liberalism that have existed, or continue to exist, across time and space, a better mode to discover the foundational core of liberalism would be to ask *what* a liberal society would look like. At least, a liberal society is an open society where freedom for individuals and groups alike allows each opportunity to flourish without fear of persecution. Since an open society would promote the value of diversity or the different ways of life (or conceptions of good) and because such diversity is best promoted by not ordering diverse ways of life hierarchically, liberalism ought to place a premium on the value of *non-hierarchical pluralism* that encapsulates a political message against different forms of discrimination, oppression, or domination.

Conclusion

Although liberalism has been on the ascendant since the end of the Cold War and the demise of communism in Soviet Russia, prompting some to even make the foolhardy claim of an end to ideology, the future of liberal theory and practice will depend largely on how precisely it meets its criticisms and shortcomings. However, as Alan Ryan (1993: 309) notes, 'the way in which liberalism institutionalizes self-criticism [will] itself be a guarantee of [its] progress'.

Points for Discussion

1. Liberalism has evolved out of struggles to limit the arbitrary uses of political authority. Discuss with examples.
2. How has the social contract tradition shaped the liberal spirit?
3. Do you agree that 'liberalism is an ideology of the West, ill-suited for non-Western contexts'? Discuss with cases from India and the West.
4. Why do most liberals now dispute the claim that faith in individualism lies at the core of liberalism?
5. Would you say that a liberal society affirms moral and cultural diversity but desires *shared* political values? Elaborate with examples in support of your argument.

Reading List

Constant, Benjamin, *Political Writings* (Cambridge, UK: Cambridge University Press, 1988).

Dworkin, Ronald, *A Matter of Principle* (Cambridge, MA: Harvard University Press, 1985).

Gray, John, *Liberalisms: Essays in Political Philosophy* (London and New York: Routledge, 1989).

———, *Liberalism* (Delhi: Worldview Publications, 1998).

Kymlicka, Will, *Liberalism, Community, and Culture* (Oxford: Clarendon Press, 1989).

Mill, John Stuart, *On Liberty and Other Essays* (Oxford: Oxford University Press, 1991).

Parekh, Bhikhu, 'Decolonizing Liberalism', in Alexsandras Shtromas (ed.), *The End of 'Isms'? Reflections on the Fate of Ideological Politics after Communism's Collapse* (Oxford: Blackwell, 1994).

Rawls, John, *A Theory of Justice* (Cambridge, MA: Belknap Press, 1971).

———, *Political Liberalism. The John Dewey Essays in Philosophy*, 4 (New York: Columbia University Press, 1993).

Ryan, Alan, 'Liberalism', in Robert E. Goodin and Philip Petit (eds), *A Companion to Contemporary Political Philosophy* (Oxford: Blackwell, 1993).

Waldron, Jeremy, *Liberal Rights* (Cambridge: Cambridge University Press, 1993).

CHAPTER 17

Socialism

Sunalini Kumar

Chapter Outlines

Introduction

> [Socialism is] a social order in which there is the maximum feasible equality of access, for all human beings, to economic resources, to knowledge, and to political power, and the minimum possible domination exercised by any individual or social group over any others.
>
> —Tom Bottomore

The world has always been an unequal place, characterized by divisions based on class, religion, race, gender, and ethnic origin, to mention a few. In particular, the wide divide between the rich and the poor has been a feature of every single era in recorded history, from the time humans moved out of caves and established settled agricultural societies, to the present. For thousands of years, individuals or groups who controlled the prized resources of society, whether land, gold, slaves or ammunition have dictated to the poor the conditions of their life and especially the conditions under which they earned their living. Occasionally, religious prophets and mass leaders have given voice to the misery of the people. Indeed, Christianity first arose as a powerful social movement due to the terrible living conditions of the poor under the Roman Empire. Ironically, however, religion itself can perpetuate unjust and unequal social practices. By the Middle Ages, in Europe, the Catholic Church became one of the wealthiest institutions in history, extending its control over society through elaborate hierarchical networks, making inequality appear divinely sanctioned. In many parts of the world, too, religious, economic and political power have historically joined hands to justify and sanction social systems that make the dream of equality impossible.

Responses to Inequality

From the Greek thinker Plato onwards, sophisticated theoretical defences of inequality have been a part of the tradition of political thought. Rulers and political philosophers alike have traditionally been in favour of some form of inequality, citing reasons from the natural right of certain individuals to rule over others (the theory of 'divine right of kings') to the argument that economic inequality is essential to maintain law and order in the society. It is only in modern times that equality as a principle and as an ideal has become widely desired. A combination of historical events has contributed to this development. In Europe, the waning of the power of the Church after the Reformation in the 15th century, the gradual decline of the hierarchical feudal system and the rise of a new class of merchant capitalists who saw profit in a more egalitarian society were prime factors. The Enlightenment of the 18th century, the growing power and changing composition of parliaments in England and other places, and the rise of liberal political thought were important steps in the same direction. The French and American Revolutions of the late 18th century were indeed milestones—they made the fundamental equality of all human beings not simply a cherished ideal but a principle that was eventually enshrined in the constitutions of many nation-states. In the non-European world, the decline of local empires and traditional forms of authority due to trade and colonialism, and the systematic impoverishment of the local population due to colonial extraction of wealth were the key reasons. A variety of radical movements and anti-colonial liberation struggles arose in these areas to speak in favour of economic and political freedom and equality. Interestingly, while some anti-colonial movements borrowed their political terminology from the nationalism and liberalism of the West, others drew upon traditional, indigenous moral and ethical concepts in order to argue for greater freedom and equality. In the United States, the appalling existence of slavery and racial discrimination against African-Americans in the southern states even after the adoption of the liberal American Constitution fuelled the 'Abolitionist' movement of the 19th century. The Abolitionists were committed to the abolition of slavery and to the promotion of equality between the races, especially in the field of civil and political rights. Interestingly, the Abolitionists allied with another group demanding equality in 19th-century America—the suffragists—who argued for equal voting and political rights for men and women.

Perhaps most important both as a cause and as a symptom of the modern concern with equality is the fact that democracy, which is a principle of political rule fundamentally based on the ideal of equality, has become the preferred form of government in the modern age. In principle, democracy confers equal political power to all through universal adult franchise, and throws open the arena of politics to all regardless of the privileges of birth or wealth. Today, with the overwhelming popularity and legitimacy of this form of rule, even some of the most autocratic dictators are keen to convey an impression of democracy to the world at large. Democracy, however, addresses only one form of inequality—*political inequality*. The question of other forms of equality, particularly economic equality, then remains unanswered. Many thinkers recognize and bemoan the fact that democracy can and does exist quite comfortably with extreme social and economic inequality. What are the consequences of this for equality? While it can be argued that political rights are sacred and necessary in themselves regardless of other conditions of life, it is equally true that without a degree of economic and social equality, the political equality afforded by democracy can become at best, limited and at worst, meaningless. As R. H. Tawney (1931) wrote in his critique of the 'religion of inequality' that permeates contemporary capitalist societies, giving rights to a desperately poor man is like extending a dinner invitation to somebody who is in no position to accept it! In our own country, despite the existence of a fully functioning democracy since Independence, we have numerous cases of socially and economically disadvantaged people being regularly denied basic rights and a fair treatment in society.

The Problem: Capitalism

With the advent of the modern age in Europe there was hope that over a period of time, the rigid feudal hierarchies characteristic of the medieval age would be 'flattened out'. The emerging economic system—capitalism—with its emphasis on free market and free enterprise was in principle accessible to every individual, regardless of whether the person possessed any rank or status in society. In addition, capitalism seemed capable of harnessing the natural resources of the world in order to end the scarcity of resources and the continuous threat of famine and mass disease characteristic of the pre-modern world. An early theoretical defence of capitalism was provided by Adam Smith who argued famously that there existed within capitalism, an 'invisible hand' capable of regulating demand and supply at the micro level, and of allocating (scarce) resources at the macro level. Thus, capitalism was a self-regulating economic system capable of thriving without interference from 'above' (the state); it performed the age-old economic tasks of managing demands, determining supplies and avoiding waste and losses with optimal efficiency. The principle of *laissez-faire* (or separation of state and market) advocated by liberal and neo-liberal economists and political scientists was based on this assumption of efficiency within capitalism, and provided the basis for government economic policy in the developed capitalist countries until the end of the 19th century.

The claims made in favour of capitalism by its advocates were not without basis—the standard of living of millions of people in the modern world has vastly improved compared to the subsistence societies of the medieval age. Income and wealth generation are at levels that were unimaginable in the pre-modern era. Modern societies, especially in the developed world, are societies of mass consumption—food production is higher than in any previously recorded time in history, and amenities that seemed like remote luxuries until recently are accessible to a majority of the working population. Scientific and technological research encouraged by capitalism has transformed the face of the earth and fuelled hopes of inventions that could permanently end scarcity in the near future.

However, capitalism has created entrenched inequalities of its own. While it may have generated enviable working conditions and leisure opportunities for white-collar workers (the managerial and corporate elite); the majority of the proletariat (the blue-collar workers) have found themselves crammed into factories and workshops for long hours, performing repetitive and uncreative tasks required for mass production. The difference in wage levels between the white-collar and blue-collar worker is vast in most capitalist economies. Contrary to the dream of free access to all, capitalism seems to have perpetuated historical and hereditary hierarchies through the institution of private property, and those individuals who have been historically disadvantaged have to a large extent remained disadvantaged within the system. Also, throughout the history of capitalism, a significant proportion of the adult working population has remained unemployed even in *successful* capitalist economies. Such a high rate of unemployment seems to be a structural tendency and not merely accidental to capitalism, resulting in the creation of a permanent class of unemployed individuals who are excluded from the fruits of the economic system.

The challenge of ordering resources efficiently to end scarcity has also remained a pressing one in capitalism. In the past two centuries, when capitalism has been dominant, the world has witnessed unprecedented economic crises—an explosive growth of world population, repeated man-made famine and drought, wars and conflagrations over depleting natural resources, especially over fossil fuels like oil. New diseases and epidemics have arisen to replace the ones conquered by modern medicine, and new patterns of scarcity have emerged. Most distressingly, the world economy has been beset by the cyclical crises—'booms and busts' that seem endemic to capitalism. Periods of economic growth, rising incomes and increased spending power among the population have been followed by spiralling inflation, poverty and economic 'slowdown'. These cycles of inflation and recession have wreaked havoc on economically vulnerable sections of the population, a fact that had become painfully clear to all by the start of the 20th century. During the Great Depression of 1929, for example, the American government was forced to resort to large-scale destruction of goods (especially agricultural produce) in order to arrest plummeting prices and looming recession. That this burning of food stocks took place at a time when millions were starving was not simply tragic, but a direct refutation of capitalism's claim of efficient allocation of resources and satisfaction of demands.

In the present world of advanced or 'late' capitalism, concentration of wealth in the hands of a few at the cost of a decent life for the vast mass of people has continued. Some argue that the world today is even more unequal a place than ever before—in the United States, for example, the foremost economic power of our times, by 1935, *one-tenth of one per cent* of all the corporations in the United States owned 52 per cent of all corporate assets—a pattern that has not significantly changed until today, and one that is representative of capitalist economies everywhere. Over the past century, as capitalism has expanded and become dominant in underdeveloped economies, too, the consequences there have been severe. Because of the impoverished condition of these countries due to the lasting effects of colonialism, their governments are usually unwilling to spend scarce resources on social security. Such social security measures (employment generation and agricultural subsidies, for example) are crucial to sustain vulnerable sections of the population during the difficult transition to capitalism, and during the structural crises endemic to capitalism. In the past few decades, under pressure from advanced capitalist countries and from international banks and lending agencies like the World Bank and the IMF, Third World countries have undertaken pro-privatization and globalization programmes that involve even lower levels of social security. This has rendered the poor more vulnerable to cycles of inflation and unemployment and has created new patterns of inequality in underdeveloped countries. Capitalist production has also led to the destruction of traditional livelihoods and traditional sources of food (like subsistence farming) in the Third World, forcibly pulling people into the 'market' and making them dependent on expensive market-produced goods.

Therefore, contrary to many of its claims, capitalism does not seem to have provided an efficient, rational solution to the management of natural and human resources. More importantly, it has been unsuccessful in bringing about equality and freedom for all in society. Thus, the challenge before us as we analyse the contemporary capitalist world is both economic and ethical—how to order the resources of society according to rational and efficient lines, and how to build a more humane and fair society where freedom is not stymied by the lack of equality for all.

The Socialist Alternative

By the 18th century, as the Industrial Revolution dramatically transformed the economies of Western Europe, making factory production dominant and turning England into 'the workshop of the world', there began a mass migration of labourers to towns to look for work in the mills. These workers found themselves without the safety net afforded by the lord–serf relationship of feudalism, or a new one provided by *laissez-faire* governments. They were forced to sell their 'labour power' whenever there was demand, working for long unregulated hours in crowded factories, living in disease-ridden slums that were springing up everywhere, and demonized as a scourge in popular opinion. It became apparent to all sympathetic observers that capitalism was creating a new underclass of impoverished workers—the urban 'proletariat'. One of the earliest thinkers to give detailed attention to the problem of inequality in modern civilization was Jean Jacques Rousseau in his work, *Discourses on the Origin of Inequality* (1754). Rousseau was not interested in capitalism specifically, but in tracing the origin of what he termed moral or political inequality between men through the ages. His ideas became one of the influences of the French Revolution of 1789, which resulted in the formation of a French Republic composed of *politically* equal citizens, or *citoyens*. The French Revolution, however, did not undertake any thoroughgoing economic transformation, accepting by and large, capitalist methods of production that were taking root in France.

By the end of the 1700s, several thinkers and reformers in France, England and elsewhere in Europe began to *specifically* address to the conditions of modern industrial capitalist society. This led to the recognition of the structural inequality within modern capitalism, and to the limitations of *laissez-faire* liberal states in providing a solution. The search for alternatives to capitalism as an economic system and of classical liberalism as its political counterpart gave rise to a distinct theoretical approach. This theory was 'socialism', and may be identified by certain central tenets. In particular, socialism involves an analysis of capitalism as a system with an inbuilt tendency towards producing and deepening inequality. Socialists seek radical equality, often devising comprehensive programmes that reduce or completely remove economic inequalities among human beings through collective, concerted action. Socialism is against the concentration of wealth in the hands of a few and, in particular, it is against the institution of *private property*, summed up in the phrase popularized by the socialist Pierre-Joseph Proudhon 'What is property? It is theft.' The aim of socialism is human emancipation through the enlightened management of society's resources. Socialists argue that the profit motive within capitalism makes owners of capital willing to sacrifice all to the principle of efficiency. It also reduces workers to a collective force called 'labour', robbed of their humanity and degraded into brute instruments of production. In order to mitigate the continual chaos, instability, and selfish individualism produced by capitalism, socialism proposes a peaceful, planned system of economic production and distribution that is perhaps best described by Marx and Engels' (1968) famous formulation— 'from each according to his ability to each according to his needs'. It is important to remember that socialism is not simply a critique of capitalism, but also of mainstream liberal notions, especially the central liberal tenet of liberty and of the meaning and status of equality. Let us examine this critique.

The liberal ideal of liberty describes freedom in purely 'negative' terms as an inviolable sphere around the (bourgeois) individual, protecting him from both society and the state. Liberal writers claim that since individual liberty is the source of all progress, its enhancement must be the paramount aim of society. To interfere with the freedom of the individual (bourgeois) man is to infringe upon the rights of the individual and to place dangerous obstacles in the way of social progress and prosperity. Against this belief, the socialists argue that the legal protection of unlimited acquisition of property by individuals amounts to the exploitation of wage-labourers by the owners of capital. According to the socialist view of freedom, man is a social animal, finding fulfilment in collective living. Thus, instead of emphasizing the liberty of the abstract individual that is the central category of liberal thought, socialists emphasize 'human emancipation' that is premised on the manner in which all human beings participate in social and economic life. In this context, Karl Marx argues that a majority of individuals perform 'alienated' labour under capitalist production; consequently, human freedom is possible only in the absence of 'alienation'. As David McLellan (1970) explains, Marx's conception of freedom involves replacement of the worker of today 'crippled by the lifelong repetition of one and the same trivial operation, and thus reduced to the mere fragment of a man, by the fully developed individual, fit for a variety of labours, ready to face any change of production, and to whom the different social functions he performs, are but so many modes of giving free scope to his own natural and acquired powers'. Genuine freedom as Marx described it, would become possible only when life activity was no longer constrained by the requirements of production or by the limitations of material scarcity. According to Marx, the external world is part of man's nature; hence it is crucial to establish the right relationship between man and his environment. Thus, in the socialist view, freedom is not an abstract ideal but a concrete situation that ensues only when certain conditions of interaction between man and nature, and man and other men are fulfilled.

There has also been a long-standing battle between socialists and liberals over the meaning of the term equality. Some liberals believe that radically egalitarian measures would result in oppressive uniformity of ideas and behaviour among the population. The 19th century writer Alexis de Tocqueville expressed this fear in his classic text *Democracy in America* (original French, 1835) when he warned against a society where similarity of ideas and achievement are so highly prized that all forms of excellence, or freedom of opinion disappear under a shroud of mediocrity. Tocqueville believed that extreme democratic tendencies could result in a tyranny of the homogenous majority, or in a society of small, helpless, and unorganized individuals over whom despotism could be easily exercised. The 19th century liberal, John Stuart Mill, felt much the same apprehensions. Mill laid elaborate emphasis on the value of a good liberal education in order to avoid what he believed were the less desirable consequences of movements towards equality.

Liberalism now contains at least two well-established positions on equality (see Chapter 4 on equality in this volume for more details). The first position seeks to ensure maximum fulfilment of the capacity of each individual. This is seen to be necessary either in the interest of justice, to prevent social disaffection, or to make maximum use of human talents for society as a whole. Notions of fair competition, equality of opportunity, merit and desert dominate this discourse on equality. The purpose is to encourage the able and provide upward mobility for the able few through a vast apparatus of testing, examination and other merit-based barriers in the fields of education and employment. The other view is best illustrated in the movement for racial equality in America, and in similar movements around the world seeking to reverse historic injustices. In this view, people must be trained and prepared for opportunities, and the pool of capacities of the entire population must be enlarged. This enhancement of opportunities may take place at any point in the individuals' life, in education or employment, in recruitment or in training, and skill development. This view on equality is more expansive than the previous one, and has resulted in policies of reverse discrimination, preferential treatment, affirmative action, and reservations. With the rise of the welfare state in the late 19th and early 20th centuries and the threat of socialist revolution especially after the Russian Revolution of 1917, measures towards greater equality have been incorporated into government policies in liberal and social democratic states. Notwithstanding these developments, however, unease about complete equality remains at the core of liberal thought and practice. In liberalism, privilege and success are explained as a result of individual rather than social factors; this success is defended through the notion of negative liberty. Consequently, lack of privilege and success are also explained as a result of individual, rather than social factors, thus relieving the state or society in general of any responsibility to promote greater equality. By contrast, equality is not a secondary value but the *central organizing principle* of all socialist thought and practice. Socialists argue that the adoption of the above egalitarian measures by liberal states have resulted in no major changes in patterns of inequality; therefore, the point is to establish social and economic institutions that fundamentally promote and preserve equality.

Apart from disagreements over individual concepts of liberty and equality, liberals and socialists have also disagreed on the relationship between the two. Liberalism is suspicious of 'too much' equality, fearing that equality beyond a certain point becomes a menace to liberty, not only in the realm of economic enterprise but also in other spheres. Unlike the liberals who would defend the right to liberty even at the cost of equality, and the democrats who would focus on political equality alone, socialists seek to make the value of liberty conditional on the attainment of equality for all. In a sense, socialism defends the *equal right to liberty of all* by maintaining that without equality, the liberty of some will be premised upon the lack of liberty for others. Further, socialists argue that since there is no inbuilt mechanism within capitalist economies and *laissez-faire* governments towards egalitarian measures, the solution is to plan an egalitarian society in advance and put it into practice.

Socialist Schemes: Old and New

Although Rousseau addressed the problem of inequality as described above, his thought cannot be labelled 'socialist'. François-Noël Babeuf, a philosopher active at the time of the French Revolution is perhaps the first socialist thinker of modern times. Babeuf established a 'conspiracy of the socialists' and called himself the 'Tribune of the People' during the Revolution. He was fiercely critical of the defence of the right to private property in the Constitution of the French Republic drafted after the Revolution in 1793. In the absence of any thorough programme to address economic and social inequality, the slogan of the Revolution—'Liberty, Equality, Fraternity'—was meaningless for Babeuf. Thus, he opposed the manner in which the Revolution and liberal slogans about human emancipation remained empty slogans without removing the primary source of inequality in society, that is, the institution of private property. Although Babeuf's conspiracy was finally crushed, *babouvisme* (the French term for Babeufism) with its emphasis on the revolutionary role of the working class had a lingering influence on the socialist theory.

Henri de Saint-Simon who wrote at the start of the 19th century was preoccupied with the challenges that the new century represented to him. According to him, with the collapse of the hierarchical feudal order of the previous era, there was a need to tackle the problem of inequality in industrial capitalism. He hoped that Christianity could be reinterpreted according to its original egalitarian principles for the modern age, and he attempted this in his best-known work, *The New Christianity* (1825). Saint-Simon's followers—the Saint-Simonians—systematized his ideas and identified the central elements of his socialism. These included the abolition of all privileges at birth, the determining of rewards according to the actual amount of work put in by the individual and the common ownership of land, capital and all instruments of labour. Tom Bottomore, a leading commentator on Karl Marx argues that Saint-Simon exercised a significant influence on Marx's thought, a fact that is not generally acknowledged.

Charles Fourier, a French socialist of the 19th century shared with his compatriot Rousseau the belief that modern civilization was rotten at the core, and consisted of deceit, hypocrisy and parasitism. According to Fourier, these were the products of the modern individualistic and competitive system of production and could be remedied by an elaborate plan for the reorganization of society according to rational principles of production and distribution. This plan included the establishing of self-contained units of cooperative workers called *phalanxes* composed of between 400 and 2,000 men and women, each. Members should unite in groups according to their tastes, which in turn according to Fourier would be determined by the character of their 'passions'—their deeply-held beliefs. By this arrangement, Fourier hoped that productivity would increase, enough for people to be active producers from the age of 18–25, and would enable them to live in leisure for the rest of their lives.

Fourier's thought is an example of the elaborate and detailed schemes for radical economic and social reconstruction imagined by socialist thinkers of his day. The Welsh socialist Robert Owen who lived and wrote in the late 18th and early 19th century is credited with not simply devising collectivistic schemes but also with managing to actually implement them in his lifetime. As mentioned above, the breakdown of old feudal relations in 18th-century Europe and the rise of industrial capitalism created precarious conditions for workers. Robert Owen was, in fact, a factory owner himself; he decided to commit himself to life-long work among factory workers of the small manufacturing town of New Lanark in Scotland. He instituted a series of measures that were designed to transform workers into a self-supporting, self-educating and self-governing community. He initiated many practices that were later fought for, and won by trade unions in the 19th and 20th centuries. In fact, most of the measures that seemed so radical in Owen's time are now a central part of all capitalist welfare states. However, Owen was not simply a reformer of capitalism; he roundly denounced private property. He proposed a blueprint for socialist communes with communal living and working arrangements and their supervision by qualified technicians.

Karl Marx and Friedrich Engels are credited with creating the most prolific and influential theory of socialism yet. They made a self-conscious effort to distinguish themselves from other socialists; to this end they started referring to their work as 'communist' rather than merely 'socialist' which they dismissed as a vague and dilute body of thought, full of pious outrage against capitalism and dimly-conceived utopian schemes for the future. Rather than framing socialism in primarily ethical terms, Marx set out to devise a systematic, scientific theory of socialism that would stand the test of actual practice. He believed that the premises from which he attempted to develop a truly scientific socialism were in his words, 'not arbitrary ones, not dogmas, but real premises from which abstraction can be made only in the imagination'. Further, instead of speaking of the need for building a socialist society as a conscious moral choice, Marx claimed that the advent of socialism was inevitable. He made this claim on the basis of his 'discovery' of what he believed were the objective laws of human society. According to scientific socialism, the ideal community cannot be planned by thinkers or well-meaning reformers and put into operation regardless of historical conditions; it must arise out of revolutionary activity and will be successful only when historically appropriate. In more specific terms, Marx and Engels argued that socialism was a stage of historical development, destined to be achieved after a worldwide revolution by the working class against the private property-owning bourgeoisie—the chief beneficiaries of the contemporary capitalist economy. The modern industrial proletariat according to Marx was effectively excluded from the benefits of the capitalist society; hence it was the class with the most compelling interest in the overthrow of that society. He sought to create a rigorous practical doctrine that would help the proletariat to develop confidence in the success of revolution as a historical inevitability, and thus resist engaging in premature revolts.

Marx characterizes man as *homo faber*, or the 'working species'. This according to him meant that the material realm—the realm of production and labour—is the most distinctive feature of human life. This was a theme found in earlier Socialists like Fourier and Saint-Simon, too, and is termed *materialism*, since in such a theory the most important phenomena in human society are explained through an examination of the manner in which human beings satisfy their material needs. According to Marx, the specific manner in which the means of production (land, labour, capital, enterprise) are organized in a society, gives rise to a particular mode of production. Further, society can be viewed in terms of a distinction between the 'base' and the 'superstructure'. The 'base' consists of the economic conditions of life including the 'means of production' and the 'relations of production'.

The 'superstructure' consisted of 'the legal, political, religious, aesthetic or philosophical' aspects of life. While in some of his writings Marx explores the influence of the superstructure upon the base; his belief in materialism leads him to stress the determining nature of the base within which the superstructure must always operate. In simple terms, the political formation of the state and the entire edifice of legal, cultural, social, and ethical systems in society are built upon the foundation of the mode of production, or the economic base. So, for example, the institution of kingship or the medieval state was the superstructural mode of political organization suitable to the feudal mode of production; the *laissez-faire* state is the organization relevant to early capitalism, the welfare state is the political form necessary for advanced capitalism, etc. In Marx and Engels' famous words, 'The mode of production of material life determines the general character of the social, political, and spiritual processes of life. It is not the consciousness of men that determines their being, but, on the contrary, their social being that determines their consciousness'.

Marx's belief in materialism led him to formulate a unique theory of historical change which he termed 'historical materialism' and may be defined thus: historical change takes place with changes in the base, which are accompanied by changes in the superstructure. Thus, it was material forces (the mode/means of economic production) rather than ideas that were the real 'motors' of history. According to Marx, every stage in human history contains within itself the seeds of its own destruction. The continual destruction of one stage and the rise of another occur due to the fact that except the final stage of communism, every other stage in history contains inherent contradictions. These contradictions deepen and express themselves in many forms, primarily in the form of class struggle, until the system itself collapses to be replaced by a new system.

Marx's analysis of capitalism followed from the above theses; under capitalism he argued, owners are forced into ceaseless competition with each other and weaker capitalists are pushed out of the market. Bankrupt owners join the ranks of the workers as their circumstances get more and more impossible, and small-scale enterprises yield to large monopolies. Society eventually comes to be divided into only two classes—the bourgeoisie, in whose hands all capital comes to be concentrated, and the proletariat, the wage earners who have no capital, no private property but only their labour power to sell. This divide between two classes is the overt manifestation of the contradictions unique to capitalism. The 'class-consciousness' of the proletariat is strengthened as workers are concentrated in large factories and as their conditions of life grow worse with every advance of capitalist production. Eventually, the capitalist system is overthrown through a workers' revolution; and a 'dictatorship of the proletariat' established to replace it. The dictatorship according to Marx and Engels would itself be eventually replaced by a truly *classless* communist society, since classes are a manifestation of the contradictions characteristic of pre-communist forms of economic production. Under socialism, marginal differences of function and of income may remain but they would not be the permanent differences of class. Further, there would be no private property, and the state—which was viewed by Marx as an instrument in the hands of the ruling class—would 'wither away'. Only in the final stage of human history would the individual be truly free, since the principle of true equality would ensure that the freedom of some is not premised on the unfreedom of others.

Conclusion

As must be clear from the discussion above, there is immense diversity within socialist thought regarding the precise problem with capitalism and the exact solution offered. Apart from the thinkers mentioned above, other influential socialists include the Bolsheviks Vladimir Lenin, Rosa Luxemburg and Leon Trotsky; the anarchist socialists Peter Kropotkin and William Godwin; the 'possibilists', including, especially, Paul Brousse; Marx's interlocutors Ferdinand Lasalle and Mikhail Bakunin; the 'revisionist' socialist Eduard Bernstein; the Russian feminist-socialist Alexandra Kollontai; the Zionist socialist Moses Hess; the syndicalists; the Austro-Marxists, including Otto Bauer; and the Fabian socialists Sidney and Beatrice Webb in England. Socialism and communism also found a dedicated set of adherents in the non-Western part of the world, including the powerful legacy of Mao Tse Tung in China, Fidel Castro in Cuba, M. N. Roy and, more recently, communist leaders like Jyoti Basu and E. M. S. Namboodiripad in India. To achieve their aims, some socialists have placed their faith in a reformed state, others wish to abolish the state altogether and establish self-governing communes; yet others speak of a historical revolution. Writers have sought to make sense of this huge variety of socialist theories by distinguishing between various schools of socialism including 'utopian' socialism, 'scientific' socialism, 'democratic' socialism, 'anarchist' socialism, 'organizational' socialism, 'reformist' socialism, etc. We must emphasize here that the above categories of socialism, while useful for understanding the differences between various types of socialist thought, are not absolute. Owen, for instance, is classified by some (including Marx himself, as mentioned above) as a utopian socialist; however, he also expressed great hope in scientific principles; in particular as mentioned above, the supervision of communes by technicians. On the other hand, Marxism sought to be 'scientific' but in fact, depended on certain concepts that were undeniably moral or ethical in their origin. Marx stated that he wished to write not about abstract individuals, but 'real individuals, their activity and their material conditions of life'. This is a deeply ethical humanist mission.

As already discussed, Marx and Engels sought to prove that the socialist society is not a distant dream but a fact of the near future promised by the scientific laws of historical development. This 'fact' never appeared in its entirety anywhere in the world; however, the 20th century is marked by attempts to establish socialism in substantial parts of the world. It was such a socialist state—the USSR—that was officially established in 1917 in Russia, an example of what has been termed 'actually existing Socialism'. It was one socialist state that came closest to achieving success in the face of huge odds in a predominantly liberal, capitalist world; however, this socialist experiment ended dramatically in 1991 with the collapse of the USSR. While North Korea and Cuba remain communist to the present day, the rest of the so-called 'Eastern Bloc' (a Cold War term for the communist part of the world) has been absorbed into the global capitalist system over the past few decades. Also, it was the widespread influence of socialism among the intelligentsia and the masses alike that to a large extent forced liberal capitalist states in the 19th and 20th centuries to reform themselves. Arguably, the welfare state that was established in England in the 19th century and spread to most of the world by the 20th century was a response within liberalism to the popularity of socialist ideas, and to the threat of socialist revolution. Policies influenced by the socialist principle of substantive equality have improved the conditions of life for millions of human beings in the contemporary world, whether they live in formally liberal or socialist states.

Socialism both as thought and practice remains an important critique of the mainstream form of economic production in the modern world, and a powerful reminder of the fact that the central liberal values of freedom and equality can be rendered meaningless in the face of the structural inequalities produced by capitalism. Socialism, as Bernard Crick reminds us, is 'both an empirical theory and a moral doctrine'. It is not an ahistorical and abstract philosophical theory of equality but a specific response to the economic and moral contradictions inherent in modernity—the existence of severe economic inequality since the Industrial Revolution along with liberal moral values. If one is truly committed to the ideal of human emancipation, one cannot ignore the stinging critique of contemporary society and the eloquent vision of a new society given by socialism.

Points for Discussion

1. Compare the standard of living of the average CEO and the average factory worker in terms of satisfaction of basic human needs, including food, clothing, shelter and means of transportation and entertainment. Do you believe the vast differences in basic conditions of life between various sections of Indian society are justified? If not, what do you believe are the reasons for these differences? If yes, how would you justify them?
2. Make a list of the major droughts/famines/economic crises that have taken place in the twentieth century (e.g., the Great Bengal Famine, the Great Depression). Do you believe these were caused entirely by 'natural' factors, or could they have been prevented by better economic management of resources?
3. In the Indian Constitution, there exists a tension between the right to property and the aim of the Indian state to redistribute wealth towards greater equality for all (for example, through land reform). If you were to choose between guaranteed liberty for a minority (including, especially, an unlimited liberty to own property) and possible equality for the masses, what would you choose?
4. Which socialist states still exist after the collapse of the USSR? What is your opinion on the 'actually-existing' socialist states in the contemporary world?
5. In the career of your choice, do you believe you will have the opportunity to work in an organization that will provide creatively satisfying work for a majority of its employees, along with an avoidance of extreme income inequalities within the organization?

Reading List

Bottomore, T. (ed.), *Karl Marx. Selected Writings in Sociology and Social Philosophy* (Harmondsworth: Penguin, 1956).
Cole, G. D. H., *Socialist Thought: The Forerunners 1789–1850* (London: Macmillan, 1953).
Huberman, L. and P. Sweezey, *Introduction to Socialism* (New Delhi: Monthly Review Press, 1968).
Marx, K. and F. Engels, *Selected Works* (Moscow: Progress Publishers, 1968).
McLellan, D., *Marx Before Marxism* (New York: Harper and Row, 1970).
Miliband, R., *Socialism for a Sceptical Age* (Cambridge: Polity, 1994).
Nanda, B. R., *Socialism in India* (Delhi: Vikas Publications, 1972).
Saint-Simon, Henri de, *The New Christianity* (1825).
Tawney, R. H., *Equality* (London: Unwin Books, 1931).
Wright, A., *Socialisms: Theories and Practices* (Oxford and New York: Oxford University Press, 1986).

CHAPTER 18

Nationalism

Sunalini Kumar

Chapter Outlines

Introduction

When you pick up the world atlas, you will see that every single inch of land in this world has been divided according to the principle of nationalism. This fact may not strike you as particularly profound unless you dwell on the fact that this was not always so. When we think of the nation that we live in today, it seems to be a natural, ancient, and stable political formation. However, the nation-state was not always the manner in which a political community was organized—ancient Greece was composed of city-states, ancient India was composed of republics and kingdoms, and since the Roman Empire, Europe has been ruled by successive monarchs or dynasties in decentralized feudal kingdoms and empires. In fact, nationalism is no more than 200 years old!

If nationalism is historically such a recent phenomenon, how did it become such a powerful and universally accepted doctrine? How and where did it arise and how did it spread around the world? What is the connection between nationalism and the modern state? The first section of this chapter answers these questions by outlining the major events and factors in the historical journey of nationalism, especially its connection with the modern state. There are several *theoretical* questions about nationalism that arise, too. These include: What is the relationship of nationalism with modern culture and capitalism? Is there a difference between 'Eastern' and 'Western' nationalism? Is nationalism an inherently progressive or regressive political phenomenon? The second half of the chapter seeks answers to these questions by examining the major theoretical debates in this field. Unlike several concepts in liberal and Marxist political theory, an in-depth theoretical study of nationalism has been remarkably absent within mainstream political science. In fact, the subject of nationalism has not existed as a distinct field of study, but has been written about in diverse ways by thinkers within the social sciences in general. There is also little agreement among writers on what exactly one means by the term 'nationalism'. The manner in which one answers the questions we have raised above depends to a large extent on the definition one adopts, the field of social science one is working within, and one's larger normative and philosophical orientation. We hope that through a close study of the historical and theoretical aspects of nationalism, you will get a clearer understanding of these questions, and arrive at possible answers to them.

It will be useful to begin by defining nationalism as the belief that a group of people are united by a common history, tradition, language, and culture, and hence that they should establish a sovereign political community of their own—the nation. The word 'nation', thus, refers to a close-knit political community with a culturally, linguistically, ethnically or even racially homogenous population, and a shared history. Although no country in the world today satisfies these criteria strictly, the idea of a nation has been a powerful force in the history of most countries. The terms 'nation' and 'state' are sometimes used synonymously; however, they are two separate entities, as will become clear from the discussion that follows. The confusion arises from one of the most fundamental beliefs of nationalism—that every community of people that think of themselves as a nation should also have a state of their own. Thus, the hyphenated term 'nation-state'. According to Hans Kohn, 'Nationalism demands the Nation-State; the creation of the Nation-State strengthens nationalism.' Max Weber argues, 'One might as well define the concept of nation in the following way: a nation is a community of sentiment which would adequately manifest itself in a State of its own'. 'Nationalism' is any ideology or movement that seeks to establish a particular nation-state, or to consolidate its power. It is the belief that the nation is/must be the primary focus of loyalty for individuals and groups within a state; that it should be the sole object of people's allegiance. It is also the sense of loyalty required for people to live and work within the modern state, and to even die for the state in wars and in internal law enforcement. The historical study of nationalism clarifies in particular its relationship to the modern state. Let us examine this history in detail.

The History of an Idea

Nationalism is commonly regarded by historians as having originated in Europe, and more specifically in Western Europe, from where it spread to other parts of the world. While nationalism, as mentioned above, arose in the late 18th and 19th centuries, certain political and military events in Europe began to create the conditions for the rise of nations as early as 14th century. These include the decline of the Holy Roman Empire and the Hundred Years War between the English and French kingdoms.

The most important factor for the rise of nationalism, however, was the rise of the centralized modern state in Europe around the 16th and 17th centuries (see Chapter 11 on the state). Nationalism has a structural connection with the state, and could not have emerged prior to its existence. Thus, it is important to first understand the rise of the state. The modern state differs from pre-modern political formations because it embodies centralized, sovereign, *undivided* political power. In contrast, in medieval Europe, political power was divided instead of being consolidated in the hands of a single sovereign ruler or government. Although monarchs and ruling dynasties existed, they shared power both 'horizontally' (with the Church) and vertically (with feudal governors or 'vassals'). The horizontal division of power at the apex of the political system existed because of the Church being as powerful as individual rulers, and often even more powerful than them. The power of the church had steadily grown ever since the adoption of Christianity by the Roman Emperor Constantine in the 4th century AD. The adoption of Christianity as the official religion of the Roman Empire meant the dissemination of Church authority to the farthest corners of the Roman Empire (i.e. most of the continent of Europe, and as far east as Turkey and Russia). By the 6th century AD, there existed overlapping zones of authority between the Catholic Church and individual rulers of kingdoms all across Europe. While on the one hand, kings justified their rule over subjects by claiming that they possessed divine sanction, the Church exercised political control in the non-religious (secular) sense; for instance, in the power to tax subjects. The presence of this uneasy alliance between religious and political authority in medieval Europe meant that neither could emerge as omnipotent, or all-powerful.

The 'vertical' check on the ruler's power in medieval Europe was provided by the feudal structure. Feudalism was a system of social stratification which existed throughout medieval Europe. It consisted of ties of obligation between superiors and subordinates which emphasized the performance of one's given duty (or one's 'station') in accordance with one's place in the hierarchy. It is important to remember that the feudal system functioned at both economic and political levels. In the largely agrarian economies of medieval European kingdoms, an individual's status was primarily determined by his/her relationship to the main economic asset—land. As a result, there were vast inequalities in status between landowners and landless tillers. These status inequalities were concretized in feudalism through the economic hierarchy between 'lords' and 'serfs'. Similarly, at the political level, the feudal structure implied a complex sharing of power vertically downwards from the monarch or emperor. The political hierarchy was expressed in distinctions between 'lords' and 'vassals'. Each lord enjoyed jurisdiction over his vassal, who in turn enjoyed jurisdiction over his vassal, and so on.

In pre-modern Europe, therefore, there were several factors that prevented the formation of a centralized political community with a fixed territory and population. Most importantly, as already discussed, the power of the kings and monarchs was limited and was often only *primus inter pares* (first among equals) when considered in relation to the Church and feudal governors. The Church commanded people's loyalty and obedience, encouraging the development of an overarching Christian identity across Europe that often overrode loyalty to individual rulers or kingdoms. Rulers were forced to depend on their vassals to execute the basic tasks of government—especially taxation and administrative control. Technological impediments like lack of advanced transport and communication networks made the sharing of political power not simply a convention but a necessity for individual monarchs. Rebellion by vassals remained an ever-present threat for individual rulers due to the latter's dependence on the former. The changing political equations between various kings, lords and vassals due to war, conquest or secession meant that the borders of medieval political communities could not be absolute. Further, marriage alliances between royal families from different kingdoms were often accompanied by large dowries and gifts of land and territory, with the consequence that subjects of one king could suddenly find themselves subjects of another king following a royal marriage! In the absence of modern rules of residence and citizenship, subjects were also free to move across kingdoms to live, work, or marry. As a consequence of all these patterns of decentralization of politics, administration, law, and culture, the daily life of populations within feudal kingdoms continued in all its local diversity and peculiarity, largely unaffected by changing political scenarios. The speech, behaviour, and social practices of populations across Europe were incredibly diverse, deriving more from local customs and conventions rather than from a centralized authority. This prevented the formation of any larger homogenized cultural identity among populations across diverse territories, and such an identity is crucial to modern nationalism.

Gradually, political conditions changed and led to the weakening and collapse of the feudal and religious forces in European society. One of the most important factors in this change was the rise of Absolutist monarchs (like the Tudor dynasty in England and the Bourbon dynasty in France). They consolidated their political power with the help of the newly emerging trading and merchant classes—the merchant capitalists, or the mercantile bourgeoisie. Merchant capitalism and trade became rich sources of wealth in early modern Europe, allowing monarchs to considerably reduce their dependence on taxation from feudal agrarian production, and thus reduce their dependence on vassals. Eventually, capitalism came to replace feudalism almost entirely, resulting in the loss of political power of feudal governors and allowing kings to exercise 'absolute' power over their kingdoms; hence the term 'absolutist'. At the same time, the religious reformation of the 15th century dealt a heavy blow to the power of the Catholic Church. With the waning of both vertical and horizontal challenges to their authority by the 16th century, monarchs were able to establish direct, effective and comprehensive rule over the entire population within their kingdoms. They strictly enforced territorial boundaries, standardized population in the realms of religion, education and language, maintained standing armies and introduced stricter rules of residence and mobility for citizens, in order that they may develop a sense of loyalty towards their respective rulers. Advancements in transport, communication, and technologies of governance meant that monarchs could achieve these political aims more effectively. These developments had far-reaching consequences. Indeed, absolutism led to the formation of the earliest form of the modern state—the absolutist state. It is important to remember that Absolutist states resembled contemporary states in many ways—they possessed sovereignty, centralized government, and fixed territorial boundaries. However, they were ruled by what we consider a pre-modern institution—the monarchy. The idea of 'absolutism' is best captured in the famous (or notorious!) statement by the absolutist king, Louis XIV of France—'I am the State'.

The doctrine of nationalism may be understood in the context of these large-scale historical events. The standardization and fixing of territorial boundaries and populations by absolutist kings had laid the *objective* foundation of nations; 'nations' being defined as a culturally, linguistically, and ethnically homogeneous population united within a state. As a *subjective* feeling, nationalism became the philosophy of the emerging elites of Western Europe, the 'bourgeoisie'. The bourgeoisie (initially mercantile and later industrial capitalists) were important political allies of the Absolutist kings in their rise to power. Ironically, they soon became restless for greater political rights and representation, dominating newly-established representative assemblies and parliaments across Western Europe. This led to the famous tussle between king and parliament in early modern Europe; the Glorious Revolution of 1688 in England is a prime example. During this tussle, the idea of the 'nation' (derived from the Latin root '*natio*', which pertains to birth, or origin) became very significant as a sense of identity for the bourgeoisie. At a time when familiar feudal social and political institutions were decaying all across Western Europe, especially after the Industrial Revolution of the 18th century, nationalism united diverse sections of the bourgeoisie through these historic upheavals. The 'nation' was used to refer to a homogenous, ancient, close-knit political community that had miraculously survived intact in the modern age, and that had to be revived. This myth of ancientness was a powerful one, expressed especially forcefully in 'Romantic' nationalism that arose later in Germany.

Nationalism, thus, arose as a powerful unifying force in the modern era, allowing the bourgeoisie to speak in the name of a seemingly *primordial* community called the 'nation' while bargaining for greater political power within their respective *modern* states. So, how did nationalism become a popular, or mass phenomenon? For the masses, nationalism served a similar purpose (as discussed above in the context of the elites)—opposition to political power. To simplify a complex picture, as absolutist monarchs struggled to hold on to their power in the face of decreasing support from the bourgeoisie, they resorted to increasingly desperate and despotic forms of rule. As a response to this, the masses took to the streets in protest, and there were successive waves of popular pressure on absolutist states (for example, the French Revolution of 1789). We may clarify here that while revolts, mutinies and uprisings against political power have existed from time immemorial, by the 18th and 19th centuries in Europe, these popular revolts were increasingly expressed in 'nationalist' terms. Often, the leadership of the national movement would remain in the hands of the elites, and the popular element would ebb and flow. Occasionally, a local rebellion against a ruler or provincial governor would be strategically utilized by the bourgeoisie in order to launch a full-scale nationalist agitation against the monarch.

To summarize and conclude this section, as absolutist states transformed into limited, or constitutional states, and finally to democratic states towards the end of the 19th century, nationalism became a rallying call for greater political power or rights for both the bourgeoisie and the masses in the modern age. It is important to remember that the above is only a simplified sketch; nationalism has differed vastly according to specific historical, cultural, and geographical conditions in various parts of Europe and elsewhere. For example, in France, the violent mass element was stronger than it was in England. Hence, it was the mass political groups that participated in the French Revolution rather than a Parliament that created and popularized the idea of the French nation as an embodiment of liberty in opposition to the excesses of absolutism. In many parts of Europe, nationalism even among the elites arose as late as the 19th century. The reasons for this phenomenon may be found in the different geographical and cultural conditions and divergent processes of state formation in these areas. In England, state formation had taken place under relatively peaceful conditions due partly to its geographical and cultural isolation from the rest of Europe; hence a distinctive English *nation* could be shaped within the boundaries of the existing English *state*. However, where large multi-ethnic, multi-linguistic empires had transformed into states, the boundaries of 'nations' and 'states' did not always neatly coincide. These empires initially became multi-national states, which gradually broke up into individual nation states. The phenomenon of nationalism was more conflict-ridden and often violent in these areas; one clear example of this could be seen in the history of nations like Bosnia and Herzegovina that were born from the debris of the old Austro-Hungarian Empire. In these areas, nationalism arose to demand the creation of the nation-state, rather than merely for the establishment of a subjective sense of loyalty among the population of existing states. In the case of Germany, too, the nation-state of 'Germany' was created in the 19th century out of the princely republics that comprised the crumbling Holy Roman Empire.

Non-European Nationalism

Within Europe, nationalism had spread from the elites to the masses by the end of the 19th century. At this time, nationalism also began to spread from Europe to other parts of the world. The salient factors in this regard were trade and colonialism. As early as the 18th century, European powers were engaged in securing lucrative trading outposts around the globe; by the end of the 19th century this search became a 'mad scramble' for colonies. As European powers opened up inner territories of Asia, Africa and Latin America for their own profit and exposed the native populations to the outside world, they ironically dug their own graves by fuelling national liberation struggles in their colonies. As the historian Benedict Anderson points out, the doctrine of nationalism was *inadvertently* 'exported' to Latin America, Asia and Africa by European colonial powers! Just as popular revolts had opposed despotic rulers within Europe, national liberation struggles in the colonies expressed popular frustration at arbitrary and unjust colonial policies. Interestingly, the leadership of national liberation movements was initially in the hands of the bourgeoisie in the colonies, too—often foreign educated, professional middle classes—who saw themselves as leaders of an indigenous nation opposing the imperialist European nations. Gradually, the mass element began to enter anti-colonial nationalism. In the Indian case, for example, historians have argued that the importance of Mohandas Karamchand Gandhi was precisely in effecting a transformation of Indian nationalism from the limited, middle-class nationalism of the Indian National Congress in the 1890s and 1900s to a radical mass movement from the 1920s onwards.

The solidarity between various liberation struggles may have been an additional factor in the demise of colonialism and the rise of non-European nationalism. Anti-colonial nationalist movements benefited from communication between colonized areas, which was ironically made possible by colonialism itself. For instance, the defeat of an imperialist power like Russia by a tiny Asian nation, Japan in 1904–1905, created a tremendous sense of confidence all over the colonized, non-European world. Similarly, the non-cooperation movement launched by Gandhi in India expressed solidarity with the anti-colonial *khilafat* movement in Turkey. Further, after World War, the legitimacy of imperialism as a principle of political rule had decreased considerably at an international level. The growing success of Asian and African anti-colonial struggles made imperialism an increasingly expensive enterprise both materially and morally. *Materially*, colonies became not simply ungovernable, but also unprofitable for many reasons. *Morally*, imperialism was opposed not simply by nationalist leaders and masses in the colonies, but also by liberal democratic governments that had been elected to power in Europe. Due to a combination of the above factors, there was a wave of decolonization in the colonized world after World War II, and by the third quarter of the 20th century, modern nation-states had been established in most of Asia, Africa and Latin America.

Theoretical Questions

Nationalism and Modern Culture

Many writers have attempted to examine the precise connection between nationalism and modern culture. These include Karl Wolfgang Deutsch who argues in his work, *Nationalism and Social Communication* (1962) that nationalism is an expression of cultural and social mechanisms peculiar to modernity, such as modern communications. Ernest Gellner's *Nations and Nationalism* (1983) is an important attempt to understand the role of cultural factors in nationalism, and vice-versa. In his now-famous words:

> Nations as a natural, God-given way of classifying men, as an inherent though long-delayed political destiny, are a myth; nationalism, which sometimes takes pre-existing cultures and turns them into nations, sometimes invents them, and often obliterates pre-existing cultures: that is a reality, for better or worse...

Thus, Gellner argues that it is not nations that create nationalism but rather, that *nationalism creates nations*, a fact that certainly seems to be true for the history of most recent nation-states. In this process, according to Gellner, the principle of nationalism exerts a homogenizing pressure on pre-modern cultures, exploiting them and transforming them to fulfil its project of creating a homogenous 'national' culture. Nationalism also obliterates obscure 'little traditions' and reinvents and homogenizes 'great traditions' in order to create a basis for the modern nation. Gellner's analysis can be used by us to understand the rise of Hindu nationalism, or Hindutva in India. Hindutva seeks to promote the development of a Indian nation by the propagation of a homogenized Hindu culture in favour of Sanskritic traditions. There is also a continuous reference in the Hindutva discourse to a glorious ancient past—the 'Vedic Age'—as the origin/root of the Hindu nation. As mentioned above, the idea of common origin or birth is a part of the history of nationalism in Western Europe, too. In this aspect, Hindu nationalism is strikingly similar to German 'Romantic' nationalism mentioned above.

Gellner also seeks to demonstrate that nationalism has a structural connection with the needs of modern industrial society. He argues that 'The social organisation of agrarian society is not at all favourable to the nationalist principle'. According to him, the need of modern industrial economies for a mobile and interchangeable workforce requires complex new skills and social formations beyond the resources of family and kinship ties. Such skills according to Gellner 'can only be provided by a public education system and integrated by (preferably) a single language and within a centralized political, economic, and educational system'; in other words, within the modern nation-state. The universality of nationalism in the contemporary world stems from the fact that it is the only form of political organization that is appropriate to the social and material conditions of modern society. Further, nationalism can unite sections of the population that would compete fiercely otherwise for valued modern occupations—jobs and political careers. Thus, seen through Gellner's eyes, nationalism is a *sine qua non* of industrialization, because it provides people with a powerful motivation for making painful changes necessary for creating modern industrial societies. The cultural homogeneity required by nationalism is also useful for industrial society in many ways. Thus, to simplify Gellner's thesis, nationalism is intrinsic to both modernity and industrialization.

Nationalism and Capitalism

The relationship between nationalism and capitalism has been analysed by the Marxists and non-Marxists alike. Marxists argue that during the four centuries old development of capitalism, nationalism has to a great extent arisen as an ally of capitalism, as a bourgeois ideology. For example, Hobsbawm believes that nationalism is a symptom of capitalism at a particular stage of its development. Nationalism unites the dominant classes—the bourgeoisie—and creates a false sense of community between them and the masses in the face of the latter's impoverishment and exploitation by capitalism (for more details, see Chapter 16 on Socialism). Marxism believes that nationalism offers individuals an identity and a means to belong to a community that seems egalitarian and unified, but actually is not so. This is because all nations are characterized by deep economic and social inequalities even today. Thus, Marxists would argue that the unity in nationalist thought can be a mythical one, and does not reflect the real conditions of human beings in the modern, predominantly capitalist world. Benedict Anderson, an influential writer on nationalism expresses this Marxist insight when he calls nations 'Imagined Communities' (1983). According to Anderson (1983: 7), nations are imagined because,

> The members of even the smallest nation will never know most of their fellow members, meet them, or even hear of them, yet in the minds of each lives the image of their communion ... regardless of the actual inequality and exploitation that may prevail in each, the nation is always conceived of as a deep, horizontal comradeship. Ultimately, it is this fraternity that makes it possible, over the past two centuries, for so many millions of people, not so much to kill, as willingly to die....

Nationalism: Western or Eastern

The question of whether there is a difference between Eastern and Western nationalism is a thorny one, since Western thinkers on nationalism have often used positive terminology to describe Western nationalism and negative terminology for Eastern nationalism. For instance, according to Hans Kohn (1945: 36), 'Western nationalism was connected with the concepts of individual liberty ... the later nationalism in Central and Eastern Europe and in Asia easily tended towards a contrary development.' Edward Shils similarly believes that one can draw a clear demarcation between the West and the East on the question of nationalism. Shils argues that rather than the secular, rational reasons that draw people into politics in the Western nations; the people of the East are drawn into politics because of what he calls their 'deep preoccupation with authority'. With the collapse of traditional sources of political authority due to colonialism in the East, the eastern individual longs for incorporation into a new, alternative collectivity. According to Shils, nationalism in the Eastern states can be understood as an expression of this overwhelming, irrational need. Theorists also argue that since nationalism is imported into non-Western states by colonialism, it tends to be a more artificial and unstable phenomenon here, spawning dangerous tendencies towards violence and extremism.

Nationalism: Progressive or Regressive

There has always existed a debate between those theorists who view nationalism as a conservative, retrograde phenomenon and those who view it as progressive and desirable. The dismissal of nationalism as a regressive or even reactionary force has come from a diverse set of political and ideological positions; Marxism, as mentioned above, has traditionally been hostile to nationalism. For example, Rosa Luxemburg (1971) believed that nationalism instils a sense of loyalty in the minds of the working class towards the existing state, and towards the ruling classes that are allied with the state. Luxemburg argued that even if the idea of the 'right of nations to self-determination' was relevant or meaningful to the mass of the world's population at some point, it had become meaningless or impossible under modern capitalist conditions. Many writers have opposed nationalism for its narrow particularism and its capacity to construct the myth of homogeneous identity. The great Indian poet and writer Rabindranath Tagore remained deeply suspicious of nationalism throughout his life for these reasons. Paul Gilroy in his book *The Black Atlantic* (1993) reminds us that marginalization of diverse traditions and experiences seems inbuilt into nationalism anywhere in the world. Gilroy's thesis is that racial immigration through slavery has been central to the history of modern Western nation-states but this is a truth that has been obliterated in the commonly held idea that all English people are white, and that the English nation has survived intact from antiquity. England is one of the most multi-racial, multi-linguistic, multi-ethnic and even multi-national countries in the world today; yet some varieties of English nationalism continue to draw on a small, homogeneous set of medieval, white upper-class traditions as the foundation of the English nation. Gellner's analysis on nationalism and culture may be recalled here.

Support for nationalism has also come from diverse and sometimes surprising quarters. The influential Marxist scholar Aijaz Ahmad understands nationalism in a manner similar to Ernest Gellner when he argues that nationalism may be a stage in the often painful transition of traditional societies to modernity. As discussed above, Marxism views nationalism as a bourgeois ideology that accompanies the rise of the modern state. Marxists like Ahmad believe that the modern nation state is a necessary historical stage in the ultimate establishment of a stateless, classless society (for more details see Chapter 16 on socialism). Therefore, Ahmad does not share the suspicion of nationalism that some other Marxist thinkers display. Rather, he argues that nationalism may be seen as a 'cementing force' in the transition of societies to modernity, and ultimately to socialism. Especially for Third World states, nationalism is viewed by many contemporary Marxist writers and activists as a powerful and useful tool to resist the forces of global capitalism. Ahmad, for instance, argues for the 'actuality, even the necessity of progressive and revolutionary kinds of nationalism' in order to defend the interests of weaker states in the international hierarchy of states. Most Third World nationalism has its roots in anti-colonial struggle. Marxists who characterize the contemporary global economic system as 'neo-colonial' would argue thus: that just as nationalism can be used to oppose colonialism, it can be employed to oppose neo-colonialism and multinational corporations (MNCs). In India, for example, sections of communist political parties have often supported even non-communist national governments in their stand against MNCs. This nationalist position, which stands directly opposed to the traditional pro-working class, internationalist stance of Marxism, is justified on the basis of the defence of weaker states against the moves of powerful Western multi-nationals.

Analysis and Critique

As regards the connection between nationalism and modern culture, the idea common to the theories discussed above is that nationalism is the 'religion of modernization' or the ideological corollary to the material fact of modernization. There is no doubt that nationalism has a structural connection with modernization as is evinced by its rise two centuries ago. Nationalism may have provided individuals from different classes with a sense of identity and connection in the face of the massive economic and political upheavals that accompanied modernity. However, it must be emphasized that neither modernization per se, nor its connection with nationalism is a straightforward phenomenon. First, nationalism often works *against* modernization, as is the case with nationalist economic opposition to international trade agreements, even where it can be demonstrated that the new rules would foster industrial modernization in the country. Gellner's analysis also becomes somewhat untenable when we consider nationalism in the developing world. Most Third World countries today are composed of combinations of agrarian and industrial forms of production. In other words, instead of having witnessed a neat transition from agrarian to industrial society, Third World societies seem to simultaneously contain all the 'stages' of historical development that Gellner speaks of. Thus, the notion of a development from traditional to agrarian society, and of nationalism as facilitating this process is unsustainable given the contemporary nationalism of the Third World.

Second, the distinction between 'Eastern' and 'Western' nationalism must be questioned. The tendency to view all 'Eastern nationalisms' as somehow lacking in the healthy values associated with Western nationalism, is very common in conventional literature. For instance, Shils in the context of 'Eastern' nationalism argues that it contains 'a deficient trend of civility'. The distinction between cultural and political nationalisms may be more useful. However, most scholars see western nationalisms as political and eastern ones as cultural. This distinction remains controversial, since some writers have argued the exact opposite—whereas most European nations emerged 'organically' from indigenous historical processes, colonized nations are highly artificial creations since their boundaries have been constructed by the imperial powers. So, they would argue that Western nations are cultural whereas Eastern nations are political. For instance, the continuing ethnic conflict in many African states may point to the fact that colonial rulers arbitrarily created their boundaries with scant respect for local ethnic loyalties. As a result, many ethnic and tribal communities were split between two nations. Conversely, a huge diversity of ethnic groups were randomly bound together in the confines of a modern nation-state, as a result of which there was a fierce and often bloody conflict between groups for political power. This random 'binding together' of groups with little cultural or ethnic similarity could be seen as the result of a conscious political action, which in turn may arise from a political form of nationalism, writers have argued.

There is undoubtedly a contrast that can be drawn between traditional political membership and modern citizenship; however, it is also true that all nationalisms share some basic features, allowing, of course, for historical and geographical differences. Therefore, to classify Eastern nationalism as non-liberal, dangerous and impassioned and Western nationalism as reasonable and cosmopolitan is inaccurate and misleading. The 'irrational' element is a characteristic of Western nationalism as much as of Eastern nationalism, as argued convincingly by theorists like Elie Kedourie, Tom Nairn and Isaiah Berlin, among others. For instance, Kedourie points to the revolutionary element in Indian nationalism, with its worship of the goddess Kali as having the same roots as the irrational, violent, spiritual, and collective elements in the Romantic nationalism of Europe. Also, the idea of a liberal, reasonable, cosmopolitan Western nationalism that is devoid of any unhealthy values including resentment and xenophobia may be a normative ideal rather than reality in Western states. Paul Gilroy's analysis of nationalism in Western states (discussed above) may be useful to remember in this regard. In fact, the historian John Breuilly believes that the welding of universalistic political discourse with a particularistic ethnic one constitutes the fundamental principle of *all* nationalisms. John Hutchinson provides a well-argued corrective to such a simplistic distinction when he maintains that 'cultural and political nationalism represent two competing conceptions of the nation, *each of which feed off each other*'.

Conclusion: The Future of an Idea

At the start of the 21st century, increasing economic globalization, mass migration, and technological advancements like the Internet and mobile phones seem to have dramatically 'shrunk the planet'. The lifestyles of the elites all over the globe are now strikingly similar; for many classes of people, national identity has become irrelevant at the everyday level—they use the same slang, travel in the same manner and even eat the same food! Migration of human beings has increased manifold, with a huge number of individuals seeking to live and work in countries far away from their own. Writers argue that in the face of an increasingly globalized world, old political formations like the nation will lose their earlier role and relevance. David Beetham, for instance, argues that the very forces that strengthened nationalism in the previous era will cause its downfall in the coming one. Some writers believe that rather than national formations, it is *trans*-national economic and political alliances that will set the agenda for the world's people in this, and in the coming centuries. In this context, writers point to the example of the EU as proof of the decline of the nation state. Europe being widely regarded as the birthplace of nationalism, the formation of the EU on this very continent has led some writers to believe that nationalism and other such 'primitive' ideologies will be overcome in this new epoch. Many writers and political commentators believe that the coming centuries will move in the direction of cosmopolitan, universal, global values, and the nationalist bloodbaths of the previous century will be distant memories.

However, well into the 21st century, a decline of nationalism seems nowhere in evidence. Nationalism as a *political* force seems alive and well, expressed in myriad forms like cultural revivalist movements in the East, debates on race and immigration all over the world, and most recently, in the controversy over business process outsourcing (BPO) in Western states. You may recall that opposition to outsourcing in Western countries was conducted in nationalist language, with implicit elements of xenophobia and racism against workers in Third World states. Further, national 'self-determination' movements are active, whether in Kashmir, in Palestine, or as witnessed in the recent liberation of East Timor from Indonesia. Nationalism has been, and will in all likelihood continue to be, at the core of many of the most bitter and important struggles well into the 21st century. The theorist Michael Billig, for example, argues that nationalism as a phenomenon is too deeply and thoroughly ingrained in modern life to study it narrowly in terms of particular social movements and make sharp and sweeping distinctions *between* nationalisms. Billig's central claim is that if all states today are *nation*-states, then nationalism is simply the ideology that maintains *all* nation-states *as* nation-states. In this context Billig (1997) refers to the idea of 'banal nationalism'—the everyday, routine forms of nationalism practised by First World states—from the restrictions on immigration to the widespread use of national symbols such as flags and songs.

To conclude, it may be useful to understand nationalism as a universal contemporary political phenomenon; not simply an occasional, spectacular outpouring of patriotic sentiment, but as a part of the history of the modern state. Nationalism has often joined hands with the democratic state and liberal politics, as the experience of Third World leaders like Gandhi, Nehru, and Kenyatta has shown. It can be a powerful transformative force that can achieve miracles in large and impoverished societies, as expressed in the idea of 'nation-building'. Nationalism has especially been an ally for post-colonial societies seeking to unite large and diverse populations and fulfil difficult developmental goals within an unequal global capitalist system. However, it has also become entwined with more dangerous ideologies like religious extremism of any sort, fundamentalism and even fascism. To understand why nationalism can be healthy or regressive, powerful or limited in its scope, one must remember above all the historical contingencies that accompanied its rise, and in particular its complex historical relationship with the modern state. The blending of the universal and the particular, the banal and the spectacular, the routine and the extraordinary, the reasonable and the irrational is what constitutes the most striking feature of nationalism anywhere in the world, and perhaps gives us a compelling explanation for the continuing power of this ideology well into the 21st century.

Points for Discussion

1. The Indian state was formally created in 1947, when the British handed over power to the Indians. However, the Indian national movement is much older: as old as the late 19th century. Therefore, is India a state or a nation? Or, like some European countries, is it a 'multi-nation state'?
2. Read the quote by Benedict Anderson on page 266. Is India an 'imagined community'?
3. Are American, French or British citizens influenced by nationalism? Is there a difference between nationalism in the West and in post-colonial states like India? Do you find Michael Billig's idea of 'banal nationalism' useful to understand this issue?
4. Nationalism may not end with the creation of the nation-state. It may continue even after Independence. Can you think of five examples from recent Indian experience?
5. Is there a difference between nationalism, 'patriotism', 'nation-building' and 'sub-nationalism'? Can you think of examples for each? Is there anything common to all of the above?

Reading List

Anderson, B., *Imagined Communities: Reflections on the Origins and Growth of National Consciousness* (London: Verso, 1983).

Anderson, P., *Lineages of the Absolutist State* (London: Verso, 1996).

Berlin, I., *The Proper Study of Mankind: An Anthology of Essays* (New York: Farrar Straus and Giroux, 2000).

Billig, M., *Banal Nationalism* (London: Sage, 1997).

Carr, E. H., *Nationalism and After* (London: Penguin, 1945).

Deutsch, K. W., *Nationalism and Social Communication* (Cambridge, MA: MIT Press, 1962).

Gellner, E., *Nations and Nationalism* (Oxford: Basil Blackwell, 1983).

Gilroy, Paul, *The Black Atlantic: Modernity and Double-Consciousness* (Harvard: Harvard University Press, 1993).

Hall, S., 'The State in Question', in G. McLennan, D. Held and S. Hall (eds), *The Idea of the Modern State* (Milton Keynes: Open University Press, 1984).

Hobsbawm, E. J., *Nations and Nationalism Since 1789* (Cambridge: Cambridge University Press, 1989).

Kedourie, E., *Nationalism in Asia and Africa* (New York: The World Publishing Company, 1970).

Kohn, Hans, *The Idea of Nationalism* (New York: Macmillan, 1945).

Luxemburg, Rosa, *The Accumulation of Capital* (New York: Monthly Review Press, 1964).

———, *Selected Political Writings* (New York: Monthly Review Press, 1971).

Seth, S., *Marxist Theory and Nationalist Politics* (New Delhi: Sage, 1995).

Smith, A., *Nationalism: A Reader*, Vol I (Oxford: Oxford University Press, 1994).

PART IV

Political Arguments

CHAPTER 19

Secularism

Rajeev Bhargava

Chapter Outlines

Introduction

Most doctrines or ideologies advocate something but also define themselves in opposition to some other things. For example, feminism advocates gender equality and justice. But it can also be understood in opposition to patriarchy, as a theory resisting institutionalized male domination. Similarly, environmentalism advocates the protection of our natural environment but it can also be viewed as against its destruction by the wilful or negligent acts of human beings.

Secularism: The Broad Definition

How, then, is secularism to be understood? The best way to understand the animating principle of secularism is to see it in opposition to religious hegemony, religious tyranny and religious and religion-based exclusion. The goal of secularism, defined most generally, is to ensure that the social and political order is free from institutionalized religious domination so that there is religious freedom, freedom to exit from religion, inter-religious equality and equality between believers and non-believers. Thus, religion defines the scope of secularism. The very point of secularism is lost either when religion disappears or if it purges itself from its oppressive, tyrannical, inegalitarian or exclusionary features. If religion is exhaustively defined in terms of these oppressive features, then the goal of secularism is to eliminate religion altogether. However, since religion is not necessarily tyrannical or oppressive, we might see the objective of secularism as the reform of religion but from a vantage point that is non-partisan. Secularism may then be seen not as intrinsically opposed to religion but as advocating critical respect towards it.

But why call this religion-related doctrine 'secularism'? The word 'secular' comes from the Latin word '*saeculum*', meaning 'this time' as distinct from some 'other time', say 'time' related to divinity. It also came to mean 'this world', as distinct from some 'other world'. In a deeply religious context, where living in this world is usually considered lower than living in some other world or where, in the last instance, freedom means a permanent escape from this world, 'this world' and 'this time' have an inferior quality. A doctrine such as secularism must deny the lowly quality of this world. But it need not be committed to its opposite view, which dogmatically asserts the absence of another world. All it must be committed to is the idea that living in 'this world' and 'this time' are significant enough for all human beings and no matter which other mode of being an entity might have, it undeniably exists in 'this world' and 'this time'. Whatever else they might be, human beings and their material and social worlds are this-worldly or secular and this is a significant enough fact about them.

Secularism is committed first to the view that, whether or not they exist elsewhere, all human beings exist on the secular plane. This view is assumed, presupposed or actually believed by all human beings. If so, even deeply religious people must accept that all human institutions including those which focus on God are entangled with everything in 'this world' and in 'this time'. Second, it presupposes that any human institutions in this world can turn oppressive or inegalitarian. If this is true, and if we are troubled about oppression, tyranny or hierarchy, then this concern must manifest itself in relation to everything in 'this world' and 'this time', including those institutions and practices that focus on some *other* world or entity. This is why some of the most religious and 'other worldly' people were concerned about religious tyranny and oppression, particularly within their own religion. Just think of Buddha, Jesus, Nanak, Kabir, Luther, Gandhi or Phule. They were all motivated by internal religious reform. Though not secular, they were, in an important sense, all part of a secular struggle. In their own way and to different degrees, they at least had affinities with secularists!

Political Secularism

I have defined secularism in rather broad terms, but still as a normative doctrine. Political secularism is narrowly defined but is also normative. It answers the question as to what should the appropriate relation between state and religious institutions be, given the background that animates secularism more generally, that is, to end religious hegemony, oppression and exclusion. The broadest and perhaps the vaguest answer provided by political secularism is that the two must be separated. Here, then, is the first initial formulation: political secularism is a normative doctrine for which the state should be separated from religious institutions to check religious tyranny, oppression or hierarchy and to promote religious and non-religious freedoms and equalities. Put schematically, it advocates the separation of state and religious institutions for the sake of values, such as the ones mentioned above.

Political secularism does not come in one unique form. It is open to many interpretations. Thus, there are many conceptions of political secularism, depending on how the metaphor of separation is unpacked, which values the separation is meant to promote, how these values are combined and what weight is assigned to each of them. I shall return to this point about different conceptions of secularism. However, to grasp its structure, it is first important to contrast political secularism with doctrines to which it is in one sense related and yet, opposed. Such anti-secular doctrines favour not separation but a union or alliance between religion and state. If political secularism advocates a state that separates itself from religion (a secular state), then doctrines it opposes seek a union with religion (theocracy) or an alliance with it (state with established religion).

Theocracy, States with Established Religions and Secular States: An Exposition

There are at least three types of states to which a secular state can be contrasted: (*a*) a theocratic state, (*b*) a state that establishes one religion, and (*c*) a state that establishes multiple religions.

A theocratic state is one where a priestly order directly administers the state by reference to what it believes are divine laws. In such states, religious and political orders are identical.

In contemporary times, the Islamic Republic of Iran, as Ayatollah Khomeini aspired to run it, or the state in Afghanistan run by the Taliban provide the best approximation of a theocracy. If the Indian state was to be run by an elite class of Brahmins in accordance with the Dharmashastras, then it would be theocratic. Such a theocratic state must be distinguished from a state that establishes religion. In such states religion is granted formal or legal recognition. There is an official alliance between the state and religion. However, a priestly order does not directly govern in such states. If so, there is a large measure of institutional differentiation in such states, i.e. religious institutions are distinct from political institutions. Likewise, religious personnel are different from political rulers. The two institutions also perform different functions. For example, the religious order or the Church is meant to secure salvation. The political order exists in order to maintain peace and order, primarily in temporal matters. This *second-order* disconnection between religious and political institutions, also referred in some contexts as Church–state separation, goes hand in hand with an overall ideological connection. For example, in the last instance, both sets of institutions share common ends. The state is subordinate to religious ends even though it has its own function, power structure, and internal norms. Because of this primary *first-order* connection of ultimate ends, there is an automatic *third-order* connection at the level of law and policy. In such states, religion is a natural object of law and policy. For example, the revenue collected by the state is available for religious purposes. The state may enact law compelling individuals to congregate for religious purposes.

States that establish religion are of two types. Some establish one religion. For centuries, England, Scotland, and Germany established Protestant Christianity. Italy and Spain promoted Catholicism. There are many states in the world today with one officially recognized religion. For example, Pakistan and Saudi Arabia are Islamic states. In the second type, a state establishes not one but many religions. With his policy of toleration for all religions, Emperor Ashoka came closest to it. It may also have been an aspiration of the Mughal emperor Akbar. Perhaps another example is the 14th-century Vijayanagar kingdom that granted recognition not only to Shaivites and Vaishnavites but also to the Jains.

Secular states are different from each of these three types of states. To understand this difference at a more abstract and general level, let me distinguish three orders of disconnection to correspond with the already identified three orders of connection. A state may be disconnected from religion first at the level of ends, second at the level of institutions, and third at the level of law and public policy. A secular state is both non-theocratic and against the establishment of religions. It establishes neither one religion nor many. The first-order disconnection from religion distinguishes secular states from both theocracies and states with established religion. A secular state has its own secular ends. The second order disconnection, Church–state separation, demarcates it from a theocracy. Table 18.1 clarifies these distinctions.

Two points follow from this. The second order disconnection, what I have called Church–state separation, is not a feature unique to secular states. If so, it cannot be its defining attribute. Why? Because this is a feature secular states share with states with an established religion. Several scholars do not fully recognize this. Many of them identify secular states with Church–state separation. However, as I have shown above Church–state separation is

Table 18.1

Levels of connection (C) or disconnection (D)	*Theocracy*	*State with established religions*	*Mainstream secular*
Ends: First order C/D	C	C	D
Institutions and personnel: Second order C/D	C	D	D
Law and public policy: Third order C/D	C	C	D

a necessary but not a sufficient condition for the existence of secular states. For a state to be secular, it must go beyond the Church–state separation and have predominantly secular ends. In societies without an established religion, the state must, in order to be secular, refrain from establishing any religion. In societies where religion is established, a state, in order to become secular, must disestablish religion(s). It must withdraw privileges that the established religion had previously taken for granted. In short, a secular state must follow a principle of non-establishment (**feature-a**). (See Box 18.1 for a list of all the features.)

The second consequence of what is stated above is this: a non-theocratic state is not automatically secular because it is entirely consistent for a state neither to be directly inspired by divine laws nor to be run by priestly order, but instead to have a formal alliance with one religion.

Amoral and Value-based Secular States

I mentioned that a secular state must have secular ends. However, these ends themselves are of two kinds. The first kind are amoral. Amoral secular states are so called because their entire purpose is to maximize power, wealth, or both. They may have moral pretensions but really no commitment to values such as peace, liberty, or equality. Usually, they are imperial and autocratic. A good example of such a predominantly secular state, despite the not infrequent allegation of its biased, Christian character, was the British colonial state in India that was motivated almost exclusively by power, wealth, and social order, but had a policy of tolerance and neutrality towards different religious communities. This is not surprising, given that empires are interested in the labour or tribute of their subjects, not in their religion. Such self-aggrandizing, amoral states may or may not disconnect with religion at the third level, that is, at the level of law and policy. They may have a hands-off approach to all religions, purely for instrumental reasons. However, if it serves their instrumental purpose, they may also connect with religion.

Values of a Secular State

Distinct from amoral states are value-based secular states. A fuller discussion of such states requires a better articulation of their connection with several important and substantive values. The first of these is peace, or rather the prevention of a society from its regression into barbarism, not an uncommon tendency where there exist two or more incompatible visions of the good life (**feature-b**). The second is toleration, that is, the state does not persecute or allow the persecution of anyone on grounds of religion. This value may be seen by some to be superseded by the discourse on rights, but in a certain context it has continuing relevance. Why so? Because there are areas of society which remain beyond the reach of the legal regime of rights. For example, we know that courts are ineffective when over-burdened with claims. To check this rot, out-of-court settlements are encouraged. In the same way, it is sometimes better to waive one's rights and rely instead on a policy of live and let live. A secular state must have room for this. Third, a secular state is constitutively tied to the value of religious liberty that has three dimensions. The first refers to the liberty of members of any one religious group (**feature-c**). It is a brute fact that in most religious communities, one or two interpretations of its core beliefs and practices come to dominate. Given this dominance, it is important that every individual or sect within the group be given the right to criticize, revise or challenge these dominant interpretations. The second aspect of this important liberty in a secular state (**feature-d**), is that it is granted non-preferentially to all members of every religious community. It is entirely possible that non-preferential treatment by the state of groups that accord religious liberty to its members is also found in states respecting multiple establishments. But religious liberty is not part of the core principles of multiple establishments. States with multiple establishments may not always secure religious liberties to individual members of every religious group. However, such liberties are a constitutive feature of a secular state. The third dimension of religious liberty (**feature-e**), inconceivable in states with multiple establishments, is that individuals are free not only to criticize the religion into which they are born, but at the very extreme, to reject it and further, given ideal conditions of deliberation, to freely embrace another religion or to remain without one.

Religious liberty, when understood broadly, is an important value of a secular state. To understand another crucial ingredient, it is necessary to grasp the point that liberty and equality in the religious sphere are all of a piece with liberty and equality in other spheres. It is not a coincidence that the disestablishment clause in the first amendment to the American Constitution institutes not only religious freedom but also the more general freedom of speech, of peaceful assembly and political dissent. It is entirely possible that a state respecting multiple establishments permits *religious* liberty and equality but forbids other forms of freedom and equality. For instance, a person may challenge the authority of the religious head of his own denomination but not be free to challenge the authority of the state. This is impossible in a secular state which is committed to a more general freedom and equality. Thus, another critical value to which a secular state is constitutively linked is the equality of free citizenship.

The value of equal citizenship has two dimensions, one active, the other passive. To be a passive citizen is to be entitled to physical security, a minimum material well-being, and a sphere of one's own in which others ought not to interfere. This lies at the root of the idea of the right to life, liberty, material welfare and perhaps, education—crucial elements if ordinary people are to lead their ordinary life with dignity. Any citizen of the state must be entitled to these benefits. The benefits of citizenship—resources that enable a dignified ordinary life—must be available to everyone and there is no room here for discrimination on grounds of religion (**feature-f**). This equal treatment is entailed by equal (passive) citizenship. State agencies and the entire system of law must not work in favour of one religious group. If the state works to protect the security and well-being of some individuals or groups but fails to secure these meagre but important benefits to others then the principle of equal (passive) citizenship is violated. Likewise, since citizenship is conditional upon education, no one must be denied admission to educational institutions, solely on grounds of religion (**feature-g**).

The active dimension of citizenship involves the recognition of citizens as equal participants in the public domain (**feature-h**). Active participation does not only mean the mere possession of the right to vote but also a right to participate in public deliberation and to stand for public office. In secular states, such active citizenship rights are available to everyone, regardless of religion.

Box 18.1

Features of a Secular State

(*a*) The principle of non-establishment of religion
(*b*) Peace between communities
(*c*) Religious liberty to any one religious group
(*d*) Religious liberty granted non-preferentially to members of every religious group
(*e*) The liberty to embrace a religion other than the one into which a person is born and to reject all religions
(*f*) No discrimination by the state on grounds of religion to entitlements provided by the state
(*g*) No discrimination in admission to educational institutions on grounds of religion
(*h*) Equality of active citizenship: no discrimination on grounds of religion

These value-based secular states differ from one another in their respective understandings of the relationship with religion at the third level. Some are committed to disconnection but understand it differently. Others have a more sophisticated relation with religion and may connect or disconnect with religion depending entirely upon whether the values to which they are committed to are promoted or undermined by one or the other way of relating to religion.

Let us briefly discuss states, which, guided by values, disconnect from religion but possess different understandings of disconnection. One type of secular state conceives disconnection at the third level in a wholly one-sided manner. To disconnect is to exclude religion from its own affairs but to have no limits on its own interventionist powers in the affairs of religion. Such states exclude religion in order to control or regulate them and sometimes even to destroy them. They may justify exclusion by claiming that religion is false consciousness or obscurantist or superstitious or they may do so in the name of a single value such as equality. Such secular states are decidedly anti-religious. Examples may be some communist states or the secular state in Turkey and the French state in the 19th century. A second type of value-based secular state conceives this third-level disconnection as mutual exclusion. Such a state maintains a policy of strict or absolute separation. Here, religion is excluded from the affairs of the state but the state, too, is excluded from the affairs of the religion. The state has neither a positive relationship with religion, for example, there is no policy of granting aid to religious institutions nor a negative relationship with it; it is not within the scope of state activity to interfere in religious matters even when the values professed by the state are violated. This non-interference is justified on the grounds that religion is a private matter, and if something is amiss within the private domain, it can be mended only by those who have a right to do so within that sphere. This, according to proponents of this view, is what religious freedom means. Mutual exclusion is justified on the grounds of negative liberty and is identical with the privatization of religion.

When a state is disconnected with religions at all three levels in this particular way, then we may say that a wall of separation has been erected between the two. For the wall of separation conception of secularism, religion must be outside the purview of state and in this sense is privatized. American political secularism exemplifies this model. This is also the *mainstream* conception of secularism.

To summarize, we have distinguished three types of religion-centred states and at least three types of secular states, the amoral self-aggrandizing secular state, the anti-religious secular state and a state that erects a wall of separation between religion and itself (see Table 18.2). We have suggested above that political secularism is a normative doctrine for which the state should be separated from religious institutions to check religious tyranny, oppression or hierarchy and to promote religious and non-religious freedom and equalities. Given this, only one of the three secular states appear to run in accordance with the principle of political secularism. Some may even run contrary to these principles.

Table 18.2

Levels of connection (C) or disconnection (D)	*Amoral secular*	*Anti-religious secular*	*Mainstream value-based secular*	*Alternative value-based secular*
Ends: First order C/D	D	D	D	D
Institutions and personnel: Second order C/D	D	D	D	D
Law and public policy: Third order C/D	C or D	Opportunistic C or D	One-sided	D Principled C or D

Crisis for Secular States

Let us turn now to the more urgent practical issue faced not only by people in India but all over the globe. Secular states the world over appear to be in crisis. This crisis afflicts not only secular political institutions but the very doctrine of secularism itself. Both have been seriously questioned in Egypt, Sudan, Algeria, Tunisia, Nigeria, Senegal, and Turkey. In the last two decades, Pakistan and Bangladesh have increasingly acquired theocratic overtones. There has been a resurgence of Hindu nationalism. Buddhist Sinhalese nationalism in Sri Lanka, and Sikh nationalism in Punjab have both undermined the secular nature of Sri Lankan and Indian states. Religiously grounded political movements arose in Poland and protestant fundamentalism, too, have become a force in American politics. In Western

Europe as well, a challenge to the secular state appears to come from both migrant workers of former colonies and intensified globalization.

Secular states are questioned not only by politicians, civil society groups, and clerics but also by academics. In India, critics have argued that the conceptual and normative structure of secularism is itself terribly flawed. There is something wrong with the ideal itself. Some claim that it is linked to a flawed modernization, that it is integrally connected with the repressive structures of the nation state and an increasingly indefensible conception of science and rationality. Others have argued that in a deeply religious society, the demand that religion be excluded from public life and be privatized is utterly impractical. Still others claim that it is tied to liberal individualism which gives little importance to communities in the life of religious people and, therefore, cannot protect the community-specific rights of communities. These Indian critics have been joined more recently by Western scholars who have drawn attention to the capacity of the secular state to trivialize faith and be just to religious believers. Others have argued that it is tied too closely to Protestantism and is neither as impartial and as removed from religion nor as inclusive as it claims to be. Indeed, it is deeply inimical to non-Protestant religions. If so, deep down it is a conflict-generating ideology that threatens peace and by an unacknowledged propensity to homogenize all faiths it also inhibits diversity.

These are important criticisms that must be taken seriously. However, the academic writing on secularism is unclear about which of the two claims it is really making. When we criticize something, we may do so either to altogether replace it by something very different or to rectify the deficiencies that have crept in. It is not clear whether secular states are to be junked or repaired. Clerics and religion-centred politicians clearly wish to get rid of the secular state. But what do these academics want? Do they want an alternative to secular states or alternative conceptions of secularism? Let me assume that some of these academics want to replace secular states with something else. The question is, what will replace secular states and what ethical gains or losses might ensue as a result of this replacement?

It was with the objective of answering these questions that I had earlier distinguished different kinds of religious states and identified the multiplicity of secular states. My interest was not in classification per se but to fulfil our need to identify the most defensible version of secularism that meets the challenge posed by whatever is valid in the objections raised by the critics of secularism.

Theocracy, States with Established Religions and Secular States: A Normative Comparison

Let us then assume that all modern societies value some version of both freedom and equality. We shall ask a somewhat unsophisticated question: How do each of the states mentioned above fare on an index of freedom and equality? Let us take first states that establish a single religion. Historically, such states, for example, the state that supported the Anglican Church in England or the Catholic Church in Italy, fared poorly on an index of freedom and equality. Such states recognized a particular version of the religion enunciated by that Church as the official religion, compelled individuals to congregate for only one Church, punished them for failing to profess a particular set of religious beliefs, levied taxes in support of one particular Church, paid the salaries of its clergy, made instruction of the favoured interpretation of the religion mandatory in educational institutions or in the media. In such cases, not only was there inequality among religions (Christians and Jews) but also among the churches of the same religion, and while members of the established church may have enjoyed a modicum of religious liberty, those belonging to other Churches or religions did not enjoy any or the same degree of liberty. When members of the other church or religious groups possessed strength or number, then such a multi-religious or multiple-denominational society was invariably wrecked by inter-religious or inter-denominational wars. If they did not, then religious minorities were not tolerated and faced persistent religious persecution. (Jews in several European countries till the 19th century.) One exception to this, however, was the Millet system of the Ottoman Empire which had Islam as the established religion but three other religious communities—Greek Orthodox, Armenian Orthodox and Jewish—were treated as equals and given a respectable degree of autonomy.

States with substantive establishments have not changed colour with time. Wherever one religion is not only formally but substantively established, the persecution of minorities and internal dissenters continues today. One has only to cite the example of Saudi Arabia to prove this point. Here the distinction between formal and substantive establishment is important. In Saudi Arabia, Islam is both formally and substantively established. Britain has a formally established Church (the Anglican Church), but this important exception apart, it is a secular state that grants liberty and equality to all. It is important to dwell on this because in so many recent critiques of secularism, a more accommodative stance towards religion is recommended with an alarming neglect of some very elementary facts about what such an alliance might entail. Consider the situation in Pakistan where the virtual establishment of the dominant Sunni sect has proved to be disastrous to minorities, including those who are Muslims. For example, under Article 260 of the Pakistan Constitution, Ahmedis have been deemed as a non-Muslim minority and forbidden from using Islamic nomenclature in their religious and social lives. A whole community has thereby been formally excluded by the state, both symbolically and materially, from its own religion. Ahmedis have been tried and convicted under the law for calling themselves Muslims or using the word 'mosque' to designate their place of worship.

Pakistan has been taken only as an illustration. Surely the result would be the same if a Hindu state was established in India. This would be a threat not only to religious minorities, but also to the plural and tolerant character of Hinduism itself and therefore to a large number of practising Hindus. The 'democratic' state of Israel suffers from the same problem. Once it was declared a Jewish state it cannot but exclude from its scheme of rights and benefits its own Arab citizens, leave alone other Palestinians.

It is, therefore, difficult to swallow the claim that in modern democratic politics there is not much reason to fear a religious majority more than a secular majority. Given the unfortunate, sectarian character of most religions, the rule of religious majority is bound to be exclusionary. This is not necessarily true of the rule of secular majority. It is also misleading to give the argument that religious majorities are no worse than secular majorities because different religious communities have lived together in the past without coming into violent conflict. This claim is misleading because the term 'secular majority' can mean many things. This statement would be true if the secular majority in question consists of hard-nosed absolutists. It would be false if the term referred to all those people who wish not to use religion in all kinds of unprincipled ways. The statement misses the point because peace between communities is entirely compatible with all kinds of exclusion from the domains of freedom and equality. A fearful minority is willing to buy peace at any cost—something that all of us painfully learnt again after the Bombay riots in 1992–93. If what we have said above is true of states that establish a single religion, regardless of whether they are democratic or not, then it is likely to be even more true of substantive theocracies that are run by authoritarian religious clerics.

What about states with multiple establishments of religions? Historically, states of New York or the colonies of Massachusetts in the middle of the 17th century officially respected more than one religious denomination. These states levied a religious tax on everyone and yet gave individuals the choice to remit the tax money to their preferred Church. They financially aided schools run by religious institutions but on a non-discriminatory basis. They may have punished people for disavowing or disrespecting the established religion, but did not compel them to profess the beliefs of a particular denomination.

States with substantive establishment of multiple churches are better in some ways than states with singular establishment. For example, such states are likely to be relatively peaceful. Members of different denominations are likely to tolerate one another. There may be general equality among all members of a religion (though, historically this has not always been the case: women and Blacks have been the usual victims). The state grants each denomination considerable autonomy in its own affairs. But states with the establishment of multiple churches have their limitations. For a start, they may continue to persecute members of other religions and atheists. Second, they are indifferent to the liberty of individuals within each denomination or religious group. They do little to foster a more general climate of toleration that prevents the persecution of dissenters. Closed and oppressive communities can thrive in such contexts. Third, they may not have legal provisions that allow an individual to exit his religious community and embrace another religion or to remain unattached to any religion whatsoever. Fourth, such states give recognition to particular religious identities but fail to recognize what may be called non-particularized identities, that is, identities that simultaneously refer to several particular identities or transcend all of them. Fifth, such states are unconcerned with the *non-religious* liberties of individuals or groups. Finally, such states are entirely indifferent to citizenship rights. States, which establish multiple religions, face similar problems but are better than states with multiple church establishments in one important respect. There is peace and toleration and perhaps equality between all religious communities.

Does this mean that all secular states are better from an ethical point of view than religion-centred states? An affirmative answer here is too hasty. Amoral secular states have no commitment to any values. Therefore, it is likely that they would fare poorly on an index of freedom and inequality. Their record at the very best will be deeply uneven. Anti-religious secular states have a poor record in promoting or even protecting religious freedoms. Indeed, states that fail to protect religious freedom, usually trample upon other freedoms also. Over time, they also develop a hierarchy between the secular and the religious. Thus, such states are also likely to fare badly on the index of freedom and equality.

That leaves us with only one other type of secular state, one that erects a wall of separation between itself and religion to protect freedom and equality. Such a state, as must already be obvious, is likely to fare very well on an index of freedom and equality. For example, it grants the right to criticize, revise or challenge the dominant interpretations of the core beliefs of their religion. Second, it grants this right non-preferentially to every member of all religions. Finally, in such states individuals are free not only to criticize the religion into which they are born, but at the very extreme, to reject it and further, given ideal conditions of deliberation, to freely embrace another religion or even remain without one. Such states also grant equality of citizenship. All citizens are entitled to the same basic benefits. They have a right to vote as also a right to participate in public deliberation and to stand for public office. In this kind of secular state, such active citizenship rights are available to everyone, regardless of religion. Such a secular state embodies the values of classical liberal democracy and might be called the mainstream conception of political secularism.

When evaluating the relative merits of religious and secular states, it is these models which must be kept in mind for comparison and not the routinely debunked, severely anti-religious or self-aggrandizing secular states. Little is to be gained from damning secularism, as Talal Asad does, by citing the atrocities of Hitler and Stalin or crimes committed by 'secularists' such as Saddam Hussain or Ali Hyder. Nor is there any point in deriding secularists for failing to realize that Sharon did not need to invoke passages of the Torah to kill and terrorize the Palestinians. Secularism, a value-based doctrine, is as committed to denouncing these secular regimes as it is to berating religious states that violate principles of liberty and equality. The more important and serious question is whether this mainstream conception itself has serious problems.

Critique of Mainstream Secularism

Many criticisms that have been mentioned earlier draw our attention precisely to this point. Let us go through some of these criticisms again. First, mainstream liberal democratic secularism asks citizens to leave their religious convictions behind in the private sphere as a condition of entering the public sphere. This is what privatization of religion means. For example, suppose a bill is coming up for discussion in the Parliament and its supporters or opponents are debating on it in the wider public domain. Mainstream secularists would want everyone not to justify their support or opposition to the bill in terms of their religious beliefs. Religious beliefs are sectarian they would say. A religious rationale can be understood by people of the particular religion from which it is drawn but is likely to remain incomprehensible to all others. If so, how can a common agreement be reached on the precise justification for the bill? Is it not a worthy goal that all citizens speak in a language that is understood by everyone, that brings people together, rather than dividing them? The goal of citizen solidarity is indeed worthy, but it is doubtful that the burden of achieving it must be placed on every issue brought for discussion. Sometimes a bad outcome is generated if you demand too much of a good thing. If we continue to demand from religious persons that on every single issue they speak in a language that everyone understands, and if this means that they will have to disconnect from their religious conviction, then the eventual result might be counterproductive. It may bring about more division rather than solidarity. Moreover, to do so may result in the deprivation of the moral agency of persons. People may want to vote an issue on the basis of their conscience. They may wish to bring their politics in line with their morality. At least sometimes, this morality is inextricably linked to their religion. For some people this is always the case. To ask them to leave behind their religion is to force them to be disconnected from their morality and conscience. It is to ask them not to act as moral agents. But this is to disrespect them. Why grant respect to some people but not to others? Is it not a violation of the principle of equal respect? If this happens persistently, religious persons may form their own public sphere whether resentment and prejudice might flourish, where identities might get frozen. This will only create walls between citizens.

A second problem with mainstream secularism is that respect for a religion is not grounded in the believers', own point of view. It is the perspective of an outsider rather than the one that flows from the inside. Liberal secularists generally value autonomy but fail to understand that some persons choose or endorse a life of discipline, a life that is restricted, rule-bound and renunciatory. A religious life may be a life in which one simply submits to the command of God.

Third, as already pointed out, mainstream secularism is sectarian. It lives comfortably with protestantized and individualized religions but lacks the resources to deal with or accommodate community-oriented religions with a strong public presence. This insensitivity to groups make it indifferent to community-specific rights. As said above, political secularism is against religious domination and exclusion, but this domination can take two forms. In the first, a small section dominates members of its own religious community. This may be called intra-religious domination. In the second, which may be called inter-religious domination, members of one community dominate and exclude members of another different religious community. Since it is indifferent to communities more generally, mainstream secularism is blind to inter-religious dominations.

Fourth, liberal secularism is a product of and is shaped by a Protestant ethic. It is therefore bound with one particular religion. However, it pretends to be universalist. This amnesia about its own religion thwarts its development as a transcultural ideal. This happens because of the pretence that it is already transcultural.

Finally, mainstream secularism relies not just on reason to which no one should have an objection to but a particular conception of reason that puts a high premium on being totally disconnected with emotions, and which encourages a dichotomous, either/or manner of thinking. Besides, its alleged universalism makes it prone to being insensitive to contexts. Mainstream secularists do not ask the question, given this context, of what an appropriate relationship between religion and politics should be, but rather the more general question of what their relationship should be at all times and at all places. This also has a bearing on how they negotiate values. Generally, they think of one or two supreme values and arrange other values in some ranking order.

These are powerful and significant criticisms of the mainstream conceptions of secularism. But do they constitute good reasons for altogether discarding secularism? I do not think so. It is true that community-oriented public religions have their own moral integrity, yet frequently these very religions continue to be a source of severe oppression and exclusion. States that are too closely aligned with these religions turn a blind eye to or endorse these objectionable practices. Take the religiously sanctioned custom within religion that excludes women from the affairs of their own faith. In several temples in India, women are not permitted entry at the time of menstruation. At the Sabarimala temple in Kerala, women between the ages of 15–65 are not permitted to enter on the grounds that their very capacity to menstruate makes their bodies impure. This is a severe violation of their religious freedom and compromises the secular character of the Indian state. Or, consider the religiously sanctioned law of evidence, *Qanoon-e-Shahadat*, in Pakistan that holds on par the evidence of two women or two non-Muslims with that of a single male Muslim, thereby establishing the intrinsic superiority of Muslim men over women and minorities. Such inegalitarian laws are inevitable in states aligned formally to a particular religion.

What does all this show? It demonstrates, first, that we must be sensitive simultaneously to the moral integrity of liberal and non-liberal religious ways of living as well as to religion-based oppression and exclusions. Second, that states that are strongly aligned to religions may be sensitive to the moral integrity of non-liberal religions but not always to their oppressions. Third, that a policy of non-interference (mutual exclusion) typical of liberal secularism is self-defeating. In short, a conception of secularism needs to be worked out that goes beyond liberal notions and does justice to both these dimensions referred to above. It shows that if we are concerned about religious and non-religious freedoms and inequalities, then religion-centered states will remain inadequate for this task. However, it also shows that available models of secularism also fall short of meeting the very basic requirements or do they? Is there no conception of secularism that meets the most significant religious objections but on balance promote the basic values of freedom and equality? Does an alternative model of secularism exist?

I believe it does. Such a conception can be culled out from the Indian Constitution and the best constitutional practices of the Indian state. Indeed, this conception may be called the sub-continental conception of secularism, because it was worked out in the first half of the 20th century well before the partition of India. Every new state professed to be secular at the time of its formation and yet for reasons I cannot go into here, the experiment was brief and failed. Though it is deeply contested and crisis-ridden, it survives only in India. Because it survives and occasionally works well in post-Independence India—I shall call this alternative conception the Indian model of secularism.

An Alternative Conception: Indian Secularism

The distinctiveness of Indian secularism is not always recognized. Many scholars believe that it is simply a Western idea on Indian soil, that like the mainstream Western model, it erects a wall of separation for the sake of two values, religious liberty and equality of citizenship, construed individualistically. On a partial reading this would be true. The state in the Indian Constitution appears to possess all the features (features-a to h) of a secular state. Feature-a is implied by Article 27 that rules out the public funding of religion and Article 28(1) under which 'no religious instruction is to be provided in any educational institution wholly maintained out of state funds'.

Articles 25, 27 and 28 guarantee religious liberty and meet the conditions specified by features-b, c and d. Under Article 25(1), 'all persons are equally entitled to freedom of conscience and the right to freely profess, practise and propagate religion' (feature-c and d). The phrase 'freedom of conscience' is meant to cover the liberty of persons without a religion (feature-e). Under Article 27, 'no person is compelled to pay any taxes, the proceeds of which are specifically appropriated in payment of expenses for the promotion or maintenance of any particular religion or religious denomination.' Finally, under Article 28(3), 'no person attending any educational institution ... shall be required to take part in any religious instruction or to attend any religious worship that may be conducted in such institution'.

Equality of citizenship is guaranteed by Articles 14, 15(1) and 29(2) of the Indian Constitution. Article 15(1) states that the state shall not discriminate against any citizen on grounds only of religion, race, caste, sex, place of birth or any of them (feature-f). Article 29(2) declares that no citizen shall be denied admission into any educational institution maintained by the state on grounds only of religion, race, etc. (feature-g). Articles 16(1) and (2) of the Indian Constitution affirm an equal opportunity for all citizens in matters relating to employment or appointment to any office under the state. They further affirm that no citizen, on grounds of religion or race can be discriminated against in respect of any employment or office under the state. The clause on universal franchise as well as Article 325 declare a general electoral roll for all constituencies and states, that no one shall be ineligible for inclusion in this roll or claim to be included in it on grounds only of religion, etc. These embody the value of equal active citizenship. Thus, feature-h is specified in the articles on equality of active citizenship.

The implications of accepting that the state in the Indian Constitution is meant to possess features-a to g are not always spelt out. First, the Constitution rules out theocracy and the establishment of religion. Second, the Indian state is not meant to be merely tolerant (in the sense specified above). Indian secularism must not be confused with a generally professed religious tolerance. It is frequently claimed that Indians have a natural, traditional affinity with secularism. In view of our traditional obsession with subtle and not so subtle hierarchies, this claim must be taken with a pinch of salt. Of course, this should not detract from the important point that tolerance, even within a hierarchical framework, forms an important background condition for the development of modern secularism. All the elements discussed above can certainly be found within traditional India and helped in the formation of Indian secularism.

There are important ways, however, in which Indian secularism departs from the mainstream version. Six features make Indian secularism distinctive. First, its multi-value character. Indian secularism is tied not only to the individualistically construed values of religious and non-religious liberty and equality but also to peace, toleration and to non-individualistically construed values of liberty and equality. It has a place not only for rights of individuals to profess their religious beliefs but for the right of religious communities to establish and maintain educational institutions crucial for the survival and sustenance of their distinctive religious traditions (Article 26, Article 30[1]).

The acceptance of community-specific rights brings us to the second feature of Indian secularism. Because it was born in a deeply multi-religious society, it is concerned as much with inter-religious domination as it is with intra-religious domination. Unlike the mainstream conception that provided benefits to minorities only incidentally (Jews benefited in some European countries such as France not because their special needs and demands were taken care of, but rather because of a change in the general climate of the society). In India, however, even community-specific political rights (political reservations for religious minorities) were almost granted and were withheld in the last instance only for contextual reasons. In fact, it is arguable that a conceptual space is still available for them within the Indian Constitution.

Third, the Indian model is committed to the idea of principled distance, poles apart from one-sided exclusion, mutual exclusion and strict neutrality or equidistance. As seen above, for mainstream Western secularism, separation means mutual exclusion. The idea of principled distance unpacks the metaphor of separation differently. It accepts a disconnection between state and religion at the level of ends and institutions but does not make a fetish of it at the third level of policy and law. (This distinguishes it from all other models of secularism—moral and amoral—that disconnect state and religion at this third level.) How else can it be in a society where religion frames some of its deepest interests? Recall that political secularism is an ethic whose concerns relating to religion are similar to theories that oppose unjust restrictions on freedom, morally indefensible inequalities, inter-communal domination and exploitation. Yet, a secularism based on principled distance is not committed to the mainstream Enlightenment idea of religion. It accepts that humans have an interest in relating to something beyond themselves including God and that this manifests itself as individual belief and feeling as well as social practice in the public domain. It also accepts that religion is a cumulative tradition as well as a source of people's identities. But it insists that even if it turned out that God exists and that one religion is true and others false, then this does not give the 'true' doctrine or religion the right to force it down the throats of others who do not believe it. Nor does it give a ground for discrimination in the equal distribution of liberties and other valuable resources.

Similarly, a secularism based on principle distance accepts that religion may not have special public significance antecedently written into and defining the very character of the state or the nation but it does not follow from this that it has no public significance at all. Sometimes, in some of its other versions, the wall of separation thesis assumes precisely that. As long as religion is publicly significant, a democratic state simply has to take it into account. Indeed, institutions of religion may influence individuals as long as they do so through the same process, by access to the same resources as anyone and without undue advantage or unduly exploiting the fears and vulnerabilities that frequently accompany people in their experience of the religious.

Principled Distance

But what precisely is principled distance? The policy of principled distance entails a flexible approach on the question of inclusion/exclusion of religion and the engagement/disengagement of the state, which at the third level of law and policy depends on the context, nature or current state of relevant religions. This engagement must be governed by principles undergirding a secular state, i.e. principles that flow from a commitment to the values mentioned above. This means that religion may intervene in the affairs of the state if such intervention promotes freedom, equality or any other value integral to secularism. For example, citizens may support a coercive law of the state grounded purely in a religious rationale if this law is compatible with freedom or equality. Equally, the state may engage with religion or disengage from it, engage positively or negatively but it does so depending entirely on whether or not these values are promoted or undermined. A state that intervenes or refrains from interference on this basis keeps a principled distance from all religions. This is one constitutive idea of principled distance. This idea is different from strict neutrality, i.e. the state may help or hinder all religions to an equal degree and in the same manner, that if it intervenes in one religion, it must also do so in others. Rather, it rests upon a distinction explicitly drawn by the American philosopher, Ronald Dworkin between equal treatment and treating everyone as an equal. The principle of equal treatment, in the relevant political sense, requires that the state treat all its citizens equally in the relevant respect, for example, in the distribution of a resource or opportunity. On the other hand, the principle of treating people as equals entails that every person or group is treated with equal concern and respect. This second principle may sometimes require equal treatment, say equal distribution of resources but it may also occasionally dictate unequal treatment. Treating people or groups as equals is entirely consistent with differential treatment. This idea is the second ingredient in what I have called principled distance.

I said that principled distance allows for differential treatment. What kind of treatment do I have in mind? First, religious groups have sought exemptions from practices in which states intervene by promulgating a law to be applied neutrally to the rest of society. This demand for non-interference is made on the ground either that the law requires them to do things not permitted by their religion or prevents them from doing acts mandated by it. For example, Sikhs demand exemptions from mandatory helmet laws and from police dress codes to accommodate religiously required turbans. Elsewhere, Jews seek exemptions from air force regulations to accommodate their *yarmulkes*. Muslim women and girls demand that the state not interfere in their religiously required *chador*. Jews and Muslims seek exemption from Sunday-closing laws on the ground that this is not required by their religion. Principled distance allows then that a practice that is banned or regulated in one culture may be permitted in the minority culture because of the distinctive status and meaning it has for its members. For many republican or liberal theories this is a problem because of their simple, somewhat absolutist morality that gives overwhelming importance to one value, particularly to equal treatment or equal liberty. Religious groups may demand that the state refrain from interference in their practices but they may equally demand that the state interfere in such a way as to give them special assistance so that these groups are also able to secure what other groups are able to routinely get by virtue of their social dominance in the political community. It may grant authority to religious officials to perform legally binding marriages, to have their own rules or methods of obtaining a divorce, its rules about relations between ex-husband and ex-wife, its way of defining a will or its laws about post-mortem allocation of property, arbitration of civil disputes, and even its method of establishment of property rights. Principled distance allows the possibility of such policies on the grounds that it might be unfair to hold people accountable to an unfair law.

However, principled distance is not just a recipe for differential treatment in the form of special exemptions. It may even require state intervention in some religions more than in others, considering the historical and social condition of all relevant religions. For the promotion of a particular value constitutive of secularism, some religion, relative to other religions, may require more interference from the state. For example, suppose that the value to be advanced is social equality. This requires undermining, in part, caste hierarchies. If this is the aim of the state, then it may be required of the state that it interferes in caste-ridden Hinduism. However, if a diversity-driven religious liberty is the value to be advanced by the state, then it may have to intervene in Christianity and Islam too. If this is so, the state can neither strictly exclude considerations emanating from religion nor keep strict neutrality with respect to religion. It cannot antecedently decide that it will always refrain from interfering in religions or that it will interfere in each equally. Indeed, it may not relate to every religion in society in exactly the same way or intervene in each religion to the same degree or in the same manner. To want to do so would be plainly absurd. All it must ensure is that the relationship between the state and religions is guided by non-sectarian motives consistent with some values and principles.

Consider laws that interfere with Hinduism for evaluating these. The relevant consideration is not whether they immediately encompass all groups but whether or not they are just and consistent with values under-girding secularism. Three reasons exist for why all social groups need not be covered by these laws. First, they may be relevant only to Hindus.

Take the abolition of child marriage and *devadasi* dedication or the introduction of the right to divorce. Here, before deciding whether it was necessary to enact a special provision for Hindus, the legislature took into account their social customs and beliefs. Similar laws for Muslims were simply redundant. Second, laws in liberal democracies require legitimacy; the consent of at least the representatives of communities is vital. If consent has indeed been obtained from the representatives of only one community, it is sometimes prudent to enact community-specific laws. It is wise to apply the general principle in stages, rather than not have it at all. Finally, 'it is perfectly within the competence of the legislature to take account of the degree of evil which is prevalent under various circumstances and the legislature is not bound to legislate for all evils at the same time. Therefore, an act passed by the legislature cannot be attacked merely because it tackles only some of the evils in society and does not tackle other evols of the same or worse kind which may be prevalent' (AIR, 1952, Bom. 84, *The State of Bombay vs. Narasu Appa)*. Thus, if the legislature acting on these considerations, wanted to enact a special provision with regard to, say, bigamous marriages among Hindus, it cannot be said that the legislature was discriminating against Hindus only on the ground of religion (AIR, 1952, Bom.84, *The State of Bombay vs. Narasu Appa)*. The Indian courts have frequently followed this line of reasoning. They have defended a policy if they found that its purpose is the eradication of a social evil traceable to religious practices, even if the policy was targeted at specific communities. It has argued that so long as the state has taken gradual steps towards social welfare and reform and has not introduced distinctions or classifications that are unreasonable or oppressive, equality before law is not breached. A state interfering in one religion more than in others does not automatically depart from secularism. Indian secularism rejects the assumption that 'one size fits all'.

Box 18.2

Secularism in the Indian Constitution

Feature A—Article 27 and Article 28(1)
Features C, D and E—Articles 25, 27 and 28
Feature F—Article 15(1)
Feature G—Article 29(2)
Feature H—Articles 16(1) and (2), Article 325

Articles that support the individualist, wall of separation thesis
Articles 15, 16, 25, 29(2), 325, 27, 28(1) and 60

Articles that depart from the individualist, wall of separation thesis
Articles 30(1), 30(2), 17, 25(2), 25(2)(B)

Fourth, it is marked by a unique combination of active hostility to some aspects of religion (a ban on untouchability and a commitment to make religiously grounded personal laws more gender-just) with active respect for its other dimensions (religious groups are officially recognized, state-aid is available non-preferentially to educational institutions run by religious communities, no blanket exclusion of religion as mandated by Western liberalism).

This is a direct consequence of its commitment to multiple values and principled distance. The Indian model accepts the view that critique is consistent with respect, that one does not have to choose between hostility and respectful indifference. In this sense, it inherits the tradition of the great Indian religious reformers who tried to change their religions precisely because it meant so much to them. Fifth, it breaks out of the rigid interpretative grid that divides our social world into the modern Western and the traditional, indigenous non-Western. Indian secularism is modern but departs significantly from mainstream conceptions of Western secularism. Sixth, it is committed to a different model of moral reasoning that is highly contextual and opens up the possibility of different societies working out their own secularisms. In short, it opens out the possibility of multiple secularisms.

This point needs more elucidation. In moral and political theory, broadly two views exist on moral reasoning. One form of reasoning about moral issues is *acontextual*. It has a list of moral values that are arranged in a hierarchy so that one value is supreme and others subordinate to it. If there is a conflict, then the value considered supreme overrides every other value. A crude version of this is sometimes found in the construction of situations in Hindi films. Some of you might have seen the film *Shakti* in which a police officer, played by Dilip Kumar is faced with a value-conflict of impartially upholding the law of the land and being partial to his only son at the receiving end of the law. The police inspector has an unambiguous preference for the value of impartiality and no place whatsoever in his moral world for even the most elementary partiality towards his son. When the conflict arises, it is clear to him what is required of him. He upholds the law and arrests his own son. He does so not through a process of contextual reasoning but because of his prior commitment to a supreme moral value. He has no wish to understand the point of view of his son, the feelings of his wife or the reasons why the illegal act was committed. He is committed to an Absolutist morality and he applies it mechanically to everyone in every situation. As I said, this is a caricature of the kind of moral reasoning to which the mainstream conception of secularism is committed, but broadly it gets the picture right.

The alternative model of reasoning is more nuanced. It simply has to be, if every value is not to be ordered beforehand. Let me take an example. Suppose that there is an important meeting on human rights violations to be held outside India. It is important for the participant not only personally but because of its larger social significance. Suppose also that a day before the person's departure her father falls ill. Now, there is a value conflict. Both are important. For those who follow acontextual reasoning, one of these values must be supreme. If issues of social significance are more important than the participant must attend the meeting no matter what happens to her father. The contextualist—and I imagine most of us fall in this category—reasons differently. If the illness is life-threatening, then the participant should abandon the trip. If it is major but not necessarily a life-threatening one, the participant may ask another family member or a friend to take care of her father. She may herself curtail the visit from five to three days and so on. Alternatively, if her own presence at the meeting is not that vital and the job she is meant to do can be performed by someone else who is willing to be a last-minute replacement, then the participant may not decide to go even when the illness is not life-threatening. When we reason in this manner in the face of a clear instance of conflict between two or more values, we are sensitive to the concrete situation at hand, and if possible, we try to find a balance between both because, after all, it is not unreasonable to hope to fulfil both these value-based desires.

Contextual secularism is contextual not only because it captures the idea that the precise form and content of secularism will vary from one to another context and from place to place but also that it embodies this second model of contextual moral reasoning. This, it does because of its character as a multi-value doctrine. To accept that secularism is a multi-value doctrine is to acknowledge that its constitutive values do not always sit easily with one another. On the contrary, they are frequently in conflict. Some degree of internal discord and, therefore, a fair amount of instability is an integral part of contextual secularism. For this reason, it forever requires fresh interpretations, contextual judgements and attempts at reconciliation and compromise. No general *a priori* rule of resolving these conflicts exist; no easy lexical order, no pre-existing hierarchy among values or laws that enables us to decide that, no matter what the context, a particular value must override everything else. Almost everything then is a matter of situational thinking and contextual reasoning. Whether one value overrides or is reconciled with another cannot be decided beforehand. Each time the matter presents itself differently and will be differently resolved. If this is true, then the practice of secularism requires a different model of moral reasoning than the one that straightjackets our moral understanding in the form of well-delineated, explicitly stated rules. This contextual secularism recognizes that the conflict between individual rights and group rights or between claims of equality and liberty or between claims of liberty and the satisfaction of basic needs cannot always be adjudicated by a recourse to some general and abstract principle. Rather, they can only be settled case by case and may require a fine balancing of competing claims. The eventual outcome may not be wholly satisfactory to either but still be reasonably satisfactory to both. Multi-value doctrines such as secularism encourage accommodation—not the giving-up of one value for the sake of another but rather their reconciliation and possible harmonization, i.e. to make each work without changing the basic content of apparently incompatible concepts and values.

This endeavour to make concepts, viewpoints and values work simultaneously does not amount to a morally objectionable compromise. This is so because nothing of importance is being given up for the sake of a less significant thing, one without value or even with negative value. Rather, what is pursued is a mutually agreed middle way that combines elements from two or more equally valuable entities. The roots of such attempts at reconciliation and accommodation lie in a lack of dogmatism, in a willingness to experiment, to think at different levels and in separate spheres, and in a readiness to take decisions on a provisional basis. It captures a way of thinking characterized by the following dictum: 'why look at things in terms of this or that, why not try to have both this and that. In this way of thinking, it is recognized that though we may currently be unable to secure the best of both values and therefore be forced to settle for a watered-down version of each, we must continue to have an abiding commitment to search for a transcendence of this second best condition. Such contextual reasoning was not a typical of the deliberations of the Constituent Assembly in which great value was placed on arriving at decisions by consensus. Yet, the procedure of majority vote was not given up altogether. On issues that everyone judged to be less significant, a majoritarian procedure was adopted. It is frequently argued against Indian secularism that it is contradictory because it tries to bring together individual and community rights, and that articles in the Indian Constitution that have a bearing on the secular nature of the Indian state are deeply conflictual and at best ambiguous. This is to misrecognize a virtue as a vice. In my view, this attempt to bring together seemingly incompatible values is a great strength of Indian secularism. Indian secularism is an ethically sensitive negotiated settlement between diverse groups and divergent values. When it is not treated as such, it turns either into a dead formula or a façade for political manoeuvres.

Is Secularism a Christian and Western Doctrine?

What then of the claim that secularism is a Christian, Western doctrine and therefore, is unable to adapt itself easily to the cultural conditions of, say, India, infused as they are by religions that grew in the soil of the subcontinent. This necessary link between secularism and Christianity is exaggerated, if not entirely mistaken. It is true that the institutional separation of the Church and the state is an internal feature of Christianity and an integral part of Western secularisms. But as we have seen this Church–state disconnection is a necessary but not a sufficient condition for the development of secularism even in societies with Church-based religions. It is clearly not a necessary condition for the development of all forms of secularisms. Moreover, as I have argued, the mutual exclusion of religion and the state is not the defining feature of secularism. The idea of separation can be interpreted differently. Nor are religious integrity, peace and toleration (interpreted broadly to mean 'live and let live'), uniquely Christian values. Most non-Christian civilizations have given significant space to each. Therefore, none of them are exclusively Christian. It follows that, even though we find in Christian writings some of the clearest and most systematic articulation of this doctrine, even the Western conception of secularism is not exclusively Christian.

One might say, secularism is not just a Christian doctrine, but is it not Western? The answer to this question is both yes and no. Up to a point, it is certainly a Western idea. More specifically, as a clearly articulated doctrine, it has distinct Western origins. Although elements that constitute secularism assume different cultural forms and are found in several civilizations, one cannot deny that the idea of the secular first achieved self-consciousness and was properly theorized in the West. One might then say that the early and middle history of secularism is almost entirely dominated by Western societies. However, the same cannot be said of its later history. Nationalism and democracy arrived in the West after the settlement of religious conflicts, in societies that had been made religiously homogeneous, or had almost become so (with the exception of the Jews, of course, who continued to face persistent persecution). The absence of deep religious diversity and conflict meant that issues of citizenship could be addressed almost entirely disregarding the religious context; the important issue of community-specific rights to religious groups could be wholly ignored. This had a decisive bearing on the Western conception of secularism. However, for non-Western societies such as India, the case is different. Both national and democratic agendas in countries such as India had to face issues raised by deep religious difference and diversity. In India, nationalism had to choose between the religious and the secular. Similarly, the distribution of active citizenship rights could not be conceived or accomplished by ignoring religion. It could be done either by actively disregarding religion (as in all political rights) or by developing a complex attitude to it, as in the case of cultural rights, where it had to balance claims of individual autonomy with those of community obligations, and claims of the necessity of keeping religion 'private' with their inescapable, often valuable presence in the public. By doing so, Indian secularism never completely annulled particular religious identities.

In addressing these complex issues, the idea of the political secularism was taken further than had been evolved in the West. Mainstream theories or ideologies in modern, Western societies have taken little notice of these features. Hence, they are struggling to deal with post-colonial religious diversity of their societies. The later history of secularism is more non-Western than Western. And by implication, the history of secularism must include the history of other non-Western societies that have sought to install and maintain secular states. To discover its own rich and complex structure, Western secularism can either look backward, to its own past or else look sideways, at Indian secularism that mirrors not only the past of secularism, but in a way, also its future. Doing so will certainly benefit the secularisms of many Western societies. For example, French secularism needs to look beyond its own conceptions of *laicité* in order to take into account its own multi-cultural and multi-religious reality. It cannot continue to take refuge in claims of exceptionalism. A good hard look at Indian secularism could also change the self-understanding of other Western secularisms, including a very individualist, American liberal secularism.

Conclusion

To sum up, I have argued that secularism is opposed to institutionalized religious domination. Political secularism is a doctrine with a narrow scope. It asks whether the relation-ship between the state and religion be, if religious domination is to be, prevented and freedom and equality are to be promoted. According to political secularism, only a separation of state and religion can fulfil this purpose. Thus, political secularism defends a secular state and opposes all forms of religion-centred states, i.e. theocracies and state that establish religion(s). However, political secularism is equally opposed to amoral and anti-religious secular states. There is a tendency in the literature to equate political secularism with a unique version developed largely in the West, which I have called the mainstream conception. I have argued that this mainstream conception is ridden with problems. The crisis of secularism the world over is also due to the internal problems of this mainstream version. One should not be too pessimistic about political secularism, however. An alternative version was developed in the subcontinent and was eventually enshrined in the Constitution of India. This model I have claimed has several distinctive features and largely avoids the problems faced by the mainstream conception. It is not sectarian, not linked to one specific religion or culture and has transcultural potential. Because it exemplifies the idea of multiple secularisms, there is, I have claimed, much to be learnt from it.

Points for Discussion

1. How important are religious beliefs and practices for people? Do you think some of them come into conflict with our mundane everyday life?
2. Do you think some religious beliefs are morally objectionable, or that some religious organizations thwart freedom and inhibit democracy? If so, what action should be taken against them?
3. Why has secularism acquired a bad name in some societies?
4. Can you imagine a state which provides an ethically sound alternative to both religious-centered and secular states?
5. Does the practice of the state in India conform to the secular principles enshrined in our Constitution? Discuss some examples that violate these principles. Can you explain why this violation takes place?
6. Can you think of any example of state action which supports the idea of principled distance?
7. Do you feel that Indians developed a model of secularism that was not an imitation of the Western conceptions?
8. Is there anything wrong in borrowing from other cultures?
9. Let us assume that you accept the Indian model of secularism. Do you think it applies only to the state and not to civil society and the wider public sphere? Or does it have wider application?

Reading List

Bhargava, Rajeev (ed.), *Secularism and its Critics* (Delhi: Oxford University Press, 1998).

Bhargava, Rajeev, 'Political Secularism', in B. Honnig, J. Dryzek and A. Phillips (eds), *A Handbook of Political Theory* (Oxford: Oxford University Press, 2006).

Chandhoke, Neera, *Beyond Secularism: The Rights of Religious Minorities* (Delhi: Oxford University Press, 1999).

Connolly, William, *Why I Am Not a Secularist* (Minneapolis: University of Minnesota Press, 1999).

Dubey, Abhay Kumar (ed.), *Beech Behas Mein Secularwaad* (in Hindi) (New Delhi: Vani and CSDS, 2005).

Jacobsohn, Gary, *The Wheel of Law* (Princeton, NJ: Princeton University Press, 2003).

Madan, T. N., *Modern Myths, Locked Minds: Secularism and Fundamentalism in India* (Delhi: Oxford University Press, 1997).

Mahajan, Gurpreet, *Identities and Rights: Aspects of Liberal Democracy in India* (Delhi: Oxford University Press, 1998).

Pantham, Thomas, 'Understanding Indian Secularism: Learning from its Recent Critics', in Rajendra Vora and Suhas Palshikar (eds), *Indian Democracy* (New Delhi: Sage, 2004).

Srinivasan, T. N. (ed.), *The Future of Secularism* (New Delhi: Oxford University Press, 2007).

CHAPTER 20

Affirmative Action

Ashok Acharya

Chapter Outlines

Introduction

In our everyday lives we confront a range of situations that compel us to engage in notions of fairness. In responding to such situations we often complain 'this (or that) isn't fair.' Very often, our complaints regarding particular injustice(s) implicitly contain a conception of justice that we may or may not articulate. In some cases, we may also realize that our conceptions of justice may not match with that of our friends or neighbours. Disagreements about conceptions of fairness may easily arise where the focus or subject of justice is debatable and there is no one correct, legitimate response to be had. Certain issues are contentious and offer multiple perspectives, and every perspective competes for our attention. Should the private lives of politicians be subject to public scrutiny? Should the state subsidize poor farmers? Should the state provide for free primary education? Should the state grant employment opportunities to every single adult? Should colleges and universities set aside a certain quota of their seats for members of a certain group? Such situations are innumerable, but within the ambit of justice let us turn our attention to a matter related to distribution of resources that gets debated very hotly, not just in our society, but elsewhere, too. Consider the following example.

Tanya and Rekha apply for admission to a prestigious medical college. Both are required to write an entrance examination. In the entrance examination, Tanya performs better than Rekha and is placed above the latter. If we care to compare their social backgrounds we get to know that Tanya hails from an upper-caste, middle-income family, whereas Rekha is a Dalit from a more modest rural background. The college decides to factor in the comparative backgrounds of the candidates but has to decide that due to limited seats only one of them, not both, can be offered admission. On the one hand, the college knows that Tanya has fared better than Rekha in the entrance exam and on the other, it recognizes that Rekha's lower rank in the merit list can be explained by her relative social disadvantage. We must ensure equal opportunity to both. Given that we are committed to giving them fair opportunities to realize their dreams of pursuing a career in medicine, how do we go about being 'fair'? The case compels us to engage some of our moral intuitions with the help of which we can then determine how we go about being fair.

It is not easy to resolve the problem of choosing between Tanya and Rekha. Both cases engage us differently and evoke different responses. Consider Tanya's case first. For anyone who thinks that merit must prevail in the allocation of scarce goods, in this case a seat in a prestigious medical college, will naturally be tempted to argue that because Tanya's relative rank is higher than Rekha's, the seat must go to the former. One may go on to add that the system of education rests on the principle of merit which, if compromised, will lead to a state of injustice. Here, we need to say something on how precisely merit promotes justice and how we should go about defending it.

One way of doing so is to subscribe to the widespread belief that the highest positions in the society should go to the talented or the best qualified. Rewarding excellence is one way of being just to individuals who may be engaged in a free competition. In the long run, it could be argued, this promotes efficiency in the system. Many argue that when it comes to certain professions, they are best served only if these professions are run by the talented. For example, you would trust a doctor who you know is efficient and can provide you with the best treatment. You wouldn't risk being diagnosed by one who has questionable skills. If every profession—medicine, education, sports, art, or administration—similarly rewards the best qualified, society will be more efficient. The idea is that the educational or the health system acts much like a market, and that it need not be hindered or regulated by another agency, say the state. In terms of this argument, then, denying Tanya that seat would amount to injustice.

The same argument will hold that Rekha needs to perform better in order to claim what Tanya is legitimately entitled to. Rekha's circumstances can be explained as her bad luck, something that she may not have chosen but something that she has to bear with. However, things may not be as simple as that. Rekha's bad luck, on another account, may owe to a variety of factors which constrain her from being as good as Tanya. Rekha may not have had the same opportunities that Tanya, for instance, had. Some account of justice must compel us to address the unequal circumstances that these two aspirants for a medical seat may find themselves in. One way of addressing this inequality is to conceive of a plan whereby we correct Rekha's disadvantage by helping her secure the coveted medical seat. Central to this conception is the argument built on a strong moral intuition that a society cannot be just if it does not address issues of inequality and disadvantage.

Justice and Social Disadvantage

Most societies that advance the cause of social justice often have a sizeable presence of disadvantaged members. Some societies have endured a long record of injustices perpetrated against certain communities or groups. Since such groups have suffered significant social disadvantages, social justice requires that such disadvantages be taken account of in any meaningful redistributive strategy adopted by the state. The challenge is to rectify historical injustices towards certain groups. Before the state can get on with the task of choosing an appropriate distributive paradigm to offset social disadvantages, it will need to know more about the nature of disadvantages and how and why these must be used as inputs for the proposed distributive strategies. Addressing social disadvantages can be a tricky affair. Sometimes our moral intuitions can educate us of certain disadvantages that individuals may face, and at times we may need to learn from our history to get a fair sense of how particular groups have suffered injustice in the past. Social justice does invoke some universal principles but cannot ignore empirical realities and hence must adopt contextualized approach.

In our own society, caste, or *jati*—a defining feature of a social order, but one that permeates in some measure other religious groups as well—is a unique identity. The caste system thrives on a belief in hierarchy, fixed occupations, endogamous marriage norms, and prescribed codes of ritual and social distance to be maintained between the caste groups. Significant inequalities and inequities of power, wealth, and status are all reflected in the caste hierarchy of India. Although the nature of interaction and attitudes between and among castes is rapidly changing in recent times due to the impact of modernization, education, and industrialization, the traditional framework of *varna* hierarchy still holds good in broadly classifying and hierarchically organizing the thousands of castes that exist in our society. Those at the lowest rung of the caste hierarchy, the Dalits, have suffered centuries of injustice. The manifestations of this injustice exist in myriad forms of discrimination that some lower castes, especially the Dalits, have faced and continue to face in matters of allocation of scarce social goods. But discrimination is not the only symptom; the question of injustice relates as much to different forms of oppression, exploitation and domination that exist as brute social realities. Parallels of caste injustice can be drawn with racial injustice in other contexts. African-Americans in the United States, for example, have roughly undergone the same fate as the Dalits in India. An appropriate conception of social justice has to respond to these challenges.

Let us be clear about one thing, however. In seeking to redress the disadvantages that may accrue to particular groups owing to persistent patterns of injustice, the social justice approach is likely to capture a certain notion of *compensation*. The idea of compensation does not strictly try to offset only particular forms of injustice; it seeks, above all, to try securing an outcome that promises some necessary goods such as increased happiness, equality of resources, and so on. There is a need, of course, to ensure whether or not the historical patterns of injustice have contributed to present structural inequalities. A compensatory approach, moreover, does not much worry about whether or not to apportion blame to a particular group for having perpetrated injustice. On the other hand, it concedes that since the injustice is an undeniable social fact, some positive programmes need to be introduced to alleviate the ensuing disadvantages. We can have various such programmes. We could, for instance, introduce policies aimed at land reforms in contexts where ownership of land is monopolized by say, a dominant caste, or provide the basic necessities at a subsidized rate to the disadvantaged groups, or increase the chances of members of the disadvantaged groups to get jobs or admissions in sectors where they might be under-represented. These policies are intended to temporarily reapportion resources and opportunities in society.

Defining Affirmative Action

Affirmative action, or reservations as we understand in India, is an idea that is deeply contested. It addresses questions of justice about disadvantages that persons of certain groups face. Some argue that affirmative action as a policy is designed to remedy injustices that a few identifiable groups have suffered. Others argue that in correcting the injustices, the policy generates a different kind of injustice. Amongst both its supporters and critics, the idea evokes passionate reactions. A deep moral disagreement exists in society on this issue as is evident from our own experiences—both past and present—in addressing the practice of reservations.

Affirmative action usually entails a state's preferential policy towards particular groups. However, not all preferential policies can be justifiably adjudged as affirmative action. Although the rationale for affirmative action varies from place-to-place, it largely seeks to address structural inequalities between different groups in societies. In a positive sense, broadly speaking, it invokes ideas of fairness toward disadvantaged groups and of redressal for unjust inequalities by way of temporarily redistributing or reallocating scarce goods.

Preferential policy, though used as a substitute for affirmative action, is a broader term and may include either considerations of fairness, political accommodations of groups, or claims of distinct groups in particular territories. For instance, preferential policies may be designed to politically satisfy dominant ethnic majorities or minorities such as the ones for Sinhalese in Sri Lanka, Bumiputeras in Malaysia, Marathas in Maharashtra, Assamese in Assam, or whites in South Africa. The political justifications for this may vary across time and space. A powerful majority or a minority in each of these cases may use the political mandate, democratically or otherwise, to entrench the groups' relative position in the society, sometimes to the exclusion of others. Affirmative action is not concerned with these instances or the logic behind them.

In contrast to preferential policy, affirmative action may be defined as *a formal effort to provide increased employment and educational opportunities for underrepresented and disadvantaged groups at a level sufficient to overcome past patterns of discrimination and present structural inequalities*. As a policy it seeks to ensure inclusion of disadvantaged groups that were hitherto excluded from full participation in citizenship. Once this is achieved, its rationale ceases to exist. In aiming to ensure justice for historic deprivations and to secure inclusion into full citizenship rights, affirmative action may need to be both forward and backward-looking.

There can be different forms of affirmative action, though. There are both weaker and stronger versions. In its least controversial form, affirmative action refers to positive procedures that employers may use to ensure that their pool of candidates is represented in some larger body where the chances of recruiting a candidate from the deprived sections is enhanced. Such procedures may be designed to make certain that the possibility of bias or discrimination is significantly reduced. A stronger form than the present one may include strategies aimed at providing the necessary skills to target groups so that more members may succeed in job competitions. However, the strongest form of affirmative action is quotas or what we understand by the rubric of reservations. In the latter case, we set aside a certain percentage of jobs or seats in educational institutions to be filled in by members belonging to the underprivileged groups. Usually, the weaker forms of affirmative action do not generate political controversy, as do the stronger versions like quotas.

The starting point for any analysis for affirmative action is usually non-discrimination. The principle of non-discrimination holds that all persons are to be treated with equal consideration. Because differences between individuals based on religion, race, caste, sex, language, and ethnicity are morally arbitrary and irrelevant for purposes of public policy, the state should ensure non-discrimination while distributing goods and opportunities. Equipped with this kind of a logic that is blind to differences, the state seeks to protect each citizen equally. As is evident, the principle allows for individuals to be treated in a just manner without any reference to their identities. However, since a certain degree of discrimination has played its part in the denial of opportunities to certain segments of the society, the principle may allow for a more favourable treatment of some members as is evident in the weaker versions of affirmative action.

At another level, the idea of equal opportunity aims to create on the one hand, a *level playing field* by guarding against discrimination, and on the other, to create formal *access* to conditions favourable to realizing the full development of human potential. The second part of the reasoning incorporates imperatives to equalize conditions of existence that go beyond merely providing formal access to social goods and opportunities. This calls for enabling the disadvantaged to acquire relevant skills that increase their chances of success.

The classic statement that justified the policy of affirmative action by drawing on a robust version of equality of opportunity is that of Lyndon B. Johnson, the former President of the United States, who argued that the policy of formal, legal equality for blacks is not enough. He said: 'You do not take a person who, for years, has been hobbled by chains and liberate him, bring him up to the starting line of a race and then say "you are free to compete with all the others," and still justly believe that you have been completely fair. Thus, it is not enough just to open the gates of opportunity. All our citizens must have the ability to walk through those gates....' In making the worse-off walk through the gates of opportunity, we surely need a stronger formulation of the equal opportunity argument, one that recognizes their collective disability.

The group-disadvantage argument makes the case for the strongest version of affirmative action, viz., quotas or reservations. When we speak of disadvantaged groups, we are referring to the objective and experiential conditions of disadvantages that are fairly concentrated and cumulative in the group. Here, we are referring to groups that suffer from being very worse-off, in addition to having had to endure being at the lowest rung of the society for generations.

The Dalits in India, who roughly comprise 16.5 per cent of the population, are in a sense the worst-off group that has occupied the lowest rung in the social hierarchy for centuries. According to recent estimates, the literacy rate among the Dalits is woefully short of the national average—about 36 per cent compared to the general literacy rate of around 55 per cent. A vast majority of Dalits—approximately 80 per cent—lives in rural areas, and almost 50 per cent of them are landless agricultural labourers. Their present lot compounds historical factors of exclusion, centuries of sub-human existence, and a clear statement of lack of self-respect. Clearly, any redistributive strategy, including affirmative action, cannot in the Indian context wish away the reality of these complex, enduring, structural inequalities. Keeping in mind these normative considerations, the Constituent Assembly set about the task of devising a complex array of affirmative action policies for the Dalits to offset their concentrated and cumulative disadvantages.

If we follow the group-disadvantage reasoning, we may concede the requirement of quotas for the most disadvantaged but may shy away from extending identical benefits to the less-deserving cases of groups whose objective conditions may not require such strong remedies. Since we are discussing the idea of group disadvantage, we must open our line of inquiry further and ask whether the Other Backward Classes (OBCs) ought to be treated at par with the Scheduled Castes (SC), for instance? It is undeniable tha Dalits are a severely disadvantaged group but the same cannot be established for OBCs, or at least most of them. This raises the issue of whether a stronger version of affirmative action is equally applicable to both, or if different strategies appropriate for each should be implemented.

Affirmative Action in India

The colonial policy of ensuring representation rights to different communities is a crude precursor to affirmative action policies in post-Independence India. Two principles ground the colonial policy of equal representation in political offices and jobs that led to communal or representational quotas: (*a*) the policy of balance between competing communities, or interests; and (*b*) the policy to divide the nationalist front by creating differences. The constitutional scheme of preferences that came to fruition during 1947–50 was, on the contrary, based on the policy of social justice (Beteille 1991: 205–6). As a democracy in search of both formal and substantive equality, India had to address on an urgent basis the cause of the historically disadvantaged groups. Whereas the requirements of formal equality meant the equal protection of law against discrimination on morally invidious grounds, the requirements of substantive equality meant recognizing the needs of the more disadvantaged. Both these commitments—one to individuals stripped of their differences, and the other to groups—run parallel in the Constitution. At a broader level, they complement each other very much like the contents and provisions of the fundamental rights and the directive principles. Some rights have inscribed onto them reasonable limits and restrictions.

Articles 15(4) (added by the 1st Amendment to the Constitution), 16(4), 46, 330, and 332 form the crux of the affirmative action policies in India's Constitution. Art. 335, which since the Constitution came into effect has been a subject of controversy and differing interpretations of the judiciary, qualifies the affirmative action provisions by adding a rider that claims of SCs and STs for federal and provincial jobs are to be taken into consideration 'consistently with the maintenance of efficiency of administration'.

Broadly, three types of preferences are sanctioned by the Constitution. First are reservations—in the sense used here they denote a broader category than affirmative action—which cover (*a*) special representation rights of SCs and STs by way of reserved seats in legislatures, and (*b*) quotas in government jobs and educational institutions. The reservation device is also used to a lesser extent in 'the distribution of land allotments, housing, and other scarce resources (Galanter 1991: 43). Second, preferences target a few groups—SCs, STs, and women—with regard to the provision of certain expenditures, services, and ameliorative schemes such as scholarships, grants, loans, land allotments, health care, and legal aid. In the course of fulfilling its developmental goals and mandate, anti-poverty measures including rural development schemes, also target some of the usual beneficiaries of affirmative action. Third, certain preferences take the form of special protections that safeguard vulnerable groups from oppression and exploitation, like measures to prohibit forced labour, and others.

In explicitly stating such sweeping and enabling affirmative action provisions, the Constitution, thus, seeks to strike a balance between formal and substantive equality. From the above account it is partially clear, however, that the state's moral commitments are more towards SCs and STs than what it loosely defines as backward classes generally. It ought to be noted here that the founders of the Constitution did not give a comprehensive view of social backwardness and who merits inclusion in it. This was left to the future governments to define and identify for preferential policies. But otherwise in its dual commitments to both individuals and groups, the Constitution brings into sharp focus the tension between individuals and groups as proper objects of state policies including those of affirmative action.

During India's constitutional deliberations, equal citizenship for lower caste members meant assuming responsibility to initiate positive policy initiatives to offset historic disadvantages faced by them. Such initiatives underscored the need for affirmative action policies for SCs and STs. Since the early 1990s, by a revision to the initial list of group beneficiaries, affirmative action policies have been extended to include OBCs as well. As affirmative action in India is constitutionally mandated and exists by way of quotas, the extension involves numerical goals in filling educational seats, government, and public sector jobs from the listed group beneficiaries—SCs, STs, and OBCs.

The Indian experience is heavily weighted towards the recognition of backward identities needing affirmative action benefits. Since the writing of the Constitution, the motif of compensatory justice has provided the moral staple for understanding the theory and practice of affirmative action in India. However, notions of justice have evolved over a period of time in judicial parlance and normative discourse. From the 1960s till date, one notices a gradual evolution of affirmative action justifications—from non-discrimination to equal opportunity to some form of equal outcome approach. The equal outcome approach is the current metric of both proposing and evaluating the fairness of affirmative action policy.

The Limits of Affirmative Action

Affirmative action policies are rife with moral and political controversies. Those who oppose such policies do so for several reasons. At one extreme are those who are not attracted by the moral appeal of social justice. For them, affirmative action policies are one form of discrimination substituting another. Critics of this line of reasoning call these policies *reverse discrimination*, mandated by the state but clearly unjust as these do not differ in any morally relevant way from past discrimination against the same groups in whose favour the state now justifies them. It must be noted, however, that this criticism originates from a procedural conception of justice intent on protecting a narrow conception of equality between individuals without reference to their social moorings or any robust vision of a just society. The critics eschew any collective moral responsibility that social justice enjoins the larger society with.

Believers in a narrow conception of equality steer close to a market logic where merit makes up for a compelling case in determining who gets what. Such critics would dismiss Rekha's case as illegitimate and instead argue for Tanya's claim to admission. In the market argument, a bad hiring practice is inefficient in the long run and in a competitive market system, the market advocates would argue, policy makers should not address practices of discrimination. The efficiency of an enterprise will depend on its hiring practices. If employers discriminate and, as a result, hire less-qualified workers, their business will falter and those who hire the best will advance. Note that all forms of discrimination are treated at par in this argument, both those that employers may display and those that the state may mandate. However, there is one problem with this criticism. What if employers find discrimination profitable? Would discrimination be warranted then? The implications of this may be very disturbing, to say the least. There are problems, then, with how far the market can have a say in ordering principles for society.

But what about merit? This calls for some serious debate, as this is a recurring theme in discussions of affirmative action. Interpretation of this principle is not straightforward. What do we understand by merit? Who defines it? How much of weight should we give to it? These are questions that cannot be easily settled. The matter gets complicated when bias toward groups or their unfavourable stereotyping gets in the way of clear-headed thinking. Merit is generally considered to include such things as intellect, skill, and competence that one achieves unaided and through one's own effort. What counts as any of these—intellect, skill or competence—is generally judged by the society. And not all societies can agree on the fundamental parameters that create these values. Within societies too, we find that there are no neutral ways of deciding what constitutes merit. A certain sense of arbitrariness creeps into the act of description, and usually the prevailing cultural norms shape the meaning of merit. In the context of a caste society, if the usual achievers belong to the higher castes, they would have an authoritative say in how the principle actually is defined. In the absence of a culturally neutral definition of the principle, we run into problems of interpretation. However, there is more than this. Many organizations also find it difficult to give a scientifically coherent view of what comprises merit; whether skills and competence are completely to be attributed to the efforts of individuals, and how precisely to measure a person's efficiency or contribution. Short of this requirement then, we may suggest that the principle has some arbitrariness built into it, and as such may need to be used with care and circumspection in making arguments. That being said, however, we do not wish to jump into the obvious conclusion that merit counts for nothing. It does, but its cause is better served if we strive to produce its content more democratically and less arbitrarily.

Second, some criticisms of affirmative action do object to the social costs of such policies. These critics might believe in the legitimacy of a social justice approach but would argue that such strategies are wrong-headed, perpetuate and exacerbate existing social divisions, and the less-deserving or the better-off members of the target groups generally corners the benefits accruing from these. An oft-repeated criticism of the policies is that although these are 'temporary' measures, they tend to not only persist but also expand in scope. In other words, the politics of affirmative action overtakes its philosophy. Any political system that once introduces these positive programmes, finds itself saddled with it forever. This is because the political system produces electoral incentives for political parties to persist with, and at times expand in scope, the policy mandate. This creates a negative effect: the society undergoes an increase in group polarization with the consequence that the non-beneficiary groups produce adverse reactions ranging from violence to backlash in the political arena.

A cause for constant worry is that among the target groups, the benefits have generally gone disproportionately to the better-off members. The crux of the argument is that the designated disadvantaged groups—the SCs, the STs, and the OBCs—are not homogeneous entities. They are marked by heterogeneity in the sense that economically not all members of the groups—and there are obvious differences between groups as well—share similar status. There is some potency to the plea that the economically better-off members of the groups in question, called 'the creamy layer', ought to be excluded from the beneficiary class. This position is even conceded to by some defenders of affirmative action.

Some of the above criticisms highlight the harm that affirmative action inflicts on the society. Part of the problem in responding to these criticisms is not having access to the relevant facts. In our own society, for instance, we have not had a caste census since 1931 and there is no system in place that periodically and comprehensively monitors the effects of redistributive strategies, including those of affirmative action.

There is one criticism, however, that suggests how these policies inflict harm on the groups themselves by a process of stigmatization. This view argues how apparently benign policies that draw upon the benevolent consent of the higher castes can promote notions of caste inferiority among the beneficiaries. However, on the other hand, there are contrary reports to suggest that instead of demeaning, affirmative action has been responsible in empowering and mobilizing the Dalits far more effectively than before.

Clearly, the arguments against affirmative action are many and some of them do confirm that arguments aside, the fact of social costs cannot be wished away. Even defenders admit that the social and political costs of affirmative action are at times too heavy to ignore. But with all its costs and imperfections, it will be imprudent to abandon the imperative of distributive justice. Jettisoning affirmative action is equivalent to turning a blind eye to the cause of social justice, which requires us to politically commit ourselves to take responsibility for past injustices. Affirmative action is, indeed, justified but only in morally compelling cases.

Points for Discussion

1. The idea that disadvantaged groups require some form of compensatory justice is a backward-looking argument. Discuss with examples.
2. What characteristics must a group have to be considered as disadvantaged?
3. Can affirmative action be defended on grounds that it will promote a more just society in the future?
4. 'One of the biggest costs of affirmative action is that the policy causes political divisions in a society'. Would you agree? Support your argument with examples.
5. How would you mediate in a conflict between defenders and opponents of affirmative action? With what arguments?

Reading List

Beteille, Andre, *Society and Politics in India: Essays in Comparative Perspective* (London: The Athlone Press, 1991).

Cohen, Marshall, Thomas Nagel and Thomas Scanlon (eds), *Equality and Preferential Treatment*. (Princeton: Princeton University Press, 1977).

Galanter, Marc, *Competing Equalities: Law and the Backward Classes in India* (Delhi: Oxford University Press, 1991).

Kumar, Dharma, 'The Affirmative action Debate in India,' *Asian Survey*, XXXII(3), 1992: 290–302.

Mandal Report, *Reservations for Backward Clases: Mandal Commission Report of the Backward Classes Commission* (Delhi: Akalank Publications, 1980 [1991]).

Rosenfeld, Michel, *Affirmative Action and Justice* (New Haven: Yale University Press, 1991).

Shah, Ghanashyam, 'Social Backwardness and Politics of Reservations,' *Economic and Political Weekly*. XXVI(11–12), 1991: 601–610.

Young, Iris Marion, *Justice and the Politics of Difference*. (Princeton: Princeton University Press, 1990).

CHAPTER 21

Freedom of Speech and the Question of Censorship

Aarti Sethi

Chapter Outlines

Introduction

This chapter examines the question of the freedom of speech and expression, juxtaposed against the question of restrictions on expression, or censorship. The chapter begins with a broad overview of the main theoretical arguments that have been made in support of freedom of expression. It then goes onto to examine the relationship between speech and harm, and the case for censorship.

Free speech is a bit of a puzzle in contemporary society. While on the one hand, almost everyone seems to agree that freedom of speech and expression are important and they enjoy unprecedented legal protection which does not extend to any other class of acts in society, at the same time there is no real agreement amongst philosophers, lawyers, legislators, and citizens as to why it is important, and how much freedom is too much freedom. Further, most liberal democracies must also deal with the consequences of incendiary and hateful speech which compromises the dignity and safety of citizens. Therefore, while the legitimacy of liberal democracies crucially hinges on the degree of freedom of expression allowed to citizens, the media and so on, there are also claims of justice that must be met which demand that citizens be protected from certain kinds of speech.

Some states, while continuing to uphold the freedom of expression, however also legislate what is fit for citizens to watch, hear, see and read. In India for instance, the Central Board of Film Certification, requires that all films must receive a censor certificate and this has often lead to films being censored which are deemed to be obscene, or liable to 'hurt the sentiments' of particular communities. Often, censorship is also seen to operate as an expression of power and the refusal to allow the circulation of certain expressions that question dominant power structures.

In this chapter, we will look at the knotty question of free speech and censorship. We will attempt to understand why and how people have defended the right to freedom of speech and expression, and think through situations that might require this right to be curtailed.

But first we will try and understand the grounds upon which a case may be made to protect freedom of expression, namely, what in the right to freedom of speech/expression singles it as worthy of the special treatment it enjoys in most liberal democracies.

In the first section of this essay we will look at some of the arguments that have been made in order to construct a 'free speech principle'. A free speech principle would need to be different from a general liberty principle in that it would have to demonstrate that speech, or that class of expressions, which we deem to be speech (such as writing, music, film, journalism and so on), constitutes a separate category which deserves greater, different, or special protection. Such a principle would have to identify qualities possessed by speech which justify this treatment.

A robust conception would also have to take into account protected speech, i.e. speech which cannot be restricted under clauses like the First Amendment in the United States Constitution or under Article 19(2) in the Indian Constitution, and protect not just 'good' speech, but also speech which is untrue, false, trite, and sometimes downright dangerous (such as racist speech or speech directed at sexual minorities or religious communities.).

And finally, a free speech principle would not need to assert that no restrictions on speech are admissible under any circumstances. But that stronger justification should be provided if the consequences of an action require the restriction of speech, than if this were not the case.

One mode of arguing in favour of free speech would be to link it with the achievement of other values we hold dear such as individual liberty, democracy, tolerance and so on. The problem with this argument is that if it could be established that the achievement of these other values would be served better through the restriction, rather than promotion of speech, speech becomes difficult to defend. Another set of arguments, therefore, ask for speech to be valued not because it has favourable consequences in the achievement of other values, but that it be valued for qualities intrinsic to itself. Such an argument would make the claim that free speech is a desirable value/good in itself, which does not need to be justified by invoking principles external to it.

Speech and the 'Lesser Harm' Hypothesis

Let us begin from the least influential philosophically, but one that nonetheless enjoys some currency in popular understanding of the power of speech, succinctly summed up in the adage, 'sticks and stones can break my bones, but words can never harm me', or what Fredrick Schauer calls the 'lesser harm principle'. The argument states that speech should be free and unregulated not because there are especial benefits to be had from its circulation; rather, speech, unlike actions, does not have the power to do any real damage to its recipients.

However, neither law nor philosophy can afford to, and indeed do not, ignore the very real consequences that accrue from speech and expression. This is especially true of misogynist or racist speech. Words are important and powerful and no clear boundaries can be drawn between speech and when speech takes the form of action. We will return to the question of just how powerful words are at several points in this discussion, but for now it leads us to another, this time extremely influential and cogent, defence, made by J. S. Mill in *On Liberty*.

Freedom of Expression and the Search for Truth

J. S. Mill in his essay, *On Liberty* remarks:

> If all mankind minus one, were of one opinion, and only one person were of the contrary opinion, mankind would be no more justified in silencing that one person, than he, if he had the power, would be justified in silencing mankind.... If the opinion is right, they are deprived of the opportunity of exchanging error for truth: if wrong, they lose, what is almost as great a benefit, the clearer perception and livelier impression of truth, produced by its collision with error.

In this lively and immensely readable essay, J. S. Mill made what remains as one of the most persuasive defences of the liberty of discussion, that without free expression society as a whole would remain bereft of the truth. It is only through the free exchange of ideas and opinions between dissenting individuals that the truth or falsity of an opinion can be ascertained. Mill's position may be read as assuming that 'truth' is a stable coherent concept which can be discovered, he, however, had interesting things to say about truth and his own position on truth is a lot more complicated, as we shall see, than it appears on first reading.

Mill makes his argument in two parts, which relate to the 'truth' of an utterance. The first relates to whether an utterance is true. If it were, to deny it a hearing would mean that the truth would be lost forever. And if an utterance were false, the truth would no longer remain a 'living truth' but become a moribund 'dead dogma' because it would not require constant justification, through arguments in its defence.

However, Mill also makes the observation that to adjudicate upon the truth-value of a statement is itself a fraught exercise because the adjudicators 'have no authority to decide the question for all mankind, and exclude every other person from the means of judging. To refuse a hearing to an opinion, because they are sure that it is false, is to assume that their certainty is the same thing as absolute certainty, and clearly no one can presume to have absolute certainty. It is only through free and open discussion and the constant tussle between individuals holding divergent opinions, ideas, and beliefs that the truth can be arrived at. And finally, Mill notes that 'The peculiarity of the evidence of mathematical truths is, that all the argument is on one side. There are no objections, and no answers to objections. But on every subject on which difference of opinion is possible, the truth depends on a balance to be struck between two sets of conflicting reasons.'

There are no certainties in social life, according to Mill, and matters can thus be resolved only when every opinion has an equal chance of being heard. There is a second related argument that Mill makes, which is closely related to the search for truth argument that privileges diversity:

> ... only through diversity of opinion is there, in the existing state of human intellect, a chance of fair play to all sides of the truth. When there are persons to be found, who form an exception to the apparent unanimity of the world on any subject, even if the world is in the right, it is always probable that dissentients have something worth hearing to say for themselves, and that truth would lose something by their silence.

The most obvious problem with Mill's argument is that often truth may not be the only, or indeed even the primary, desirable outcome in a given situation. Other considerations, such as justice, or maintaining peace, or individual privacy might far outweigh the value placed on what is 'true'. States are often loath to reveal 'sensitive information' relating to military matters, and courts often rule against the exposure of the private lives of celebrities. Therefore, often precisely because something is true, requires that it not be made public.

Mill also seems to assume that all individuals share an equal capacity to speak freely and that they will understand each other in the same language. By language here is meant not really English or Hindi or French, but a shared set of understandings of the values, codes, and norms through which people make sense of the world and their place in it. Often, the bitterest contests in society are between individuals and groups whose perception of the world do not share the same rules, and therefore cannot make sense to each other. The conflict between customary law (norms developed by communities over time, often unwritten, based on patterns of usage, such as rights to inheritance, pasture-lands, water and so on) and constitutional law is one such instance. The latter and its understanding of private property, often come into conflict on the question of community rights over the usage of natural resources such as land, forests, and water. Communities are often faced with situations in which they are unable to translate a claim on resources, into a language that can be acknowledged as such in the courtroom. Constitutional law and community understanding are based on differing views of the world and sometimes there is no easy way to translate between worlds. Indeed, 'life', 'property', 'freedom', might mean different and incommensurable things, and one 'truth' which everyone might agree on might be difficult, even impossible to find, even through discussion.

Freedom of Speech and its Relation to Self-Government

Another argument, which relates to the 'social' dimensions of free speech, that is, which views free speech as deserving of protection because through it important social objectives are met, is made by Alexander Meiklejohn. According to him, freedom of speech and expression are important because they are crucial for the functioning of a democratic system of government. Besides, popular discourse and literature in which the press is hailed as the 'fourth estate', invoke this argument, where the vibrancy of a democracy is seen as relating crucially to the freedom of the press.

The interesting fact in Meiklejohn's argument is that he focuses not so much on the speaker's right to speak, but the listener's right to hear. The basis of a democratic government is citizens' consent. It is only through the free exchange of ideas and a free press that citizens will be exposed to the ideas, opinions and views which they require in order to participate effectively in democratic decision making, and hold government responsible for its actions. Only when citizens are able to hear all sides of an argument can they effectively make up their mind, and this is only possible when 'public speech' enjoys untrammelled protection.

The problem, of course, arises in the event that the goal of democracy is in restricting rather than promoting free speech. For instance, the government in power might refuse to allow political campaigning during elections on the grounds that the opposition is spreading false information. Also, what would happen to speech which served no democratic purposes at all but was merely fun, enjoyable, and pleasurable? Further, Eric Barendt asks, would incessant advertising campaigns qualify for protection? Could it not be argued that they hinder rather than promote democracy? The huge advertising budgets of Coke and Pepsi mask the public from the ongoing conflict between these companies and the rights of local communities over water resources (such as the ongoing struggle in Plachimada in Kerala).

The question of the relationship between different classes of people in society and the function of speech brings us to the next argument, which links freedom of speech and expression to the capacities for tolerance within society.

Free Speech and Tolerance

In *The Tolerant Society* (1986), Lee Bollinger attempts to arrive at a free speech principle which begins not with trying to establish the benefits that flow from it per say, but the relationship between its reception and other values; in this case what he terms tolerance, in society. His treatment of the issue thinks through 'free speech in relation to our dealings with social behaviour in general.' On this view a defence of free speech may be constructed by invoking its function in inculcating an ethic of tolerant listening.

Bollinger recognizes that speech can be harmful. However, this recognition does not lead him to demand that speech be regulated; rather that recognition of the very real harms that speech can affect and to nonetheless, 'let the injury pass' countermands the widespread societal impulse of excessive punishment. Free speech allows us to develop the 'virtue of magnanimity'.

There is a further social benefit to be had from the free circulation of diverse, and often contentious views. In the societies in which we live, everyday life is necessarily an encounter with enormous diversity. People hold different views, opinions, beliefs, and practise different ways of living, not all of which can comfortably accommodate each other. For Bollinger, free speech performs the function of a 'zone of tolerance' in which individuals are forced to confront and tolerate views not in keeping with their own.

Tolerating free speech makes us more receptive to the idea that things do not always go our way, and no one has the right to impose their way of living on anyone else. We may not agree with someone's life choices, indeed we might have very strong objections to them, but we do not have the right to impose our ideas of what is right on them. For Bollinger, tolerating speech performs the important task of teaching us this.

It is not hard to see why there have been several criticisms of Bollinger's thesis. David Richards notes that given that tolerance is the 'central normative term' in Bollinger's argument, it is necessary for him to provide, at the outset, a critical theory of tolerance. In its absence the contention that the toleration of speech creates the conditions for a general increase of tolerance levels in society, leaves several questions unanswered. Why, for instance, does the toleration of speech have this special attribute, why not the toleration of actions? Tolerating the right of all adults to choose their sexual orientation and partners (currently criminalized as 'sexual acts against the order of nature' under Section 377 of the Indian Penal Code) might go a long way in promoting a more inclusive society in India. Furthermore, why value tolerance at all? Surely, it can be argued, there are some things, which no democratic society should tolerate such as racist, misogynist or casteist speech? And finally, could it not be argued that excessive speech can sometimes lead to less rather than more tolerance? For instance, the February 2002 genocide in Gujarat was preceded by widespread propaganda on the part of politicians and leaders from which could be argued, helped in no small way to create conditions wherein a massacre could have occured.

Clearly then, it seems from the above, that it is difficult to construct a robust free speech principle by invoking the positive consequences of free speech and the negative effects of restrictions, because this leaves free speech vulnerable when it can be argued that there are benefits to be had from restrictions.

The autonomy defence of free speech seeks to rescue it from the tenuous terrain where consequentialist defences, i.e. defences which argue from the positive outcomes or consequences of free speech, often leave it stranded, by grounding a defence of free speech in the idea of individual autonomy. A convincing autonomy argument would be able to 'free' free speech from the burden of demonstrating desirable results. If successful, it would also be able to protect free speech as a value in itself, restrictions on which would require stronger justifications than if it were merely a condition for the attainment of other values.

The Autonomy Defence of Free Speech

The autonomy defence of free speech asserts that freedom of speech must enjoy state protection because restrictions on the same would violate the autonomy of individuals. While 'autonomy' is a difficult conception to pin down, and different formulations will deploy it differently, a sufficient conception for our purposes here is one that underpins liberal philosophy in general. An autonomous person is one who is a self-governing, rational individual, who takes responsibility for the beliefs he/she holds.

In 'A Theory of Freedom of Expression' (1972), Thomas Scanlon employs this notion of autonomy, which he terms the 'Millian principle'. For Scanlon, freedom of speech and expression are important because restrictions on them seriously compromise individual autonomy. To be autonomous a person must be able to view oneself as sovereign in deciding what to believe and what not to believe. He/she must be able to weigh competing opinions and courses of action and come to independent decisions based on his/her own judgement and discretion. An autonomous person, therefore, will not accept another's pronouncements on the merit of an issue, without exercising his/her own independent judgement on the issue in hand. This extends even to views and opinions which are aimed at persuading the person to believe in something which is untrue and dangerous.

The powers of the state thus must be restricted to those that citizens will be willing to accept, while still regarding themselves as equal, autonomous and rational. Restrictions on speech do not meet this requirement because they undercut the capacity of people to decide matters for themselves.

Scanlon's Millian principle states that though there are certain harms which would not occur but for certain acts of expression, these harms cannot justify legal restrictions on these acts of expression. These include harms to individuals because they come to hold untrue beliefs as a result of expression (such as people believing the world is flat because a book says so), and the negative consequences of acts which are performed by people because certain acts of expression lead them to believe these acts were worth committing (such as someone robbing a bank because they heard someone saying that robbers would go to heaven).

An autonomous individual cannot allow the state to withhold certain views because it is the individual's prerogative to decide whether these views are to be believed or not. And, while the state might outlaw certain kinds of actions as harmful and prosecute people who commit them (such as murder), it cannot restrict their advocacy (such as encouragement to kill) because the decision on whether the law ought to be followed or not, again devolves onto individuals.

Thomas Nagel (1995) invokes an idea of autonomy similar to Scanlon's in his defence of free speech. He notes that recognition of individual sovereignty over reason and beliefs requires that a person must be permitted to discuss his/her views and elicit reactions. Further, it also requires that he/she should not be 'protected against exposure to views that might influence him in ways others deem pernicious, but that have the responsibility to make up his own mind about whether to accept or reject them'.

Susan J. Brison (1998) points out that Scanlon's claim that an autonomous individual will refuse to allow another to decide on her behalf because she will take responsibility for her beliefs, may be countered by the reasoning that false information, by making people believe that a group is inferior or unworthy, might compromise autonomous decision-making capacities. Second, she argues that not all speech is processed rationally. Indeed, the socialization of young men and women into occupying differential power roles in society is the result of processes which are not rationally mediated. And finally, Scanlon's argument that autonomous rational agents would not be willing to grant government the power to legislate speech may be countered with the claim that rational agents might, indeed, ask for such regulation precisely through a rational evaluation of the harms that certain speech acts can affect. We might decide that the consequences of certain speech are so harmful that we do not wish their circulation in our society. The recent government ban on cigarette advertisements on television could be viewed in this light.

What do we do with Hate Speech?

The question of speech becomes even more problematic when we enter the realm of what has been termed 'hate speech', that is, speech directed at certain people or communities with the intent to cause harm by asserting their natural inferiority (such as racist speech), or speech that by its nature asserts the domination of one group of people over another (such as pornography, or misogynist speech). This would also include speech, which while ascribing certain negative traits or characteristics to groups and individuals also asks others to take actions meant to cause harm to this group.

In terms of demands for the legal regulation of hate speech, the initiative came from America and Europe in the context of racist speech. In India, concerns have centred on inflammatory speech directed at religious minorities, and this question has acquired greater urgency after the Gujarat genocide in 2002 in which there was widespread propaganda against the Muslim community.

Hate speech requires us to address a number of critical questions that have to do with the relationship between language and harm. The first assumption in hate speech regulation is, of course, that speech can cause harm. Further, this harm is akin to, or must be treated as being at par with, physical harm or injury.

The link between the capacity of words to hurt, which are of an almost physical nature, pervades much of the literature on hate speech. For instance, in *Words that Wound* (1993), Richard Delgado argues that racist speech leaves deep psychological wounds on its victims. By perpetuating social stereotypes of inferiority, racist speech leads to feelings of self-hatred, humiliation and isolation in its victims. By linking achievement and merit with skin colour, it also leads to the internalization of feelings of inferiority in those it addresses. Delgado points to several arenas in which racist speech causes minority groups to suffer, such as children's scholastic achievements, parenting skills on the part of single mothers, and problem in the workplace. For Delgado, racist speech is inflected with the desire to cause harm. He goes further and notes that Black Americans are more prone to high blood pressure, hypertension and stroke as compared to their white counterparts, and this probably has to do with the physiological manifestations of stress caused by racial abuse.

People are more likely to cause harm to those they believe are inferior and less powerful than themselves and racist speech also creates the conditions in which certain groups are more vulnerable to violence than others. The legal regulation of racist speech, for Delgado and others who demand it, is recognition of the capacity for words to wound, and an assurance to its victims that attacks on the equal worth of all members will not be tolerated in a free and democratic society. For Delgado, while speech causes identifiable harm, speech and the harmful actions it leads to are nonetheless different order of things. Another way of thinking about the relationship between speech and harm is to complicate the relationship between 'speech' and 'action' which have traditionally been seen as separate. Noted philosopher J. L. Austin (1975) complicates this distinction by introducing the idea of the 'speech act', i.e. an action that is enacted through speech.

Austin refers to two kinds of speech acts: illocutionary and perlocutionary. An illocutionary speech act is one that both describes and does—that is utterance is equal to the performance of the act. When the judge in a courtroom hands down a verdict saying, 'I pronounce you guilty,' or a minister officiates at a wedding ceremony with the words, 'I now pronounce you man and wife,' they are performing illocutionary speech acts where there is no time lag between saying and doing. As he says the words, he does the action.

A perlocutionary speech act, on the other hand, is one where there is a temporal lag between the utterance and the consequences of the action it encapsulates. For instance, when I ask you, 'Can you bring me the book on the table?' I am asking you to perform a certain action (which is an action in itself), the results of which will be demonstrated after the utterance.

Rae Langton (1993), the feminist theorist, invokes the Austinian schema in her discussion and defence of Catherine Mackinnon's argument calling for laws against trafficking in pornography. Langton argues that pornography does not simply advocate the subordination of women (the consequences of which are felt later), but it is the subordination of women and must therefore be viewed, for purposes of regulation, as violent action, not merely as violent speech. While not explicitly invoking Austin, Andrea Dworkin and McKinnon, too, identify the capacity of words to effect actions in themselves. Therefore, for Dworkin, pornography is the theory of subordination, which translates into the practice of rape. The problem with this position, Judith Butler (1997) argues, is in assuming the stability of language where a statement always does what it says; it bestows on individuals a sovereignty, which in actuality only belongs to the state. It is only the state, which has, through the language of law, an illocutionary power to always make language mean precisely what it says.

Let us return to our example of the illocutionary speech act to understand this better. Let us assume you and I disagree over something I say. You say I am guilty of misconduct and I say you misunderstood the import of what I was saying. Things come to a head, we both threaten each other with dire consequences and since we cannot resolve this dispute amongst ourselves, we approach the court. The court considers the evidence, and decides that there was no misunderstanding; that my words did indeed have the effect you claim they did, and prescribes suitable punishment. The judgement by the court does not only redress a harm done unto me, but it also 'fixes', in perpetuity, the import of what I said. The court decides once and for all, not just what I said, but what my speech meant. And because it is backed by the coercive power of the state, the court is the only institution in society which has the sovereign authority to decide the consequences of language.

Hate speech is a purely legal category. It is the law that defines certain kinds of speech as hate speech. The category of hate speech thus cannot exist without the state deeming it to be so, and it produces, through legislation, speech that does what it says: victimization, degradation, and subordination. When this category of hate speech is applied to the things people say to each other, the law produces subjects who have the illocutionary linguistic power of the state. The state then re-enters this arena as the neutral arbiter of speech between citizens, without recognition of the power of the state in prefiguring the arena of speech acts in society.

Butler's work provides us with a way to reflect on speech and the ethical questions that surround speech acts, which moves outside the juridical framework presumed in liberal theory, where the state is the sole arbiter of what is publicly speakable or otherwise, and so defines in this way the effects of language itself. It might help us to negotiate the liberal conundrum where the state's commitment to a liberal order is precisely why it cannot allow certain speech acts which attack the normative foundations of this order. It also cautions us against turning to the state too easily for solutions particularly where the state itself is imbricated in the configurations of power in society. In India, therefore, Section 153A of the Indian Penal Code, which prohibits the promotion of enmity between groups, has been used against Taslima Nasreen, in relation to her book *Amar Meyebela* (My Girlhood) for offending the sentiments of some Muslims, and against M. F. Hussain for his depictions of a nude Saraswati (for offending the sentiments of some Hindus), while Praveen Togadia's incendiary language prior to and during the Gujarat genocide did not invite legal restriction.

In Butler's formulation, the subject of hateful speech can render the skeins of language itself vulnerable. We see this, for instance, in the usage of the words 'nigger' and 'queer' for the black and queer community as instances of the appropriation and re-signification of language. In India, one of the most powerful instances of such appropriation is the use of the word 'Dalit' which literally means 'oppressed', as a self-descriptive term. Words that are used with the intent to harm, are appropriated to mean their opposite. Words can and do wound, but they can also be re-signified and appropriated, their potential to hurt turned into affirmations of strength.

When we think of speech this way it allows us to be open to non-juridical forms of intervention which in recognizing the power of speech and the complicated terrains in which it operates in society, do not flatten out complications by nominating the state as the only arbiter with the power to decide what can and cannot be said.

Conclusion

We need to recognize that speech and speech acts have a real impact on people's lives, and it is because they cannot be dismissed that we need to consider with a great deal of seriousness how best they may be governed. Are all kinds if speech pemissible? Should the speech that incites violence and hatred be curtailed? Who decides what is violent and hateful, and on what grounds? What if silence can be seen on some occasions to be as injurious, or as productive, as speech? Can silence be regulated? What is the difference between mere utterance and considered speech? How is the content of this difference arrived upon? Should different norms, rules, and regulation apply to private and public instances of speech?

Each one of these is an open question, and it is difficult, if not impossible to arrive at answers that will satisfy all of us, or even some of us, all the time. Much depends on context, the identity of the speakers and the listeners, and the history of what has been said before. The choice of when to privilege speech, when to emphasize the virtue of coded forms of speech, and when to pass over things in silence, are matters that require us to take into account various intersecting ethical and pragmatic constraints. Sometimes there are no satisfactory answers.

All we can safely say is, by and large, if something erroneous, mistaken, untrue, dangerous, hateful or injurious is said, then that utterance can always be responded to by various acts of counter-speech. However, the silent prejudice, the unspoken hatred, and the inaudible threat can never be challenged. It is the absence of challenge towards such sentiments that allows them to accumulate prestige and grow in stature, until they threaten to overcome the very foundations of an open, tolerant, and democratic polity. For this reason alone, the risks of the freedom of speech may be seen by many committed to an open society to be preferable to the safety of regulated expression.

Points for Discussion

1. Should a liberal democratic society allow the airing of racist, sexist and misogynist views in the national media?
2. If we were to extend the definition of speech to all forms of expression, how would we think of the place a body like the Central Board of Film Certification occupies in society?
3. Can you elucidate examples of cultural subversion and the re-signification of derogatory speech from popular culture?
4. Is it possible to think of the freedom of expression and its relationship to the right to information?
5. What, in your view, is the importance of freedom of speech and expression in a multi-cultural, democratic society?

Reading List

Austin, J. L., *How to Do Things with Words*, 2nd ed. (Harvard: Harvard University Press, 1975).

Barendt, Eric "Why Protect Free Speech?", *Freedom of Speech*, Oxford University Press, USA; reprint edition (December 10, 1987).

Bollinger, Lee C., *The Tolerant Society* (New York: Oxford University Press, 1986).

———, 'The Tolerant Society: A Response to Critics', *Columbia Law Review*, 90(4), 1990: 979–1003.

Brison, Susan J., 'The Autonomy Defense of Free Speech', *Ethics*, 108(2), 1998: 312–39.

Butler, Judith, 'Sovereign Performatives in the Contemporary Scene of Utterance', *Critical Enquiry*, 23(2), 1997: 350–77.

Delgado, Richard, *Words That Wound: Critical Race Theory, Assaultive Speech, and the First Amendment* (Boulder, CO: Westview Press, 1993).

———, 'Words that Wound: A Tort Action for Racial Insults, Epithets, and Name-calling', *Harvard Civil Rights-Civil Liberties Law Review*, Spring 1982.

Langton, Rae, 'Speech Acts and Unspeakable Acts', *Philosophy and Public Affairs*, 22(4), 1993: 293–330.

Meiklejohn, Alexander, *Free Speech and its Relation to Self Government* (New York: Harper Brothers Publishers, 1948).

Mill, J. S., 'On the Liberty of Thought and Discussion', in *On Liberty and Other Essays*, new ed. (New York: Oxford University Press, 1998).

Nagel, Thomas, 'Personal Rights and Public Space', *Philosophy and Public Affairs*, 24(2), 1995: 83–107.

Richards, David, 'Toleration and Free Speech', *Philosophy and Public Affairs*, 17(4), 1998.

Scanlon, Thomas, 'A Theory of Freedom of Expression', *Philosophy and Public Affairs*, 1(2), 1972: 204–226.

The Editors and the Contributors

The Editors

Rajeev Bhargava was until recently a professor at the Centre for the Study of Developing Societies, New Delhi, and between 2007–2014 served as its Director. He is currently the founder-director of the Centre's Parekh Institute of Indian Thought. He is a permanent (honorary) fellow at Balliol College (Oxford). He has been a professor of political science at Jawaharlal Nehru University and was between 2002–2005, the HOD, Political Science, University of Delhi. He has been a fellow at Harvard University, Columbia University, Stanford University, New York University, Institute of Advanced Studies (Jerusalem), Wissenschaftskolleg (Berlin), Institute for Human Sciences (Vienna), Australian Catholic University (Sydney), and University of Leipzig.

His many publications include Reimagining Secularism (2023), Between Hope and Despair (2022), The Promise of India's Secular Democracy (2010), Politics and Ethics of The Indian Constitution (2008) and Secularism and its Critics (1998) and Individualism in Social Sciences (1992). His work on secularism and individualism is internationally acclaimed.

Ashok Acharya is Professor in the Department of Political Science, University of Delhi and Global Justice Fellow, Yale University. He received his PhD from the University of Toronto as a Commonwealth scholar. He is the editor of *Citizenship in a Globalizing World* (Pearson, 2012; 2nd revised edn., 2022) besides publishing in areas of multiculturalism, social justice and affirmative action. He has been a Fellow at the Australian Social Science Academy, Canberra, the India Fellow at the University of Birmingham, UK and has also held the Henry Hart Rice Visiting Professorship at Yale University for the year 2012–13, besides being a visiting scholar at the universities of Oslo, Humboldt, Nanjing, Gadjah Mada, ANU, Sydney, Monash, and Griffith. His areas of research interest include comparative and contemporary political theory, ethics and politics, and themes surrounding global and social justice. He has led the interdisciplinary *Nyaya: Global Justice* research programme at the University of Delhi in partnership with various global institutions and funding from the British Council. He is the Director of the Delhi School of Transnational Affairs, University of Delhi (Institution of Eminence) and the Founder-Director of the Centre for Ethics, Politics and Global Affairs.

The Contributors

Swaha Das is Associate Professor at the Department of Political Science, Indraprastha College for Women, University of Delhi. Graduated in Political Science from Lady Shri Ram College for Women, University of Delhi, she received a Ford Foundation fellowship for completing her Master's Degree at the School of International Studies, Jawaharlal Nehru University.

She has also contributed chapter in *Citizenship in a Globalizing World* edited by Ashok Acharya (Pearson 2022).

Sunalini Kumar is Associate Professor at the School of Global Affairs, Ambedkar University, Delhi. Educated at Cambridge University, Delhi University and JNU, she has been awarded the Nehru Chevening Cambridge Scholarship, the Oxford Cambridge Society of India scholarship and the Fulbright Nehru Fellowship for postdoctoral research at MESAAS, Columbia University.

Krishna Menon teaches political science at the Lady Shri Ram College, New Delhi. She has a PhD in the subject from the University of Delhi. Her areas of interest include political theory, Indian politics, and feminist theory and politics. Apart from academics, classical music and dance are her other areas of involvement.

Nivedita Menon is Professor at Centre for Comparative Politics and Political Theory, Jawaharlal Nehru University, Delhi. Her latest book is *Secularism as Misdirection: Critical Thought* from the Global South (2024).

She has translated fiction and non-fiction from Hindi and Malayalam into English, and from Malayalam into Hindi, and received the AK Ramanujan Award for translation instituted by Katha.

Anupama Roy is Professor at the Centre for Political Studies in the School of Social Sciences in Jawaharlal Nehru University, Delhi. She was Sir Ratan Tata post-doctoral Fellow at the Institute of Economic Growth in Delhi and Key Technology Partner Fellow at University of Technology, Sydney, Australia.

Her most recent publication is *Citizenship Regimes, Law and Belonging: the CAA and NRC in India* (2022).

Papia Sengupta teaches at the Centre for Political Studies in Jawaharlal Nehru University in India. A PhD in Linguistic Diversity and Group Rights, she was awarded the Distinguished Teacher Award in 2009 by the President of India and the Solidarity Award in 2021 by the International Association for Applied Linguistics Netherlands for her work on multilingual among marginalised communities.

Her recent publication is an edited volume *Critical Sites of Inclusion in India's Higher Education* (2022).

Aarti Sethi is assistant professor at the Department of Anthropology at UC Berkeley. She is a socio-cultural anthropologist with primary interests in agrarian anthropology, political-economy, and the study of South Asia. She holds degrees in political science, and cinema and cultural studies, from University of Delhi and Jawaharlal Nehru University, and went on to receive her Ph.D. in Anthropology from Columbia University.

Mohinder Singh teaches at Centre for Comparative Politics & Political Theory, School of International Studies, Jawaharlal Nehru University. Political Thought and Theory: India, Western, Global South; History of political concepts in modern India.

Janaki Srinivasan teaches at the Department of Political Science, Panjab University, Chandigarh. She holds a PhD from Jawaharlal Nehru University, New Delhi. Her research work is in the areas of political theory and development studies.

V. Sriranjani was associated with Lokniti at the Centre for the Study of Developing Societies (CSDS) as a research associate for a project titled *State of Democracy in South Asia*. She has taught for a brief period at Lady Shri Ram College and Gargi College, University of Delhi.

Index